Service Etiquette

FIRST EDITION BY
REAR ADMIRAL BRUCE MCCANDLESS, USN (Ret.)
CAPTAIN BROOKS J. HARRAL, USN
ORETHA D. SWARTZ

SECOND EDITION BY
CAPTAIN BROOKS J. HARRAL, USN
AND ORETHA D. SWARTZ

REVISED BY
ORETHA D. SWARTZ

ρ

THIRD EDITION

Service Etiquette

By Oretha D. Swartz

NAVAL INSTITUTE PRESS
ANNAPOLIS, MARYLAND

Contents

Preface to the Third Edition

OLD AXIOMS have a way of coming true. And it is a fact that times have changed. In the past there have been definite times of social change: the Victorian Age, the Jazz Age. Perhaps one could say that today is the age of informality. As with any great change in social customs there are fads that come and go. But good behavior never goes out of style.

Informality does not mean letting down the bars to gracious living. Many of the old established customs are blended with today's less restricted ways of life—of entertaining with little or no help, in communicating with others, and in coping with everyday problems that once were handled by a staff. The full integration of women and races into the services brought more changes. Service people now have a more knowledgeable way of life. Still, as in bygone years, there are certain rules to be followed in order to reach the goal of easier, gracious living.

As with any rule of the road, a charted course will get you to a specific place at a given time for a certain occasion. Should you plan to drive from the East to the West Coast you would get a comprehensive chart for the entire distance, or pick up road maps along the way. These maps show the best highways, the mileage, the exits, and posted speed limits.

Should you decide to drive on uncharted highways and go as fast as you please, you can expect to run into trouble: your way will be longer, with penalties and roadblocks. There is little difference in life's highways and those for the military road: both are time tested, both are constantly upgraded, and are charted in *Service Etiquette* for the single purpose of bettering your daily living.

However, no official book comes into being without the help of those involved. Many persons have given of their knowledge in order to make this book of equal value to men and women officers in all branches of the armed forces, and their families. This revised third edition not only is updated but is enlarged to include more about the women in the services, the Reserves, the retired, the military family, and the Maritime Service—an important force though not an armed one.

First, I want to express special appreciation to Rear Admiral Brooks J. Harral, USN (Ret.), who co-authored the first edition that was published in 1959 for the naval service. The creation of this book was his original idea, and without his help and support it would never have come into being. Space does not permit the inclusion of the names of all persons who have helped with this present edition, but acknowledgment is hereby given to those who gave specific information including: Rear Admiral Sheldon H. Kinney, USN (Ret.), president of the State University of New York Maritime College; Mr. Robert J. Blackwell, the Assistant Secretary for Maritime Affairs, Department of Commerce, and Mr. E. J. Bernhardt, the Maritime academies program officer; Rear Admiral Arthur B. Engel, USCG (Ret.), superintendent of the U.S. Merchant Marine Academy, and Captain Charles M. Renick, USMS, Director, Office of External Affairs, USMMA; Rear Admiral John W. Smith, USMS, superintendent of the Texas Maritime Academy.

The title of director of women in the services has been or is being phased out due to the full integration of women in the services, but the following officers have until recently held such titles, and thanks go to Brigadier General Mary E. Clarke, USA, Colonel Bianca D. Trimeloni, USAF, Colonel Margaret A. Brewer, USMC, and Captain Jeanne Gleason, USCGR. In the Navy there has been no director since 1973, and in the Bureau of Naval Personnel acknowledgment is given to Lieutenant Commander Louise C. Wilmot, USN, Lieutenant Commander Joyce Kilmer, USN, Lieutenant Commander Bonnie Hampson, USN, Lieutenant Commander Betty Anderson, USN, and Lieutenant (jg) Artelia Green, USN.

As always, the cadet and midshipmen hostesses (social directors) at the service academies have cooperated fully in giving up-to-date information concerning the social life at the academies. My appreciation goes to these hostesses: Mrs. George Brown, U.S. Military Academy; Mrs. Edward McComas, U.S. Air Force Academy; Mrs. James G. Marshall, U.S. Naval Academy; Mrs. Robert Pope, U.S. Coast Guard Academy, and Mrs. Janice Hawley, U.S. Merchant Marine Academy. Special thanks go to Mrs. Forrest J. Agee, cadet hostess at The Citadel, a military institution with ROTC programs for four services.

Among Army personnel who have given important data are Lieutenant Colonel Hugh G. Waite, USA, Chief, News Branch, Public Information Division, Office of the Chief of Information; Lieutenant Colonel Patricia A. McCord, USA, executive officer, Office of Director WAC; Major Arnold Kendall, USA, protocol officer, Department of the Army; Colonel Michael Fletcher, USA, logistics officer, Lieutenant Colonel M. S. Sirkis, USA, and Captain Barbara J. Yost, USA, cadet activities officers, U.S. Military Academy.

Air Force personnel include Lieutenant Colonel M. E. Bodington, USAF, Chief, Magazine and Book Branch, Office of Information; Colonel Ellis C. Stewart, Jr., USAF, Director of Information Headquarters Air University; Colonel William T. Schwob, USAF, Chief, Procurement Division, Director of Personnel Procurement, Headquarters Air Force Personnel Center; and Lieutenant Jeffrey Bircher, USAF, protocol officer, Andrews AFB.

Naval service personnel include Rear Admiral C. F. Rauch, Jr., USN, Assistant Chief, Naval Personnel for Human Goals; Commander Joseph J. Andrilla, USN, personnel and administrative officer, Captain Maurice E. Roberts (ChC) USN, senior chaplain, Commander Robert K. Lewis, Jr., USN, public affairs officer, Commander Harry A. Seymour, Jr., USN, aide to the commandant of midshipmen, and Lieutenant Cynthia Atwell Madey, USN, visiting services officer, U.S. Naval Academy.

And Lieutenant Colonel J. D. McNamara, USMC, head of the External Information Branch, Division of Information, Marine Corps Headquarters; Major Ruth D. Woidyla, USMC, administrative assistant, Marine Corps Headquarters.

Also, Rear Admiral Walter A. Jenkins, USCG, superintendent, U.S. Coast Guard Academy, and Lieutenant Commander Paul G. Patrinos, USCG, secretary of the Uniform Board, Coast Guard Headquarters.

A number of individuals have given considerable time in their help, among them Mrs. Betty Anne Myers, Defense News Branch, Directorate for Defense Information, Office of the Assistant Secretary of Defense; Mrs. Lynn Gunn-Smith, Office of the Chief of Information, Department of the Army, and Mrs. Mary Chapoutot, Air Staff Protocol, Air Force Headquarters.

Assistance was given by Mrs. Betty Allred, social secretary to the superintendent of the Naval Academy, and information of value to young officers and their families by Marijo Heyworth, whose husband is a line officer. Facts about ASH were received from Mrs. Richard H. Olsher, president of the Baltimore Regional Chapter of Action on Smoking and Health; her husband served as an Army officer.

While writing the first edition, the second edition which was revised to include all members of the armed forces, and the present third edition, I have had the support of Capt. and Mrs. Joseph K. Taussig. The careful editing by Carol Swartz (no relation), a manuscript editor at the Naval Institute, is noteworthy.

Annapolis, Maryland   ORETHA D. SWARTZ
December, 1976

Introduction

WHAT IS ETIQUETTE? According to Webster, the word *etiquette* means: "The forms required by good breeding, social conventions, or prescribed by authority, to be observed in social or official life; the rules of decorum." Good manners are the rules of the game of life—the rules which you observe in your daily living with your fellow men. Good manners are more than a way of holding your fork, the proper words spoken in an introduction, or the correct form for going through a receiving line. These tools of etiquette are important, but there is more to being a well-bred person than the mechanics of good manners.

Good manners also mean kindness to others, respect for the other person's feelings, an acknowledgment of right and wrong, an awareness of someone—*anyone*—whom you meet in a hallway, on the street, or at a party. Good manners mean the consideration you grant someone as a person—not because he is important or of high rank, but because he is a human being. George Bernard Shaw expressed it this way, "The great secret . . . is not having bad manners or good manners or any other particular sort of manners, but having the same manner for all human souls . . . ."

And what is service etiquette? It is all these aspects of everyday good manners combined with the traditions and customs of the various branches of the armed forces. Servicemen and servicewomen are considered not only as representatives of their service, but of the United

States government. They are judged not only by their professional ability but by their manners in social and official life, at home and abroad.

This book was written for all officers in the armed forces, men and women, and for retired officers and members of service families. But it was written especially for the young officers. As cadets and midshipmen, they must undergo the transition from civilian to military life; and upon graduation must adjust to a second transition of blending both military and civilian social customs, since they will be a part of both.

To you, the prospective new officers—cadets and midshipmen of the service and maritime academies, students in the Reserve Officer Training Corps units, the Officer Candidate and Officer Training Schools, and the military schools—it is to *you* that this book is dedicated.

Manners & Dress

CHAPTER 1

Everyday Good Manners—
In Uniform & Out

GOOD GROOMING

A good first appearance depends to a great extent upon your personal grooming. As a midshipman or cadet you are trained during your years at the academies, in the ROTC units or in any military school to take care of your gear and your person—and this training should be observed for the rest of your life.

A first appearance may be one of the most important events of your life. It is impossible to foresee which day, which hour, may be that most important event, or what casual meeting may lead to your being accepted—or refused—by a person of value to your career.

It is important that you keep your uniform, cap cover, and gloves in neat and clean condition; your shoes must be shined, and your hair well cut and shampooed.

For military women in uniform, care in grooming and dress is essential. Extremes in hair styling, nail polish, and makeup are not acceptable. Back hair may touch but not fall below the collar.

Out of uniform, you dress pretty much as you please—but always using good taste.

ON TIME!

One of the most valuable habits that you can acquire is that of being on time. All officers are trained to be punctual in their official duties—

and this habit should not be laid aside in your daily or social life. It is said that promptness and responsibility go hand in hand—therefore a habitual lack of punctuality must be considered irresponsibility.

At official or state occasions, you are expected to be on time. When royalty, very high-ranking officers, or dignitaries of state are guests at a luncheon or dinner, you must arrive before they do; but do not leave before they do.

While you are not expected to be late at a dinner party, neither should you arrive before the hour named in the invitation and catch your hosts unprepared. It is permissible to arrive up to 10 minutes after the stated time, but no later.

There may be times when you are late through no fault of your own—when the plane is late, when the car has a flat tire, or when fog closes in and your boat cannot leave the ship.

When a man is unavoidably late at a dinner and the guests have already gone into the dining room, he should go directly to the hostess and briefly apologize, then take his seat at the table. For reasons of her own, the hostess may not be able to wait more than 15 minutes.

When a woman is late, she should also briefly apologize to the hostess; then take her place at the table. Her dinner partner should rise and assist with her chair. The hostess does not rise; thus, other men guests at the table do not rise—which would further embarrass the late guest and also inconvenience the other seated guests.

You should never deliberately be late at a party in order not to be the first guest to arrive. This is inconsiderate to the hosts and does *not* show sophistication on your part.

At an afternoon reception, at-home, or cocktail party, you may arrive at any time after the first hour named in the invitation, but not later than about a half-hour before the last hour indicated in the invitation.

When you are a guest at a family dinner, be on time. Older children may join the family group at the table, and they are invariably hungry and impatient to be fed. Most hosts feed small children early and have them squared away before guests arrive. In this case, the dinner hour is a little later than usual.

Of course, a host and hostess are *never* late.

TIME TO GO?

There are no set regulations that will tell you exactly when it's time to leave after a party, but many a weary host and hostess wish there were.

The aim of any host is to ensure that guests enjoy the occasion—but sometimes a guest exceeds his host's hospitality.

In the services, officers of high rank are frequently the busiest persons on the base or station. Other than their official responsibilities, senior officers have many social, community, and station obligations. Sometimes, such an officer makes only a token appearance at a reception, or cocktail party.

If you are a junior officer at an official or very important social function, you should not leave until after the guest of honor or the high-ranking guest departs. This person may leave within 30 minutes after a dinner, and then you may also leave. The ranking lady always makes the first move to leave.

However, a junior officer may have an official reason to leave before the guest of honor at a smaller occasion, such as a dinner, and this should have been explained to the hosts beforehand. When it is time for you to leave, briefly tell the guest of honor why you are leaving early, then say goodnight and quietly go.

Customarily, the high-ranking guest will stay from 30 to 45 minutes after dinner, and should stay no longer than an hour afterwards. If you are the high-ranking guest, always remember that no one can properly leave until you do—and another guest may have a real reason to leave on time. Altogether, when nothing has been planned afterwards, the time involved at a formal dinner is between three and three and a half hours.

When to leave after an official luncheon is determined by the station duty of the host and the guests, and upon the time schedule and what is planned for the visiting dignitary. Customarily, guests stay about half an hour after luncheon. Altogether, the time involved is about an hour and a half.

At an afternoon reception, at-home or cocktail party, or tea, you should stay no less than 20 minutes, but you should not stay uncomfortably close to the probable dinner hour of your hosts.

At an evening reception, you will probably stay about 45 minutes, but you may possibly stay longer at a smaller reception or cocktail party—say an hour or an hour and a half.

A young couple making a call on a senior couple usually stay about 20 minutes. Although the husband or wife—or single officer—must not be obvious in watching the time, watch it one must. Senior officers have many demands on their time.

Should you, a junior officer, make a call and should a senior officer and his wife also call, you leave at the proper time. There is no discourtesy in your leaving before the senior officer.

A midshipman or cadet should not form the habit of calling at all hours and staying for hours. If the host invites you to his quarters and insists that you stay on for TV or tennis, you may feel free to do so. When you call unannounced and stay too long, you may be upsetting plans made by your host and hostess. Half an hour is long enough to stay, customarily.

RANK TERMINOLOGY

In the Navy and Coast Guard, *junior officers* are those of the grades of ensign, lieutenant, junior grade (j.g.), lieutenant, and lieutenant commander; *senior officers* are of the grades of commander and captain; *flag officers* are of the grades of commodore (wartime or retired rank), rear admiral, vice admiral, and admiral.

In the Army, Air Force, and Marine Corps, *company grade officers* are those of the grades of second lieutenant, first lieutenant, and captain; *field grade officers* are those of the grades of major, lieutenant colonel, and colonel; *general officers* are of the grades of brigadier general, major general, lieutenant general, and general.

When introducing or addressing a junior officer in the Navy or Coast Guard, a man or woman of the rank of ensign through lieutenant commander is "Mister" or "Miss." All officers in the Army, Air Force, and Marine Corps, are introduced and addressed by rank. (*See* Chapter 8, Service & Civilian Forms of Address.)

FORMS OF ADDRESS

When you, as a young junior officer, report to the office of a senior, you announce yourself either through the orderly or by knocking. You wait until told to enter. If you are a male, you uncover, holding your cap in your right hand by the visor. You go up to the officer, or to within a few paces of his desk, and precede your report or request by announcing, "Lieutenant John (or Jane) Doe, Sir." When the business has been terminated, you leave promptly.

You, as the junior officer, call the senior by his or her title and name, "Colonel Jones," rather than by the impersonal "Sir" or "Ma'am." On board ship or in any naval organization, there is only one "Captain" (the regularly assigned commanding officer) who is addressed as "Captain," regardless of his actual rank, without adding his name.

Juniors reporting to senior women officers announce themselves in the same way as they would to senior male officers.

"Miss" or "Mrs." is used for junior or company grade officers (lieutenant commander and down in the Navy and Coast Guard, and captain and down in the Army, Marine Corps, and Air Force). "Ma'am" is used in place of "Sir," and "Yes, Captain," or "Yes, Miss Smith" in lieu of "Yes, Ma'am."

You should always be careful not to obtrude your greeting upon your senior. For instance, if the senior is engaged in conversation, working on a chart, or concentrating on some problem, the necessity of replying to the greeting could be distracting.

Even though you, the junior, are on a first-name basis with a senior officer, do not call him or her by their first name during official occasions.

Always remember that a senior sends his *compliments* to a junior; the junior sends his *respects*. In written correspondence the senior may "call" attention to a problem or whatever, but the junior may only "invite" it.

Service academy women are addressed in the same way as their male counterparts: "Midshipman" or "Cadet." The terminology is of military rank, not title. At unofficial occasions she is "Miss Doe."

EVERYDAY MANNERS

By the time you have been a cadet or midshipman, ROTC, OTS, or OCS student for a few weeks, your practice of showing respect to military seniors will be automatic. Such things as saying "Sir," or "Ma'am" or "Miss," rising when spoken to, all these and many more fine points become instinctive.

But what about your courtesy to nonmilitary seniors and to your contemporaries? Courtesy and consideration are not to be turned on and off because of rank. Generally speaking, the older the person, the more respect you show him. Therefore, age is an acceptable yardstick, since civilians do not wear such convenient things as insignia of rank.

Undue familiarity from you, a junior, will not be appreciated by a doctor, lawyer, or college president any more than it will be tolerated by an officer of rank considerably higher than your own.

HATS ON—AND OFF

THE MALE OFFICER

In uniform, it is a custom of the naval services that you do not raise your cap when greeting a man or woman in passing out-of-doors. Instead, you give a hand salute. When greeting and passing a woman, a man may accompany the hand salute with a slight bow, but the bow is not necessary. You do not uncover when you are introduced to a woman out-of-doors, and you may salute again when leaving.

In the Army or Air Force, you may salute or raise your hat or cap when introduced to a person out-of-doors. If a lady engages you in conversation, remove your hat and keep it off while talking with her. If the conversation is prolonged for several minutes, or if it is raining, replace your hat or cap.

Indoors, you generally take off your hat or cap as you would when in civilian dress. However, although a civilian generally does not remove his hat in an elevator, the military man should apply the rule in reverse: he should remove his hat or cap in an elevator unless removing it would make him conspicuous.

Aboard ship, junior officers should uncover when passing through captain's or admiral's country, except when in evening dress uniform or wearing sword.

Male officers should remove their caps on entering sick bay and when passing through messing compartments while meals are in progress.

In civilian dress, it is easy for an officer to forget to take off his hat as custom demands in civilian life, so make a habit of not forgetting. Take off your hat when you stop to talk, or are introduced, to a woman out-of-doors, and leave it off unless the weather is bad.

You must take off your hat in a place of worship, except in Orthodox Jewish synagogues and in some conservative synagogues; you take it off whenever you pray or witness a religious ceremony, including a burial or outdoor wedding, or a dedication.

You remove your hat indoors except in stores, lobbies, corridors, and in such public buildings as an airport terminal, post office, bank, etc. Your hat is safer on your head in a crowded elevator than when held in front of you, but you should take it off in hotel or apartment elevators.

Inside an office building leave your hat on—but take it off when entering an office. If you stop to ask directions of the receptionist, you should touch your hat. Touching your hat means touching the crown of a soft hat or the brim of a stiff one.

Your hat may be lifted momentarily when saying *hello, good-bye, thank you, excuse me.* Grasp the front crown of a soft hat or the brim of a stiff one, then lift it slightly up and forward as you bow your head or smile.

A young man lifts his hat to an older man, and a man of any age lifts his hat in respect to a dignitary or an elderly gentleman. An abbreviated hat tip, something of an informal salute, is always a friendly gesture from one man to another.

You may check your hat before entering a public or club dining room, and it may be checked in a theater or placed in the rack under your seat.

THE WOMAN OFFICER

In uniform you always wear a hat or cap out-of-doors; when you are a passenger in an automobile, taxi, bus, train, or aircraft; and when in naval ships.

Indoors, hats are generally worn at luncheons and in church. Remain covered in such public areas as hotels and department stores, and never carry your hat in your hand.

At formal official ceremonies, you cover indoors if military men remain covered, and uncover if they uncover. However, at some formal official ceremonies, such as a military graduation, memorial service, or invocation, at which military men uncover during the ceremony, you remain covered.

You uncover in the dining rooms and cocktail lounges of officers' clubs. It is optional to uncover when making social calls and when making a long trip in a bus, train, or plane. Hats are worn or removed in conformance with local custom when meeting the commanding officer in his office and when visiting in hospitals and other military buildings.

In civilian dress, you comply with customs established by civilian women; at most functions you don't wear a hat.

BOWING

A man should return any bow directed to him—on the street, in a bus, or across the room. When he is being introduced to a woman, he may bow slightly while shaking hands.

A bow is a slight inclination of the body from the waist up, feet together. A deep bow expresses great respect. A too-deep bow is strictly a continental custom and is not customary in the United States.

When he is seated at the table and it is awkward or impossible to rise without disturbing others, a man may half-rise and give a slight bow. But do not remain seated and bow, unless to someone junior to you. Whenever you bow, don't give the effect of bobbing your head.

SALUTING IN CIVILIAN DRESS

As all servicemen and servicewomen know, in uniform you salute whenever the national anthem is played, when the flag is passing in parade or in review, or when the flag is hoisted or lowered.

Out of uniform, a man stands at attention, removes his hat with his right hand, places the hat over his heart—but no higher than shoulder level—or if he is uncovered, then he stands at attention.

A woman in civilian dress should stand quietly as she faces the flag or the direction of the music.

If wearing a hat or a cap, as you step on the quarterdeck of a ship, you face aft and salute the national ensign and then salute the officer-of-the-deck. On leaving a ship, the procedure is reversed.

Out of uniform, you don't return a salute by a uniformed man or woman, but give a verbal greeting instead. For example, at a base or post gate you would return a guard's salute by saying, "Good morning," etc.

GLOVES

When in uniform, you wear or carry gloves as prescribed. If you should be introduced outdoors, you may remove your right glove—if you have time. It is better to shake hands with your gloves on than to keep a person waiting—and you need not apologize for leaving them on.

A man removes his gloves indoors except when ushering at a wedding or funeral, or when he has official guard duty. When introduced to someone during any of these occasions do not take off your glove.

At an academy hop or dance, midshipmen and cadets leave their white gloves with their hats upon arrival at the hop. It is optional for ladies in the receiving line, as well as young ladies going through the line, to wear gloves, but usually they don't.

Men wear white gloves at a formal ball, such as a debutante cotillion, and leave them on throughout the receiving line and dance, removing them only when eating or smoking or wear them through the receiving line and then remove them.

Women may wear gloves when going through the line at a formal reception—but when shaking hands with a head of state or a church dignitary, the right glove is removed. Afterwards, gloves are removed.

Unless in working uniform, military women wear gloves when out-of-doors. In general, gloves should be worn when covered. Exceptions are: when eating or drinking, driving an automobile, visiting an office, traveling in short-haul carriers, or shopping. You wear white gloves at official formal occasions; it is optional to wear them otherwise, unless authorized.

YOUR HANDS, AND HANDSHAKE

Men shake hands upon being introduced or saying good-bye to other men—with the senior making the first move. It is unforgivable not to accept a proffered hand. A man should wait until a woman offers her hand before extending his. If he is seated, he should rise to his feet when introduced to anyone, and upon the departure of anyone.

A good handshake is at elbow level. Avoid a handclasp that crushes or is too limp. Do not hold another's hand too long, or pump it up and down. A slight bow usually accompanies a man's handshake.

As mentioned before, you remove your right glove before shaking hands with anyone—if you have time. And of course, when shaking hands, always look the person you are greeting in the eye.

Kissing a woman's hand is not a customary social gesture in the United States. However, if a continental woman should extend her hand to be kissed, here is the correct technique. Take her hand lightly in yours, then with a slight bow over her hand, merely touch your lips to the back of her hand. It is improper to kiss the hand of an unmarried woman unless she is an older woman.

When women shake hands, a younger woman customarily waits for an older or high-ranking woman to extend her hand in greeting first. The younger woman should rise when introduced to the wife of a senior officer or a much older woman, and remain standing until that woman is seated. A woman need not rise for an introduction to a contemporary other than a military woman when the contemporary is her senior.

Your hands should be in your lap when you are not eating at the dinner table. Avoid awkward positions with your hands at all times—such as locking them behind your head, thrusting them in your suit pockets in unattractive bulges, or standing with clasped hands behind your back or pressed together steeplewise in front.

To stroke your chin, pick at your ears or head, or to drum on a table or chair shows a lack of poise. When you are walking or standing, your hands should be in a relaxed position at your sides.

Midshipmen and cadets do not hold hands or link arms with others in public; any ostentatious show of affection indicates a lack of tact and training.

When dancing, a man's left or leading hand should hold the woman's lightly and naturally. Your right or holding hand should be placed firmly yet easily just above her waist.

When you wish to help a woman down from a bus or train, extend your hand to her, palm up. Don't put your hand under her arm.

Women in uniform conform with military etiquette; in civilian dress, they conform with civilian etiquette on social occasions.

OFFERING YOUR ARM

A man should offer a woman his arm only to give assistance when needed, or as an escort at a formal dinner, or as an usher at a wedding. Never grasp or take hold of the woman's arm—unless an accident is to be avoided. She will take your arm—you do not take hers.

You don't offer your arm in the daytime unless a woman needs help over rough ground, in a crowd, or when you assist an elderly or invalid man or woman. Do not offer your arm to a woman at a luncheon.

When you offer your right arm at a formal dinner, bend your arm slightly at the elbow with your forearm parallel to the floor. Your partner should hold your arm lightly, but not hang onto it. When a guest at a wedding, a woman customarily takes the usher's right arm. A man does not take an usher's arm at a wedding unless he is elderly or an invalid.

Military women, either in uniform or civilian dress, do not hang on a man's proffered arm.

ON YOUR FEET

At a social occasion, such as a dinner party, men should stand whenever a woman enters the room, and remain standing until she sits down, and rise again upon her departure from the room.

However, common sense will dictate how long you should remain standing when a woman thoughtlessly continues to stand and keeps all the men on their feet. When a woman prefers to remain standing with a group, you may return to your own group and sit down.

A man is not expected to rise to his feet every time a hostess re-enters or leaves a room. And he need not rise to his feet at a business or organization meeting when a woman arrives late. He should stand when an elderly or high-ranking man enters the room.

You stand up—not jump up—for introductions, greetings, fare-wells, and whenever a person wants to pass in front of you at the movies, football game—or any place where someone must pass in front of you and you do not want your feet stepped on.

When a woman, senior officer, dignitary, or elderly person comes to your table in a restaurant, a man should rise to his feet. When it is very difficult to stand at a crowded table, a half-standing gesture is better than upsetting something on the table or annoying others.

A junior servicewoman should stand when introduced to a senior officer—male or female—or when the senior enters the room. When in civilian dress at social functions, she conforms to civilian etiquette: the junior woman will stand when introduced to an elderly lady or a promi-nent personage, or to the wife of her commanding officer—regardless of her age.

It is not necessary in this modern age of equality among the sexes for a man to offer his seat in a bus or subway to a strange woman, but he may if he chooses to do so, particularly if the person is elderly, disabled, burdened, or obviously tired.

When you rise to leave a party, say "good-bye," and don't continue in conversation or otherwise dawdle and delay. Just—go.

WALKING OUTDOORS

When a man is walking with a woman outdoors, he walks on the curb side or on her left, if there is no curb. When walking with two women, he may walk between them when crossing the street or if both ladies are elderly or are in poor health and need assistance. Although the old rule of a man never walking between two women is outmoded, most American men still prefer to walk to their left or curbside. When abroad, learn the local custom and follow it.

When two men are walking together, the junior always walks on the left of the senior. When two or more men in uniform are walking together, they keep in step, with the senior setting the pace.

When passing a senior approaching from the opposite direction, salute well in advance. When overtaking a senior, pass to the left if possible (otherwise to the right), salute and say, "By your leave, Sir," just before coming abreast.

A servicewoman follows the same rules and defers to seniors, unless a senior indicates otherwise. The senior may prefer to walk on the left or curb side.

OPENING DOORS

When a man is escorting a woman, he should hold any door open, then follow her through and close the door. If she gets to the door first and opens it, he should not make an issue of it, but hold the door for her to pass through.

A man may start a revolving door for a woman or a male senior to pass through. He should precede a woman through any door that opens onto a dark street or leads down steep stairs.

A junior officer, or any younger man or woman, opens a door for his or her senior. Junior officers stand aside for seniors to pass through doors, then they follow.

To be militarily proper, upon official occasions or in his office, the senior male officer would not hold the door open for the junior woman officer, nor would he follow her through the door.

Unofficially, common courtesy prevails.

WHO GOES FIRST?

When a man is with a woman, she does—except:

When assistance is needed, such as when she is stepping down from a bus
or train.

When there is no waiter to precede you to a table in a restaurant, or no
usher at the theater or movies.

In a crowd, when you will clear the way.

When going down the White House or an official formal receiving line.
It is the title that takes precedence.

At official occasions the senior male officer precedes a junior woman
officer.

MILITARY COURTESY IN BOATS, CARS, AND AIRCRAFT

The procedure for getting in and out of a boat, car, or aircraft is similar:
normally, the senior officer enters last, and the junior enters first. This
procedure may be reversed in entering at a left-hand curb. Then the
senior may enter first, in order that he may sit to the right without
stumbling over juniors who are seated to the left. Seniors are always accorded the most desirable seats. When three persons are in the back seat,
the junior is in the middle.

In a boat, the junior officer sits forward, with the senior sitting aft.
In a car, the junior sits on the left, the senior on the right. In cases of
full cars, the senior officers sit in the back seat and the juniors sit in front.

In getting out of the boat, car, or aircraft, the order is reversed: the
senior officer disembarks first, and the junior last. However, if a car draws
up to a left-hand curb, it may be more appropriate for the junior to step
out first. In an aircraft, if the senior officer is engaged in flying the plane,
the disembarkation procedure applies only among the passengers.

When you travel aboard the personal aircraft of a high-ranking
senior—for example, the aircraft of a flag or general officer—unless instructed otherwise, you should be aboard in a designated seat before the
senior arrives at the aircraft. You should also remain in your seat until
after he leaves the plane at its destination.

CUSTOMS IN AIRCRAFT

Air Force customs while traveling in military aircraft include:

1. Passengers are subject to the orders of the first pilot or airplane
commander, regardless of rank, seniority, or service.

2. Dependents are loaded and unloaded after dignitaries, but before officers, regardless of rank.

3. An aircraft with general and/or flag officers aboard is marked with a detachable plate carrying stars appropriate to the highest rank aboard.

4. Passengers do not enter the flight deck or pilot's compartment unless invited to do so.

5. All safety regulations must be observed, including no smoking on takeoff and landing, and during flight, if so announced. Parachute rules must always be observed.

6. Flights are decided by weather conditions; thus, the pilot's decision to fly or not to fly is never questioned.

IN EVERYDAY LIFE

It is customary for a younger man to follow an older man into any vehicle—boat, car, or aircraft—and to sit where he will least inconvenience him.

When accompanying women in a car, a man should be the first to get out. He should hold the car door open, assist the woman out, then close the door. He should be the last person to get in the car and should close the door. On official or formal occasions the woman is customarily seated at his right.

When driving a car, a man should, if possible, get out, walk around the car and open the door for any woman or older person. If it is not possible for him to get out, he may excuse himself and reach across and open the door.

When a man is the driver and a doorman opens the car door, the woman will get out first. When a man and woman are passengers in a car or taxi and not in city traffic, he should get out first—even if she is closer to the door—and then walk around the car and open the door for her. In traffic, whoever is closer to the door on the safe side gets out first.

A young woman—service or civilian—defers to the senior woman in the same way.

MANNERS AT THE WHEEL

When driving a car, be considerate of others on the road. It is inconsiderate to stop suddenly in the middle of the street to pick up a friend or to talk with him when it is just as easy to pull over to the curb.

On dates, it is good manners for a man to go to the door of his date's house and properly call for her rather than just blowing the horn and waiting for her to come out.

RIDING IN TAXIS

When escorting a woman, a man should give the directions to the driver and pay the taxi fare. If he is not accompanying her to her destination, he should ask the driver what the amount will be and pay him. He should pay the driver's tip along with the charge.

When a man shares a taxi with a woman member of the armed forces or a business woman, she will want to pay for her share of the fare. If she gets out first, she should pay her share to that point, plus her share of the tip.

A man should not ask an unknown woman to share a taxi, but if he knows her slightly and if she is going his way, he may offer to share the taxi, particularly in the case of bad weather or at a rush hour. When he has an important schedule to keep, he should drive there first.

Two or more men (or two or more women) may share a taxi fare. If one person insists upon paying, you may agree and say, "Next time it's mine." Then be sure there is a next time.

Taxi tips vary, but usually they are 15 percent of the bill. Do not tip less than 25 cents, which is adequate for a fare of $1.50 or less.

SEATING A WOMAN

A man assists the woman to his right with her chair when she sits down at the dining table, and when she rises. The chair is pulled back as she steps into place from the left, then he slides the chair under her as she bends to sit down. When she rises from the table, he should draw the chair back without jerking it.

Although it seems easier for a woman to sit down from the left, there is no established rule to this effect. A man should be alert to note from which side the ladies nearest him are being seated by their dinner partners, and then, to avoid confusion, seat his own dinner partner accordingly. If he is the host, he should assist the lady at his right; if he is seated at the right of the hostess, he should assist with her chair.

HOLDING COATS

When a man helps a woman with her coat, he holds the coat with the armholes at a comfortable height for her to slip her arms into them, and is careful not to muss her hair.

A woman usually does not check her coat in a restaurant or the theater. The coat may be laid across a vacant chair at the table, or across the back of her chair at the table or in the theater. He should see that the coat does not trail on the floor. A fur may be folded and laid across a chair or chair back.

A man may check his own coat and hat after entering a hotel but before going into the dining room. These articles may also be checked at the theater, but time may be saved if he takes them with him. He generally places his hat on the rack under the seat.

SENDING FLOWERS

When sending flowers to a woman, a man should choose them to fit her type, as well as to the occasion at which they will be worn. Try to find out what she is wearing, and send flowers that are appropriate. Chrysanthemums are appropriate for attending a football game, and gardenias or an orchid for a dance. Flowers are pinned on a costume heads up— just as they grow.

A very short woman may not care for a very large corsage but she would like a small corsage or nosegay to pin on her gloves or evening bag. A bouquet of flowers may be sent to a hostess by a guest of honor for the party given for him, or as thanks for a favor received or a special party attended.

It is not advisable to send a potted plant to a hostess whose husband has orders, as she may be moving. In such a case, the plant and your money would be wasted.

At the service academies, college ROTC units, and most colleges, corsages are not sent to dates before hops or dances, except on special occasions, such as the "flower formal" at the Coast Guard Academy, and ring and graduation hops. Then, the midshipmen and cadets cut expenses by placing group orders for flowers.

CHANCE ENCOUNTERS

A man does not have to pay for the lunch or dinner at a chance encounter with a woman. If you should happen to run into an acquaintance at a restaurant or lunch counter, you do not need to pay his or her bill— unless you want to. When you chance to meet a man or woman at a bus stop, or decide to share a taxi, you pay only your share of the charges.

If you must speak to a woman who is a stranger, or hand her something—such as returning an object she dropped on the sidewalk—you may touch her arm lightly when you catch up with her, to get her attention; then turn away as soon as you have accomplished your mission.

When you give your seat to a woman in a bus, subway, or train, you may touch your hat when you rise to your feet, but you need not say anything. When a man gives his seat to the woman you are escorting, you should touch your hat when acknowledging his courtesy.

A man should avoid calling out a woman's name in public in loud tones, even when he is surprised and pleased at the encounter.

TELEPHONE COURTESY

You should always be courteous when talking on the telephone. When answering or placing a call, identify yourself. "Hello" may be used in answering when at home, but in an office or upon an official occasion it is discourteous, for the other person must then ask to whom he is talking. Say, "L Two Company orderly room, Cadet Abbott speaking, Sir."

When telephoning a stranger or someone you do not know well, say "This is Lieutenant Jones," then state your business. When you know the person, simply say "This is John (or Jane) Jones," and so on.

In an office a secretary would say, "Captain Smith's office, Miss Jones speaking." A wife calling her husband at his office would inform the secretary, "This is Mrs. Smith. Is Captain Smith in?"

At home, when the caller's name is not requested or given, a young member of the family, or a maid, would call an adult to the phone by saying, "A lady (or gentleman) is calling."

You must always be careful of the time you phone. Unless necessary, do not call a private residence before nine in the morning or after ten o'clock at night. Avoid calling at meal hours.

When you are placing a call and get a wrong number, always apologize to the person who answers—and make certain that you have the right number before placing the call again.

After making a long-distance call in another person's home, ask the operator how much the call cost, then pay for it.

When abused, the telephone is a nuisance. It is inconsiderate to engage in lengthy chitchat when others may urgently need to use the telephone or are trying to call in. Therefore, conduct your business and allow others to do the same.

SMOKING

Smokers should observe the following rules.

Do not smoke in nonsmoking areas, such as in commercial airplanes and elevators.

Do not blow smoke or allow it to drift from a cigarette in your hand or ashtray into another person's face.

Never use a saucer, dish, or plate at the dining table for an ashtray—ask
 for one, when needed.
Never smoke at a formal or official occasion such as a wedding, a re-
 ception, or parade.
Smoke in Navy ships and military aircraft at specified times and places.
A servicewoman does not smoke on the street.
In uniform you may smoke out-of-doors at an athletic contest or other
 type of informal activity.
When there are no ashtrays in a home, or on the dining table, the hostess
 does not want any smoking.
When a person asks if you mind if they smoke—say so if you do.
Do not spill ashes on the floor, flip ashes into a wastepaper basket, or
 put a lighted cigarette on a table.
Never toss a lighted cigarette out of a car window—particularly in a
 wooded area.

There is no need to go around a room and offer cigarettes or a
light to everyone at a dinner party. Cigarettes and ashtrays should be conveniently placed nearby for the guests to help themselves. You may
offer a light to those near you; hold the match or lighter high enough so
that the person does not have to bend over it.

You may smoke during intermissions at the theater. If a guest does
not care to smoke, that person may remain seated while you go to the
lobby. If a woman wishes to smoke, and you don't smoke, you may
accompany her to the lobby.

PIPES AND CIGARS

Some people find the smoke from pipes and cigars stronger and a little
more offensive than cigarette smoke, so the smoker should ask those
nearby if they mind if you smoke. You should be especially careful in a
car or closed area.

Smokers should always have an ashtray large enough to accommodate all the ashes. A chewed cigar or piles of ashes from a pipe are not
attractive in any room.

NONSMOKERS' RIGHTS

Nonsmokers know that it is your business, not theirs, if you smoke—
but they also know that it is their business to protect their own health.
An organization formed throughout the country is Action on Smoking
and Health, called "ASH." They are people who cannot tolerate smoke—
it irritates their eyes, makes them cough, brings on an asthma attack,
or makes them dizzy. They are not crochety people, they are allergic
people.

ASH members feel that they have the right to breathe clean air, that doctors, dentists, and hospitals should have waiting rooms free of smoke, as should various public places other than elevators and churches. And many state governments are beginning to feel this way, too, and are banning smoking in certain places.

Nonsmokers feel that they should have the right to express firmly and politely their discomfort when smokers light up without first asking permission, and when permission is asked to say, "Yes, I do mind," and explain why. Furthermore, they feel that no-smoking regulations should be adhered to at organizations and club meetings, and in business offices, where many work hours are lost when illness occurs. Smoking areas should be established in such places.

SOUNDING OFF

There is an old rule: "Never volunteer information." If you don't give free information about someone or something, you can't be quoted. Gossip is not confined to the feminine sex—a study of military history through the ages forces one to the conclusion that there would be no Mata Haris if servicemen didn't talk.

A young officer should learn early in his or her career not to discuss carelessly military subjects of a classified nature. You should never speak critically of your seniors.

A gentleman does not discuss such subjects as personal business or women in the officers' mess or in the wardroom. If you must discuss these, do so elsewhere—and discreetly. Always remember that your business ceases to be personal if made public.

Everyone has been bored to distraction by the conversationalist who drones on and on. But—are *you* sometimes guilty of being a bore by going overboard on a subject that interests you greatly? When you suspect that you are becoming long-winded—and you may detect this by observing the reactions of those around you—then change the subject and let someone else talk while you listen. Don't be a know-it-all.

In reverse, there are times when you are exhausted beyond endurance by a monologue, and the only way to break the spell is to interject a remark at the end of a sentence or when the bore needs a fresh breath. A favorite phrase is, "Oh, that reminds me—!"

When you unintentionally interrupt a speaker, you should say, "I'm sorry," or "I'm sorry, but I thought you had finished." You should try not to interrupt a speaker, and you should pay him the attention that you hope he pays you.

EXHIBITIONISM

Exhibitionism means drawing attention to yourself in a public place. This is accomplished by shouting, whistling, clowning, loud laughter, booing, or doing something foolish or unusual. A person of refinement does not care to make himself, or his friends, conspicuous.

You should not make a public display of your emotions or affections. Kissing in public is frowned upon in the services, except in cases of farewell when the separation is expected to be a long one. It is a better custom for men to shake hands in greeting and farewell with women as well as with men, although some women insist upon kissing when meeting—other women as well as men. Kissing and holding hands should be considered a private rather than a public demonstration.

One example of exhibitionism is the couple on the dance floor who execute too-intricate steps or who hold each other in exaggerated positions. No couple should monopolize the dance floor.

Although everyone enjoys talking about friends and acquaintances of high rank or position, and interesting or amusing anecdotes about them, you can overdo it. A name-dropper can be a bore.

Another form of showing self-importance is the overuse of foreign words and phrases. Although an occasional foreign expression can be very appropriate in good English conversation, too many such expressions can become tiresome to the average person who does not speak that particular language.

When you use foreign phrases, be sure that you are proficient in their usage and pronunciation—you may be among linguists who are really adept!

APOLOGIES

No one likes to apologize, but apologies are in order when:

You are late at a luncheon or dinner party—or any social occasion such as a reception where the receiving line has already been dispersed. Then you go directly to the hostess and briefly apologize.

The host and hostess have waited for your arrival at a luncheon or dinner party and have not gone into the dining room. Then you apologize and tell them why you were late—and the reason must be excellent!

You fail to keep an appointment. You should telephone or write a brief note, explaining your failure to keep the appointment—and again, the reason must be a good one.

You cannot grant a request. In this case you must not only give your regrets, but if possible add some explanation, such as, "I'm sorry,

but due to the great sentimental value attached to the object, I can't
lend it for the exhibition, etc."
You break or damage something. You must attempt to replace the article
exactly, but if you cannot, then send flowers with your calling card.
You should, of course, state on the card that you are sorry concerning the mishap.
You step or pass in front of someone, or bump into them. In such cases
you say "Please excuse me," or "I beg your pardon," or "I'm sorry."
You have caused harm, or have hurt someone needlessly, or through
carelessness. In this case you must do more than apologize—you
must ask the other person's forgiveness.
You dial a wrong telephone number—particularly at a late hour.

SOCIAL OBLIGATIONS

A single officer, or a young married couple, cannot be expected to repay
in the same fashion the hospitality of an established or older married
couple. The young couple may repay their hosts' hospitality in their own
way—at a small cocktail party, informal lunch or dinner, or by performing some small act or favor that is sincere and without ostentation.

As a general rule, when you accept someone's hospitality, you are
expected to reciprocate in some fashion. The perennial guest will eventually wear out his or her welcome by always being a guest, but never a
host or hostess. No one wants the young couple to repay an expensive
dinner party with the same kind of party, dollar for dollar. But the genu-
ineness of the juniors' desire to repay is all-important. As the younger
couple advances in seniority and rank through the years, they in turn
will extend hospitality to junior officers and young couples.

Single officers, widows, or unmarried women frequently repay
their hosts by inviting them to the theater, or to lunch or dinner in an
officers' club or restaurant.

There is no requirement for a junior officer to repay an official
social obligation, such as a "calls made and returned" type of party.
Junior officers frequently combine their efforts and finances in repaying
unofficial social obligations by giving a dinner, cook-out, or cocktail
party.

YOUR THANKS

You do not have to write or telephone a hostess after all social occasions. A sincere expression of thanks at the time of leaving the party is
generally sufficient. If you and many of the other guests phoned a hostess
after a very large party, she would be on the line for hours.

But after any very pleasant or special occasion (especially a very small one), any hostess is pleased to know that you enjoyed her hospitality, and a note or phone call is in order.

If the occasion was a very special one, you *should* write a note of thanks. When you are the guest of honor at a party or dinner, when a cadet or midshipman was a Christmas or Easter dinner guest, when a luncheon or any occasion was very much enjoyed, express your appreciation in a note or by phone.

Occasionally, after a very special occasion—say, when you have been an overnight guest and a dinner was given in your honor, or when a cadet visited his classmate's parents over the weekend, flowers may be sent to the hostess by the individual or couple. When you are a frequent guest, you do not need to write a note after every visit—but do thank your hostess with simple sincerity before or upon departure.

All social invitations should be answered promptly, preferably within a day or two. Thank-you notes should be written within forty-eight hours after the occasion. A note will take only a few minutes of your time, but this small courtesy is invaluable in matters of manners and good will.

Anyone who has many social engagements should keep a record of them in order not to overlook an obligation. Such a record should include the names of the hosts, with rank, address, and type of occasion—dinner, lunch, cocktails, etc.—as well as any social calls and the date they were made.

MORAL OBLIGATIONS

You must always remember that your word—or signature—is your bond. Therefore, think twice before you make promises. Signed to a check your signature means that you are good for the amount indicated. Signed to the endorsement at the end of an examination, it means that you subscribe to the work submitted and that it is your work. Signed to a letter it means that the ideas expressed are your own.

It is of the utmost importance that men and women in the services be honest and direct in all their dealings. Juniors can avoid a great deal of embarrassment by giving a complete but to-the-point answer in replies to questions put by their seniors.

If you are the junior and do not know or cannot give a complete or correct answer, then you should answer *only as much of the question as you can without being evasive or misleading.* An honest "I don't know, Sir (or Ma'am), but I will find out and let you know," is a better answer than an indirect one that gives misinformation on which your senior may be basing an important decision. An evasive answer can seriously affect your service reputation.

FINANCIAL OBLIGATIONS

It is mandatory that all members of the services discharge their acknowledged and just financial obligations. As a member of a service you remain a citizen and, as such, you have a continuing obligation to obey certain civil statutes and to carry out any civil court orders, decrees, or judgments to which you are a party. You cannot use your service status as a pretext for evading your financial obligations.

This doesn't mean that you must pay unjust claims just to avoid unpleasant publicity. You are protected by the fact that your commanding officer must make a careful investigation into the justness of any claim you disavow. But be sure you are in the right before you put your commanding officer to that trouble.

However, commanding officers are not supposed to act as agents for claimants in business transactions or claim collections. Usually the CO only makes sure that the claimant's communication reaches the officer or man concerned and that a prompt reply is made. But a commanding officer cannot tolerate actions of irresponsibility, gross carelessness, neglect, or dishonesty in the financial dealings of service personnel. If it is determined that the officer is negligent or careless in regard to his or her personal finances, an entry will be made on the officer's fitness report and, if the circumstances warrant such action, a trial by court-martial will be recommended.

If you are assigned to a job involving the custody of funds—such as mess treasurer—you should make a careful check to ensure that you get everything you sign for when you take over. If you should be a member of an auditing board, be sure that what you certify to be on hand is actually present. Never be careless in making audits and taking inventories. The fact that someone else may have signed does not mean that you can sign blindly and assume that all is well. Usually, the junior signs first, at the bottom of the page.

Officers should never lend money to, or have any financial dealings with, enlisted personnel. Your service regulations are definite in directing you not to make such loans. If someone asks for a loan, you must decline and say that regulations prohibit your making the loan. If the case is a deserving one, there should be no trouble in his getting a loan from the ship's Welfare Fund or the Navy Relief Society, the Air Force Aid Society, the Army Emergency Relief, or other established welfare societies. While there is no similar regulation prohibiting financial dealings between officers—there should be. It is better to avoid such dealings.

YOUR SERVICE COMMUNITY

The armed services are friendly services. No matter where you go on active duty, there will be service people near you in your own age group and financial circumstances. It's difficult to be lonely in the service, whether you are at home or abroad.

Most service communities are also friendly—however, a few service people make themselves undesirable in a town or community because of their lack of consideration for other people's feelings and possessions. Perhaps this lack of responsibility stems from the fact that service people are not in one place very long and thus grow careless in caring for another's property.

You should take care of another person's property with at least as much respect as you would your own—and this is taking for granted that you *do* take care of your own things. When you are in quarters, or rent a house or apartment, you should not abuse it. Don't leave dirt and trash lying around, or generally wreck the place—you will not be welcome again nor will you leave a favorable impression of the service you represent.

It is thoughtless to borrow another person's property and not return it—no matter whether this be a book, a golf club, or a pound of coffee. You must always return what you borrow—and develop the habit of not borrowing.

A wise person will try to fit into a new community rather than attempt to change it. Always be thoughtful of your neighbors. It is extremely unwise to walk into a store and say, "That can be bought at the Exchange for one third your price!"

THE SEA OF MATRIMONY

Good manners in marriage mean loyalty to and respect for the other partner—but this loyalty and respect should be earned, not demanded. A man and his wife should share the responsibility in the management of the family finances, with the wife fully understanding the limitations of a paycheck and the obligations which must be met each month. Since an officer is away from home during much of his career, it is necessary that someone carry on the family's financial obligations and keep an accurate account of the family expenditures during his absence.

A young wife may have had little experience in financial matters before marriage—and a young husband may have had almost as little financial experience himself. It is important that a young couple work together as a team in sharing the household responsibilities.

A partnership in marriage includes a sound evaluation of each other's responsibilities: a man with his busy career and its problems and worries; a woman with a house to clean, food to cook, and children to care for. Today a woman often combines these household activities with a career, or a part-time career, with little or no household help.

A husband often lends a hand—and the wife will do the same—in jobs formerly considered the specific chore of the other.

A partnership in marriage means that both partners say "we" instead of "I" and "our" instead of "my"—with the exception that official service business is the husband's concern only. Unless she is a service-woman with her own rank, it is *his* orders, *his* crest, *his* rank.

A partnership, however, does not mean that one or the other cannot have any liberty of thought or action. Partnership and domination do not go hand-in-hand.

A happy household is one where both the man and woman have a certain money allowance for their own personal use—with no strings attached whatsoever.

As partners, a man and wife should never belittle each other. Any family dissension should be discussed in private—but *not* before the children or anyone else. It should be a matter of personal pride for both a man and his wife to be as neat and attractive, and as mentally stimulating, after marriage as before.

HOSPITAL MANNERS

THE VISITOR

Nothing is more exhausting to a hospital patient than to have a visitor who comes too soon after surgery or a serious illness, or who stays too long, or talks too loudly. If patients were in good health and feeling fine, they would not be in the hospital. Some visitors, however, seem to regard a hospital room as a fine place for a chat.

Any visitor in a hospital should observe these rules:

Walk and talk quietly in hospital corridors, and in patients' rooms. Women particularly should guard against heels clacking on tiled floors.

The length of time of your visit depends upon the patient's condition and how he is momentarily feeling. Five minutes may be too long. Fifteen minutes is generally long enough, unless you are a relative—and even then the patient may not care to see anyone.

There are definite visiting hours in most hospitals, and visitors should check them before going there. Make sure in advance that a patient wants visitors, by telephoning to the hospital or the patient's home.

Do not visit anyone in the hospital when you have a cold. Sick people
are apt to be more susceptible to contagious diseases.

Do not sit on the patient's bed, and avoid jostling it.

If there are other visitors ahead of you, wait outside until some leave. If
the patient has many visitors, he may be getting weary so cut your
own stay—unless you are urged to stay. Better still, leave and go
back another day.

Don't smoke in a hospital room unless the patient is smoking, or doesn't
mind if you do. Some hospitals do not permit smoking in patients'
rooms, but have smoking areas.

Do not visit a new mother immediately after the event—unless it is
your wife! You may always see the new baby by looking through
the glass door of the nursery.

When you want to take the patient a small gift, flowers are always nice—
but don't overdo it; too many flowers remind some people of
funerals. When a patient is to be in a hospital for some time, a
potted plant is appreciated.

THE PATIENT

When you are the patient in a hospital, there are some do's and don'ts
for you:

Do be considerate of your nurse or corpsman—they are there to help
you, not to wait on you. A nurse or corpsman is a professional man
or woman—not a servant.

Do cooperate with hospital rules, and don't make too much fuss about
pills, needles, etc.

In a private room, you can suit yourself (within reason) concerning the
volume of your radio or TV, or airconditioner, but in a semiprivate
room or a ward, you must be considerate of your fellow patient
or patients, who may feel worse than you do. Smoke can be disagreeable to another patient and your TV may drive him wild.

Do not give orders to your nurse, and call her by name: "Miss Smith."
When the nurse doesn't tell you her name, you may properly ask
her what it is. Do not ask her the details of your illness—ask your
doctor.

Patients do not tip a trained nurse or a corpsman. You may give them a
gift when you leave, or buy a large box of candy which will be
available for the staff on your floor.

If you do not want to see a visitor—*don't*. A "no-visitors" sign can be
placed on your closed door by your nurse who can also notify the
desk that no one is to be admitted to your room. No explanation
need be made to any visitor—after all, this is not your home.

CHAPTER 2

Service & Civilian Dress

THE BRIEF UNIFORM CHARTS which appear on the following pages have been compiled for the convenience of men and women officers. These charts show the type of uniforms, with prescribed medals or ribbons, which are worn to informal, semiformal, and formal occasions.

The uniforms in the charts are the equivalent of the civilian formal afternoon dress and of the evening "black tie" and "white tie." However, the distinctions between black tie and white tie, and when each is worn, have necessitated further description of civilian dress. There is also a more general description of the civilian clothes needed by officers for everyday living out of uniform.

Decorations, medals, and ribbon bars are worn on the left breast pocket of the uniform coat or jacket, and are pinned or sewed from the wearer's right to the left in the order of official military precedence. Insignia, such as aviator's wings, are worn above the pocket.

In general, *regular size medals* are worn with semiformal dress; *miniature medals* are worn with mess dress, formal evening, and dress white uniforms; *unit award emblems* are worn with service, semiformal dress, and dress whites; *ribbons* are worn with service, semiformal dress,

NOTE: The local uniform regulations differ in various parts of the country, according to climate and locale. The change from one uniform to another differs in various sections, according to the season. Details of all uniforms will be found in the *Uniform Regulations* of each service.

mess dress, evening dress, and dress whites. Decorations and service medals, regular size, are worn with semiformal dress uniforms in lieu of ribbons.

Insignia of speciality, grade, and branch of service are worn according to regulations, and aiguillettes are worn when authorized.

AWARDS

Awards is an all-inclusive term covering any decoration, medal, ribbon, badge, or an attachment thereto which is bestowed on an individual.

A *decoration* is an award conferred on a person for an act of gallantry or for meritorious service, or given to units distinguished for gallantry in action against the enemy. Certain decorations carry the word "medal," for example the Medal of Honor and the Distinguished Service Medal. The Medal of Honor is worn from the neckband ribbon.

A *miniature medal* is one-half the size of the original large medal, with the exception of the Medal of Honor which is not in miniature. A *ribbon* is a part of the suspension ribbon of a medal which is worn in lieu of the medal. The dimensions of all ribbons are 1⅜ inches by ⅜ inch. A *badge* is an award to an individual for some special proficiency and consists of a medallion hung from a bar or bars.

Miniature medals are worn by men and women officers with formal and semiformal winter and summer uniforms. The holding bar is no longer than 4⅛ inches in length. When six or less medals are worn, they are attached in a single row, fully exposed. When the number exceeds six, each medal may overlap the medal to its left, but not more than 50 percent. Thus, the maximum number worn in a single row is 11. If more than this number are worn, they are arranged in two rows; if more than 22, in three rows evenly divided. If this cannot be done, the top row will contain the lesser number of medals with the center of the row placed over the center of the row below it.

When ribbons are worn, badges, such as the Navy command insignia, are worn immediately below the bottom row of ribbons. When large medals are worn, badges are placed directly below the bottom row of medals so that the medallion of each badge may be seen.

MEDALS ON CIVILIAN DRESS

The Medal of Honor may be worn with civilian dress. Likewise, miniature medals may be worn with black or white tie in the same manner as prescribed for service evening dress uniforms.

Miniature replicas of ribbons made in the form of lapel buttons, or

UNIFORM CHARTS

ARMY (Men)

Uniform	Coat/Jacket	Trousers	Cap	Shirt	Necktie	Shoes	Socks	Gloves
ARMY BLUE AND ARMY WHITE UNIFORMS[1] Wear at general official/social occasions.								
Army Blue	Army blue	Army blue	Blue	White	Black bow[2], or four-in-hand[3]	Black	Black	White
Army White	Army white	Army white	White	White	Black bow[2], or four-in-hand	Black	Black	White

1. Wear ribbons, miniature or regular medals
2. Constitutes black tie.
3. Constitutes semidress.

Uniform	Coat/Jacket	Trousers	Cap	Shirt	Necktie	Shoes	Socks	Gloves
ARMY GREEN UNIFORM:[1] General duty wear; for informal social functions after retreat.								
Army Green	Army green	Army green	Green	Tan	Black four-in-hand	Black	Black	Black

1. Wear full size medals or ribbons.

Uniform	Coat/Jacket	Trousers	Cap	Shirt	Necktie	Shoes	Socks	Gloves
ARMY BLUE MESS AND WHITE MESS UNIFORMS:[1] Constitutes black tie.								
Blue Mess[2]	Army blue	Army blue mess	Blue	White evening dress	Black bow	Black	Black	White
White Mess[3]	Army white	Black dress	White	White evening dress	Black bow	Black	Black	White

1. Wear miniature medals.
2. Wear black cummerbund. With white vest constitutes evening dress uniform.
3. Wear white vest. Optional, black cummerbund. Gold studs.

ARMY EVENING DRESS UNIFORM: Equivalent to white tie.

Evening Dress	Army blue	Army blue	Blue	White full dress, wing collar	White bow	Black	Black	White

Wear miniature medals
Wear blue cape
White studs.

ARMY (Women)

Uniform	*Coat/Jacket*	*Skirt*	*Shirt*	*Necktab*	*Shoes*	*Gloves*
ARMY BLUE AND ARMY WHITE UNIFORMS: For general social/official occasions.						
Army Blue[1,3]	Army blue	Army blue	White		Black pumps	White
Army White[2,4]	Army white	Army white	White		White pumps	White

1. Wear ribbons, miniature or full size medals.
2. Wear miniatures.
3. Black handbag; Army blue hat.
4. White handbag; Army white hat.
   Wear stockings complimentary to uniform.

Uniform	*Coat/Jacket*	*Skirt*	*Shirt*	*Necktab*	*Shoes*	*Gloves*
ARMY MESS UNIFORMS:[1] Equivalent to black tie.						
Army Black Mess[2,5]	Army black	Army black street length	White blouse	Black	Black pumps	White
Army White Mess[3,4]	Army white	Army white street length	White blouse	Black	Black pumps	White
Army All-White Mess	Army white	Army white street length	White blouse	Black	White pumps	White

1. Wear miniature medals.
2. Wear black cummerbund.
3. Wear white cummerbund.
4. White handbag.
5. Black handbag.

ARMY EVENING DRESS UNIFORMS:[1] Equivalent to white tie.

Uniform	Coat/Jacket	Trousers	Shirt	Necktie	Shoes	Gloves
Army Black Evening Dress[2,3]	Army black	Army black long	White blouse	Black	Black pumps	White
Army White Evening Dress[2,3]	Army white	Army white long	White blouse	Black	Black pumps	White

1. Wear miniature medals.
2. Wear black cummerbund.
3. Black dress handbag.

NOTE: The Army green uniform is for general year-round wear. The Army green cord uniform is for summer wear.

NAVY (Men)

Uniform	Coat/Jacket	Trousers	Cap, Combination	Shirt	Necktie	Shoes	Socks	Gloves
SERVICE DRESS UNIFORMS:[1] For general wear.								
Service Dress Blue[2]	Blue	Blue	White	White	Black four-in-hand	Black	Black	Black (optional)
Tropical White, Long		White	White	Tropical white		White	White	
FULL DRESS UNIFORMS:[1] Wear at official/social occasions.								
Full Dress Blue	Blue	Blue	White	White	Black four-in-hand	Black	Black	White
Full Dress White	White	White	White	White		White	White	White

1. Wear ribbons.
2. For Service Dress Blue (Yankee) substitute white trousers, white socks and shoes for the dark.
3. Service Dress White is the same as Full Dress White except that ribbons are worn and gloves are optional.

1. Wear large medals.

DINNER DRESS UNIFORMS:[1] Equivalent to black tie.

Uniform	Coat/Jacket	Trousers	Shirt	Necktie	Shoes	Gloves
Dinner Dress Blue[3]	Blue	Blue	White	Black bow	Black	White
Dinner Dress White	White	White	White	White	White	White
Dinner Dress Blue Jacket[2]	Blue jacket	Blue evening	White[3,4]	Black bow	Black	White
Dinner Dress White Jacket[2]	White jacket	Blue evening	White[3,4]	Black bow	Black	White

1. Wear miniature medals.
2. Wear gold cummerbund.
3. Optional, stiff bosomed shirt or pleated soft front shirt.
4. Turndown collar.

FORMAL DRESS UNIFORM:[1] Equivalent to white tie.

Uniform	Coat/Jacket	Trousers	Shirt	Necktie	Shoes	Gloves
Formal Dress	Blue dress jacket	Blue evening	White stiff bosomed	White bow	Black evening dress	White

1. Wear white waistcoat. Miniature medals.

NAVY (Women)

SERVICE DRESS UNIFORMS:[1,2] For regular official/social occasions.

Uniform	Coat/Jacket	Skirt	Shirt	Necktie	Hat, Combination	Shoes	Gloves
Service Dress Blue A	Blue	Blue	White	Black	Complete	Black	White
Summer Blue	Blue	Summer Blue	White	Black	Beret optional	Black	
Light Blue	Light blue	Light blue	Light blue		Light blue	Black	Black optional

1. Wear with ribbons.
2. Black handbag.
Note: Service Dress White is the same as the Blue except for color. Service Dress Blue and White Uniforms, worn with large medals and white gloves, are referred to as *Full Dress Blue* and *White Uniforms*.

NAVY (Women) (Continued)

DINNER DRESS UNIFORMS:[1] For general official and social functions, or black tie.

Uniform	Coat/Jacket	Trousers	Cap	Shirt	Necktie	Shoes	Socks	Gloves
Dinner Dress Blue[2]	Blue	Blue		White	Black	Complete	Black dress	White
Dinner Dress White[3]	White	White		White	Black	Complete	White dress	White
Dinner Dress[4,5] Blue Jacket	Blue	Blue		White	Black	Tiara optional	Black formal dress	White
Dinner Dress[4,5] White Jacket	White	Blue		White	Black	Tiara optional	Black formal dress	White

1. Wear miniature medals.
2. Black handbag.
3. White handbag.
4. Black dress handbag.
5. Black cummerbund.

FORMAL DRESS UNIFORM: For official formal evening functions, or white tie.

Uniform	Coat/Jacket	Trousers	Cap	Shirt	Necktie	Shoes	Socks	Gloves
Formal Dress Blue	Blue	Blue long		White dress	Black dress	Tiara optional	Black formal dress	White

Miniature medals.
Black cummerbund.
Black dress handbag.

Note: The long Formal Dress Blue Skirt is optional with the Dinner Dress Jacket Uniforms, when prescribed.

AIR FORCE (Men)

Uniform	Coat/Jacket	Trousers	Cap	Shirt	Necktie	Shoes	Socks	Gloves
SERVICE UNIFORMS: For general wear.								
Blue Service[1]	Blue	Blue	Blue	Blue	Blue	Black	Black	Gray or black, optional

Tan Summer Service[2]	Tan	Tan	Blue	Tan		Black	Black

1. Wear ribbons.
2. Ribbons optional.

Note: The *Winterweight* or *All Season Uniforms* are the same as the Blue Service Uniform except for materials.

INFORMAL DRESS UNIFORMS: For informal daytime and evening occasions.

Informal Black[1]	Black	Black	Black	White	Black four-in-hand	Black	White
Informal White[2]	White	White	White	White	Black four-in-hand	White	White

1. Wear miniature medals.
2. Wear ribbons.

DRESS UNIFORMS: For black tie occasions.

Mess Dress Black[1,3]	Black	Black	Black	White, soft bosom	Black bow	Black	White
Mess Dress White[1,3]	White	Black	White	White, soft bosom	Black bow	Black	White
Semiformal[2]	Blue	Blue	Blue	White	Black bow	Black	Gray or white

1. Wear miniature medals.
2. Wear ribbons.
3. Wear black cummerbund.

FORMAL EVENING DRESS UNIFORM: Equivalent to white tie.

Formal Evening Dress	Black	Black	Black	White, wing collar	White bow	Black	White

1. Wear miniature medals.
   Wear white vest.
   Pearl studs.
   Black cape optional.

AIR FORCE (Women)

Uniform	Coat/Jacket	Skirt	Shirt	Tabs	Hat/Cap	Shoes	Gloves
SERVICE UNIFORM COMBINATIONS: For general wear.							
New Service Uniform Combination A	Blue	Blue	Light blue overblouse	Blue	Blue	Black pumps	Black
Overblouse and Skirt Combination B		Blue	Light blue overblouse	Dark blue	Beret optional	Black pumps	White

1. *Wear ribbons; optional for "B."*
Neutral shade hose will complement uniforms.
Black handbag.

Uniform	Coat/Jacket	Skirt	Shirt	Tabs	Hat/Cap	Shoes	Gloves
INFORMAL DRESS UNIFORMS: For daytime and evening functions.							
Black Informal[2,4]	Black	Black	White	Black		Black pumps	White
White Informal[1,3]	White	White	White	Blue	Blue beret optional	White or blue pumps	White
Blue Semiformal	Blue	Blue	White shirt or overblouse	Blue		Black pumps	White

1. Wear ribbons.
2. Wear miniature medals.
3. Blue clutch or white purse.
4. Black clutch purse.

Uniform	Coat/Jacket	Skirt	Shirt	Tabs	Hat/Cap	Shoes	Gloves
MESS DRESS UNIFORMS: For black tie occasions.							
Winter Mess Dress[1,2,3]	Black	Black, long or short	White mess	Black		Black pumps	White
Summer Mess Dress[1,2,3]	White	White, long or short	White mess	Black		White pumps	White

1. Wear miniature medals.
2. Silver cummerbund, with long skirts; black or white with short skirt.
3. Black clutch handbag.

FORMAL DRESS UNIFORM: White tie occasions.

Formal Dress	Coat/Jacket & Belt	Trousers	Cap	Shirt	Necktie	Shoes	Socks	Gloves
	Black mess	Black long	White mess	Silver			Black pumps	White

Wear miniature medals.
Silver cummerbund.
White pearl earrings optional.
Black clutch handbag.
Cape.

MARINE CORPS (Men)

Uniform	Coat/Jacket & Belt	Trousers	Cap	Shirt	Necktie	Shoes	Socks	Gloves
BLUE DRESS A, B, C, AND WHITE DRESS UNIFORMS:[1] Wear at general/official occasions.								
Blue Dress A[2]	Blue	Blue	Dress	White		Black	Black	White
Blue Dress B[3]	Same as "A"—except with ribbons.							
Blue Dress C[3]		Blue	Dress	Khaki		Black	Black	Black
White Dress A[2]	White	White	Dress			White	White	White
White Dress B[3]	Same as "A"—except with ribbons.							
Blue/White Dress A[2]	Blue	White	Dress	White		White	White	White
Blue/White Dress B[3]	Same as "A"—except with ribbons.							

1. Wear badges; sword.
2. Wear large medals.
3. Wear ribbons.
   Black leather gloves with outercoat.

MESS DRESS UNIFORMS:[1] Black tie.

Mess Dress	Coat/Jacket & Belt	Trousers	Cap	Shirt	Necktie	Shoes	Socks	Gloves
	White mess, scarlet cummerbund	Black mess	Dress	White pleated bosom	Black bow square ends	Black	Black	White

1. Wear miniature medals.

MARINE CORPS (Men) (Continued)

EVENING DRESS A AND B UNIFORMS:[1] White tie.

Uniform	Coat/Jacket		Dress		Shoes	Gloves
Evening Dress A	Black evening, waistcoat	Black evening	White stiff bosom	Black	Black	White
Evening Dress B	Same as "A"—except with cummerbund.					

1. Wear miniature medals.

MARINE CORPS (Women)

Uniform	Coat/Jacket	Skirt	Shirtwaist	Scarf	Cap and Necktie	Shoes	Gloves
BLUE DRESS UNIFORMS: General official/social occasions.							
Blue Dress A[1,2]	Blue	Blue	White	Red	Blue	Black pumps	White
Blue Dress B	Same as Blue Dress A—except ribbons are worn.						
White Dress A[1,3]	White	White	White	White	Dress green	White pumps	White
White Dress B	Same as White Dress A—except ribbons are worn.						

1. Wear large medals.
2. Black or clutch purse with black cover.
3. Clutch purse with green cover.
   Hose to complement uniform.

Uniform	Coat/Jacket	Skirt	Shirtwaist	Scarf	Cap and Necktie	Shoes	Gloves
MESS DRESS UNIFORM: Equivalent to black tie.							
Mess Dress	Mess, cummerbund	Black short		White		Black pumps	White

Wear miniature medals.
Clutch purse with black cover.

	Coat	Trousers	Cap Cover	Shirt	Necktie	Shoes	Socks	Gloves
Evening Dress A	Evening, cummerbund	Long black		White		Tiara	Black pumps	White
Evening Dress B	Same as Evening Dress A—except short black evening skirt.							

Wear miniature medals.
Clutch purse with black cover.
Cape.

COAST GUARD (Men)

Uniform	Coat	Trousers	Cap Cover	Shirt	Necktie	Shoes	Socks	Gloves
SERVICE DRESS UNIFORMS: General duty wear.								
Service Dress[1]								
Blue	Blue	Blue	White	Light blue	Blue	Black	Black	Gray
White	White	White	White			White	White	

1. Wear with ribbons.

Uniform	Coat	Trousers	Cap Cover	Shirt	Necktie	Shoes	Socks	Gloves
FULL DRESS UNIFORMS: Wear at official/social functions.								
Full Dress[1]								
Blue	Blue	Blue	White	White	Blue	Black	Black	White
White	White	White	White			White	White	White

1. Wear large medals; sword.

Uniform	Coat	Trousers	Cap Cover	Shirt	Necktie	Shoes	Socks	Gloves
DINNER DRESS UNIFORMS: Equivalent to black tie.								
Dinner Dress								
Blue[2,5]	Blue	Blue	White	White dress[4]	Black bow	Black	Black	White
Blue Jacket[1,2]	Blue Dinner	Blue Evening[3]	White	Formal soft front	Black bow	Black	Black	White

COAST GUARD (Men) *(Continued)*

Uniform	*Coat*		*Shirt*	*Necktie*	*Hat Cover*	*Shoes*	*Gloves*
White[2]	White	White	Formal soft front	Black bow	White	White	White
White Jacket[1,2]	White Dinner	Blue Evening[3]			Black	Black	White

1. Optional for lieutenants and below.
2. Wear miniature medals.
3. With gold cummerbund.
4. Stiff turndown collar.
5. Primarily for lieutenants and below not possessing the jacket uniforms.

EVENING DRESS UNIFORMS: Equivalent to white tie.

Uniform	*Coat*		*Shirt*	*Necktie*	*Hat Cover*	*Shoes*	*Gloves*
Blue[1,2]	Blue evening	White	Formal stiff bosomed[3]	White bow	Black	Black	White
White[1]	White	White			White	White	White

1. Wear miniature medals.
2. Wear white waistcoat.
3. Wear winged collar.

COAST GUARD (Women)

Uniform	*Coat*	*Skirt*	*Shirt*	*Necktie*	*Hat Cover*	*Shoes*	*Gloves*

SERVICE DRESS UNIFORMS: Regular official/social functions.

Uniform	*Coat*	*Skirt*	*Shirt*	*Necktie*	*Hat Cover*	*Shoes*	*Gloves*
Service Dress[1]							
Blue[2]	Blue	Blue[4]	Light blue	Lt blue w/stripe	White	Black dress	White
White[3]	White	White	White	Black	White	White	White

1. Worn with ribbons.
2. Black handbag.
3. White handbag.
4. Slacks optional.

FULL DRESS UNIFORMS: Wear at official/social functions.

Uniform	*Coat*	*Skirt*	*Shirt*	*Necktie*	*Hat Cover*	*Shoes*	*Gloves*
Full Dress[1]							
Blue[2]	Blue	Blue	White	Black	White	Black dress	White
White[3]	White	White	White	Black	White	White dress	White

1. Worn with large medals.
2. Black handbag.
3. White handbag.

DINNER DRESS UNIFORMS: (Worn in lieu of evening dress uniforms) Equivalent to black tie.

Dinner Dress Blue[1]

Blue[4]	Blue	Blue	White	Black	White	Black dress	White
Blue Jacket[5,7]	Blue dinner	Blue dinner[2]	White dress	Black dress	Tiara[3]	Black formal	White
White[6]	White	White	White	Black	White	White dress	White
White Jacket[5,7]	White dinner	Blue dinner[2]	White dress	Black dress	Tiara[3]	Black formal	White

1. Worn with miniature medals.
2. Formal dress blue skirt optional.
3. Optional.
4. Wear with black handbag.
5. Wear with black dress handbag.
6. Wear with white dress handbag.
7. Required for all lcdr's and above, optional for others.

EVENING DRESS UNIFORMS: Equivalent to white tie occasions.

Evening Dress[1,5]

Blue[2]	Blue dinner	Formal blue	White dress	Black dress	Tiara[4]	Black formal	White
White[3]	White	White	White	Black	White	White dress	White

1. Wear with miniature medals.
2. Wear with black dress handbag.
3. Wear with white dress handbag.
4. Optional.
5. Required for all officers captain and above.

MERCHANT MARINE

UNIFORMS: Officers of the Merchant Marine who are officers of the U. S. Naval Reserve wear the Naval Reserve Merchant Marine insignia on their Merchant Marine uniforms. Members of the Naval Reserve who are serving as officers under licenses issued by the U. S. Coast Guard in ships under contract with the Federal Maritime Administration, or those serving as staff officers on certificates of registry issued by the Coast Guard, wear the USNR Merchant Marine insignia. Other members of the Naval Reserve serving in merchant ships in positions which require them to wear a uniform appropriate to an officer, wear the insignia on their uniforms.

SERVICE INSIGNIA

ARMY	AIR FORCE	MARINE CORPS	NAVY	COAST GUARD
GOLD BROWN / GOLD BROWN — W-1 WARRANT OFFICER / W-2 CHIEF WARRANT OFFICER	GOLD SKY BLUE / GOLD SKY BLUE — W-1 WARRANT OFFICER / W-2 CHIEF WARRANT OFFICER	GOLD SCARLET / GOLD SCARLET — W-1 WARRANT OFFICER / W-2 CHIEF WARRANT OFFICER	W-1 WARRANT OFFICER / W-2 CHIEF WARRANT OFFICER	W-1 WARRANT OFFICER / W-2 CHIEF WARRANT OFFICER
SILVER BROWN / SILVER BROWN — W-3 CHIEF WARRANT OFFICER / W-4 CHIEF WARRANT OFFICER	SILVER SKY BLUE / SILVER SKY BLUE — W-3 CHIEF WARRANT OFFICER / W-4 CHIEF WARRANT OFFICER	SILVER SCARLET / SILVER SCARLET — W-3 CHIEF WARRANT OFFICER / W-4 CHIEF WARRANT OFFICER	W-3 CHIEF WARRANT OFFICER / W-4 CHIEF WARRANT OFFICER	W-3 CHIEF WARRANT OFFICER / W-4 CHIEF WARRANT OFFICER
(GOLD) SECOND LIEUTENANT	(GOLD) SECOND LIEUTENANT	(GOLD) SECOND LIEUTENANT	ENSIGN	ENSIGN
(SILVER) FIRST LIEUTENANT	(SILVER) FIRST LIEUTENANT	(SILVER) FIRST LIEUTENANT	LIEUTENANT JUNIOR GRADE	LIEUTENANT JUNIOR GRADE
(SILVER) CAPTAIN	(SILVER) CAPTAIN	(SILVER) CAPTAIN	LIEUTENANT	LIEUTENANT
(GOLD) MAJOR	(GOLD) MAJOR	(GOLD) MAJOR	LIEUTENANT COMMANDER	LIEUTENANT COMMANDER
(SILVER) LIEUTENANT COLONEL	(SILVER) LIEUTENANT COLONEL	(SILVER) LIEUTENANT COLONEL	COMMANDER	COMMANDER

SERVICE INSIGNIA

ARMY	AIR FORCE	MARINE CORPS	NAVY	COAST GUARD
COLONEL	COLONEL	COLONEL	CAPTAIN	CAPTAIN
BRIGADIER GENERAL	BRIGADIER GENERAL	BRIGADIER GENERAL	COMMODORE	COMMODORE
MAJOR GENERAL	MAJOR GENERAL	MAJOR GENERAL	REAR ADMIRAL	REAR ADMIRAL
LIEUTENANT GENERAL	LIEUTENANT GENERAL	LIEUTENANT GENERAL	VICE ADMIRAL	VICE ADMIRAL
GENERAL	GENERAL	GENERAL	ADMIRAL	ADMIRAL
GENERAL OF THE ARMY	GENERAL OF THE AIR FORCE	NONE	FLEET ADMIRAL	NONE
AS PRESCRIBED BY INCUMBENT GENERAL OF THE ARMIES	NONE	NONE	NONE	NONE

rosettes, may also be worn on the left lapel of civilian clothes, with the exception of civilian evening dress. Honorable discharge and service buttons may be worn on the left lapel of civilian clothes, except on evening dress.

RETIRED OFFICERS' DRESS

Although retired officers wear civilian dress at most official and social occasions, there are occasions when the uniform may be worn.

The number of years of retirement has nothing to do with the retired officer's decision to wear—or not to wear—his uniform; the elements of good taste and propriety are the key to his decision.

Retired officers on active duty wear the same uniforms prescribed for officers on active duty.

When not on active duty, a retired officer may wear the uniform corresponding to the grade at the time of retirement, or as authorized, upon the following occasions:

At military ceremonies.
Military weddings or funerals.
Memorial services, inaugurals, patriotic parades on national holidays.
Other military parades or ceremonies in which any active or Reserve
    United States military unit is taking part.
At educational institutions when giving military instruction or when responsible for military discipline.

Retired officers wear civilian clothing when riding in military aircraft, except when engaged in a military activity, then they wear the uniform.

The uniform is *not* worn when you are visiting or living in a foreign country, except when attending by formal invitation a ceremony or social function at which the wearing of the uniform is required. Under these circumstances, authority to wear the uniform may be granted by the service secretary and/or the nearest military attaché.

RESERVE OFFICERS

Reserve officers on active duty have the same minimum outfit of uniforms and insignia, as well as accessories, as prescribed for the regular service, except that the sword, sword accessories, and formal evening dress uniform are not required.

When not on active duty, reserve officers wear the uniforms upon the same general occasions as listed for the retired officers.

SEPARATED PERSONNEL

Any person who has served in the Army (including personnel assigned to the air components prior to the establishment of the Department of the Air Force), Navy, Air Force, Marine Corps, or Coast Guard during wartime, and whose most recent service was terminated honorably, is entitled to wear the uniform of the highest grade held during his or her war service, upon the following ceremonial occasions:

Military funerals or weddings, memorial services, inaugurals.

Patriotic parades on national holidays, or other military parades or ceremonies in which any active or reserve United States military unit is taking part.

The uniform worn may be the one authorized at the time of separation, or it may be that prescribed by authorization at the time of the ceremony.

CIVILIAN DRESS (MEN): FORMAL

BLACK TIE (AFTER 6 P.M. WHEN INDICATED IN INVITATION)

"Black tie" means your dinner jacket or tuxedo. The term "tuxedo" came about in the 1890's when the dinner jacket was introduced into the United States from England and was first worn at the Tuxedo Club.

This is the favorite form of men's evening dress and is worn at almost any formal occasion—receptions, weddings, theater or opera, dances, dinners, etc. Guests may wear dinner jackets at a formal evening church wedding, although members of the wedding party wear full dress. Black tie is not properly worn before six o'clock in the evening.

Jacket—Of black, or dark blue tropical worsted or one of the new blended materials of good quality, usually single-breasted. The lapels are faced with satin, rolled or peaked. For summertime, white linen, dacron, etc. The dark jacket may be worn in the summertime—but it is hot. Nowadays, the plaid or more colorful dinner jacket is worn for cruises and less formal occasions.

Trousers—Material matches the coat, with single stripe of matching colored braid or satin. Trousers are without cuffs. (Black trousers are worn with white, plaid, or colored jackets.)

Waistcoat—Not worn with a double-breasted jacket; with a single-breasted jacket, the waistcoat will be of white piqué or black plain, ribbed, or self-figured silk. Instead of a waistcoat, a *cummerbund* is usually worn, black, maroon, or midnight blue silk; in the summertime it may be plaid or figured.

Shirt—The popular (and comfortable) attached fold collar with pleated or piqué bosom. White or light blue.

Tie—Black bow, or color to match cummerbund.

Socks—Black or dark blue to match trousers.

Shoes—Black patent leather, or black kid, plain-front shoes or pumps.

Hat—Rarely worn. A gray fedora goes with everything but white tie. A straw in the summer.

Gloves—Gray or white evening.

Topcoat—Black, charcoal gray, or dark blue.

Accessories—White linen handkerchief; white silk scarf; studs and cuff links.

Boutonniere—Red or white carnation. (*See* "White tie.")

WHITE TIE (AFTER 6 P.M.)

"White tie" means full-dress evening wear, or "tailcoat." Tails are not worn often except by men in the diplomatic service, senior officers, or at a very formal wedding or ceremonial occasion. When you need tails, a good rental service will furnish all the items necessary.

Like dinner jackets, tails should never be worn before six o'clock. Also, tails are not worn in the summer.

Boutonniere—White carnation for left buttonhole, for full dress; or a small white gardenia, lily-of-the-valley, rosebud, or miniature rose. At a wedding, the bridegroom usually wears a white carnation, with the ushers wearing a white flower that differs from those of the best man and groom. Do not wear a boutonniere when wearing decorations or when you are in uniform tails—or in any uniform.

FORMAL DAYTIME CLOTHES (BEFORE 6 P.M.) (MEN)

Formal daytime clothes—the *cutaway* or *sack coat*—are mainly worn at diplomatic or governmental affairs. A man taking part in a formal daytime wedding party, or a pallbearer at a state funeral, also wears such dress. For a formal wedding, the cutaway is worn; for the semi-formal wedding, the sack coat. A pallbearer or any other man wears a black four-in-hand tie with a fold-down collar instead of an ascot. There are few occasions for the average man to wear a cutaway or sack coat, therefore they should be rented.

Concerning certain accessories, boutonnieres other than white or red carnations may be worn at various occasions. Cornflowers and small white gardenias are sometimes used, and a groom at a wedding occasionally wears an orange blossom or a small sprig of lily-of-the-valley.

Such flowers are always worn in the left buttonhole of a suit but are *never* worn when you are in uniform.

A handkerchief placed in the breast pocket of your suit is entirely for show. It must, of course, be clean and folded, and only an inch or two shows. When you use a colored handkerchief in your breast pocket, it must blend with the colors in your tie.

A dress handkerchief is white linen and can be initialed with a single letter or with all your initials. For evening use, the initials are white, gray, or black, but other colors are correct for daytime use.

CIVILIAN DRESS (MEN): INFORMAL

Any serviceman faces a distinct problem in the matter of his clothes. This is because he must possess two wardrobes—service and civilian. Since uniforms are a necessity, they are purchased first.

When an officer of average financial circumstances purchases his uniform wardrobe and maintains it in the high state of excellence in which it should be kept, usually there is only a modest amount left over in the clothes budget. It is wise to start off with a conservative civilian wardrobe which can be worn for many occasions and seasons.

The best clothes are always those of good quality, subdued color, and the best possible tailoring. Such colors as gray, blue-gray, dark blue, or tans and brown, are best. Sports jackets in moderate-toned greens, browns, blues, and gray mixtures are always in good taste. The same conservative overtone is important in all other items of dress—such as socks, ties, shirts.

However, if you want more color in your wardrobe, it could be confined to such items as sports shirts, bathing trunks, pajamas. Although more color is used in men's clothing today than ever before, do purchase shirts and ties, particularly, with care; don't succumb to extremes in color and style.

In the long run, cheap clothes are the most expensive because they don't last as long and must be replaced earlier than expected.

It is well to remember that what is good taste in one part of the country may be poor taste in others. The bright and unusual sports shirts and slacks which are so familiar in Hawaii or southern and western states may not fit in with the more conservative—and cooler—northern and New England states—or vice versa.

Although it is difficult to state any rule for wearing or buying clothes—particularly when you are transferred from one coast to another—appropriate dress is usually the more conservative type of clothes which are usually in good taste anywhere. Dress in foreign countries is generally on the conservative side, and a "loudly" dressed American is not a good representative of his service or country.

The question often arises as to the clothes needed for a young officer's civilian wardrobe. The following suggestions are based on the consensus of a cross section of officers who have learned through experience.

MINIMUM CLOTHING LIST FOR MEN

1. *A conservative suit.* One such suit will be adequate at first, but you should plan on getting two as soon as the financial situation permits. One or both suits should be suitable for wearing after six o'clock when informal conditions are to be met. The dark blue business suit is traditional, is worn at daytime and less formal evening weddings and receptions. A gray suit is frequently worn at the office or during daytime activities. Texturized polyester and worsted materials wear well and are not heavy or bulky; coats may be double breasted or single breasted, with peaked or notched lapels. Leisure suits are worn to many less formal occasions. These are sports coat/jacket, with trousers/slacks.

2. *A sports jacket.* This jacket will probably be the most useful and the most worn item in your wardrobe. You should be sure to get a good one that will stand many cleanings; choose one that can be worn with almost any color slacks.

3. *Slacks.* At least two pairs. Gray and tan are standard colors anywhere.

4. *Topcoat.* If you find that you cannot afford a topcoat in the early stages, you can always use your officer's raincoat without the insignia. But making the raincoat "double in brass" reduces its longevity, and you should plan on getting a topcoat in the near future.

5. *Summer clothes.* It may develop that you will need summer suits and slacks immediately. Eventually you will need one or two summer suits—and leisure wear—but don't spend too much money on this type of clothes. Duty calling for winter wear will surely turn up.

6. *Dinner jacket*: Optional. Early in your career you may not be able to afford a dinner jacket and, in any case, have little need for one. When the need arises at a nonmilitary affair, there are rental services available almost everywhere. See earlier section on "black tie."

7. *Shirts.* Polyester sport and dress shirts.

8. *Ties.* For all occasions; currently no wider than 3 to 3¾ inches, but styles in tie widths change frequently.

9. *Shoes.* Dress and casual. Crepe-soled moccasins are comfortable, long-wearing for casual wear and for traveling. Black patent or kid for formal wear. Brown or black for less formal dress.

10. *Socks.* Dress and casual. Black for formal wear; black, dark

blue, gray, or brown with business suits; almost any color for casual wear. Avoid the angle-length sock that shows your skin below trousers—particularly when you sit down.

11. *Sweaters, pullovers.* A good washable sweater and several pullovers are needed in everyday living.

12. *Bathing trunks*, and any special wear for sports participation.

13. *Robe.* Packable but not bulky. Washable.

14. *Hat.* Hardly worn nowadays. A gray felt snap-brim is worn with any business suit; a straw for summer wear.

CIVILIAN DRESS FOR SERVICEWOMEN

The types of civilian clothes which are needed by women in the services must be determined by the climate and season, the size and location of your base, post, or station, and your specific needs. The rapid changes in women's fashions make it impractical to give a detailed list of clothing for a civilian wardrobe.

In an area where civilian clothes are worn at work, the woman officer should select her wardrobe with care. She should dress as her civilian counterpart—the executive woman. Appropriate clothes—suits, tailored dresses, and street dresses—in becoming colors and of excellent quality are always in good taste for daytime wear.

Since the junior officer may be able to acquire only a limited civilian wardrobe, she would be wise to select fashions of such quality that they can be worn frequently and can be expected to remain in style for more than a season or so. Large and/or bright designs soon become tiresome, and such a dress may seem old after being worn only once or twice. On the other hand, an older dress of subdued shade and design may seem new when worn with different accessories.

Appropriate outfits and accessories for "after five" should be included in a woman officer's wardrobe. However, the number and kind of social affairs you attend will dictate your needs. In such areas as Hawaii or Camp Pendleton, you may need more sports or casual clothes; in Washington, D.C., you may have more need for cocktail and evening dresses.

In selecting your civilian clothes, always pay attention to good workmanship and quality of fabrics, and choose styles which are becoming to your individual figure.

VARIATIONS IN STYLE

Almost any woman knows that very short women should select dresses with long lines rather than those broken at the waist by a band of another color or by a wide belt. Some suit styles will "cut you in two." Horizonal stripes should not be worn.

On the other hand, the very tall woman should avoid vertical stripes and select dresses with a break in the middle. Most suits are very becoming.

A plump woman should not wear a dress of clinging material or one of large design. A slightly flared skirt is flattering. Care must be taken in the selection of shorts, slacks, and bathing suits.

CIVILIAN WARDROBE

In general your civilian wardrobe should include the following:

1. *Raincoat or all-purpose coat.*
2. *Coat.* A cold-weather coat should be of basic color to go with almost anything.
3. *Casual suit.* Weight in accordance with the climate; preferably of dacron knit or easy-care material; washable, drip-dry.
4. *Pantsuit.* Washable and machine or drip-dry.
5. *Slacks.* Washable and machine or drip-dry.
6. *Jacket and/or sweater.* For sports or casual wear.
7. *Blouses.* Plain or print, polyesters, or any washable material, to wear with a suit, pantsuit, slacks, shorts, skirts.
8. *Skirt.* Short and/or long.
9. *Afternoon dress.* Of polyester, dacron knit, silk, wool, etc.
10. *Cocktail dress.* Of any becoming style and material. Short skirt. Dressy.
11. *Evening dress.* For formal occasions. Long skirt.
12. *Shoes.* Dress and casual. Comfortable walking, low or moderate heels for casual; probably pumps for dress.
13. *Hats and gloves.* Optional.
14. *Handbags.* For casual and dress.
15. *Robe.* Packable and washable. And house slippers.

WHAT TO WEAR AT WEDDINGS

Servicemen and servicewomen may wear the uniforms prescribed for formal, semiformal, and informal occasions such as weddings and receptions, as described in the uniform charts for each service on pages 30 to 41 (For civilian dress at weddings, *see* Chapter 25, Planning the Wedding.)

GENERAL WEAR—MEN AND WOMEN

Although there is a great deal more informality (and color) in men's dress today, there are occasions where sports jackets are not worn. However, before 6 P.M. almost anything goes. A rule of thumb is that when a wife or date wears a cocktail dress, a man does not wear a sports jacket, but wears a conservative suit appropriate for possible dinner and the theater later.

Sports jackets and slacks—or the leisure suit—are often worn to informal suppers, cookouts, and to late afternoon cocktail parties when the invitation states casual dress. There is a difference in the meaning of "casual" and "informal." Very casual dress is not worn at most informal occasions—unless the hosts say so.

There is no question about what to wear at a very formal reception, dinner, or ball; it is spelled out on the invitation, either by the hour stated or by the "White tie" or "Black tie" written in the lower corner of the card. When a ball starts after nine or ten at night, it means white tie. An officer, cadet, or midshipman may wear their evening dress uniform instead.

Servicewomen at formal civilian occasions wear uniforms in accordance with male officers, or evening dress in accordance with local custom. When you have a doubt about what to wear at a dinner or luncheon—or any occasion—ask the hostess. It is better to phone and find out than to be sorry when you get there.

SPORTS WEAR

Sports and physical fitness enthusiasts need clothing in keeping with the sport. Shoes are most important for comfort and security. The skier will need leather ski boots; the angler, hip-high waders; the golfer, cleated shoes; the mountain climber, rugged boots or shoes with a grip. Golf shoes, tennis shoes, soft-soled deck shoes for boating—for your protection as well as the boat's deck—are some of the types worn.

The skier must have a warm jacket or parka and pants; the mountain climber's gear must be rugged but not heavy. Slacks are generally worn for bowling. Women golfers like shorts or short skirts; men wear shorts or slacks and a wide variety of sports shirts, turtlenecks, or pullovers. Women tennis players wear brief dresses or shorts; men usually prefer shorts. Jeans are worn by western riders—and almost everyone else; and bathing suits and trunks in a rainbow of colors are at the beach or pool.

The Social Side of Life

CHAPTER 3

Hops & Dances

YOUNG MEN AND WOMEN in training at the service academies, ROTC units, or Officer Candidate Schools—or, for that matter, any young officer anywhere—will find that the etiquette observed at the academy hops* and the college dances will generally be the same at any other dance or ball. The earlier the correct etiquette at a dance is learned, the easier it will be for you to attend with complete poise and confidence any debutante ball or embassy dance.

The new fourth classmen at the academies each year are young people from all walks of life. Many have had previous college or preparatory school training, and know how to escort or be escorted to fraternity or class dances. Others, directly out of high school, may not have had the opportunity to learn what to do at formal dances, or how to greet those in the receiving line.

A midshipman or cadet, or any student, should be well versed in such courtesies before being graduated and receiving an assignment in a service that may take him all over the world and into various social situations.

---

* Hop is a word for dance long used at the older service and maritime academies, but is less used today and never used at the Air Force Academy.

THE ACADEMY HOPS

There are two kinds of dances: *informal* and *formal*. The distinction between them is mainly in dress.

Informal hops are held for fourth classmen, as well as for upperclassmen, on weekend afternoon or nights. Women dates wear casual dress but never jeans, and sport shirts and slacks are worn by the civilian dates of women midshipmen and cadets.

The uniform is prescribed for all formal hops and dances, usually evening dress uniform. Women dates wear long dresses. The civilian date of a woman midshipman or cadet wears black tie or the equivalent of what the male midshipman or cadet wears. But at any hop or ball, the important thing for a date to remember is to dress in accordance with the formality—or informality—of the occasion.

An academy hostess is always on hand at the hop to receive, or assist in receiving, guests.

HOP TIME

Formal dances at the service academies are usually held from 9:00 P.M. until midnight, or later upon special occasions. Upper classmen attend on a voluntary basis, but must return to their barracks or quarters by a designated time after the hop is over.

When you arrive at the dance, the man waits while his date takes her coat to the coatroom. There will be needles, thread, etc. for any emergency.

At the informals, you arrive and leave at designated times.

RECEIVING LINES AT HOPS

It is a courtesy—and therefore mandatory—that you go through the receiving line at formal dances. This is good training for future events and is similar to receiving lines at dances, balls, receptions, or similar functions.

The receiving line customarily forms near the entrance to the ballroom and is kept as short as possible. At a very large function there may be two lines. Standing first in line is the hop manager or chairman, with the person who is receiving standing next. The wife of an officer on active duty on the base or station, or the commanding officer, will be invited to receive the guests, with their husband or wife.

The hop manager or chairman always keeps his hands at his sides, or at his back, so that guests will not shake hands with him. It is his duty to announce the names of guests to the receiving person at his side, who will shake hands with each guest and greet everyone in a friendly manner. When the commanding officer of the station receives, such as the superintendent of the academy, it is optional for him to stand next to the hop manager (or chairman) or his wife.

Receiving lines are not held at informal hops and mixers. Academy hostesses are always on hand to mix with the guests.

At a formal dance at West Point, the officer stands to the right of the hop manager, with the officer's wife to his right, then the cadet hostess. The receiving line may be as follows:

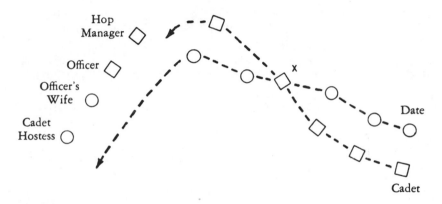

The Receiving Line at a West Point Formal

The young lady is on the right of the cadet as they enter the ballroom. At point "x," the cadet has passed behind the young lady and is now on her right.

PROCEDURE

The steps in going through the receiving line at West Point are:

1. The hop manager (chairman or escort) stands first in line, in order to present the guests to the receiving officer at his side. He does *not* shake hands with the guests, but the officer does.

2. As the cadet and his date approach the line, she will be on his right. She does *not* hold his arm.

3. Nearing the line, the girl steps ahead and the cadet is now behind and to her right, in position to give their names to the hop manager.

4. The cadet gives the girl's *last* name only: "Miss Smith."

5. When the girl steps ahead of the cadet, the hop manager turns to the receiving officer and says the *receiving officer's name first:* "General Brown, Miss Smith."

6. The receiving person shakes hands with the young lady and says something similar to, "Good evening, Miss Smith, it's nice to see you." The girl may answer, "Good evening, General Brown," or "Good evening, it's nice to be here."

7. After the hop manager presents the girl to the receiving person, he turns to you the cadet, and you give your last name: "Cadet Jones."* Do not fail to give your name, regardless of how well you know him. If a guest does not state his name, the hop chairman may say, "Your name, please?" The civilian date of a woman cadet (or midshipman) would say "Mr. Jones."

8. The hop chairman then presents you to the person who is receiving: "General Brown, Cadet Jones." You respond in this manner: "Good evening, Sir," or "Good evening, General Brown." It is always correct to say, "How do you do, Sir?"

9. You may bow slightly when you shake hands, you should look at the person addressed—escort, receiving lady, etc.—and not attempt a conversation.

10. The line does not form again at the end of the dance. It is always courteous, however, to thank those receiving, and the hostess, and to say good-bye.

At any social function where the person receiving is a lady, her name is given first.

INTERMISSIONS

Fruit punch and cakes are served during intermission at formals, and smoking is permitted, but in authorized areas only. You may have the minor problem at very large dances of finding your date if she was dancing with someone else when intermission was called.

If you, a man, should pass her, you may extend your arm and tell her partner that you will take over, which will release him to find his own young lady. If something unexpected happens to the escort of the girl with whom you have had that dance and he has not reclaimed her, *then it is your duty*—and your date's—to stand by until he appears.

---

* A midshipman or Coast Guard cadet is introduced or addressed as "Mister" at social or official occasions, except at certain military, state, or social occasions when he is introduced or addressed by title for purposes of identification or designation. At the Air Force and Military Academies, cadets are introduced (or give their names) as "Cadet Doe," but are addressed thereafter as "Mr. Doe." Cadets and midshipmen at the Merchant Marine Academies are introduced in the same way.

CONDUCT AT DANCES

Midshipmen and cadets are expected to conduct themselves with decorum at all times—on or off the dance floor. Displays of affection on the dance floor are not tolerated, and Hop Committee members will ask those who violate courtesies to leave the hop. Members of the Hop Committee at the Coast Guard and Naval Academies are distinguished by their gold aiguillettes; at the Air Force Academy by silver aiguillettes; at West Point by red sashes. They have the authority to enforce regulations.

A man never leaves his date sitting alone, or embarrasses her with boisterous conduct. Never leave her in mid-floor. If an occasion arises when you must leave, you should leave her with a group before excusing yourself. If you are not adept at certain steps, such as in the more intricate dances, you may suggest "waiting this one out."

However, since it is the gentleman who invites the lady to dance, it is up to her to suggest that you stop. She might say, "Shall we rest a moment?" or "Please, let's have some punch."

When you complete a dance with a girl who is not your guest, take her back to her escort or to her party, and thank her.

Since the general tone of a ball is formal, rather formal dancing is expected. Contemporary dancing is permitted, but not so strenuously as to demand a wide area.

It is inconsiderate to remain talking in groups on the dance floor. If you want to talk, rather than dance, you should move to the side of the floor.

OBLIGATIONS

The *first* obligation of a midshipman or cadet—or anyone—is to the person you are with. He or she should be shown every consideration, and in turn, it is your date's duty to you to make this one of the most memorable of occasions.

You should dance with your date frequently, but not exclusively. You should introduce him or her to other couples. A man must see to it that his date is never neglected, even though this might be a blind date and she is not "Miss America."

Your *second* obligation is to the others in your party or at your table. You must join in the general conversation, bring your date or others into the conversation, suggest refreshments during intermission, and dance with others in the group.

Your *third* obligation is to the midshipmen or cadet hostess, to those in the receiving line, and other seniors present.

Each cadet or midshipman in the host company for that evening has this particular obligation: he or she must make it a point to talk briefly to the receiving officer and to any senior guests, and to dance with their spouses. Do not neglect your academy hostess. Seniors are well aware of your desire to dance with others of your own age, so don't be afraid of being "stuck."

In asking an officer's wife for a dance, a male cadet or midshipman would first approach Colonel and Mrs. Rank, greet them, and introduce his date, although she has already met them in the receiving line. After a brief exchange of small talk, he asks Mrs. Rank if she would care to dance. Colonel Rank then talks or dances with his date.

At the end of the number—or earlier, if indicated by Mrs. Rank—you both return to the place where you started. Thank her for the dance, as you would any partner, before you and your young lady move away.

SPECIAL HOPS AND DANCES

The hops and balls held during Graduation (or Commissioning) Week are considered the most important of all. They are the final dances for the first classmen. Informals and formals for all classes are held throughout the week, with the graduation dinner and ball held after the final parade and Color Girl presentation on graduation eve.

The ring dance is the highlight for the second class at the Naval and Air Force Academies, held during the week, with West Pointers and Coast Guard cadets receiving their rings a month earlier. Customs vary at the different academies but at Annapolis couples pass through a replica of the class ring and each young lady receives a kiss. At the Air Force Academy the ring presentation and dining-in are for cadets only, followed by a formal dance in Arnold Hall.

During the ring banquet weekend at West Point, second classmen receive their rings at a dining-in, and the formal dinner-dance is held the following night in Eisenhower Hall. At the Coast Guard Academy the ring dance is held in Leamy Hall. At the Citadel the ring dance has a Junior Sword Drill composed of sergeants from the second class who form an arch of sabers through which pass the first classmen and their dates.

The ring dance is a tradition at the State Maritime Academies and the Merchant Marine Academy, with each observing a special custom. At the Massachusetts State Maritime Academy, for example, a feature is a precision drill by the Honor Guard. The ring dance at King's Point is held in August.

The occasion of the ring dance and dinner is considered a prime time for cadets and midshipmen to give their "One and Only" a miniature of their class rings.

INFORMALS

An informal is held almost weekly at most academies, usually on a weekend in the late afternoon. They are also held following pop or rock concerts. On nights when there are no dances, a popular time is disco night when all kinds of records are played.

A hop, an informal, a mixer, all mean about the same thing. At the academies an informal means that the midshipman or cadet invites his own date. At a mixer the social director may send out invitations to young ladies at least sixteen years of age from nearby colleges and communities. Dress is a little more casual for the mixer, but jeans and shorts are never worn. In turn, nearby women's colleges often invite the midshipmen and cadets to their mixers.

The informals serve as times to get acquainted with other young people as well as a means of improving dance steps and learning social mores. Dance instruction is available for those who want it.

SPECIAL DANCES

Each academy, each military school and college in the country, has a special dance all its own. Each class has its own, also, such as the plebe parents' formal held during Parents Weekend after spring break at West Point, with parents and dates dancing in Eisenhower Hall. There is a homecoming dance, a Christmas ball, a spring formal, and a Valentine's Day dance.

At Annapolis, the International Ball is an annual formal with young ladies and men invited from nearby embassies. At the Air Force Academy, there are the all-class Dean's Ball and the Commandant's Ball, and the Recognition Ball held for all classes during Graduation Week; at West Point the Camp Illumination formal highlights the end of summer training for the third class at nearby Camp Buckner.

The formal held during King's Point Weekend in early June at the Merchant Marine Academy is held on an outside dance floor overlooking the Sound.

SERVICE BALLS

Each service has its own special ball, which usually is a charity fete with proceeds going to their personnel for financial or educational assistance.

The Navy Relief Ball committee in Washington, D.C., issues some two thousand invitations for their annual formal dinner-dance. The Air Force has two main balls: the Iron Gate Ball, held annually on the East and West Coasts, with guests other than Air Force officers including industrial personages; and the Air Force Charity Ball which is held in Washington, D.C., with senior officers in the area attending as well as government officials and industrial leaders. Both are black-tie affairs, with dinner preceding dancing.

The occasion of the birthday of the Marine Corps on 10 November 1775, is observed throughout the world—aboard ship and at all posts and stations. Distinguished guests from other services and from civilian life attend the formal ball in Washington, D.C.

The cake-cutting ceremony follows a time-honored procedure including the playing of "The Marines' Hymn," while the cake escorts bring in a Mameluke sword on a serving cart with the cake.

Army Branch Balls (infantry, artillery, etc.) celebrate the founding of the particular branch, at formal balls held throughout this country and abroad.

SERVICE JUNIOR DANCES

Among the service dances held throughout the country is the Army-Navy-Air Force Cotillion in Washington, D.C., which is open to service juniors who are sons or daughters of active, retired, or deceased officers of the Army, Navy, Air Force, Marine Corps, and Coast Guard. Members must be at least sixteen years old.

A representative from one of the services and his wife act as official hosts. There usually are three informals held during the year. The one formal—the Christmas cotillion—is attended by midshipmen and cadets on Christmas leave.

Informal hops are held for cadets and midshipmen following the Army-Navy game in Philadelphia, and in cities where other service academy games are played. When time permits, dances may be planned at universities where games with service academies are scheduled.

Commanders of various posts, bases, and stations, and service organizations such as Alumni Association chapters or ROTC units, often invite cadets and midshipmen to attend dances held during leave.

COLLEGE DANCES

A college man wears black tie—his tuxedo, or a white dinner jacket in the summer—to a formal college dance.

Midshipmen and cadets, ROTC students, OCS, OTS—or any officer

—may wear the uniform that is the equivalent of black tie, or civilian dress.

When a dinner precedes a dance at a women's college, the girl usually pays for the dinner—in advance, so no one will be embarrassed. But if you invite her out for dinner, you pay for the meal. You pay for all taxi fares during the weekend and for any flowers, movies, etc.

DEBUTANTE BALLS

In metropolitan cities throughout the country, debutantes (girls about eighteen years old) are introduced to society in large groups at cotillions and assemblies. Such balls are usually held for the benefit of various charity organizations, with the young ladies' fathers making contributions to charities in lieu of the greater expense of private debuts. Dinners honoring individual debutantes are customarily held before the ball.

Daughters, or daughters of close friends and relatives, are frequently honored by their parents or sponsors at afternoon tea dances, which are usually held in private clubs or hotel ballrooms, and are less elaborate.

Each girl attending a formal ball subscribes for two or three partners—or more. Debutantes wear long white dresses and white gloves for their presentation. Midshipmen, cadets, and young bachelor officers are often invited to become dancing partners at a ball, or to attend as "stags." Officers wear evening dress uniform or white tie. Midshipmen and cadets wear evening dress uniform. Civilian gentlemen wear white tie.

Partners of the debutante, as well as her close relatives and friends, send flowers to the girl before the ball, with one corsage or bouquet selected to be worn. The other flowers are used as a background at the place the debutante is presented.

A buffet supper is served after midnight, and the ball is over in the early morning hours. No line is formed at the conclusion of the affair, but guests are expected to thank the debutante's parents or sponsors. If a dinner, at which you were a guest, was held before the ball, then you thank the host and hostess of that dinner, also.

Since each cotillion has various customs and traditions, it is important that you learn the ground rules in advance, from the person who sent you the invitation.

THE FORMAL DANCE

A formal dance, or private debut, may be held in a large room or club, usually starting about ten o'clock, with dancing getting underway an hour later. For a very formal affair, a carpet may run from the curb to the front entrance, with an awning overhead and guests are announced.

The hostess and the guest of honor—say, a debutante—stand near the entrance to the ballroom, where they greet guests. Should the host stand in the receiving line during the early part of the evening, he will leave the line before the hostess and guest of honor, to mix with the guests. The receiving line usually breaks up after three-quarters of an hour, then the girl is free to join the dancers. Her first dance is with her father, who has been circulating among the guests, then with the young man who is her escort for the evening and who will take her in to supper.

There is a stag line, with an extra man for each nine or ten girls. If you are invited as a stag, your duty is to see that the girls receive the proper attention and never lack for dancing partners.

A buffet supper is served after midnight, with no announcement made concerning its serving. The hostess usually initiates the movement of a few guests toward the buffet table, and other guests follow.

When you attend as a stag, you may ask any unattached woman to have supper with you. You fill both your plates, and sit wherever you like. Usually, small tables are arranged to sit at. At a large dance, the food may be served directly to guests seated at small tables.

DUTY DANCES

"Duty" dances are those that good manners require a man to have with certain ladies at a private dance, or dinner dance. Such duty dances are those with your hostess, the guest of honor, and any feminine member of the hostess's family.

If you attended a dinner before the dance or ball, then you should also dance with the hostess and the guest of honor at that occasion. You have a certain duty (but it is not required) to dance also with the two women who sat at your left and right at the dinner. If the woman at your right was your assigned dinner partner, then you are obligated to dance with her.

When you are the guest of a woman at a party, or are the guest of a subscription party member, you should dance several times with her, and invite her to have supper with you.

At a service dance, you dance—or sit and talk for a few minutes— with the wife of the senior officer present, whether she is the hostess or not.

CHAPTER 4

The Hop Weekend

WHEN YOU INVITE a date to your service academy, ROTC, or military college for the first time, write the letter in a simple but sincere manner. If your date has never been to the academy before, you should include a brief but general idea of the plans for the weekend. Write three or four weeks in advance of a special hop or dance; if the invitation is for Graduation Week, then many more details must be included.

A hop weekend is for one or two nights. Usually, Graduation Week (Commissioning Week at the Naval Academy) starts the Friday before graduation, which currently takes place at most academies the end of May.

After your date accepts your invitation, then write a more specific letter in return. Dates do not want to arrive either unprepared or overloaded with luggage, and should be told the best way to come—by bus, train, plane, or car. And they should also be told whether you can, or cannot, meet them, owing to drills, classes, etc. If you know that others from the same area or college will be arriving that weekend, you might mention their names so that they have company on the trip.

For a regular hop weekend, you should inform your date about any formal or informal dances, and advise him or her about any activities such as a football game or a play. At all academies, a full week is planned during Graduation Week, including parades, formals and informals, dinners, sailing, picnics, baseball, tennis, and for first classmen the graduation reception which parents and dates attend.

Your date will want to know about the accommodations you have arranged, and reservations should be made as early as possible—frequently a year ahead—for the week of graduation.

ARRIVAL BY BUS OR PLANE

When a person is not arriving by private car, a bus may be the most convenient method for a fairly short trip. For the person coming from a distance, a plane to the nearest large city will save time, then a bus or taxi to the academy. But taxis and airport limousines are expensive. When several are traveling together, this expense is shared and thus becomes reasonable.

There are regular bus schedules out of New York City for West Point, New York (or to Highland Falls), some fifty miles north; and to New London, Connecticut. And there are regular schedules out of Washington, D.C. for Annapolis, Maryland (about thirty-five miles), and out of Baltimore for Annapolis, about twenty-five miles. The Air Force Academy is located about twelve miles north of Colorado Springs, and sixty miles south of Denver. There is a regular bus schedule on weekends out of Colorado Springs which takes visitors to the academy complex, which is about six miles from the entrance to the main buildings.

The New York State Maritime College at Fort Schuyler, and the Merchant Marine Academy at King's Point, both on Long Island Sound, are readily available by car or bus, with parkways leading to them from almost any direction. The sites of all maritime academies are accessible by plane or car.

Air lines have daily schedules—subject to change—at airports near all large cities close to the academies. Arrival and departure information is ascertained at the time the plane tickets are reserved.

PLEBE DATES

Women plebes at the service academies may date men plebes or civilian men, but regulations do not permit them to date upper classmen.

A civilian man who is dating a woman cadet or midshipman wears black tie to a formal dance in accordance with the dress uniform worn by his counterpart. Casual dress is worn to the informals and mixers.

Since civilian dress is now authorized to be worn on base at some informal and recreational occasions by the midshipmen and cadets, similar dress is worn by civilian men.

DRESS FOR DATES

Your date will want to know what clothes to bring for a hop weekend or for Graduation (Commissioning) Week, and what type of events will be attended. For a girl, a formal hop means a long dress. The informal means an attractive but simple short dress or pantsuit—but never jeans.

Sunday morning chapel services require a girl to wear daytime dress, but hats and gloves are not necessary. A man wears a suit and tie.

Shoes are probably the most important item of dress—there is considerable walking at all academies. Nowadays most girls wear shoes with moderate heels for any occasion, but high heels may be worn for formal occasions when desired. Soft-soled shoes are mandatory when sailing (this protects the deck) and on the tennis court. Durable shoes are needed for hiking or a mountain climb.

For a sports weekend, the slacks or pantsuit worn on the trip may double for any contest. In cold weather, such as a late-season football game, a warm coat or jacket, a warm skirt and sweater, slacks or pantsuit, boots and scarf—these are essential. A wise date may bring along a blanket to help keep warm. A lightweight raincoat or an all-purpose coat is indispensable for the sudden storm.

In warm weather shorts may be worn for sailing, tennis, and other sports, but the too-brief shorts are frowned upon; along with bathing suits they should not be worn away from the beach or swimming pool.

And don't forget to bring dark glasses!

EXPENSES OF DATES

When dates come for a hop weekend, or for graduation, they pay for their own transportation. They also pay for their own meals en route and for any during the visit that have not been arranged for them by their cadet or midshipman host.

Dates will pay for their own room during the stay in a motel, hotel, or guest house, even though the reservation was made for them. Frequently, officers' quarters are open to young friends, who are invited as nonpaying guests. A Squadron Sponsor Program at the Air Force Academy is backed by staff officers and airmen who "adopt" the cadets in the forty squadrons, and invite members of their families and dates as guests in their quarters. At the Hotel Thayer on the grounds of the Military Academy, dormitory rooms are available for dates at very reasonable rates. Motels are conveniently located near all service and maritime academies. A list of rooms in accredited homes, and of hotels and motels in the area are available in the office of each service academy social director (hostess). Upon request, the list will be sent to the date.

When you, a cadet or midshipman, ROTC, or college student, invite a guest for a meal, movie, or whatever, you pay for it. A man pays for flowers for his girl. However, sending a corsage is an exception rather than the rule of former years, and is for very special occasions. Giving flowers is determined by class decision, with considerable savings gained by group purchase.

Although cadets and midshipmen receive a larger monthly allowance than in former years, they are not affluent. For those who have little or no financial assistance from home. the allowance does not go very far.

CAR AND BICYCLE REGULATIONS

A date should be aware of the regulations regarding the driving of cars and riding in them by the midshipmen and cadets. The regulations vary at each academy, but in general first classmen may own cars and leave them in a posted area on the academy grounds during the final academic year. They may drive them during weekend leave—when their grades are up—and return them by a specified time.

At all academies, all classes may ride in cars, and at certain academies second classmen may drive them. Fourth classmen do not drive.

Regulations also vary at the academies concerning bicycles, with some midshipmen and cadets permitted to own and ride them at specified times, and others riding them as members of bicycle clubs. At the Naval Academy all classes may own and ride pedal-driven bicycles; at the Air Force Academy motor-driven bicycles and motorcycles may be owned and driven by the cadets.

DRINKING

Midshipmen and cadets, or any college student, are considered mature young men and women. Usually the voting age is considered the age of maturity, but the laws of each state determine the age when men and women may drink hard liquor—usually 21. Beer cannot be served to anyone under 18.

In general, a beer-call may be held in a specified area at the academies at times designated by the commandant; wine may occasionally be served at a dining-in or a formal occasion, but hard liquor is not permitted at the academies. Midshipmen and cadets during liberty may accept a cocktail when in the quarters of officers or in the homes of professors, but at all times a date—or anyone—should remember not to offer drinks except at prescribed times and occasions and when their guests are of legal age.

CHAPTER 5

Receptions & Cocktail Parties

RECEPTIONS

According to Webster's dictionary, a reception is a "ceremony of receiving guests." There are many kinds of receptions—afternoon or evening, formal or informal. They are of a limited duration of time, and a few or many people may be invited.

Receptions are usually held in honor of someone—a dignitary, a bride and groom, a debutante, or a newcomer. They are also held to mark a special occasion, such as an officer's retirement, after a parade, the christening or commissioning of a ship, a golden wedding anniversary, or the baptism of an infant. But no matter what the occasion may be, the routine of holding a reception is basically the same.

The purpose of a reception given in honor of someone is to have as many friends and acquaintances of the hosts as possible meet the guest (or guests) of honor. In the services, one type of reception is an "at-home," when, for example, the senior officer of a large command designates a certain day for "calls made and returned." (For more about this, *see* Chapter 6.)

When this type of reception is held, it means that the senior officer of a very large command cannot possibly receive and return individual calls made by all the officers and station personnel and their families. Thus the at-homes are held as often as necessary, ranging from one or two a year, to one every month or so.

It is no longer customary for guests to leave cards, and their call is considered repaid.

TIME

The hours of the reception are indicated on the invitation and usually span a two-hour interval. They are held at various hours, according to their nature, with less formal receptions frequently held from six to eight o'clock in the evening. Afternoon receptions and at-homes are often held from five to seven o'clock. An informal reception may be held in mid-afternoon or early evening; a formal debutante reception may be at five o'clock, or at half past ten at night.

An official or formal reception usually starts at nine o'clock in the evening, and a very formal reception and dance may be held at ten or half past ten o'clock at night.

DRESS

At *informal daytime receptions*, men wear the uniform of the day or dark business suits. Women wear afternoon dresses or suits. Ladies in the receiving line do not wear gloves. Such words as *informal*, or *service dress white* and *civilian informal* are written or engraved in the lower right-hand corner of the invitation.

At *formal daytime receptions*, a man wears the uniform of the day or the prescribed civilian dress for the very formal occasion—the cutaway —which is worn at an inaugural reception, or any formal state or public function. Such dress is also worn at a very formal wedding when you are a member of the bridal party. Women wear afternoon dresses and white gloves. The gloves are not removed until after you have gone through the receiving line, with the exception of shaking hands with a head of state or a dignitary of the church; then, the right glove is removed.

At *formal evening receptions*, the formality of the occasion is indicated by the words *black tie* written or engraved in the lower right-hand corner of the invitation. *White tie* indicates a very formal occasion. *Decorations* always indicate full evening dress.

A reception is usually black tie, unless specified otherwise. Women wear evening dress and long gloves, and men wear mess or dinner dress uniforms, or the prescribed uniform according to the season. (*See* Chapter 2, Service and Civilian Dress.)

At *semiformal receptions black tie* or *civilian informal* (your best dark business suit) with corresponding uniform designation, indicates the type of dress to be worn.

At large official receptions, or at a large reception of a somewhat public nature, *dress optional* is frequently engraved or written on the lower right-hand corner of the invitation.

Small cards stating the type of uniform to be worn are usually enclosed with naval and military invitations for official occasions.

WHITE HOUSE RECEPTIONS

Dress for a reception at the White House is the same as at any reception. A woman wears her most becoming dress, and gloves, and military personnel usually are in uniform.

As a guest, you must be on time. You should arrive at the White House gate no less than ten minutes before the hour of invitation, which will give you time to be checked at the gate where names of all guests are posted and to leave your hat and coat in the designated room.

You will be directed to the place of reception. Guests are expected to be in the room before the President, followed by his wife, enters. A military aide announces the guests' names. Since it is the title that takes precedence at an official occasion, the men precede the women they are escorting through the receiving line. Before shaking hands with the President, a woman should remove her right glove. You say, "Good evening, Mr. President," and "Good evening, Mrs. ———," and move on— unless they stop you briefly to say a few words. Otherwise, do not open a conversation with either the President or the First Lady while going through the line. You do not leave cards, and you don't leave the reception until after the President and his wife have left the room.

ARRIVAL AND DEPARTURE

There is no particular time limit as to how long you stay at a reception. You may arrive at any time between the hours indicated on the invitation, but guests are expected to arrive before the receiving line disbands. It is imperative that you first pay your respects to your host and hostess. You may stay a little longer at small receptions than at large ones.

Usually, you stay about 45 minutes, but you may stay until the closing hours at a formal reception and dance. You should not arrive uncomfortably near the closing hour of the afternoon reception unless you have been asked to stay on for supper by the hosts. A guest who arrives late at an afternoon reception and lingers on through the dinner hour can be a problem to the hosts, who may have other social obligations.

RECEIVING LINE

There are differences in the way receiving lines are formed at various official, formal, and informal receptions. Customarily, the host stands first in line at *official* receptions, with his wife at his side. The hostess stands first in line at social, *nonofficial* functions, with her husband at her side.

At *official* receptions, an aide stands either at the head of the line or facing the host and announces the names of guests as they arrive. The protocol established by the State Department, not counting the aide, is:

1. The official host
2. The guest of honor
3. The guest of honor's wife or husband
4. The official host's wife
5. Extra man, if possible, to avoid leaving a woman at the end of the line.

When the guest of honor is the president of any country, a reigning king and/or queen, or a dignitary of the Church, the host and hostess relinquish their positions in favor of their guest. The line would be:

1. President, King (or reigning Queen)
2. The honored guest's wife (or husband of Queen)
3. The official host
4. The official host's wife.

At many Washington receptions, when the honor guests are of high rank or position (for example, when the Secretary of Defense gives a reception in honor of a service Secretary), the receiving line is frequently arranged in the following manner:

1. The host
2. The hostess
3. The guest of honor
4. The guest of honor's wife.

Some hosts invite a man appropriately connected to the occasion to stand at the end of the line, in order that a woman need not be in this position. Other hosts feel that this is incorrect, since a reception is to honor certain individuals only.

At very formal *nonmilitary receptions*, a butler may announce the names of guests as they arrive. At most formal—and at some less formal —receptions, guests are received in the same way as at a formal dinner. The hostess greets each guest and presents him or her to the guests of honor; then the guest is greeted by the host, who is near the hostess but is mixing among the guests and introducing newcomers into groups.

The receiving line at receptions should be kept as small as possible. Usually, those in the line are the host, hostess, and guest or guests of honor. No one likes to go down a long line—which generally means that a guest's name is mixed up midway in the line. Names are not announced at small and informal receptions.

The receiving lines at wedding receptions, at-homes, and formal dances, are discussed in chapters pertaining to those subjects.

When a president, king, queen, or dignitary of the Church, or a person of very high rank, attends a reception, all other guests should arrive before they do. In the case of a king, president, or dignitary of the Church, women are presented to them, rather than the customary rule of presenting men to women.

RECEPTIONS FOR GRADUATES

It is customary each year for the superintendents and presidents of the various service academies and colleges, and their wives, to entertain at an afternoon or evening reception in honor of the graduates, their parents and other members of their families, and their guests.

This custom prevails not only at the academies, but also at the Officer Candidate and Officer Training schools, Marine Corps schools, ROTC and Maritime units, etc.

When the reception is held in the evening, after 6:00 P.M., and is followed by a formal dance, officers wear evening dress uniform and civilian women wear long or short formal dresses.

GARDEN PARTY

The procedure for guests going through the receiving line at a large reception may be illustrated by the superintendent's garden party, which is held at the Naval Academy each spring during Commissioning Week for the parents and guests of the first classmen. In recent years two parties have been held, because of the size of the graduating class.

The superintendent and his wife receive guests inside the superintendent's house. The guests greet their hosts; then they go into the garden where punch and small cakes are served.

At an evening party, guests go on to a dance after the reception, which will continue until midnight. In case of rain, the receiving line forms inside Dahlgren Hall. Staff officers and their wives assist in hospitalities throughout the evening. Although the majority of parents and other relatives of the midshipmen will wear evening dress—the men in dinner jackets and the women in evening attire—many persons coming from a distance may not be able to bring formal clothes. In this case, women are properly attired when they wear their prettiest afternoon dress. Men wear a dark or conservative business suit, with white shirt.

Customarily, the superintendent is first in the line—owing to his official position—with his wife at his side. The aide announces the names of guests as they arrive, and he stands nearer the entrance to the reception room, either at the head of the line or facing the host—whichever way names are more clearly heard. As the guests approach the line, the aide turns and faces them. Guests do not shake hands with the aide, and last names only are given.

The midshipman steps forward and clearly states the name of each person in his or her party, starting with the parents: "Mrs. Jones"—then "Dr. Jones"—and the date, "Miss Smith" or "Mr. Smith."

If there are other members of the family, they would be presented in this order: the mother, father, grandmother, grandfather, aunt, uncle, sister, brother, and lastly, the date.

After each person in the midshipman's party has been presented, the aide turns to the midshipman, who gives his or her name: "Mr. Jones," or "Miss Jones." The aide turns to the superintendent and says, "Admiral Blank, Mr. Jones," or simply, "Miss Jones." The superintendent and his wife shake hands with each guest.

The midshipman (or cadet) may say, "Good evening, Sir," or "Good evening, Admiral Blank," or "How do you do, Sir."

Remember to shake hands lightly—but with a degree of firmness. Your hosts have many hands to shake during the evening, and a pressure grip is to be avoided. Guests may arrive at any time between the hours stated in the invitation, but it is customary at this type of academy reception that the midshipmen or cadets attend by battalions at certain designated hours. When the line is very long, guests may dance first, then later go through the line—but all guests *must* go through the line.

Upon leaving, do not look up your hosts and say good-bye. This is a very large recepiton, and it is not expected or desired that guests again shake hands.

TITLES

Midshipmen and naval officers, as well as Coast Guard cadets and officers, up to and including the rank of lieutenant commander, give their titles as "Mister" or "Miss" at official and social occasions at the base or station, unless it is desirable that identification of the officer be made.

Officers of the rank of commander and above state their rank, with admirals of all grades stating their rank as "Admiral."

Officers of the Marine Corps, Army, and Air Force, regardless of rank, use their titles, rather than "Mister" or "Miss."

RECEPTION FOOD

The type of food served at receptions is as simple or as elaborate as the hosts desire and the occasion requires. Fruit punch may be served by nonalcoholic drinking hosts, but cocktails, highballs, fruit punch, and coffee, are offered at most receptions, with waiters to serve them.

One room is usually set aside for food, but more rooms may be needed at large receptions. After being received by their hosts, guests then go into the room where the table is set with a cloth and centerpiece of flowers, and serve themselves. Food ranges from various kinds of roasts, breads and biscuits, shrimp, lobster, or salmon, to finger-foods freqeuntly served at cocktail parties or formal teas.

DEPARTURE

At receptions other than the superintendent's garden party, the receiving line may form again at the end of the evening, and once again you go down the line. You thank your hosts as you shake hands, express pleasure for the evening, and say good-bye.

At a reception to meet a newcomer, the line is usually broken up after the first hour, but the hosts and guests of honor usually stay near the door, mingling with other guests. At a large affair, you do not look them up; at a small reception, you do. In the latter case, you thank them—and leave.

COCKTAIL PARTIES

Cocktail parties vary in size from a handful to many people. They are, perhaps, the easiest means of entertaining a large number of guests—who may arrive at any time within the customary two hours stated in the invitation.

The main difference between cocktail parties and receptions is that cocktail parties usually are informal, with no receiving line, and alcoholic drinks are always served. (However, alcoholic beverages are forbidden aboard Navy ships.) Cocktail parties are customarily held during or near the close of daylight hours.

Hosts frequently give cocktail parties for a special guest or guests, or "to meet" newcomers to the station or neighborhood. The guest or guests of honor stand near their hosts, in order to be introduced to other guests as they arrive.

The hosts stand near the door when guests arrive, and greet their guests in an informal manner. If you are a stranger, your host or hostess should introduce you to someone nearby—but after this, you are on your own. You may talk with stranger or friend, and you may stay as long as the invitation specifies.

Customarily, a choice of two or three drinks are offered at cocktail parties. Soft drinks should be available for nondrinkers. A host should never insist that a guest take a drink when he doesn't want one. If you do not drink, say so. When a drink is offered to you, simply say, "No, thank you," without explaining why you don't want it. In case of a toast, however, you go through the motions of drinking.

SMALL PARTIES

Some cocktail parties may be small affairs, for perhaps a dozen friends, with the host mixing and serving drinks from a tray placed at a convenient spot in the room. Cocktail food may consist of a bowl of nuts or potato chips with a dip, with guests serving themselves or assisting in passing the food around the room. But at any party, have plenty of glasses of various sizes.

At the average party, a host should figure on three cocktails per person. Drinks are frequently served from a bar, which has been set up in a designated room, with a waiter in attendance. Guests are expected to order their choice. When you arrive, the host may say, "Won't you go over to the bar and have a drink?" A man will ask his date—or anyone whom he has brought—what she would like to drink; then get both drinks. Do not set a damp or cold glass on a table without something underneath it—a coaster, napkin, magazine, or anything convenient when coasters are not provided.

Some hosts prefer that drinks be served on a tray by a waiter. If your host, or the waiter, should ask if you prefer a drink not offered, you may state your preference; otherwise do not request a drink not offered, other than nonalcoholic beverages. If you must request anything at a party—such as a glass of ginger ale or water—you make your request to the waiter, not to your busy host or hostess. If you want a nonalcoholic drink, it is proper to ask for it. You may say, "I'd like a ginger ale or a Coke, if you have some."

At small cocktail parties, the host usually acts as bartender. If he does not limit or state what he has to drink, you may ask, "What are you serving?" However, a wise host will first state what is on hand, and then ask each guest which he prefers. Most hosts mix drinks beforehand, such as martinis and old-fashioneds.

PAY-BACK PARTIES

The very large cocktail party is the way many people return a large number of social obligations. It is often necessary for those who have many cocktail obligations to return them at one big party. This, however, should not be a substitute for a formal dinner—other than a cocktails-buffet party where elaborate and substantial food is served.

The pay-back cocktail party can either be a way to pay back a large number of invitations, or to insure the hosts that they will remain on a continuous cocktail circuit—so almost anyone is invited. Such a party is usually crowded, and too often gives little more than was intended: a pay-back. A discriminating host may prefer to give several smaller parties rather than one blockbuster—even though they will cost more. Then, he will have a chance to talk with his guests and enjoy the evening.

COCKTAILS-BUFFET

A popular type of cocktail party is called *cocktails-buffet*. The time is usually 6:30 P.M.

The main purpose of the hosts in indicating *cocktails-buffet* on their invitation is to inform the guests that they need not make other plans for supper. As a guest, you are expected to partake of the buffet-style food which is more elaborate than the usual cocktail fare. The table is usually covered with a white or pastel cloth, with a centerpiece of fruit or flowers. You can expect such food as roast beef, ham, seafood, and a number of hot dishes.

COCKTAIL FOOD

Cocktail food should be delicious, but a guest invited to a cocktail party other than cocktails-buffet, should eventually move away from the table or tray of food. Roast ham, turkey, or beef, with hot and cold breads, seafood, elaborate dips, broiled olives wrapped in bacon, bite-size biscuits filled with hot mixtures, miniature meat balls on toothpicks—many of these may be served at a large party, and several are often served at small affairs.

Appetizers—called canapes, hors d'oeuvres, or finger-food—may be the only food served at a small party. This could be toast or bread rounds topped with caviar or cream cheese, olives wrapped in broiled bacon, or any tasty food you can hold in your fingers.

Most cocktail food is eaten with the fingers, except that some food, such as shrimp or meatballs, is served on or with toothpicks. Food, however, is not offered until after a guest has been served a drink. Napkins are either handed to guests or are available on a buffet table nearby.

ORGANIZED PARTIES

The organized group party—for officers in a unit, headquarters, division, wing, group, squadron, department, and their wives, husbands, or dates is a popular type of party.

A committee is appointed to make arrangements for the party, which is frequently held in an officers' club at a designated time. Notices may be telephoned or posted, stating the proper dress, and the estimated cost for each couple.

Such parties are usually informal, with their purpose the opportunity for the officers of each unit, etc., and their wives and husbands, to become better acquainted. Or they may be of a more formal nature, with an evening of cocktails, dinner, and dancing.

Junior officers should remember to greet the senior officers and their spouses upon arrival.

ARRIVAL AND DEPARTURE

Although cocktail parties never start or end at the time stated in the invitation, the guest who arrives toward the end of the closing hour cannot expect the party to go on and on. The hosts may have made other plans for the evening—for dinner, or the theater.

No party should be expected to last for more than forty minutes after the closing time—unless the hosts want it to. Frequently the hosts invite several guests to stay on for a late supper, but without such an invitation in advance, no guest should linger so long that he forces himself to be invited.

The best way to move the slow guest on his or her way is to have the liquor removed and close the bar. For the diehard, the host might say, "Sorry, but Jane and I are meeting the Dows in a few minutes—" or state whatever plans you have made.

For the guest who has had too much to drink but wants another, this knotty problem may be handled by trying to bring up a subject of interest to him, or to introduce him into a trusted group—"I want you to meet my classmate Les Smith who made that fantastic eagle on the greens last week. . . ." Or forget to bring him the drink. The barmen will be aware of a problem guest and will do what they can to deter him.

If this doesn't work, call on a pal to maneuver the unwise drinker into another room—or, hopefully, on his way.

CHAPTER 6

Official Calls, Visits, & Personal Cards

IN TIMES OF WAR or national emergency, the social life in the services is relatively informal. Many social customs were held in abeyance during World War II and the later conflicts; some have been slow to come back, and others may never return, owing to the changing times.

One of the customs which has changed since the days of the more recent wars is that of making formal calls. Formerly, there was a rigid system of etiquette observed in making official and social calls. The system of official calls is modified, but that of making and returning social calls is changed to the point of extinction.

In most parts of the country, social calls are extinct; in a few others, they are being reestablished. Many old hands in the services desire the return of such calls as a gracious way of living. The more formal system of calling in the prewar services had its merits—mainly in the promotion of friendships between senior officers and their wives, and junior families.

However, there are problems involved in today's living that did not affect the services of the past particularly. With few servants in the modern household, there is far less time to make calls; junior officers frequently have no one with whom to leave their children when making calls. There are many more officers serving at larger bases than ever before—thus more officers' families on whom to call.

The commanding officer of a large station cannot possibly take the time today to receive and return all the calls that once were required. In order to extend hospitality to the officers in the command, and members of their families, and to become better acquainted with them, the commanding officer will hold one or more receptions which are considered "calls made and returned."

OFFICIAL CALLS

A long-time custom that is still carried out at many stations is that of the official call, which is made by newly assigned officers on their commanding officer in his office ashore or aboard ship. The call should last no less than 10 minutes and no more than 15, unless the caller is requested to stay longer.

In the naval services, a junior officer calls on his or her commanding officer on the first day after arrival, if possible, or within 48 hours. In the Army, you pay your official call within the first three days of your arrival.

However, in the past few years such calls have been eliminated in many areas because of the size of the station or area—such as in Washington, D.C., where great numbers of military personnel are stationed. Therefore, the newly assigned officer must find out what is expected of him upon arrival. Usually, an officer attached to the station will take the newcomer to the various offices and introduce him to fellow co-workers; later the newcomer will be introduced to the commanding officer at a staff meeting.

SPONSORSHIP PROGRAM

In the Air Force, in lieu of official calls, regulations require that a sponsorship program be carried out at all bases. The sponsor is a base officer who acts in liaison with a newly assigned officer by contacting him or her at least a week (preferably much earlier) before arrival. The sponsor is required to send any information which will be helpful to the new arrival, such as a map of the base, the type of work that can be expected, something about the social activities, housing, and the climate. The sponsor is charged with the introduction of the new officer to others in the office, and to the seniors at the first staff meeting.

CALLS MADE AND RETURNED

It is a widespread and popular custom for the senior officer (and his wife or her husband) to entertain at one or a series of receptions or at-homes, to which the officers in the activity, and their families, are invited. It is announced in advance that attendance serves as "All calls made and returned." The hours are usually 5:00 to 7:00 P.M.

At a large command, an aide stands near the entrance to the reception room and announces the name of each guest to the commanding officer, whose spouse stands at his (or her) side. A man gives the name of his lady to the aide, giving the last name only, "Mrs. Jones." The aide announces her, then he turns to you and you say, "Captain Jones." The commanding officer and his spouse greet and shake hands with each guest.

Staff officers do not stand in line, but assist in greeting guests and in directing them to the punch bowls and food placed in the various rooms, or in a single room. You should stay about 45 minutes. The line does not form again at the end of the reception, but if your host and hostess are nearby and not busy with other guests, you may thank them and say good-bye.

VISITS

A visit in the quarters of a newly married couple or a couple newly arrived at the station, means a welcome into the service community. It is the accepted custom all over the country to phone first and find out when it is convenient for you to stop by. When you stop in to see a new baby in the family, this shows a sincere interest in the family of a fellow officer.

Whenever time permits, it is desirable that midshipmen, cadets, ROTC students, or any young person, make a short visit with their senior officers and professors in the area. This gives them the opportunity to become better acquainted and more at ease with their seniors.

Ask beforehand when it is convenient to call on a certain day, and stay only about 30 or 40 minutes, unless asked to stay on for a game of tennis or for supper.

CALLING PROCEDURES

At bases and stations where calls are still being made, you leave cards when making first calls. A card tray is usually placed on a table in the entrance hall, or in the living room. Cards should be left on the tray at a convenient moment either upon your arrival or departure, but you never hand them to the host or hostess.

The number of cards that you leave depends on the number of adults in the family you are calling on, and the type of card that you use. A man calls upon each adult member of the family, man or woman; therefore, he leaves a card for each. If he is married, his wife leaves a card for each adult woman only; she never calls on a man, not even the President.

In contrast, the woman officer does call on and leave a card for the man who is the official for whom a call is required. Otherwise, and in addition, she leaves calling cards upon the same occasions as a civilian woman, one for each adult woman in the household.

When you wish to be received, but the family is not at home, you may leave the cards and the call is considered made. Otherwise, do not leave your cards but return at another time.

When a member of the household opens the door, you may introduce yourself—but do not give him or her your card. If admitted, you leave your card on the table; when your host is not in, you may ask if you may leave your card, then you step inside and lay the card on the table yourself.

A woman may make or return a call and leave cards for her husband when he cannot accompany her. A man cannot leave cards for his wife when she does not accompany him. All calls should be returned within two weeks. The procedure for returning calls is the same as when making them.

CALLING CARDS

At no time does any *individual* leave more than *three cards*. The following rules apply to the individual cards a husband and wife leave:

When calling on a senior officer and his wife—2 officer cards and 1 "Mrs." card.

When calling on a senior officer and his wife, and his mother—3 officer cards and 2 "Mrs." cards.

When calling on a senior officer, his wife, his mother, and his father—3 officer cards and 2 "Mrs." cards.

When calling on a senior officer, his wife, his mother, his mother-in-law, and adult daughter—3 officer cards and 3 "Mrs." cards.

When a husband and wife use *joint* calling cards (Lieutenant and Mrs. John Smith Jones), these rules apply.

When calling on a senior officer and his wife, leave—1 officer card and 1 joint card.

Cards in addition to joint cards are left in accordance with the general rules given for individual cards.

CALLS ON FOREIGN STATIONS

The prevailing custom of official calls must be determined upon your arrival in a foreign country. The protocol officer of the American Embassy will provide guidance on the local requirements.

Officers on military and diplomatic assignment are sometimes expected to call on officials within their own embassy and military activity, on officials of the host government, and on diplomatic representatives of other governments. In many countries, calls are greatly simplified.

When calls are expected, the following procedures may be helpful:

Upon the arrival of a new member of an embassy, such as a service attaché at a foreign capital, introductory calls are arranged by his predecessor and made promptly upon the civilian heads of foreign military establishments which correspond to the Secretary of Defense and/or the Secretaries of the Army, Navy, and Air Force. Calls are also made upon the military chiefs of these activities, and any other person, if according to local custom. These office calls are made in uniform and usually cards are left.

The Chief of Mission (ambassador or minister) is the highest-ranking American on the diplomatic staff in a foreign embassy or legation. The attaché and his wife should call on the wife of the Chief of Mission at the Residence within 24 hours after their arrival. You should first inquire of the protocol officer or her secretary if she would like to receive you in person, or if you should leave cards instead. When received, you should stay no longer than 15 minutes.

Then you should call on the wife of the Counselor of Embassy, who will advise you concerning any additional calls necessary to make. However, some foreign officers do not wish to be called upon at home, and this information can be determined in advance by asking the Secretary of Embassy.

It is customary in diplomatic circles that the new arrival calls first on those of equal rank and above; those of junior rank call first on the newcomer. Such calls should be made within one week of your arrival.

In addressing high officials, you say "Mr. Ambassador" or "Mr. Minister," but his wife is "Mrs. Doe." If married, you refer to your wife as "my wife," *not* "Mrs. Jones." And she refers to you as "my husband," or by your first name.

When leaving a country, you may need to leave cards on the Ambassador and his wife, or the Minister and his wife, and the Economic Minister and his wife. Then, "p.p.c." (*to take leave*) is written in pencil in the lower left-hand corner of the top card. Cards for Counselors, Army, Navy, and Air Attachés (and any others whom you wish to inform that you are leaving) may be mailed. When mailing cards, write "p.p.c."

When an officer and his family are going on home leave, no cards need be left. When returning from home leave, single officers and wives of officers should again leave cards and sign the book at the Residence. You should write in pencil "returned from home leave" in the lower left-hand corner of the top card.

Should a Minister, Counselor, Army, Navy, or Air Attaché, or the officer's Section Chief have arrived during your home leave, cards should be left on him and his family.

Upon detachment, courtesy calls in the chain of command may be expected. When detached on short notice, cards marked "p.p.c." may be mailed when you do not have time to leave them.

All calls must be returned; first calls within a week.

OFFICERS' CARDS

An officer's personal (calling) card is narrow and may vary slightly in size, according to the length of his name and title, and the type of engraving selected. The length and width of the cards are approximately:

Male officer (or civilian): 3⅛ inches by 1⅝ inches.
Single woman officer: 2⅞ inches by 2 inches.
Married woman officer (or civilian): 3⅛ inches by 2¼ inches.
Attaché: 3½ inches by 2 inches.
Joint cards (man and wife): 3½ inches by 2½ inches.

RANK AND TITLE

The placement on the card of rank (or title), name, and service, is in one of three ways:

The rank precedes the name in the center of the card, with service designation in the lower right-hand corner.

The rank precedes the name in the center, with service designation directly underneath.

The name only is in the center of the card with rank and service designation in the lower right-hand corner. It is now correct for officers of all services and of all ranks to use this placement.

In the *Navy* and *Coast Guard*, an officer's rank of commander and above may precede his or her name in the center of the card, with the service in the lower right-hand corner. Junior officers (lieutenant commander and below) place rank and service in the lower right-hand corner.

In the *Army, Air Force,* and *Marine Corps,* the rank of major and above may precede the name in the center of the card with the service in the lower right-hand corner. Company grade officers (second and first lieutenants and captain) place their name in the center of the card with rank and service in the lower right-hand corner. All Air Force officers usually place rank and service in the lower right-hand corner. First and second lieutenants are designated "lieutenant" in the Army and Marine Corps.

Retired officers in all services use the word *Retired* centered beneath the service designation in the lower right-hand corner of the card. On a joint card for married couples the word retired is not used.

A Cabinet officer is entitled to use only his title on his card, but his wife uses their surname. The Service Secretaries and the Under Secretaries are also entitled to use only their rank or title on their cards.

Senior flag officers and department officials are entitled to use their rank or title and surname on their cards. However, many officials prefer to use their full name, for purposes of identification.

When a man's name is the same as that of his living father, you add *junior* written out in full—unless the line is too long, and junior may then be written *Jr.* The Roman numeral II is used to identify a younger man who has the same name as an older living relative, such as a grandfather, uncle, etc. Other numerals, III, IV, and so on, would be used accordingly.

Do not put a home address on a personal card. Matching envelopes should be ordered with the cards, since they have many uses. But *never* place a card in an envelope when making a social call. When the cards are used for informal invitations, remember that postal regulations require mailing envelopes to be at least 3½ by 5 inches. It is proper to write only the name, "Miss Smith," on the envelop of the card and to enclose this in a larger envelope for mailing, similar to wedding invitations.

MIDSHIPMAN OR CADET CARDS

A midshipman or cadet, ROTC, or any student, is not required to have personal cards, but you will need them for certain social occasions, for use with gifts, and for brief notes. Your full name is engraved in the center of the card and your rank in the lower right-hand corner as follows:

CADET

UNITED STATES MILITARY ACADEMY

SELECTION OF CARDS

Your choice of cards will reflect your good taste. According to American usage, your name, rank, and service should be engraved or printed in full, without abbreviations or initials.

Clear lettering should be chosen rather than a heavy or unusual type, with script, shaded roman and antique roman among the popular styles. Go to the very best engraver and take his advice in the matter. Your service Exchange also will advise you.

Cards should be of excellent quality paper; this is customarily white, but may be a very light cream color. The lettering is always black. If engraved, the engraver will give you the engraving plate, and you can have additional cards made up at any time thereafter. However, you should order only the number that you anticipate using; when you advance in rank, the old cards should never be used.

In the business world cards may be of thinner paper in order that they are not bulky and are more easily carried. Thermography, a form of printing, is more often used than engraving, since it is attractive and much less expensive.

ATTACHE'S CARDS

On the cards of all officers attached to a diplomatic office, two sizes of lettering are used, with the larger for the name and the smaller for the title. Such officers sometimes have two sets of calling cards; one engraved in the language of their own country, the other engraved in the language of the country to which they are assigned. It is customary for such an officer serving in the Orient to have his name and title in the characters of the Oriental language on the back of his cards.

The official card of an attaché is larger than the regular card since it will carry some five or six lines of engraving. The customary size is about 3½ inches long and 2 inches wide, corresponding in size to official cards of State Department representatives.

Official Cards

Admiral John Paul Smith
United States Navy

Chief of Naval Operations

General Randolph Henderson

Commandant
United States Marine Corps

General George Washington Jones

Chief of Staff
United States Army

Flag or General Officers' Personal Cards

Vice Admiral Jones

United States Coast Guard

Robert Edward Decatur

Major General
United States Air Force

Flag or General Officer's Joint Card

GENERAL AND MRS. SMITH

Including and below the rank of rear admiral or brigadier general, full names are used for both active and retired officers.

Brigadier General and Mrs. Robert Edwards

Personal Cards, Senior Officers

Captain Stephen Sidney Preble

United States Coast Guard

Colonel Paul John O'Bannon

**Judge Advocate General Corps
United States Army**

Captain James Lee Briggs

United States Maritime Service

John Carl Brown

**Lieutenant Colonel
United States Air Force**

Married Woman Officer's Card

Major Mary Ames Smith

United States Marine Corps

Single Woman Officer's Card

> *Eleanor Sarah Harris*
>
> *Lieutenant Commander*
> *United States Navy*

Personal Cards, Retired Officers

> **Albert Edward Dewey**
>
> **Captain**
> **United States Army**
> **Retired**

or

> **Rear Admiral Willard Arthur Saunders**
>
> **United States Coast Guard**
> **Retired**

Junior Officer's Joint Informal for active and retired couples

The retired status is not used, but the officer's title may be abbreviated if the name is very long.

Lieutenant and Mrs. Peter Winston

Midshipman's or Cadet's Personal Card

William Orrmond Paul

Cadet
United States Military Academy

Reserve Officer's Card

Joan Doris Puller

Ensign
Medical Service Corps
United States Naval Reserve

Air Force Attaché

Colonel Albert Paul Truxton
United States Air Force
Air Attaché
Embassy of the United States of America

Athens

Marine Attaché

Richard Brinton Butler
First Lieutenant, United States Marine Corps
Assistant Naval Attaché
Assistant Naval Attaché for Air
Embassy of the United States of America

Paris

Staff Corps Attaché

Commander Dan Murray Hill
Supply Corps, United States Navy
Assistant Naval Attaché
Embassy of the United States of America

Paris

WOMEN'S CARDS

A woman's calling card is about the same length as a man's card, but is wider. The customary size is about 3⅛ inches long by 2¼ inches wide, but the size varies slightly according to the length of the name. It is desirable that a wife's card match her husband's in color, style, and type of engraving.

```
+-----------------------------------------------+
|                                               |
|                                               |
|                                               |
|                                               |
|         Mrs. Henry George Dickinson           |
|                                               |
|                                               |
|                                               |
|                                               |
+-----------------------------------------------+
```

A *married woman officer* in the services uses a similar card with the same type of information engraved in the same way as a male officer's personal card. A *single woman officer's* card is narrower, about 2⅞ by 2 inches in size.

Since a woman officer may legally retain her maiden name in the services upon marriage, she may have her own personal cards, and forego her title on the joint cards which could read: "Major and Mrs. John Doe." Otherwise, when they are in the same service, both titles could be used.

A *professional civilian woman* may use her title on both her social and business cards. After marriage, she may assume her husband's title on their joint cards, "Mr. and Mrs. John Doe," but her professional card may read "Jane Doe, R.N."

A *widow's* card is the same as before her husband's death. A wife takes her husband's name for life—or until a divorce or remarriage. She is "Mrs. James Doe," *not* "Mrs. Jane Doe"—unless she prefers to use her first name.

A *divorcee's* card customarily has her maiden name before her former husband's last name: "Mrs. Smith Doe." When she legally takes back her maiden name she is "Miss Jane Smith." When she has children she usually retains her status "Mrs. Jane Doe" or "Mrs. Smith Doe."

JOINT CARDS

The *joint card* that married couples frequently use is about 2½ by 3½ inches in size. When used in making formal calls, one such card may be used along with any additional individual cards as needed, or two joint cards are used in accordance with the number of adults in the family. The officer's branch of service is never indicated on the card, but the individual card will provide this information.

A senior flag or general officer's joint card may have only the rank and surname engraved in the center of the card; a brigadier general or rear admiral and officers of less rank use their full names. The active or retired status is not used. It is customary for junior officers to have their rank precede their names on joint cards.

The joint card is also useful for extending and replying to invitations, and is frequently enclosed with gifts. Notes of thanks, condolence, etc., are written across them; an address is sometimes engraved in the lower right-hand corner of the card. Matching envelopes should be ordered with the cards.

INFORMALS

The fold-over cards, known as *informals*, are widely used for informal invitations and brief notes, but they are *not* used for calling cards. The name is engraved or printed on the outside, and the message or invitation is written on the inside of the card. They are about 3 by 4¼ inches in size.

Another style of informal is a single flat card about 3½ by 4½ inches in size. The address is engraved above and to the right of the name, with the name engraved in the center or near the top center of the card. Matching envelopes come with the cards.

ABBREVIATIONS ON CARDS

There are a number of conventional abbreviations on calling cards. Although some are rarely used in this country, you should be aware of their meaning. Such abbreviations are penciled in the lower left corner of the card.

p.p.c. (*Pour prendre congé*)—*To take leave.* This indicates that one is leaving the station or country.

p.c. (*Pour condoléance*)—*To extend sympathy.*

p.f. (*Pour féliciter*)—*To congratulate.*

p.p. (*Pour presenter*)—*To introduce.* This means that the friend who left the card is introducing a stranger to whom the receiver should send cards, phone, or call on. The stranger's name is written on the card.

p.r. (*Pour remercier*)—*To thank*; to reply to a "p.f." card.

n.b. (*Nota bene*)—"*Note well*"; this calls attention to any words or messages written on the card.

R.s.v.p. or R.S.V.P (*Répondez s'il vous plaît*)—*Please reply.* These initials are customarily written on invitations when an answer is requested.

Easy Conversation

CHAPTER 7

Introductions & Farewells

IT IS FORTUNATE that the mechanics of making introductions are simple and natural, because you probably will be introducing people to each other for the rest of your life. The simplest form of introduction is illustrated by a young child who introduces a hero-worshiped older child by announcing, "Mommy, this is Johnny!"

Brevity and accuracy are the two requirements that must be kept in mind when introducing people. The person making the introduction is completely in charge of the situation for the length of time that it takes to effect it. When you are that person, you are momentarily the ringmaster who must be sure not only of what you are going to say but how you are going to say it.

INTRODUCTIONS

When making introductions, all names must be clearly and correctly stated. You must know instantly whose name is stated first. There are a few simple rules you should remember:

A man is always presented *to* a woman—with the exception of the president of any country, a king, or a dignitary of the Church, or when a junior woman officer is officially presented to a senior male officer.
The honored or higher-ranking person's or woman's name is stated first, then the name of the person being presented.

Young people are presented *to* older people of the same sex.
A single person is introduced *to* a group.

To illustrate these rules, you should introduce these persons in this manner:

"Mr. President, may I present Mrs. Jones?" or: "Mrs. Jones, may I present Admiral Smith?" or, "May I present Admiral Smith . . . Mrs. Jones."

"General Smith, may I present Lieutenant White . . . Miss White is an Army nurse."

"General Smith, may I present Colonel Jones?"

"Mrs. Jones, this is my daughter Ann," or "Mrs. Jones, Miss White."

"Miss White (or, This is Miss White—)—Ensign Fields, Miss Lewis, Midshipman Brown, Miss Smith, Cadet Long," and so on. In this case, when you wish to indicate individuals in the services, junior rank is stated.

VARIATIONS IN SERVICE INTRODUCTIONS

In the Navy and Coast Guard, junior officers are those of the rank of lieutenant commander and below, including midshipmen and Coast Guard cadets. They are introduced and addressed as "Mister" or "Miss" at both social and official occasions—with the exceptions of certain military, state, official, or social occasions when the designation of title is necessary. Commanders and up are introduced by rank.

In the Air Force and Marines, company grade officers—second and first lieutenants and captains—and up are introduced by rank. In the Army, officers of both grades of lieutenant are introduced and addressed as "Lieutenant."

Cadets at the U. S. Military Academy and at the U. S. Air Force Academy are introduced as "Cadet"—and addressed thereafter as "Mister" or "Miss."

Servicewomen are officially introduced in the same way as are servicemen. A junior woman officer is presented to a senior male officer upon official occasions. Socially, as with any lady, the senior officer—as any man other than the President or very high dignitary—is presented to her.

Women cadets and midshipmen are addressed and introduced the same as their male counterparts: Cadet Jane Doe, Midshipman Mary Doe on certain official occasions; otherwise they are Miss Doe.

A doctor, nurse, and chaplain are introduced by rank. Upon such occasions as a speaking engagement, they would be introduced as "Major Doe who is a doctor in the Air Force Medical Corps," or ". . . a nurse in the Army Nurse Corps," or "Colonel Jones is command chaplain at the Air Force Academy." Since their titles are distinguished, it is equally proper to call them Doctor Doe or Chaplain Jones.

WHAT TO SAY

In making introductions, the easiest way is simply to state the names of the two persons concerned: "Miss White, Mr. Jones," or "Commander Brown, Mr. Smith." The phrase, "May I present," is more formal, but it is always correct to say, "Miss White, may I present Mr. Jones?" You may then add, "Jack is a second classman."

Midshipmen and cadets may introduce fellow classmates in this manner: "Mary, this is my roommate, John Jones—Miss. White." If the friendships are less intimate, the introduction may be "Miss White, Mr. Jones." When you introduce your sister or your best girl friend (or your financée) to your roommate who knows her name well, you may say, "Mary, this is John Jones." However, this form is reserved for intimate friends only.

Although it is proper to use first names in introductions, it is important that those being introduced are contemporaries or are on equal footing. When a very close friend or relative is introduced to a stranger, the last name must be worked into the introduction: "Mary, may I present Midshipman John Jones . . ."; then turning to Midshipman Jones, you add, "—Miss White." Otherwise he will have no idea who "Mary" may be.

You should be careful about making personal comments when introducing people. Biographical data or human interest stories that are too long may cause embarrassment rather than establishing the topic of conversation for which they were intended. However, a brief comment can be very helpful in breaking the ice between strangers, and can be the start of a lasting friendship. "Mrs. Wilson, may I present Mrs. Smith? Her husband, as you know, served with General Wilson at Iwo Jima."

INTRODUCTIONS IN GROUPS

Introductions made in groups must be handled in an efficient way, with the person or persons presented *to* the group. It is impossible to introduce everyone at a large function, but do introduce all guests at small gatherings of a dozen or so. A host and hostess should introduce a guest into a small group upon his or her arrival, and to the others later, when it is convenient. Otherwise, after the first introduction, the guest is on his own.

To introduce a latecomer to a small group, the easiest way is to announce to all present, "This is Jane Brown." Then the names of those present are stated in rotation around the room as they stand or sit. Should part of the group be actively engaged in a game or conversation at the time, introductions should be made only to those closest to you and the latecomer.

FAMILY INTRODUCTIONS

When introducing a member of your family, usually you omit the last name of the person you are introducing. A midshipman or cadet may say, "Mother, this is my roommate, James Smith." If your mother has re-married, you would say, "Mother, this is my roommate James Smith";—then turning to Midshipman (or Cadet) Smith, you would say, "—Mrs. Northrop."

When the person to whom you wish to introduce your relative may be vague concerning your own name, then you add the last name of your relative. For example: "Colonel Wilson, this is Roger Doe, my brother." After the customary courtesies are exchanged, you might add: "Colonel Wilson is my regimental commander, Roger. Sir, my brother is going to Exeter and hopes to be a plebe next year."

A married man refers to his wife as "my wife" to people who do not know her, and by her first name to people who do. Introduce your wife in this manner: "Mrs. Smith, may I present my wife?" If you want to encourage the friendship, you may add your wife's first name: "Mrs. Smith, may I present my wife, Ruth?"

A man introduces his wife to a man in this manner: "Ruth, this is Captain Jones . . . my wife." *Never* refer to your wife as "Mrs." at a social occasion, except when you are going through a receiving line when you present your wife as "Mrs. Brown." When speaking with very junior officers, enlisted personnel, tradespeople, and servants, however, you do refer to your wife as "Mrs.———."

When a wife introduces her husband, she says, "Mrs. Smith, this is my husband," and refers to him as "husband"—not as "Mr." or "The lieutenant." She only refers to him as "Mr. Brown" with tradespeople, servants, etc.

When introducing or referring to your wife, never use humorous forms such as: "Jim, I want you to meet the missus," or, "Meet the greatest little wife in the world."

STEPPARENTS

A stepparent is introduced, "My stepfather, Mr. White," but the relationship need not be mentioned unless you care to.

Half-brothers or sisters are usually introduced as brothers and sisters even though their last name is different from your own. You must give their names, however, when they are different from your own. "Mary, this is Cadet Smith—my sister, Miss White." Relatives, such as cousins, uncles, etc., are so designated at the end of the introduction, rather than in the body of the introduction.

IN-LAWS

When introducing your mother- or father-in-law, you may use the term "My mother-in-law" or "father-in-law," but it is preferable that you say, "Mother (or whatever she is called), may I present Lieutenant John Smith?" Then turning to Lieutenant Smith you add," "Mrs. Woods is Mary's mother."

FORMER IN-LAWS

Members of a family who have kept a warm relationship with former in-laws following a divorce or death, are sometimes puzzled about the best way to introduce them.

A former father-in-law could say, "I want you to know Jane Doe who was my son's wife and is now married to John Doe." If she was a widow who has remarried he would say, ". . . she is my son's widow and is now married to John Doe." She would introduce you as, "Colonel Smith, my first husband's father." In-laws, past or present, should be friends.

FORGOTTEN INTRODUCTIONS

When you are presented to someone you have met previously but who apparently has forgotten that introduction, you may say: "I believe that I met Miss Lewis at the ring dance last year," or make other reference to the place of introduction. But do not blurt out, "Oh, I've met Miss Lewis—don't you remember?" It is obvious that she does not remember, and such a remark only causes embarrassment.

The fact that a junior officer, midshipman, or cadet is not remembered by a senior officer does not imply that the senior officer is rude, or that you, the junior, did not make a good impression. A senior officer meets many people in his career, at many places, and the person who "never forgets a name or face" is a rarity in this accelerated world of today. Introductions made at large social functions, or made long ago, are easily forgotten.

When someone momentarily forgets your name when introducing you, help him out by giving your name, "John Jones." This momentary lapse of memory sometimes happens even to your best friends, and, in reverse, to you. When someone seems to have forgotten you, you may say, "How do you do, Mrs. Smith—I'm John Jones. We met at the station Christmas party."

If a person deliberately appears to forget you were introduced previously, you should not mention having met before. But don't be too quick to take offense at a forgotten introduction.

When a person joins a group and his last name is unknown—or you have forgotten it—it is best to say, "I'm sorry, but I have momentarily forgotten your last name," before attempting introductions.

ACKNOWLEDGMENTS

The customary answer to an introduction for both persons concerned is, "How do you do?" You may add, "So nice to see you." If you want to be certain that you understand the name correctly, say "How do you do, Mrs. Smith." You are *not* expected to answer, "I'm fine, how are you?"

It is good training to listen carefully when introductions are made so that it will not be necessary to have the name repeated. To acknowledge an introduction with a flip remark or with an attitude of indifference is not only improper, but insulting. Introductions should always be treated wtih the respect that they deserve; they invariably constitute first impressions, and first impressions should be good ones.

Young people frequently say "Hello," to each other, following an introduction. Although the expression "How are you?" is frowned on, it is correct and is used in certain sections of the country. The temptation is to answer the query, which makes for an awkward situation.

Some people acknowledge another's introduction by saying, "It is nice to know you" which phrase the other may repeat, or merely say, "Thank you."

Always avoid such acknowledgments as, "I am pleased to make your acquaintance," or, "Pleased to meet you." But—a hostess will cordially greet a guest's friend who is a stranger by saying, "I am so pleased you could come." And when you are introduced to someone who is an intimate friend of a friend of yours, you will probably say that you are pleased to know him!

Never use such trite phrases as, "Cadet Jones, shake hands with Jim Brown," or, ". . . I want you to make the acquaintance of. . . ." Embellishments on introductions can be confusing; it is best to keep introductions as simple and as direct as possible.

SELF-INTRODUCTIONS

Self-introductions are sometimes necessary, but they should be treated with care. Too often, the self-introduction has been used by presumptuous persons, with the result that others are wary of the custom.

There are occasions, however, when self-introductions are necessary. For instance, when you are a stranger at a large reception or cocktail party and the host and hostess are busy elsewhere and cannot introduce you into a new group—then you may introduce yourself. A man may shake hands with each man near him and with any woman who offers her hand first. A single woman introduces herself.

However, when two persons are of the opposite sex, it is preferable that the lady speak first to the gentleman. If she doesn't, extreme care must be exercised by the man and he should talk about something impersonal—the decor of the room or a floral arrangement or even the weather—and then introduce himself.

When you introduce yourself at a social or nonofficial occasion, do *not use your rank or title.* Say, "My name is John Jones" or, "I am John Jones." When your name is mispronounced and it seems advisable to correct it, say "Excuse me, my name is Jones (or John Jones)." Do not say, "Lieutenant Jones" or "Mr. Jones."

When you are telephoning someone who is your senior, you should introduce yourself "Colonel Brown, this is John Jones." If it is an official conversation, state your rank or title. A woman would say to the Colonel's wife, "Mrs. Brown, this is Mary Jones. My husband is Lieutenant John Jones, who is serving under Colonel Brown. . . ."

· At an occasion when a junior officer is not in uniform but wishes to identify himself to a senior officer, he might say something like this: "Colonel, I'm Lieutenant Hawkins. I was the forward observer in your battalion in the Alaskan maneuver. . . ."

WHAT TO DO

MEN

When introduced to a man or woman, a man rises if he is seated. He shakes hands with another man when being introduced—but waits for a woman to extend her hand before offering his. If he should forget and extend his hand first, it is no breach of etiquette since he is showing friendliness; however, he will probably feel more comfortable if he remembers to wait. He may bow slightly when presented to a woman, but does not bob his head.

When you are at an inconvenient distance from a person to whom you are being introduced, you may nod or bow slightly. At a crowded table in a restaurant, you may half-rise when a person stops at your table and introductions are made. But if you are the one *making* the introductions, you always stand.

Outdoors, in uniform, the hand salute may be given when you are introduced to a man or woman. In the naval services you do not remove your cap; in the other services, you may salute or remove your cap. In civilian dress, you remove your hat and leave it off, weather permitting. However, if you should be the only Navy man in uniform in a mixed group, you may feel more comfortable by deferring to civilian practice, and accordingly remove your hat when introduced to a woman.

Usually, you do not lift your hat to men when women are not present. It is awkward to lift your hat, and then shake hands. But if you are presented to a dignitary or very high-ranking man outdoors when you are in civilian dress, you may as a matter of courtesy remove your hat with your left hand before shaking hands.

If you are wearing gloves when introduced to a woman, remove your right glove—that is, if you have time. But do not keep a person waiting while you peel it off. When ushering at a wedding or funeral, or when attending a formal dance where white gloves are worn, do *not* remove your glove when introductions are in order. At no time do you need to apologize for leaving gloves on.

In Europe, a man shakes hands with anyone presented to him. The gallant custom of kissing the hand of a continental woman is not expected of American men visiting in a country where this custom prevails —or when the woman is visiting here.

WOMEN

A woman does not rise when introduced to another woman of about her own age, but she stands when introduced to an elderly woman or the wife of a senior official. She should remain standing until the elderly or senior woman is seated. A woman may shake hands with another woman, when convenient. But the younger or junior woman usually waits for the elderly woman, senior officer, or senior officer's wife to offer her hand.

A woman does not rise when introduced to a man—unless he is the President, a king, or a dignitary of the Church, or when she is a junior woman officer being introduced to a senior officer. When a young woman is in the presence of a very high-ranking officer or dignitary, she should rise. A woman customarily extends her hand first to a man of *any* age or rank except to heads of state or members of royal families. Children and teen-agers should stand when introduced to an adult.

THE JUNIOR WOMAN OFFICER

On duty or at an *official* occasion, when a junior woman officer is introduced to a senior officer, male or female, she stands. Thereafter, she does not rise every time the senior enters or leaves the room—but she does upon the senior's departure when nearby.

She should also stand upon being introduced to a dignitary or senior civilian, man or woman.

Socially, the junior woman officer does not stand when she is introduced to a contemporary woman officer or when they are a grade or two ahead.

If, at an informal occasion out of uniform, she is introduced to the wife of her commanding officer who is about her own age, she need not stand but she may want to in order to show respect to her CO. Common sense will tell her whether or not to stand; if she is in a group of contemporaries and the CO's wife is also a contemporary, it may be pointed to do so when the others do not.

Since the junior woman officer stands to greet her female commanding officer, she remains standing, of course, to be introduced to her CO's husband, civilian or military.

At social functions and in everyday living, men of all ages and positions prefer that women not stand for introductions.

THE PRESIDENT OF THE UNITED STATES

If you have the good fortune to present someone to the President of the United States, stand straight, look directly at the President, and say, "Mr. President, may I present Admiral Brown?"

If you—a man—are the person being presented, you wait for the President to offer his hand, and bow as you shake hands. A woman being presented to the President also waits for him to offer his hand first. But most men—regardless of rank or title—usually prefer the customary form of a woman offering her hand first.

If you are called upon to make a formal presentation of the President at a banquet, you give his full title: "Ladies and gentlemen—the President of the United States." In conversation, you address him as "Mr. President."

The Vice President is addressed and introduced in the same way as the President. The wives of Presidents and of Vice Presidents are introduced and addressed as "Mrs." When introduced and when in conversation, a former President is called "Mr." Although he is never so called while in office, an ex-President is given the courtesy title of "The Honorable."

FAREWELLS

After an introduction, the first person to move away might say, "I hope that I see you again soon." The other person will probably answer, "Thank you." He may wish to add such a comment as, "I hope so, too."

In taking leave of a group of strangers, it makes very little difference whether a person has been introduced all around or merely included in certain conversations. The most courteous action is to bow "good-bye" to anyone who happens to be looking at you. No attempt should be made to attract the attention of those who are apparently unaware that you are leaving. When saying good-bye to an acquaintance, you may say, "Good-bye, it was so nice to see you," or "I hope we can meet again soon."

It is impossible to say good-bye to all guests at a large party, but you can do so to those with whom you were most recently talking. You say good-bye to all guests at a very small party, such as a dinner, and you *always* say good-bye to your host and hostess.

When saying good-bye, both men and women stand. A hostess rises to her feet when she sees that a guest is ready to leave. A woman guest makes the first move to leave, and her husband or escort immediately rises and joins her. The hostess and host shake hands with their guests on departure the same as on arrival.

A departing guest should make some appreciative comment to the hostess, then to the host: "It's been a very pleasant evening, thank you so much." The hostess might answer, "Goodnight, I'm so glad you could be with us."

At a formal dinner, the hostess remains standing inside the living room when saying good-bye to guests, and the host walks to the door of the living room or into the hall with a high-ranking guest. The high-ranking guest is always the first to leave. In very senior quarters, an MS (mess management specialist), airman or Army aide, or a butler in a civilian home, opens the door for guests and says, "Goodnight, Sir (or Madam)." A guest answers, "Thank you, goodnight."

At informal parties, or when the host lives in the country, the host usually walks with guests to their cars—and always makes certain that everyone has a way to get home.

CHAPTER 8

Service & Civilian Forms of Address

A. NAVAL SERVICES: Full rank *precedes* the name of commissioned officers; customarily, rank may be abbreviated in official correspondence, but is *written out* in social correspondence. Likewise, the names of the services are often abbreviated in official correspondence, but are written out in business or social correspondence. The rank also precedes the names of warrant officers, midshipmen, Coast Guard cadets, and Merchant Marine cadet/midshipmen. When in civilian dress, a captain and a lieutenant are introduced as *of the Navy* to distinguish the rank from the Army, Marine Corps, and Air Force. In conversation, all admirals are *Admiral*.

Official:

Rear Admiral John Jones, U.S. Navy　　　Admiral Jones
Superintendent　　　　　　　　　　　　*Or formal:*
United States Naval Academy　　　　　　Rear Admiral John Jones,
Annapolis, Maryland　　　　　　　　　　Superintendent of the
　　　　　　　　　　　　　　　　　　　United States Naval
　　　　　　　　　　　　　　　　　　　Academy

Social:

Rear Admiral and Mrs. John Jones　　　　Admiral and Mrs. Jones
Superintendent's House
U. S. Naval Academy
Annapolis
Maryland

Note: Zip codes are not included in this chapter. On less formal/official addresses the abbreviation may be used, such as USN, USCG, USAF, etc. However, when these regular, less official addresses are abbreviated, the rank is also abbreviated, thus it would be, for example: *LCdr. John Jones, Jr., USN.*

Written Address	*Spoken Address and Introductions*
Official:	
Lieutenant Commander John Jones, U. S. Navy Gunnery Officer USS *Los Angeles* c/o Fleet Post Office San Francisco, California	Mr. Jones (Commissioned officers of the rank of lieutenant commander, and down, are addressed and introduced as "Mister," except for official or social occasions when designation of rank is necessary.)
Social:	
Lieutenant Commander and Mrs. John Jones 7100 Atherton Drive Long Beach California	Mr. and Mrs. Jones
Official:	
Chief Warrent Officer John Jones, U. S. Coast Guard USCGC *Eastwind* c/o Fleet Post Office New York, New York	Mr. Jones
Social:	
Chief Warrent Officer and Mrs. John Jones 1125 Ocean Drive New London Connecticut	Mr. and Mrs. Jones
*Official or Social:**	
Midshipman John (or Jane) Jones, U. S. Navy Room 3654, Bancroft Hall United States Naval Academy Annapolis, Maryland	Mr. Jones or Miss Jones (Upon certain occasions, midshipmen are addressed and introduced as "Midshipman" for purposes of designation.)

Note: Women and men students at the service and maritime academies are *midshipmen* and *cadets*; these are grades of rank, not titles.

* The social address for a midshipman or cadet need not include the service after the name. For example: Midshipman John Jones, Room 3654, United States Naval Academy, Annapolis, Maryland.

Written Address	*Spoken Address and Introductions*

B.   *ARMY, AIR FORCE, AND MARINE CORPS:* Although the Marine Corps is an integral part of the Navy, the rank is similar to that of the Army and Air Force, and therefore is included with these services. In written correspondence, both official and social, full rank and ratings precede the name and are written out. In conversation, all generals are *General*; all colonels are *Colonel*; and all privates and sergeants are *Private* and *Sergeant*.

Official:

Brigadier General John Doe, U. S. Army Commandant of Cadets United States Military Academy West Point, New York	General Doe *Or formal:* Brigadier General John Doe, the Commandant of Cadets at the United States Military Academy

Social:

Brigadier General and Mrs. John Doe Quarters 101 United States Military Academy West Point New York	General and Mrs. Doe

Official:

Lieutenant Colonel John Doe, U. S. Air Force 335th Bomber Squadron Langley Air Force Base Virginia	Colonel Doe *Or formal:* Lieutenant Colonel Doe, of the 335th Bomber Squadron

Social:

Lieutenant Colonel and Mrs. John Doe Quarters M Langley Air Force Base Virginia	Colonel and Mrs. Doe

Official:

First Lieutenant John Doe, U. S. Marine Corps Marine Corps Base Camp Lejeune, North Carolina	Lieutenant Doe *Or formal:* First Lieutenant Doe, of the Marine Corps Base, etc. (In the Army, first and second lieutenant are designated "Lieutenant.")

Written Address	*Spoken Address and Introductions*

Social:

First Lieutenant and Mrs. John Doe
1073 East Peleliu Drive
Tarawa Terrace 1
Camp Lejeune
North Carolina

Lieutenant and Mrs. Doe

Official:

Colonel John E. Doe, U.S. Air Force
Senior Chaplain
Cadet Chapel
United States Air Force Academy
Colorado

Colonel Doe
Or *Formal:*
Colonel Doe, the Senior
Chaplain at the Air Force
Academy

Social:

Colonel and Mrs. John E. Doe
Chaplain's Quarters
United States Air Force Academy
Colorado

Informally:
Chaplain Doe

Official or Social:

Cadet John (or Jane) Doe
Company C, Corps of Cadets
United States Military Academy
West Point, New York

Mr. Doe, Miss Doe
(For purposes of identification or designation, the title
"Cadet Doe" is used upon
certain official or social occasions.)

Cadet John (or June) Doe
Room 3A20, Vandenberg Hall
United States Air Force Academy
Colorado

Cadet Doe or Miss Doe
(A cadet at the Air Force
Academy is introduced as
"Cadet Doe" and addressed
thereafter as "Mr. or Miss
Doe.")

Official or Social:

Sergeant Major Mary Doe
U. S. Marine Corps
Marine Corps Air Station
Cherry Point
North Carolina

Sergeant Major Doe
(The spoken address for
first sergeants is "First Sergeant" and for all other
Sergeants "Sergeant." A cor-
poral is addressed "Cor-
poral.")

Written Address	*Spoken Address and Introductions*

Official:

(Senior woman officer and husband)   Colonel Doe and Major Doe
Colonel Mary Doe, U. S. Air Force
    and Major John Doe, U. S. Air Force
Commander, 6940th Security Wing (her office)
Goodfellow Air Force Base
Texas

Social:

Major and Mrs. John Doe   Major and Mrs. Doe
Quarters Nine
Goodfellow Air Force Base
Texas

C. *SERVICE ABBREVIATIONS:* In official correspondence, rank and ratings are abbreviated and fully capitalized in the naval services, and are partially capitalized in the other services. The abbreviations for the relative ranks of commissioned officers of the U.S. Armed Forces, according to the Abbreviation Manual of each service, are as follows:

NAVY AND COAST GUARD

Fleet Admiral (Navy only)	FADM
Admiral	ADM
Vice Admiral	VADM
Rear Admiral	RADM
Commodore	COMO
Captain	CAPT
Commander	CDR
Lieutenant Commander	LCDR
Lieutenant	LT
Lieutenant, junior grade	LTJG
Ensign	ENS

MARINE CORPS

General	Gen
Lieutenant General	LtGen
Major General	MajGen
Brigadier General	BGen
Colonel	Col
Lieutenant Colonel	LtCol
Major	Maj
Captain	Capt
First Lieutenant	1stLt
Second Lieutenant	2dLt

Note: For the insignia of rank of all commissioned and warrant officers see pages 42 and 43.

WARRANT OFFICERS—ALL SERVICES EXCEPT ARMY

Chief Warrant Officer (W-4)	CWO
Chief Warrant Officer (W-3)	CWO
Chief Warrant Officer (W-2)	CWO
Warrant Officer (W-1)	WO

Army: WO4, WO3, WO2, WO1

ARMY

General of the Army	(No abbr.)
General	GEN
Lieutenant General	LTG
Major General	MG
Brigadier General	BG
Colonel	COL
Lieutenant Colonel	LTC
Major	MAJ
Captain	CPT
First Lieutenant	1 LT
Second Lieutenant	2 LT

AIR FORCE

General of the Air Force	(No abbr.)
General	Gen
Lieutenant General	Lt Gen
Major General	Maj Gen
Brigadier General	Brig Gen
Colonel	Col
Lieutenant Colonel	Lt Col
Major	Maj
Captain	Capt
First Lieutenant	1st Lt
Second Lieutenant	2d Lt

BRANCH OF SERVICE

United States Army	USA
United States Navy	USN
United States Marine Corps	USMC
United States Coast Guard	USCG
United States Air Force	USAF
United States Merchant Marine	USMM
United States Maritime Service	USMS
National Guard	NG

RESERVE OFFICERS

Reserve officers of all the services add the letter *R* after the branch. For example: USAR, USCGR, etc.

Reserve and National Guard officers use their titles only when on active duty.

Written Address	*Spoken Address*	*Introductions*

D. *UNITED STATES—Federal, State, and Local Dignitaries: The Honorable* is the preferred form for addressing most American officials in office or retired, and is always written out in full on the line above and even with the name. The phrase is always used with the full name—and *never* with any other title such as *The Honorable Admiral Jones,* or *The Honorable Mr. Jones.* In the salutation and close of a letter to the President, you would write, officially or in business, *Dear Mr. President*:; and socially, *My Dear Mr. President*:; and, officially and in business, *Respectfully yours,* or socially, *Very respectfully.* In writing to all other American officials, the official or business closing is, *Very truly yours,* or socially, *Sincerely yours.* Wives of American officials are addressed and introduced as *Mrs.—.*

The President		
The President	Mr. President	The President
The White House		*Or formal:*
Washington, D.C.		The President of the
		United States
		Abroad, add:
		. . . of America
Social:		
The President		
and Mrs. Doe		
The White House		
Washington, D.C.*		
The President's Wife		
Mrs. John Doe	Mrs. Doe	Mrs. Doe
The White House		
Washington, D.C.		
The Vice President		
The Vice President	Mr. Vice President	The Vice President
United States Senate	or	*Or formal:*
Washington, D.C.	Mr. Doe**	The Vice President
		of the United States
		Abroad, add:
		. . . of America
Social:		
The Vice President		
and Mrs. Doe		
(home address)		
The Vice President's Wife		
(home address)	Mrs. Doe	Mrs. Doe

* Formally written *District of Columbia*, although the abbreviation *D.C.* is generally used.

** In continued conversation, *Mister*—is used.

Written Address	*Spoken Address*	*Introductions*
The Chief Justice of the Supreme Court		
The Chief Justice of the Supreme Court Washington, D.C.	Mr. Chief Justice or Mr. Doe	The Chief Justice *Or formal:* The Honorable John Doe, Chief Justice of the Supreme Court of the United States *Abroad, add:* . . . of America
Social: The Chief Justice and Mrs. Doe (home address)		
Associate Justices Mr. Justice Doe The Supreme Court Washington, D.C.	Mr. Justice Doe or Mr. Doe	Mr. Justice Doe *Or formal:* The Honorable John Doe, Associate Justice of the Supreme Court of the United States *Abroad, add:* . . . of America
Social: Mr. Justice Doe and Mrs. Doe (home address)		
A Cabinet Officer (man) * The Honorable John Doe Secretary of State Washington, D.C.	Mr. Secretary or Mr. Doe	The Secretary of State, Mr. Doe *Or formal:* The Honorable John Doe, Secretary of State
Social: The Secretary of State and Mrs. Doe (home address)		
A Cabinet Officer (woman) The Honorable Jane Doe Secretary of Labor Washington, D.C.	Madam Secretary or Miss or Mrs. Doe	The Secretary of Labor, Miss (or Mrs.) Doe *Or formal:* The Honorable Jane Doe, Secretary of Labor

* All cabinet officers except the Attorney General and the Postmaster General use the title of Secretary. Although the service secretaries do not have cabinet rank, they may be addressed and introduced as *Mr. Secretary*, or *The Secretary of the Army*, etc. The Secretary of Defense has cabinet rank.

Written Address	Spoken Address	Introductions
Social, when married: The Secretary of Labor and Mr. Doe (home address)		
The Attorney General The Honorable John Doe Attorney General Washington, D.C.	Mr. Attorney General or Mr. Doe	The Attorney General, Mr. Doe *Or formal:* The Honorable John Doe, Attorney General
Secretaries of Defense, and *of the Army, Navy, and* *Air Force (Under Secre-* *taries and Assistant Secre-* *taries)* The Honorable John Doe Secretary of the Air Force Washington, D.C.	Mr. Secretary or Mr. Doe	The Secretary of the Air Force, Mr. Doe *Or formal:* The Honorable John Doe, Secretary of the Air Force
Social: The Secretary of the Air Force and Mrs. Doe (home address)		
Former Presidents of *the United States* The Honorable John Doe San Francisco, California	Mr. Doe (or any title, such as military)	The Honorable John Doe, the former President of the United States
The Assistant to *the President———* The Honorable John Doe Assistant to the President The White House Washington, D.C.	Mr. Doe	The Assistant to the Presi- dent, Mr. John Doe *Or formal:* The Honorable John Doe, Assistant to the President of the United States
Social: The Honorable John Doe and Mrs. Doe (home address)		

Written Address	Spoken Address	Introductions
The Special Assistant to the President with Military Rank Major General John Doe, U. S. Army Special Assistant to the President The White House Washington, D.C.	General Doe	The Special Assistant to the President, General John Doe, United States Army
Social: Major General and Mrs. John Doe (home address)		
The Speaker of the House of Representatives The Honorable John Doe Speaker of the House of Representatives The Capitol Washington, D.C.	Mr. Speaker or Mr. Doe	The Speaker, Mr. Doe *Or formal:* The Honorable John Doe, Speaker of the House of Representatives
Social: The Speaker of the House of Representatives and Mrs. Doe (home address)		
American Ambassador (man)* The Honorable John Doe American Ambassador London, England	Mr. Ambassador *Or on leave:* Mr. Doe *Or with military rank:* General Doe	The Honorable John Doe, the American Ambassador (When he is not at his post, the name of the country to which he is accredited must be added: "to——.")
Social: The American Ambassador and Mrs. Doe American Embassy London England or		

* When a woman is a United States ambassador, or a United States minister, the word *Madam* is substituted for *Mr.* in the spoken address.

Written Address	*Spoken Address*	*Introductions*
His Excellency The American Ambassador and Mrs. Doe London England	Your Excellency or Mr. Ambassador	His Excellency the American Ambassador
American Ministers (men) The Honorable John Doe American Minister Dublin, Ireland	Mr. Minister or Mr. Doe	The American Minister *Or formal:* The Honorable John Doe, the American Minister *Or not at his post:* . . . to—" (name of country)
Social: The American Minister and Mrs. Doe American Legation Dublin Ireland		
American Chargé d'Affaires *and Consular Officers* John Doe, Esquire American Chargé d'Affaires (or Consul General, or Vice Consul) Paris, France	Mr. Doe	Mr. Doe *Or formal:* Mr. John Doe, the American Chargé d'Affaires
Social: The American Chargé d'Affaires and Mrs. John Doe (home address)		
United States Senator (or State Senator, with ap- propriate State address) The Honorable John Doe United States Senate Washington, D.C.	Senator Doe or Senator	Senator Doe *Or formal:* The Honorable John Doe, Senator from Oklahoma
Social: Senator and Mrs. Doe (home address)		

Written Address	Spoken Address	Introductions
United States Congressman		
The Honorable	Congressman	Congressman Doe†
John Doe	Doe	*Or formal:*
House of Representatives	or	The Honorable John Doe,
Washington, D.C.	Mr. Doe	Representative from South Carolina
Social:		
The Honorable and Mrs. Doe		
(home address)		
Governors*		
The Honorable	Governor Doe	Governor Doe or
John Doe	or	The Governor
Governor of Maryland	Governor	*Or formal:*
Annapolis, Maryland		The Honorable John Doe, Governor of Maryland or . . . of the State of Maryland
Social:		
The Governor and Mrs. Doe		
Or outside the State:		
The Governor of Maryland and Mrs. Doe		
or		
His Excellency the Governor and Mrs. Doe		
Mayors		
The Honorable	Mayor Doe	Mayor Doe
John Doe	or	*Or formal:*
Mayor of Boston	Mr. Mayor	The Honorable John Doe, Mayor of Boston
Boston, Massachusetts		or . . . Mayor of the City of Boston
Social:		
Mayor and Mrs. Doe		
or		
The Honorable and Mrs. John Doe		
(home address)		

† The title *Congressman* seems to be widely used in informal introductions by the Representatives themselves and by others when introducing them. It is not incorrect to call a Congresswoman *Congressman*. The prefix *Representative* is never used in correspondence.

* The Governor is given the title *Excellency* in many states, but the title *Governor* is the one used by the Department of State.

Written Address	Spoken Address	Introductions
Judges		
The Honorable	Judge Doe	Judge Doe
John Doe		*Or formal:*
Judge of District Court		The Honorable John Doe,
(or whatever court)		Judge of the District Court
Wheeling, West Virginia		
Social:		
Judge and Mrs. Doe		
or		
The Honorable and Mrs.		
Doe		
(home address)		
Head of a Federal Agency		
The Honorable	Mr. Doe	Mr. Doe
John Doe		*Or formal:*
Administrator (name of		The Honorable John Doe,
agency)		Administrator of (name of
Washington, D.C.		agency)
Social:		
Mr. and Mrs. John Doe		
or		
The Honorable and Mrs.		
John Doe		
(home address)		
Head of a Division or Bu-		
reau of a Department		
Mr. John Doe	Mr. Doe	Mr. Doe
Chief, Federal Bureau of In-		or
vestigation		Mr. John Doe, Chief of the
Washington, D.C.		Federal Bureau of Investiga-
		tion
Social:		
Mr. and Mrs. John Doe		
(home address)		

E. AMERICAN CLERGY AND CHURCH DIGNITARIES

The Presiding Bishop of		
the Protestant Episcopal		
Church in America		
The Most Reverend John	Bishop Doe	Bishop Doe
Doe, D.D., LL.D.		or

Written Address	Spoken Address	Introductions
Presiding Bishop of the Protestant Episcopal Church in America (local address)		The Most Reverend John Doe, Presiding Bishop of the Protestant Episcopal Church in America
Protestant Episcopal Bishops The Right Reverend John Doe, D.D., LL.D. Bishop of— (local address)	Bishop Doe	Bishop Doe or The Right Reverend John Doe, Bishop of—
Roman Catholic Cardinal His Eminence John Cardinal Doe Archbishop of New York New York, New York	Your Eminence	His Eminence or Cardinal Doe or His Eminence, Cardinal Doe
Roman Catholic Archbishop (or *Bishop*) His Excellency, The Most Reverend John Doe, S.T.D. Archbishop (or Bishop) of Chicago Chicago, Illinois	Archbishop (or Bishop) Doe	Archbishop (or Bishop) Doe or His Excellency, The Most Reverend John Doe, Archbishop of Chicago or His Excellency, The Archbishop of Chicago
Methodist Bishop* The Very Reverend John Doe, D.D., LL.D. Bishop of Denver Denver, Colorado	Bishop Doe	Bishop Doe or The Very Reverend Bishop Doe, Methodist Bishop of Denver
Roman Catholic Monsignor The Right Reverend Monsignor John Doe (local address)	Monsignor Doe	The Very Reverend (or Right Reverend) Monsignor John Doe or Monsignor Doe
Protestant Episcopal Archdeacon The Venerable John Doe, D.D.* Archdeacon of— Diocese of Virginia	Archdeacon Doe or Mr. Doe	Archdeacon Doe or Dr. Doe or The Venerable John Doe, Archdeacon of— in the Diocese of Virginia

Written Address	Spoken Address	Introductions
Deans and Canons		
The Very Reverend John Doe, D.D. Dean (or Canon) of Washington Cathedral Washington, D.C.	Dean (or Canon) Doe or Dr. Doe	The Very Reverend John Doe, Dean (or Canon) of Washington Cathedral
Priests who are addressed as "Father"		
The Reverend John Doe, S.J. St. Mary's Church Washington, D.C.	Father Doe	Father Doe or The Reverend John Doe
Mormon		
Mr. John Doe President of Manti Temple Manti, Utah	Mr. Doe	Mr. John Doe, President of Manti Temple
Rabbi		
Rabbi John Doe Kneseth Israel Congregation Annapolis, Maryland	Rabbi Doe or Rabbi *Or with scholastic degree:* Dr. Doe	Rabbi Doe *Or with scholastic degree:* Dr. Doe
Mother Superior		
The Reverend Mother Mary (and the initials of her order) The Convent of— (address)	Reverend Mother	Reverend Mother
Sisters		
Sister Mary (and initials of her order (local address)	Sister Mary	Sister Mary
Brothers		
The Reverend Brother John Doe Fordham University Bronx, New York	Brother John or Brother	Brother John

* Protestant clergymen with a doctor's degree may be addressed and introduced as *Dr. Doe,* and *The Reverend Dr. Doe,* respectively. Without such a degree, they are addressed and introduced as *Sir,* and *The Reverend Doe,* respectively. In conversation, say *Dr. Doe* or *Mr. Doe.*

Written Address	*Spoken Address*	*Introductions*
Cantors		
Cantor John Doe	Cantor Doe	Cantor Doe
Kneseth Israel Congregation		
Annapolis, Maryland		
F. *INDIVIDUALS*		
Professor and Doctors		
Professor (or Assoc. Pro-	Mr. Doe	Professor Doe
fessor or Asst. Professor)	or	
John Doe	Professor Doe	
Or with		
Doctor's Degree:		
Dr. John Doe	Dr. Doe	Dr. Doe
Columbia University		
New York, New York		
Divorcées		
Mrs. Smith Doe (or Mrs.	Mrs. Doe	Mrs. Doe
Jane Doe)		
(the maiden surname or		
given name is followed		
by the ex-husband's name)		
(local address)		
Widow		
Mrs. John Doe	Mrs. Doe	Mrs. Doe
(the same as when her		
husband was alive)		
(local address)		

RÉSUMÉ OF DIFFERENCES IN THE FORMS OF ADDRESS

IN THE NAVAL SERVICES:

All grades of admiral are addressed and introduced as "Admiral"—with the exception of a formal presentation when the full grade would be stated.

Medical and dental officers are addressed and introduced by rank including and above the grade of commander; including and below the rank of lieutenant commander they are called "Doctor."

In a mixed group it is customary to introduce a captain in the Navy as "Captain, United States Navy," since the rank of captain in the

Navy and Coast Guard corresponds to the rank of colonel in the Army, Air Force, and Marine Corps—and the rank of captain in these services corresponds to the rank of lieutenant in the Navy.

A woman officer is addressed and introduced in the same way as a male officer. For example, a lieutenant commander is "Miss Jones"; a commander is "Commander Jones."

Navy enlisted women are addressed by ratings, in the same manner as the men. A warrant officer is "Miss."

Marine servicewomen, officers and enlisted, are addressed and introduced by rank.

On board ship, the captain of the ship is *always* "Captain"—regardless of his rank.

IN THE ARMY, AIR FORCE, AND MARINE CORPS:

All officers are addressed and introduced by rank.

It is not correct in a spoken address to use the title by itself, such as "Colonel." It is correct to say, "Colonel Doe," etc.

At a social occasion, the various ranks are not necessary to mention (for example, all generals are "General," and first and second lieutenants are "Lieutenant"), but at a formal presentation the full title is stated: "Brigadier General," "First Lieutenant," etc.

Warrant officers are addressed and introduced as "Mister" or "Miss" (except for formal occasions, or reasons of designation when the full rank is stated).

Noncommissioned officers are addressed and introduced by their rank, such as "Private Doe," not "Doe" or "John."

Servicewomen, both officers and enlisted, are addressed and introduced by rank.

IN THE MARITIME SERVICE:

The captain of the ship is Captain Doe. Graduates of the Merchant Marine Academy and the State Maritime colleges and academies become third engineers or third mates or are commissioned as ensigns in the U.S. Naval Reserve; they are addressed as "Mister."

IN CIVILIAN LIFE:

"The Honorable" is the preferred form for addressing most American officials, in office or retired. The phrase is always used with the full name—and never with any other title.

"His Excellency" is used in addressing an ambassador but his wife is *not* called "Her Excellency."

Some of the American officials addressed as "The Honorable" are

American ambassadors and ministers, governors of states and territories, cabinet officers, senators and congressmen, the assistant to the President, assistant secretaries of executive departments, judges (except judges of the Supreme Court), commissioners of the District of Columbia, American representatives on international organizations, heads of independent federal agencies, and mayors of cities.

High officials such as presidents, ambassadors, and cabinet members are addressed by their titles only, never by name.

In addition to the above-mentioned persons addressed as "The Honorable," you should remember that "Once an Honorable, always an Honorable," and that a person out of office may be addressed in writing as "The Honorable."

The word "Honorable" is never used by the person who holds this distinction in issuing or answering invitations, or on personal or calling cards—or in any other way.

IN FOREIGN COUNTRIES:

American service attachés and other officials serving in foreign countries should consult the protocol section of the American Embassy. In Washington, the foreign liaison section of the office of your service will advise you on problems of customs and protocol.

CHAPTER 9

The Art of Conversation

FOR MANY PEOPLE, the art of conversation is of little importance. In some walks of life this may be true—but not for you as an officer in the armed forces, or anyone who chooses to become a professional leader of men and women.

The general public considers an officer in the services to be a person of position and so renders judgment upon this basis. You must, therefore, devote significant thought and effort to the development of proficiency in general conversation, since you are, so to speak, "on the spot."

The first thing you must do in order to be a good conversationalist is to *have something to say*; second, you *must be able to say it well.*

MANNER OF CONVERSATION

Poor grammar, rude or vulgar talk, and the persistent use of improper and uncouth phraseology are representative of careless personal habits that can be corrected if you take sufficient interest. There are officers who perform their duties acceptably—occasionally, excellently—despite their inability to express themselves clearly and in good taste. But this is the exception rather than the rule.

Errors of a gross nature in conversation are particularly noticed by those officers junior to the speaker—and, paradoxically enough, even by those juniors who themselves use poor grammar.

Juniors, despite shortcomings of their own, expect high standards in their superiors, and justly so. Such use of careless speech will inevitably result in the loss of prestige. The juniors are likely to suspect that a senior who tolerates carelessness in his own speech may well tolerate carelessness in other phases of his official behavior. Such a suspicion is something that every officer wishes to avoid, so it is well that a cadet or midshipman, ROTC or OCS student, recognize this fact early and cultivate the habit of proper speech in everyday conversation.

OFFICIAL AND SOCIAL CONVERSATION

"The tongue is but three inches long, yet it can kill a man six feet high." This old Japanese proverb can, too often, be only too true.

In the services, the essential difference between official and social conversation is one of situation. Conversation in an *official situation* requires that the conversationalists recognize differences in rank even while carrying on their conversation. Regardless of how pleasant and congenial such conversation may be, the speaker should always remember that such congeniality is never any excuse for not giving due deference to rank.

Social conversation means general talk between persons during which no conscious recognition of rank, as such, is made. Social conversation is more informal and is made up of considerable "small talk." This is pleasant talk that is not important—and not at all harmful. But small talk that is fitting and proper at a dinner party is not carried on during an official conversation.

In both types of conversations, the objectives are the same: to create a personal relationship without tension in which thoughts and ideas may be exchanged. The tone of official conversation is generally more serious, but not necessarily so. Senior admirals and generals are only midshipmen and cadets grown older, and they, like anyone else, often enjoy a light conversation that does not concern career or business problems. Official business, of course, should never be discussed at social gatherings.

When talking with a senior or very high-ranking officer, a junior officer shows deference and allows the senior to take the lead in the conversation—but should never freeze up while desperately trying to think of something brilliant to say. At a social occasion, the officer should be attentive—but not "at attention."

FAMILIARITY

There is an old military maxim that you should always remember: in the relations between seniors and juniors, the senior will never think of the difference in rank—but the junior will never forget it. This adage is true in both social and official relations. Adherence to it will lead to ease and harmony, but violation of it often leads to unpleasantness and, sometimes, to downright embarrassment.

Official conversations between seniors and juniors follow a basic principle: seniors may call you, the junior, by your first name, but this does not grant you similar privileges. It is a gesture of friendly consideration on the part of the senior to call a junior by his first name, and this should be accepted as approbation by the junior.

Upon occasion, a senior will ask a junior to call him by his first name—but such informality must be handled with care on your part, and it must be clearly understood that the familiarity of the first name is *not* to be used in official conversations. Neither does the privilege of calling a senior by his first name automatically carry with it a "back slapping" familiarity—in fact, quite the opposite. The senior must have expected you to exercise the utmost propriety, or he would not have lowered the bars in the first place.

In talking with your contemporaries in the mess or anywhere else be on guard against telling your personal affairs. Your mess mates and station friends will become very good friends in time, but they are not the same as your parents or your immediate family. When you talk "just a little" with others about your personal affairs, a "little" quickly becomes "too much," and you will find that constraint and unease begin to develop in your formerly easy relationship.

When on duty, conversations between seniors and juniors, and between commissioned and noncommissioned officers, should always be kept on the official and impersonal level. This does not mean that you should resemble Captain Hornblower when talking with those of junior rank, but it does mean that you should avoid undue familiarity.

Enlisted personnel appreciate your consideration for their welfare and your interest in their interests, but they do not appreciate—or want—familiarity. They know that familiarity in manner tends to cause an officer to forfeit his status as an officer; they distrust an officer who talks as thought he wants to "join the gang" one moment, and shortly thereafter issues even a minor reprimand in his official capacity. Any such occurrences hurt the sensibilities of the junior who is reprimanded.

The necessity for reprimands is not frequent, but the same situation will hold when you must make even minor criticisms: their significance is clouded over by the personal element. In positions of command, "Familiarity breeds contempt."

DISSENSIONS

Be careful of dissensions! You will find that you can disagree in your mind completely, and furthermore, can express that disagreement in conversation with a group without "leaving the sea strewn with burning wrecks." It merely takes tact. And tact, as some wit stated, is the talent for not saying that you were right in the first place. But there are those who cannot disagree with any expressed opinion without seeming to launch a personal attack on the person who stated the opinion.

An effective way to disagree with an expressed conversational opinion is to make no return comment at all—or, to make a rather roundabout comment which tends to veer the conversation away from the offensive statement without being obvious about it.

Religious discussions in dissimilar groups are generally unwise because statements, seemingly innocent to the speaker, may seem offensive to a listener. This does not mean that you should refuse to state an opinion on a religious subject, or to enter into a discussion, but it does mean that you should be careful of the company in which a religious discussion is carried on. Unless the group is composed of men of good will, intelligence, and tolerance, such discussions tend to break down into heated arguments and end in violent wrangles.

When you feel it necessary, however, to go on record as disagreeing with something that has been said, you may do so in a number of polite ways. For example, you may say, with a pleasant smile, "I'm afraid that I don't agree with that," or "I have given the matter considerable thought and have come to an entirely different conclusion." A light but disarming remark could be, "I'm from too far south to agree with such a Yankee idea." In brief, learn how to disagree without being disagreeable.

You may politely, but firmly, express disagreement by obviously changing the subject. Since this maneuver is not in the best social taste, it should be reserved for situations which require drastic treatment—as when a person enters upon a tirade concerning a religious sect, and you know there is a member of that sect present. In such cases you are within the safest grounds of propriety to change the subject swiftly and decisively in order to avoid an unfortunate situation.

There may come a time, however, when a senior officer states an opinion which is radically against your own convictions. Unless some action on your part is imperatively called for, you naturally avoid comment, out of deference for your senior's greater age and experience. But if your senior then asks you to give an opinion, you may say "I have not entirely made up my mind, Sir," or "I'm not too well versed in that subject, Sir."

When the senior officer persists in an answer, you must state your honest opinion, or you will not be true to your own convictions and risk being labeled as a "yes man." With due respect, you may say "Sir, that is a matter of opinion, but my experience has been to the contrary."

IMPORTANCE OF REMEMBERING

Names are important to remember. You do not like your own name forgotten or mispronounced—so do not forget or fumble another's. Some people have excellent memories for names and faces, others must work at remembering. Most memory courses depend upon associating the name with an object, or repeating a name over and over in your mind after an introduction. If you miss the name on first being introduced, you can quite properly ask to have the name repeated.

When you cannot remember a person's name, and yet it is your duty to make the introduction to a conversational group, it is better to admit your lapse and say, "I'm sorry, but I will have to ask you your name," or "Please tell me your name again." The question should be asked with poise and no embarrassment.

In conversations, it is complimentary to remember another's personal concerns: a birthday or wedding anniversary, or an accomplishment by a member of the family. Any pleasant occurrence—an award, or a recent promotion in grade—that has happened to an individual, often serves to provide a background for conversation.

WHEN YOU DON'T KNOW THE ANSWER

Does it hurt your pride to admit that you do not know something? It takes a big person to admit that he (or she) does not know the answer to a question that he should know, particularly when the questioner is an important person whom he would like to impress.

Can you do this? If so, it is to your credit. Always remember that even though you may be an expert on some subject, no one knows everything about every thing.

WHEN YOU DO KNOW

Have you been in a conversation—say at a party, when someone sounds off on a subject that he knows little about but you do?

If you are a sensitive person you will consider the type of individual sounding off: is he making small talk, trying to keep the conversation going? If so, he could be shattered by your pointing out his lack of knowledge by your giving the correct version. An inhibited person not only would be embarrassed, but you might drive him into a deep shell from which he would be afraid to emerge for fear of further blundering. In such a case, the kindest thing would be to change the conversation to another subject as quickly as possible.

THE JOKER

Some people just love to tell a joke. They must be the life of the party, and quite often they are. But when the joke discredits another person—intentionally or not—then "the insult with a smile" is not funny at all.

Sometimes the joker merely wants to show a little self-superiority by his cleverness. But when the joke stings or hurts another because of some social or business error that he has made, he is being put down.

TABOOS

Controversial subjects—such as religion, race, and frequently, politics—and unpleasant subjects should not be discussed at social functions, and are treated carefully at any time. Examples of such subjects are death, disasters, accidents, battle losses, or serious illness.

Never discuss a person's age in his or her presence. Elderly people do not enjoy being considered decrepit, neither do young people want to feel immature and inadequate. Both the very young and the very old are frequently sensitive about their ages.

EASY CONVERSATION

An essential part of your everyday living is the art of simple, easy conversation. A good conversationalist always has something interesting to talk about, is not overbearing in his attitude, and never irritates his listeners.

In general, plain words are preferable to ponderous phrases, and trite expressions are tiresome. The topics for conversations are endless: newspapers, books, magazines; television personalities and news analysts can always be discussed, and art, music, and concerts appeal to the artistic. Any sport event in season is of interest to most men and many women.

A topic of conversation may be discussed as long as the listeners find it of interest, then new ones must be introduced. When you are talking, look at your listeners and observe their reactions. No monologue is of interest—except possibly to yourself. When you are the listener, pay attention to what is being said. It is extremely discourteous to openly show obvious disinterest—such as allowing your glance to wander off to other people or things.

A good conversationalist does not interrupt or contradict another. He learns to draw out the shy person by finding out his interests, then adroitly asks leading questions concerning that hobby or interest. When talking with a horticulturist, you could ask him about his garden; an author would be interested in a new book.

When you want to start a lively conversation, ask a question which presents a challenge: "I hear the Army is strong—who do you think will win the Army-Navy game?" or, "Would it be better to return to the Three R's than to continue with progressive education?"

When you wish to have a certain subject discussed without coming right out with it, bring up a related subject or experience that will open the door to the desired subject. For example, if you wish to hear a man who wears the Congressional Medal of Honor talk about his experiences, you might pave the way by saying, "Sir, how many patrols did you make during World War II?"

In order to talk intelligently on a certain subject to a person of authority, it is well to brief yourself on that subject beforehand. In this way you can converse easily with the personage about his work or accomplishment and at the same time increase your own store of knowledge.

In your desire to make a good accounting of yourself, however, do not be so obvious that you appear insincere. It is an insult to your seniors, or to anyone else, to express more interest than common courtesy allows.

POISE AND GOOD MANNERS

When you talk, do you keep your hands and feet quiet, or do you gesture wildly and shuffle your feet? Do you drum on a table with your fingers, or tap your feet on the floor? If you do—stop it. To shift from one foot to the other makes you appear ill at ease and detracts not only from your appearance, but also from what you are saying: Finger or foot tapping draws attention to what you are *doing*, rather than what you are saying.

A good conversationalist is always a considerate one; he will reflect upon a new thought before blurting out a remark that may be regretted later. He is tolerant of other's ideas, and does not ridicule or laugh at an unfortunate remark, or tell an amusing story to the discredit of anyone.

Poise in conversation includes the ability to time a conversation—to know when to talk and when to be silent. Relaxation is an essential ingredient for a poised conversationalist; an incessant chatterer will soon exhaust his listeners.

Sometimes two people start talking simultaneously. Such a situation generally happens when there has been a lull in a conversation and both persons attempt to relieve the situation at the same time. In such cases, if you are one of them, give way amiably and quickly. To fail to do so makes you seem rude and domineering.

A skilled conversationalist can be compared to a ship's captain; he can steer thoughts and ideas into interesting conversational channels, but when necessary, he can chart the course of an unfortunate subject away from the reef to the safety of calmer seas.

TONE OF VOICE

A well-modulated voice is an asset to anyone. Words should be enunciated clearly, in a pleasant tone which is pitched neither too high nor too low. If you aren't aware of how your voice sounds to others, try speaking naturally or reading a news item into a recording machine; then play it back. Do your words run together? Do you bark them out? Are you too loud? To high-pitched? Shrill? The range of your voice is always important; speaking in a monotone makes any topic dull and monotonous.

With some effort on your part, you can control your voice by breathing from your diaphragm and developing a range in tone which will improve both your voice and your conversational appeal.

NAMES AND TITLES

Sometimes it's hard to know just what to call a person when he is very junior or senior to you. A senior officer and his wife may call a junior officer and his wife by their first names in an informal and friendly manner—but they are still "Colonel and Mrs. Smith" to you, the junior officer, unless you are requested to call them by their first names.

Officially, senior rank is always observed when speaking with or referring to an officer, regardless of how well you know him. Socially, close friends call each other by their first names regardless of age or rank.

A man does not call a woman by her first name until she takes the initiative, such as calling you by your first name or asking that you call her by hers. Then, you are free to use her first name.

ASKING FOR FIRST DATES

Although the majority of young men at the service academies and in ROTC units are experienced in asking girls for dates, there are some who have had little time or inclination to date before entering these institutions.

Upon first meeting a girl, a rather shy young man usually "talks around" the problem of asking for a date the first time. If you are that young man you might say something like, "Do you like sports?" If she replies in the affirmative, you might mention a game you might attend, and in her manner will be a clue as to whether or not she would like you to ask her.

If she seems favorably interested, then you can say. "How would you like to meet me after the game and go on to the hop?"—or to the movies, or whatever the occasion might be. In the case of a fourth classman, you could ask the girl to meet you at the place or occasion limited to your opportunities of meeting girls.

Some young men are afraid that a girl will turn them down, thus hesitate to ask for a date. In turn, the girl may be afraid to seem overeager when you show interest, and what appears to be coolness on her part may be a bit of stage fright. So *ask*.

If a girl, however, refuses you twice, then you should hesitate to continue the pursuit. But do learn to take an occasional refusal with poise— she may have a very sound reason why she cannot accept your invitation.

RULES TO REMEMBER

Do:

Have something to say—and say it well. Brief amusing stories, a news item, unusual incidents, a TV personality—all are conversation starters.

Be a good listener.

Develop the art of small talk; this is pleasant talk about nothing in particular, but does *not* include official or harmful subjects.

Learn to remember names and faces; nothing will make you more popular.

Put a shy person at his ease by getting him to talk about his hobbies, pets, children, or known interests.

Put yourself at ease—by thinking of the *other* person.

As a host, act as moderator and intervene in a monologue, a "dead" group, or a controversial discussion, by changing the subject.

Talk in a moderate tone of voice.

Keep your eyes and ears open—and, occasionally, your mouth *shut*.

Be able to say "I don't know"—when you don't.

Do not:

Gossip. Say nothing about a person that you would not want him to hear.

Talk business at a social gathering.

Substitute sarcasm or ridicule for wit.

Interrupt or contradict others.

Monopolize any conversation.

Talk over anyone's head, or "talk down" to anyone.

Flatter others; insincerity is unwelcome.

Talk endlessly; silence, at times, *is* golden.

Allow a guest to be stranded with a conversational bore.

"Clam up"; a shy guest is a burden to a host, who thereupon must force conversation.

Exclude anyone from a conversational group.

Give the state of your health when someone says, "How are you?" This is simply a polite expression, generally used in greetings or "small talk."

Talk about a party you have been invited to—when others have not been invited.

Be ingratiating with your seniors. Deference expresses respect for authority; bootlicking does not.

CHAPTER 10

Good Manners Before
an Audience

ANY OFFICER MUST be able to speak effectively in any situation. At the Naval Academy, the need for public speaking is considered so important that midshipmen receive formal classroom instruction in speech, and after-dinner speaking is required of the first class. In this course, small formal dinners are held at the Academy, with each first classman delivering a certain number of brief speeches during the year. The dinners are complete with toastmaster, guest of honor, and an instructor who gives helpful criticism. The dinners are prepared under conditions approximating those which can be expected later.

After graduation from the academies, Officer Training Schools, Officer Candidate Schools or ROTC units, an officer will find that one of the most important aptitudes which he (or she) can possess is skill in addressing a group. From the very beginning of his career, he will find himself called upon to address a division aboard ship or a company ashore, to enter into general meetings in the wardroom or barracks, and to discuss professional matters before groups of other officers at critiques, etc.

Later on he will find himself drawn into the public life of his community. He will be called upon to deliver speeches upon patriotic occasions, to present proposals in public meetings, and to be an active member of service clubs and civic organizations.

Preparedness for such a role is one of the responsibilities that you will assume as a person in public life, where the general public expects experienced leadership from officers in the services. The responsibility for group leadership may not be something that you desire—but it may be something that you must assume.

When you are asked to be president of a PTA or chairman of service night at Rotary or to speak to a women's club, you cannot plead inability to speak in public or ignorance of parliamentary procedure. The public knows better. They know that you had the opportunity to learn these things, and they expect to find you, if not an expert, at least well grounded in the fundamentals. The best grounding that any officer can have is a clear understanding of the proprieties of public speaking, and the forms of courtesy to be followed when addressing a group.

In effect, public speaking is based upon one's ability to win the interest of the audience, to "get over" to the group, and to treat every person with courtesy and consideration.

It is an axiom in public speaking that your first important objective is to create a favorable relationship between your audience and yourself before attempting to deliver your message. The impression that you leave with an audience is almost as important as the message that you have delivered.

Dale Carnegie recognized the relative importance of this relationship of a speaker to his audience in the title of his book on public speaking: *How to Win Friends and Influence People.* You will note that *friendship* ranks ahead of *influence.*

PREPARATION

A speaker should never accept an invitation to talk on a subject about which he is not well informed. If you have time to research the subject, then you should feel free to accept.

Any serious speech should be prepared well in advance, with all facts, dates, and names carefully checked out. Thoughts should be well organized and presented in logical order. You will want to know how long you are to talk—and try to stay within this limit.

APPEARANCE

The *appearance* of the speaker is the first thing an audience notes; then his *mannerisms*, and next his *voice.* A speaker in uniform should be at his or her best—your uniform immaculate, your posture relaxed. A man in civilian dress should be conservatively dressed, tie in order, suit pressed, and hands out of pockets. A woman should make certain that her skirt hangs evenly, and that her stockings do not wrinkle. Loud colors and prints are distracting. A speaker should not stand or sit ramrod-stiff; neither should his hands or feet be in constant motion.

An audience expects the speaker to recognize and address properly the leader or chairman of the meeting. It also expects him to use correct forms of address when speaking to the group as a whole, or to an individual member. A speaker can be as polite—or as impolite—to a group of people as he can be to a single person.

PERSONAL CONDUCT IN SPEAKING

You should always avoid "talking down" to a group, or "over their heads." It is insulting to an audience to address them as though you are the only one who knows anything about a given subject—even when you are an expert in that particular field. You should avoid the over-use of the first person pronoun: "*I* think—," "*I* know—," or "*I* did—." Simplicity and ease of speech are as important as your subject matter.

Your yardstick in speaking (or writing) is: Can people understand what I mean? A familiar word is better than a "show-off" word or phrase; a short word is preferable to a long one.

No audience likes to hear a speaker apologize for himself or for what he has to say. Any apology puts the speaker on the defensive. Apologetic and self-conscious gestures such as clearing the throat, jutting the chin up and down, straightening a tie, rebuttoning your coat, shifting from one foot to another—all such gestures make an audience as uneasy as the speaker.

Although most words spoken in private conversation are just words, some of these same words may set up a chain reaction against you when used in a speech or before an audience. Experience will teach you what these words and expressions are and they should be mentally catalogued as *fighting words* and not used again.

From various viewpoints, such fighting words could be; "We of the intelligentsia . . .," or "You military dictators . . .," or, "You civilians couldn't understand. . . ."

To the listener, such words and expressions indicate a disregard for his personal feelings. The listener may merely consider you highhanded—but you will still be unpopular. A joke which seemed so amusing to one may seem like ridicule to another—if the shoe fits, so to say.

You should be respectful of others' opinions at a meeting, and should try to look at various viewpoints from all sides before making up your own mind on a subject. Always be fair—but firm.

Always give credit whenever credit is due, but be careful of the timing in expressing a compliment made in public. An ill-timed compliment may embarrass the recipient as well as give an impression of "fawning" upon him.

In order to achieve a feeling of communication between himself and his audience, some speakers find it helpful to select a person in the audience and talk to him or her, armchair fashion.

THE FUNNY STORY

A brief amusing story of reminiscence, a good joke, or a good quotation are all ice-breakers at the opening of a meeting. Such stories must be *good*, however, or the speaker will lose his audience and will have to try harder than ever to win them over.

The first rule in telling a story is that it must be amusing to you, the speaker, or you cannot expect it to be funny to your audience— unless you presume them to be of lower intelligence than yourself. In this case, you have played down to your audience.

The second rule is that a joke sparkles best in brevity.

The third rule is not to laugh heartily at your own joke.

You must, of course, be fully aware of the type of audience you will address when speaking before a club or organization: large or small, mixed or stag, rural or cosmopolitan. You should take into careful consideration the racial, religious, political, and age groups involved. The type of club or organization will determine the tone of your talk, and you must make certain that your material is in keeping with the spirit of the occasion.

An off-color story is a dangerous story to tell before an audience at any time. Such a story told in a locker room or in a foursome may seem hilarious—but when the same story is told at a public or private gathering, particularly before a mixed group, the one telling the story may be marked as vulgar or uncouth.

Lastly, at no time must you allow your sense of humor to desert you. A good sense of humor will protect you from a seemingly disinterested audience and also from becoming "too full of yourself."

YOUR GRAMMER

The grammar you use when you are making a speech or in everyday conversation tells much about you. If you are unsure of your grammar, it probably will be reflected in your talk. Hesitations, some "uhs" or "wells," will slow your train of thought as well as the listener's interest. Today, the words "you know" are sprinkled through innumerable sentences. Avoid this whenever possible.

An academy professor has stated that in his opinion cadets and midshipmen have a poorer background in English grammar than in any other subject. If you are uncertain of your usage, check out a book in the library or hunt up a school grammar book which explains everything about verbs and sentence structure.

YOUR VOICE

A well-modulated voice is pleasing to your audience. If you have a tendency to talk too fast and rush your sentences, slow down. Learn to space important words and phrases, then for emphasis wait a second or so after a very important remark is made.

If nature did not provide you with a pleasant speaking voice, then cultivate one. Take courses in public speaking and voice control. Practice pitching your voice down, should it be high or shrill.

Although it is better to talk slowly than to rush your words, the man or woman who talks very slowly in a droning fashion can lull his audience to sleep.

PARLIAMENTARY PROCEDURE

It is essential that you have some knowledge of parliamentary procedure, whether you are the presiding officer at a meeting or the member of an organization who sits in the back row and just listens. You can never tell when you might be moved to "rise to a point of order."

The nationally recognized book on parliamentary procedure is *Robert's Rules of Order Revised*. Incidentally, this book was written by a West Pointer—Class of 1857—Brigadier General Henry Martyn Robert, who became Chief of Engineers, U.S. Army.

General Correspondence, Invitations & Replies

CHAPTER 11

Business Correspondence

IN CONVERSATION you are judged by what you say; in correspondence you are judged by what you write. Plain words and phrases are preferable in letter writing, just as they are in conversation. A letter difficult to compose is handled with more ease when written as though you were speaking to the person addressed.

When you choose your stationery, consider its use: whether for official or business correspondence, or social or personal. White paper is customarily used for all types of business correspondence in the services, but personal stationery may also be cream color, gray, blue-gray, or a light tan. These and other pastel colors are used by women.

All engraving is much more expensive than printing. The tremendous amount of correspondence at any large post or station, the thousands of invitations issued each year, make the cost of engraving prohibitive except for the very official or important formal occasion. And it is prohibitive for many individuals.

A process called *thermography,* a raised type, is widely used for the more formal types of invitation cards and official or personal stationery. It is almost indistinguishable from engraving—and is much less expensive although it cost more than plain printing. Today, plain printing is perfectly acceptable for all but the most formal or official correspondence. Any good stationery store or the PX can advise you about this.

BUSINESS PAPER

Official or business stationery is white, with black or dark blue engraving or printing. The official letterhead is usually at the top center of the sheet, but may also be placed at the top left-hand side.

There are various sizes of business paper most frequently used:

> The traditional white bond paper, single sheet, 8 by 10 inches, with standard matching envelope of oblong shape and plain flap.
>
> A slightly larger sheet, with or without telephone number in the letterhead, 8½ by 11 inches.
>
> A slightly narrower sheet for business-personal use, 7¼ by 10¼ inches, used for both longhand and typewirter.
>
> A smaller business-personal sheet, 7 by 8½ inches, used for business invitations.

BUSINESS LETTERS

There are several styles generally used for official or business letters with letterheads:

1. The *full block* style with everything flush left on the page: the date, the name and address, the salutation, all paragraphs and lines, the complimentary close and signature. Double spacing separates the single-spaced paragraphs.

2. The *modified block* style with the date at the upper right; the name and address, the saluation, all paragraphs and lines flush left; the complimentary close and signature to the right in line with the date. Paragraphs are separated by double spacing.

3. The *modified semi-block* style with the date at the top right; the name and address, the salutation flush left, each paragraph indented (5 or 10 spaces) and single spaced, separated by double spacing. The complimentary close and signature are at the right, in line with the date.

The dates in business letters, civilian form, may be written, "May 7, 1977," but the official service form is "7 May 1977." No letter should be dated "5/7/77."

Customarily, there is a colon after the salutation, and a comma after the complimentary closing of a letter.

The *inside address* is written in the same way as on the envelope, with no punctuation at the end of the lines. The title may be abbreviated when it precedes the name, as "Dr. John B. Jones," but it is written in full in the salutation, as "Dear Doctor Jones." In official service correspondence, the order of address usually is: (a) administrative position; (b) station; (c) city, zone, and state. Sometimes, rank and name are "(a)."

In business, the order usually is: (a) title and name; (b) administrative position; (c) company name; (d) company address; (e) city, zone, and state.

The *salutation* is "Dear Mr. Jones:" or "Dear Captain Jones:". When names are unknown, "Dear Sir:" or "Gentlemen:" is used. A business woman is addressed "Dear Miss Jones:" or "Dear Mrs. Jones:"—but when it is not known whether she is married or not, use "Miss" or "Ms." Two or more women are addressed as "Mesdames."

Paragraphs in business letters are not numbered as they are in official correspondence, but items in paragraphs may be lettered and numbered.

The body of the letter should include all necessary information, with well-constructed sentences and no errors in spelling, punctuation, or grammar. Avoid stilted or trite phrases; be courteous, and not annoying. Whenever possible, write a one-page letter. The second page is usually indicated by "—2—" at the center top.

The *complimentary close* is the polite phrase or word (adverb) with which you end your letter. Business letters are customarily closed by the "yours" phrase, with "Very truly yours," the most formal. "Sincerely yours," or "Cordially yours," is used for a more personal-business letter and "Very respectfully yours" when writing to a superior. The complimentary close is typed *two-lines* below the preceding line of typing.

Your *signature* is typed or stamped *four lines* below the complimentary close, and hand-signed above the typed signature. For an officer, the order of signature is:

1. Name in capitals
2. Rank or
3. Functional title
4. Authority line, if any.

The signature for a business man usually is:

1. Name, not capitalized throughout
2. Functional title
3. The company name (usually not used, since it is in the letterhead).

Signatures on the official service letter vary from the business-form letter in the following respects: (1) the rank, if any, is included; (2) the functional title is added; and (3) the authority line, if any, is expanded to include the title of the command at whose direction the letter is prepared. Examples:

John B. JONES
Assistant Secretary for Maritime Affairs
U.S. Department of Commerce

J. B. JONES
Brigadier General, U.S. Air Force
Director of Telecommunications

JANE B. JONES
Lieutenant, U.S. Army
Defense Advisory Committee
on Women in the Services

J. B. JONES
Rear Admiral, U.S. Navy
Head, Division of Administration
By Direction of the Chief of Naval Operations

J. B. JONES
Captain, U.S. Coast Guard
Commandant of Cadets

JOSEPHINE B. JONES
Colonel, U.S. Marine Corps
Women's Equal Opportunity Branch

In signatures it is incorrect to use titles such as "Mr.," "Mrs.," "Capt.," "Dr.," "Prof." Men and women in business usually use the company's writing paper for all business correspondence, but important executives often have specially engraved or printed paper. Under the company's letterhead, at the *left-hand* margin, the full name is engraved with the title of office directly underneath. For example:

Rear Admiral John E. Doe, USN (Ret.)
President

THE MODIFIED BLOCK STYLE:

Department of the Army
Office of the Chief of Information
Washington, D.C. 20310

(seal)
DAIO-PI   (date)

Miss Jane Jones
Sunday Magazine Editor
The St. Louis Dispatch
St. Louis, Missouri 63106

Dear Miss Jones:

In response to your 24 February request for information needed
for your news article concerning women cadets at the United
States Military Academy at West Point, the following documents
are attached:

Incl. 1. Current Army Regulations on Uniform and
Insignia, Female Personnel.

Incl. 2. Chart listing uniforms worn by USMA cadets
(female) starting July 1976.

Incl. 3. Booklet on Information for Women Cadets published by the United States Military Academy.

Incl. 4. ODWAC Notes, January 1983.

We hope the above-listed items will answer the questions you
posed in your letter.

Sincerely,

Incls: James E. Doe
As stated   Lieutenant Colonel, GS
                                Chief, News Branch
                                Public Information Division

A MODIFIED SEMI-BLOCK LETTER:

(letterhead)

(date)

Major Mary Smith, USA
Cadet Activities Officer, Women
United States Military Academy
West Point, New York 10996

Dear Major Smith:

You are cordially invited to be our guest speaker at a luncheon to be held for junior girls of Plains High School on Friday, April 5. The luncheon will be held at 12 noon in the school's new activity room, with about 100 students attending.

Many of our girls have expressed a keen interest in becoming women cadets, and we think that your being with us will give them an opportunity to learn how to achieve an appointment and what to expect in cadet life.

We hope very much to have you with us on April 5.

Very sincerely yours,

JED:v   John E. Doe, Principal

ENVELOPES

Business envelopes usually match the paper and are in sizes ranging from 3⅞ by 8⅞ inches to 4½ by 10⅜ inches. They are usually imprinted with the title of an official or company, or the name of the command, with return address in the upper left corner.

Envelopes are addressed in the same manner as inside addresses, and are single spaced and frequently indented. The letter is folded in horizontal thirds and inserted in the long envelope, or folded first in half and then in thirds for the shorter envelopes.

In business, the address may be from two to five lines. Titles are used in the address: "Mr.," "Dr.," "Prof.," "Capt.," etc.

Mr. John Doe
Executive Vice President
Supreme Book Stores
115 East 53rd Street
New York, New York 10022

The address could begin with the last three lines and the notation: "Attention Mr. Doe" written in the lower left-hand corner. When necessary to signify PERSONAL that word is capitalized above the address.

CHAPTER 12

Social & Personal Correspondence

MEDIUM WEIGHT PAPER approximately 7 by 10 inches is often used by men for personal correspondence. A service crest or insignia, monogram, initials, or name and address may be engraved but usually is printed at the top center or upper left corner of the paper. The conventional colors of white or cream, blue, gray, blue-gray, or light tan are most frequently used, with matching envelopes.

Men's correspondence cards do not fold over and usually are about 4 by 5 inches, or larger. Your rank, name, and address, if retired, are engraved on the card which usually has an embossed insignia or seal at the top. Such cards may be used for invitations to stag luncheons, dinners, cocktails, etc.

Women's personal notepaper is smaller, about 5½ by 7 inches, and the full name and address are in the top center or the upper left corner of the page. Color combinations are more varied than those for men.

A married woman's notepaper is engraved or printed "Mrs. John Doe" rather than "Mrs. Jane Doe." An unmarried woman is "Jane Doe," but "Miss" is used on the envelope; a business woman might prefer "Ms."

A woman officer will use her rank on official stationery and she may use it on her personal paper if she so desires.

The fold-over notepaper is widely used for brief notes, for acknowledging and issuing invitations.

CRESTS

An admiral's or general's flag, a family crest or any military insignia of note are often used on a man's official and personal writing paper. They also are used by a married couple on wedding invitations or joint cards.

However, the admiral's flag and the family coat of arms are the exclusive property of the male members of the family—they are not used by the wife on her notepaper or invitations or in any personal way. The flag or crest is not hers to use any more than she is "Mrs. General."

INITIALS

Initials may be engraved, or die-stamped in color or in simple block form, at the top center or left of the sheet. Initials are usually 3/16 of an inch high, and are spaced to take up no more than ¾ of an inch over-all. On large sheets of paper, they may be ¼ inch high, and cover about the same amount of space. Initials are preferable to a monogram, but an address is better than either.

HANDWRITTEN LETTERS

Certain types of informal letters may be typed, *but others must be written by hand*, in a legible manner. It is obligatory to handwrite "bread and butter" and "thank you" letters, as well as letters of congratulation, condolence, and notes of welcome to a prospective son- or daughter-in-law.

Invitations to small weddings (and their reply), and engagements and birth announcements may be handwritten. But answers to formal invitations are always handwritten.

ADDRESSING ENVELOPES

Addresses on the envelopes of social correspondence are written by hand (unless the contents are typewritten), such as a note or letter to a friend or relative.

Write out the name in full, unless the envelope is small, then such abbreviations as Lt.Col., Brig.Gen., Rear Adm. or RAdm., are used. Write out names rather than using initials, such as "Col. and Mrs. John Lee Jones," rather than "Col. and Mrs. J. L. Jones."

When addressing a letter to a boy of twelve or under, you may use the word "Master": Master John Jones. There is no title for him until his teens or high school age when he is addressed "Mr. John Jones." Messrs. is the French abbreviation of the plural of "Mister" and may be used to address brothers but not a father and son.

A young girl is addressed "Mary Jones" until she reaches her teens when she is addressed "Miss." When you do not know the title of a person to be addressed, such as a business woman, you may write "Ms." A married woman is addressed "Mrs." unless she has a title or rank, which is used: "Dr. Mary Jones" or "Lieutenant Mary Jones, U.S. Air Force."

A man may use "Jr." after his name as long as his father is living, when it may be dropped. If his mother is living nearby he may prefer to retain the "Jr." for postal and business reasons.

A confidential letter may have the word *Personal* written above the address if addressed other than to that person's home. When you are uncertain of an address, *Please Forward* may be written in the lower area.

At all times, write the zip code. And write legibly.

SOCIAL OR PERSONAL LETTERS

A social or personal letter follows basic rules. A long letter has the date at the upper right-hand corner of the page. The date may also be written on the last page, or at the bottom of the first page, near the left-hand margin but slightly below the signature. Only very informal letters have abbreviated dates: the more formal the letter, the fewer the abbreviations.

The basic steps are:

1. *Date:*

Near the top right: "June 15th" (very informal)

or   Near the top right: "June 15, 1983" (civilian form)

or   Near the top right: "15 June 1983" (civilian or service form)

or   Near the lower left: (same form)

or   Near the lower left: "Saturday" (very formal or very brief).

2. *Salutation:* Flush with left margin, no inside address. For example:

"Dear Mary,"

or   "My dear Mary,"

or   "Dear Mrs. Jones," etc.

3. *Body of letter:* Indented paragraphs, or one paragraph, brief note. Avoid over-use of the pronoun "I."

4. *Complimentary close:* Start at center of page; or, start at the right, even with date line. For example:

"Sincerely,"

or   "Sincerely yours,"

5. *Signature:* Directly under, or under and slightly at right, of complimentary close. No title or rank, with first name for close friends—or

when the body of the letter gives no clue to the identity of the signer, then write full name, "John Jones." Otherwise, write your name in full.

The conventional salutations and closings for informal or personal correspondence are:

June 15th

(To a woman)
    Dear Mary,

. . . .
. . . .

As ever, (or "Yours ever,")
John (or "John Jones")

(To a man)
    Dear George,

. . . .
. . . .
. . . .

Sincerely, (or "As ever,")
John Jones

In letters to a relative or intimate friend, the closing would probably be "Affectionately," "With love," "Devotedly," etc., with the last name of the person writing omitted from the signature. Last names are added to the signature in informal letters when the body of the letter does not give a clue to the identity of the writer.

The date is usually written at the upper right-hand corner of the paper, with no address. On a short note, the day instead of the date may be written at the bottom left of the page, two spaces lower than the signature. On an informal note, the month is sometimes abbreviated; otherwise, it is written out.

THANK-YOU LETTERS

"Thank-you" letters should be written within a week after you have received a gift or a favor, or have been a houseguest or a guest of honor at some occasion. When you have been a houseguest, your thank-you note is called a "bread-and-butter" note. Although the envelope is addressed to the hostess, there is no inside address and mention should be made of the host in the body of the letter when it applies.

A basic form to follow in both the bread-and-butter letter and the thank-you note is printed herewith, with parts as indicated:

(date)

Dear Mrs. Doe,

(A) "Thank you for . . . (the gift or occasion, etc.)"
(B) A sincere comment concerning the occasion or gift; an expression of appreciation; a comment concerning something of mutual interest.
(C) A looking-forward-to-seeing-you-again (soon) sentence.
(D) A "thanks again," and a request to be remembered to the host and/or to any other members of the family.

Sincerely,

For a bride's thank-you notes, *see* Chapter 26 Wedding Invitations, Announcements, & Replies.

PERSONAL LETTERS

It is a wise man or woman who observes certain rules in writing very personal letters:

Never state anything that can be used against you.
Be careful of making direct promises or of stating familiarities.
Never write anything which might damage another's reputation or harm him in any way—for the person who might eventually be harmed most might be yourself.

You should guard against writing angry or abusive letters. If you must write a letter of complaint, wait several hours or overnight, and then re-read the letter before mailing it.

Letters of apology are sometimes required of even the best of us. Brief and sincere notes of explanation are always advisable when you are unable to keep a certain appointment, or when there has been some other misunderstanding.

RESERVATIONS

When you write a hotel or motel for a reservation, give brief but full information.

For example:

Quarters M
Fort Sam Houston
San Antonio, Texas
(date)

The Manager
Hotel Thayer
West Point, New York

Dear Sir:

Will you please reserve a room with bath for my wife and
me, from June first for one week?

If such accommodations are not available at present, please
let me know the earliest date you can take us.

Yours truly,
James Smith
Major, U.S. Army

A telegram to a hotel should include the title or rank in the signature:

PLEASE RESERVE SINGLE ROOM WITH BATH FOR ONE WEEK
STARTING SATURDAY 8 JUNE. WIRE CONFIRMATION COLLECT.

LIEUTENANT MARY ANN BROWN, USAF
14 NAVAJO PLACE
COLORADO SPRINGS, COLORADO

A man or wife may wire reservations ahead to a bus, plane, or train
terminal in this form:

UNITED AIR LINES
DULLES INTERNATIONAL AIRPORT
CHANTILLY VA.

PLEASE RESERVE TWO SEATS TO STOCKHOLM WIFE AND SELF
FIRST AVAILABLE JUNE, REPLY COLLECT.

MAJOR JAMES SMITH (address)

For reasons of clarity, other than in telegrams, use the term "my
wife and me." Upon arrival at the hotel or motel, however, you register,
"Major and Mrs. James Smith," *not* "Major James Smith and wife."

LETTERS OF CONDOLENCE

One of the most difficult letters to write is a letter of condolence—but no
letter is more appreciated than the one expressing sympathy at a time of
sorrow. Respect and obligation, affection and friendship are the grounds

for writing such letters. They should be addressed to the most bereaved, with reference to other members of the family in the letter.

The brief letter of condolence has a traditional form, with parts as follows:

1. An expression of sympathy.
2. A kind comment or observation concerning the deceased person.
3. A last word of affection and sympathy.
4. The complimentary close and your signature.

Always be careful of your choice of words in sending a message following a death that resulted from an accident, suicide, or any catastrophe.

The essentials in writing a letter of condolence are the expressions of sympathy, encouragement, and a desire to help. An example of a letter written to the mother of a classmate killed in an accident is:

Dear Mrs. Ledbetter,

I have just heard of Larry's fatal accident, and I want you to know that you have my deepest sympathy. Our friendship, which began when we roomed together at the Academy, has always been a solid reality on which I have leaned many times.

Since I am being transferred to Washington next month, I plan to stop over in Memphis en route. At that time, I want to call on you and, if possible, be of some service.

Sincerely,
John Jones

Telegrams are frequently sent, and follow this form:

OUR DEEPEST SYMPATHY.

MARY AND JOHN JONES

or

DEEPLY SHOCKED AT YOUR LOSS, ALL MY SYMPATHY. SINCERELY.

JOHN JONES
(OR MARY AND JOHN, for very close friends.)

REPLIES TO MESSAGES OF CONDOLENCE

Letters, telegrams, and other messages of condolence, as well as floral tributes, charity contributions, and such gifts as food for the family, should be personally acknowledged by the individual to whom they were addressed. This brief reply of thanks should be handwritten and mailed within six weeks after the message (or gift) has been received, and preferably earlier.

A sentence or two will be enough, particularly in cases of ill health or extreme grief. In cases of illness, extreme age, or shock, a member of the family may write the note of thanks.

All-white paper is used more frequently for correspondence in connection with bereavement than the traditional black-bordered paper of former years. Mourning paper for men is usually all white, or white with an address or initials engraved or printed in black. Women may use all white, or white with a black or gray border about 1/16 of an inch wide, or with a black monogram or address. A light gray paper is also used.

A reply to a message of condolence may be very brief:

Dear Mrs. Smith,

Thank you so much for your very kind expression of sympathy.

Sincerely,
John Jones

Or, to a long-time friend, you would write a more personal note:

Dear Mary,

Your very kind letter gave me great comfort. Thank you so much for the roses, and for writing. I will call you and Bill as soon as I can.

Very sincerely,
John Jones

In order for the bereaved to acknowledge accurately the messages of condolence, flowers, etc. an accurate list must be kept by a close friend or a member of the bereaved family. When the services take place at a funeral home, a member of the staff will collect the cards for the family.

Although letters of condolence are usually handwritten, a letter may be dictated and typed from a business office to someone related to a person the writer has known in official or business life.

MOURNING CARDS

In case of bereavement, it is correct to send engraved cards of acknowledgment in response to expressions of condolence when they are comparatively impersonal but are in the hundreds or thousands. For example:

SECRETARY OF THE AIR FORCE AND MRS. DOE
ACKNOWLEDGE WITH GRATEFUL APPRECIATION
YOUR KIND EXPRESSION OF SYMPATHY

CHRISTMAS CARDS

Christmas cards are sent to close friends and acquaintances, and these may be limited to those you cannot greet personally. Usually cards are not sent within a service activity or base.

Envelopes for Christmas cards are always addressed to *both husband and wife*, even if you know only one or the other. A printed or engraved card without your name carries the signature at the bottom of the greeting, and the rule for signatures is: the person who is signing writes the other person's name first. When cards are engraved or printed with the name, the husband's name may come first, but either way is correct. Or you may sign for both, as: "The John Jones." When the names of several members of a family are listed on the card, the father's name should be written first. It is wise to place your return address in the upper left-hand corner of the envelope when you are unsure of the mailing address. In addressing the envelope to a family, write "The John Jones" rather than "Mr. and Mrs. John Jones and family."

From the strictly religious point of view, Jewish people should not celebrate Christmas or send Christmas cards. However, many Jewish people observe Christmas as a national rather than a religious holiday and send out nonreligious cards as well as receive them.

LETTERS OF REFERENCE

When you are asked to write a letter of reference—for example, for someone leaving the service or your place of employment, you will want to write an honest, straightforward account of that person's ability and character. It is important that the letter be fair both to the future employer and to the employee. The letter should always be dated.

A letter of reference, or any letter written to an unknown reader, needs neither salutation nor closing. The letter is a statement of fact, and is attested to by the signature. The outmoded phrase "To Whom It May Concern" is infrequently used. When you know to whom the letter will be addressed, you of course may use that person's name.

Letters of reference can be typewritten or written by hand. The general points covered in the typical letter of reference are:

The name of the person or employee.
The length of his (or her) service or employment.

The nature of his service or work—and *his competence.*

His honesty and character; his loyalty to the service or business.

His sobriety.

His ability to get along with others.

The reasons for his leaving the service or business; an expression of your
regret at losing him, if such is the case.

Your willingness to answer any further questions concerning him, and
an expression of your confidence in him in his new field.

When a person has been unsatisfactory in his or her work, or when
he has a questionable reputation, omissions in your reference are the best
way of indicating it. However, you are under no obligation to give any
reference at all.

LETTERS OF INTRODUCTION

A letter of introduction can be useful in business as well as in social
matters. Since the writer is stating approval of the one he or she is introducing, extreme care must be used: he is recommending someone as a
potential friend, or possibly for a job.

When the letter is handed to the receiver in his office, it is unsealed.
A business letter does not commit the receiver to anything, but he will
talk several minutes with the stranger in his office and if time permits—
and if he is favorably impressed—a suggestion for cocktails or luncheon
may be offered.

Nor is the receiver committed socially. A woman should mail her
letter of introduction, then wait until it is acknowledged. If the receiver
so desires, he or she may invite the stranger to luncheon or some informal occasion.

When a note of introduction is written for a retired officer to a
long-time friend in the business world, he could use his personal card in
this simple manner:

Introducing John Smith

Robert Edward Decatur

Major General
United States Air Force

A personal note, or longer letter, should be mailed several days before the time of arrival of the person being introduced. Such as:

Dear Mary,

A good friend of mine, John Doe, will be in Washington the week of April fifth, and I want very much for him to get acquainted with you. He is reading a paper at the Medical Center and will be doing research there.

John is a fine person, a very efficient doctor, and a specialist in his field. As a speech therapist you would have much in common with him. I do hope that you can find time to get together.

Affectionately,
Jane Smith

BIRTH ANNOUNCEMENTS

The announcement of the birth of a baby is made soon after he or she is born. Usually the choice of cards is made in advance. Fill-in cards may be purchased at a stationers or in the greeting cards department of a store, or the PX. Or you may want to send handwritten notes.

When cards are ordered—and they are more expensive—one frequently used is a small white card, with the baby's name and birth date printed on a smaller card attached by a pink or blue ribbon to the one with the parents' name. Sometimes the card is edged with pink or blue. Such a card is:

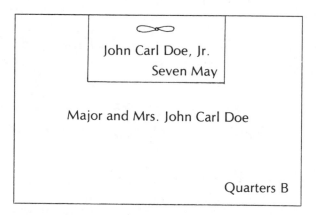

In the case of twins, both names appear on the smaller card, and when of mixed sexes the ribbon bows are of both colors.

ADOPTION ANNOUNCEMENTS

Parents usually make public in the very beginning the fact of their adoption of a child. Announcement could be worded in this manner:

> Lieutenant and Mrs. John Doe
> have the pleasure of announcing
> the adoption of
> Mary Jane
> age two months

Adopted children receive all the usual baby or children's gifts, as any other child.

CHANGING YOUR NAME

Should you want to change your name, this can be done legally. You should select your new name with care—either your first name, surname, or both names. Perhaps the name should be fairly similar to your old name, to avoid too much confusion with people you know.

Sometimes a name of Mediterranean or Slavic extraction is very long and hard to pronounce, and a citizen of this country—new or old—finds it easier to simplify it, particularly in the military or business world. But you must *want* to change it, not feel that you should just because it is long and hard to pronounce and spell.

Occasionally foolish parents bestow "cute" names on their infants—which they grow up to detest. For example, a name such as "Ima Nutt" could be changed to "Emma Nutt."

If you wish, you may inform your friends concerning your new name in person, by note, or by announcement. When a family prefers to send out printed announcements, on plain white cards, these could read:

> Ensign and Mrs. Konrad Mieckelmeister
> wish to inform you
> that they have adopted the names of
> Ensign and Mrs. Conrad Michaels

Or the second and third lines could read: ". . . announce that by permission of the court/they have changed their names to . . ." or, ". . . they will be known as. . . ."

If you do not care to send out announcements, the change in your name may be noted on your Christmas or any seasonal card, when you would sign it "The Conrad Michaels (formerly the Mieckelmeisters)."

A serviceman or servicewoman must send a request to his or her service Bureau of Personnel, including the court order authorizing the name change. Copies of the Bureau's letter of authorization will be sent to all offices having custody of your various official records.

CHAPTER 13

Informal Invitations
& Replies

THE ISSUANCE OF INVITATIONS, as well as the acknowledgment of them, follow definite social rules which should be observed. These rules may be considered a framework within which you can extend or answer invitations with maximum advantage and minimum effort for both the guest and the host. In general, the types of invitations that you will receive are:

Informal—These may be issued in person, over the telephone, by handwritten note, informal card, or on a calling card enclosed in a matching envelope.

Formal—These may be fully engraved, partially engraved, thermographed, telephoned, or handwritten in the same form as the fully engraved invitation. Thermography is a less expensive but effective way of simulating engraving.

Envelopes for both the informal and formal invitation are addressed by hand.

Although most invitations are informal during the early years in the career of a midshipman, cadet, or young officer, formal invitations are issued by the superintendent or commandant at the various academies, or by presidents of college ROTC units, OCS, OTS, and military schools in all states. Junior officers, as well as midshipmen and cadets, will receive formal invitations to debutante dinners and dances; official occasions as well as informal parties are encountered during the annual summer cruises to foreign countries. Senior officers will receive many invitations to state, official, and social occasions throughout their service careers.

GENERAL RULES

When invitations are extended in person, you must be alert and be prepared to accept or refuse without advance notice. When the invitation is one that you will enjoy accepting, there is no difficulty in expressing pleasure. But when you do not care to accept the invitation, your feelings must be concealed.

When you refuse any invitation, your answer should be plausible. Do not fumble with generalities, such as, "Well, I may have the duty that night so I don't know whether I can come or not. . ." when you do not care to go. Instead, you may say, "I'm sorry, I'm not free that evening—but thank you."

When you are not sure if you are free to accept the invitation, be frank with the person extending the invitation and say why you cannot commit yourself at the moment; for example, you can truthfully say that you believe you have the watch, etc. You may ask if a delayed reply will be inconvenient, and that if not, you will check your schedule immediately and let the hostess know as soon as you can. If a delay is inconvenient, you should refuse at once, but graciously.

Telephone invitations follow the same pattern as those given face-to-face. The information concerning the time, date, and place, should be repeated in order that no mistake is made. It is wise to write the information immediately in an engagement book or on a pad; it is embarrassing, to say the least, if you forget and arrive at the wrong hour or day.

Oral invitations usually are issued for smaller occasions, including luncheons, dinners, cocktails, teas, children's parties, christenings, informal dances, picnics, and morning coffees. Invitations by card—either personal or the informal—are used for such occasions as cocktails and receptions, afternoon and evening; suppers, teas, children's parties, dances, at-homes.

Remember to order matching envelopes with the cards. Calling (personal) cards used for invitations should have outer envelopes at least 3½ by 5 inches in size, in accordance with postal regulations.

Written invitations are also extended to those who cannot be reached by telephone, or when the location of the house or place of entertainment is difficult to find. Pertinent information concerning the location of the party is sometimes illustrated by charts or clever sketches either drawn or imprinted on the card.

When you receive an invitation for a time when a friend will be visiting you, you may state in your answer that you are sorry that you cannot accept the invitation because a houseguest will be with you at that time. Common sense will dictate whether you should do this, however, since you do not want to place the hostess in the position of *having* to invite your guest.

When it is convenient to your hosts, the hostess probably will invite you to bring your houseguest with you. Otherwise, she may say something like "I'm sorry; we're only having ten guests, and the dinner isn't buffet—but perhaps another time?" Because, as anyone will realize, when mixed guests are to be seated at the dining table, an extra guest would upset the seating arrangement.

INVITATION CARDS

For informal or formal invitations, fine quality cards are used, about 3½ by 5½ inches or 4 by 6 inches in size, with matching envelopes. The card may be plain or partially engraved with a crest.

At most commands, particularly large ones, the cost of engraving is prohibitive and good printing is used.

The popular *fill-in* cards are white or ivory, with the crest or insignia engraved in dark blue or black at the top center. Your name (or administrative position) is directly under the crest, followed by the line: "request the pleasure of the company of." A few key words complete the engraving. For example:

THE SUPERINTENDENT OF THE

UNITED STATES COAST GUARD ACADEMY

AND

MRS. DOE

REQUEST THE PLEASURE OF THE COMPANY OF

AT

ON

          AT   O'CLOCK

R.S.V.P.

The name of the guest and other information is written by hand in blue or black ink. The cards are used for almost any occasion; formal or informal dinners, receptions, luncheons, etc.

When an officer's station will not change for some time and many cards are used, or when a retired officer has a permanent address, the address may be engraved (or printed) in the center of the card directly under the "at . . . o'clock" line. Or the address may appear under the R.s.v.p., and the place of entertainment written by hand under the "at . . . o'clock line.

INFORMALS

Fold-over cards are about 3 by 4 inches in size, and are frequently used for invitations to luncheons, cocktail parties, buffet suppers, etc. These cards are called informals and are of smooth heavy paper in white or cream or pastel color, with contrasting engraving or printing, and matching envelopes. Your name is centered on the outside of the card, and the invitation written on the lower half of the inside of the card.

A single flat informal, which is about 3¼ by 4 inches in size, is often used in place of the fold-over informal. Your name is engraved in the center—or slightly above the center—of the card, with the address in the upper right corner. If desired, a telephone number is engraved in the top left corner.

The message or invitation is written below the name, and an *R.s.v.p.* or *Regrets only* would be written in the lower left corner. They are never used for calling cards. When required, replies to informals are addressed to the hostess only.

REGRETS ONLY

It is customary today for a host and/or hostess, or aides and secretaries, to write or have printed or engraved, *Regrets only* in place of the R.s.v.p. on invitations (other than wedding and very formal invitations). This means that only those who cannot attend the party or occasion need reply. At a very large occasion this saves considerable time.

Frequently, a telephone number is listed under the *R.s.v.p.* or *Regrets only* on the invitation, for the convenience of the guest in replying— usually to an aide or social secretary who firms the guest list.

Telephone numbers are never placed on wedding or very formal social invitations but are used on official or less formal invitations.

ENVELOPES

Matching envelopes should be ordered with all informals and fill-in cards, and with some calling cards when they are to be used for invitations, replies, or to send with gifts.

Postal regulations require that envelopes be at least 3½ by 5 inches. When your calling card envelopes are smaller, it is correct to write only the name on this envelope and to enclose it in a larger envelope addressed for mailing.

REMINDER CARDS

To confirm invitations, particularly those sent to a guest of honor, to VIPs, or those issued verbally, reminder cards are sometimes sent out a short time before the occasion to those who have accepted.

The regular invitation may be used again, with a line drawn through the telephone number and/or the *R.s.v.p.*, with the words, "To Remind," written underneath. Such cards are not acknowledged.

A smaller, fill-in card may be used, with specific information written by hand. For informal occasions, a calling or joint card may have this sentence written on it: "To remind you—Thursday 12th, 7 P.M."

INFORMAL INVITATIONS, REPLIES

An invitation given by a married couple is customarily extended by the hostess. An oral invitation, given in person or by telephone, may be stated in a simple manner: "John and I are having a few friends in for supper on Saturday at seven; we do hope that you and Bill can join us. It will be informal."

An invitation to an older couple might be extended in this form: "This is Mary Jones. Could you and Colonel King have supper with us next Saturday at seven?"

When the host extends the invitation, it is given in the name of the hostess: "Mary would like you to have supper with us on Saturday at seven."

An invitation written on personal note paper is usually brief, but will give full information. For example:*

> *Quarters 15*
> *Fort McNair*
> *Washington, D.C.*
>
> *Dear Mr. Jones,*
>
> *Captain Swanson and I are having as our houseguests during Christmas leave, Miss Betty Hallam, the daughter of an old friend, and several of her friends from Mary Baldwin College.*
>
> *We are asking several midshipmen and cadets for dinner and dancing at our quarters on Saturday, the twenty-ninth, at seven o'clock. We sincerely hope that you can join us. Dress is informal.*
>
> *I am sure that you will find Betsy and her friends most attractive.*
>
> *Cordially,*
> *Mary Swanson*
>
> *Monday*

* In this chapter, *italics* are used to indicate handwriting when used in invitations, acceptances, and refusals.

Your *reply* should be written on personal stationery, by hand, and must be mailed within a day or two, or as soon as possible. Replies are addressed to the hostess only. For example:

Room 2045, Bancroft Hall
(date)

Dear Mrs. Swanson,

I am very pleased to accept your kind invitation for dinner at your quarters on Saturday, the twenty-ninth, at seven o'clock.

The occasion will be of added pleasure since I met Miss Hallam at the Thanksgiving Hop a few weeks ago. Thank you for including me.

Sincerely,
John Jones†

When your reply is a *regret*, you should explain the refusal:

Room 2634, East Barracks
(date)

Dear Mrs. Swanson,

I appreciate your invitation to dinner on Saturday, the twenty-ninth, but unfortunately I am not able to accept since I will be in Montreal during the holidays.

It was very kind of you and Captain Swanson to include me, and I regret very much that I will not have the opportunity to meet Miss Hallam and her friends.

Very sincerely,
James Smith

Invitations for luncheons and dinners may be sent on *personal cards* or *informals*. When an *R.s.v.p.* or *regrets only* is written on the cards, an answer is mandatory. Your acceptance or refusal of the invitation may be made on your personal or informal card, by brief note, or by telephone.

Examples of informal invitations written on personal cards and informals are as follows:

† Sign your full name only; it is not proper to add your title or any other information.

ON A CALLING (PERSONAL) CARD:

Lunch
Saturday, 7 May, 1 P.M.
Captain Stephen Sidney Preble

Officer's Club   **United States Navy**

or

Dinner
Saturday, 2 March, 8 p.m.

Major Mary Jane Dickinson

Army Navy Town Club
R.S.V.P.   **United States Air Force**

ON THE JOINT CALLING CARD:

To meet
Captain and Mrs. Henry Roy Smith

Lieutenant and Mrs. John Doe
At home

Fri. May 18
6-8

420 East
Douglas Valley

ON THE FLAT INFORMAL:

34 Upshur Road

Captain and Mrs. John Henry Jones

Reception
Wednesday, October tenth
after parade

(If no parade—five o'clock)

On the *joint informal card*, the officer's title may be abbreviated if the name is very long.

ON THE INFORMAL:

(Outside)

Colonel and Mrs. Lee Adam Smith

3700 Connecticut Avenue

(Inside)

Cocktails
Wednesday, June 9th
5–7 P.M.
Regrets Only

or:

Cocktails-Buffet
Wednesday, June 9th
6:30–8:30 P.M.
Regrets Only

A REPLY ON A PERSONAL CARD:

Will be happy to come
Saturday at eight

William Paul Ormond

Bill

Lieutenant
United States Air Force

It is not necessary to write your name under your engraved name on the card, but close friends do.

FILL-IN CARDS

The most favored form of invitation is the fill-in engraved or printed card which is much less expensive and is adaptable to any date or occasion. It is used mainly for large functions, such as dinners, receptions, luncheons, dances, change of command and other ceremonies, parades, and many others.

The following example is an invitation to the Marine Corps' famous Moonlight Parade:

The Commandant of the Marine Corps and Mrs. _____

request the pleasure of your company

at a Reception and Parade
Tuesday, the twenty-fifth of July
at seven forty-five o'clock
                        Service Dress White
                        Commandant's House

R.s.v.p.

Oxford 4-1872   *Marine Barracks*

Parade begins nine o'clock

Invitations to receptions, garden parties, teas, and at-homes do not require an answer unless a response is requested.

CHAPTER 14

Formal Invitations
& Replies

FORMAL INVITATIONS, REPLIES

Invitations to formal occasions may be fully engraved, partially engraved, thermographed, or they may be handwritten on the first page of folded white or cream-colored note paper, in the third person. Invitations to formal occasions may also be telephoned. Invitations are issued between two and three weeks in advance of the occasion, but wedding invitations and other invitations when advance notice is necessary, should be sent out three or four weeks in advance.

Invitations to very important functions may be fully engraved and carry the phrase "request the honour (or pleasure) of your company." Popular letterings are script and shaded antique Roman. An admission card to be shown at the door is frequently enclosed. With today's stress on the importance of economy, invitations to large general receptions and parties are usually printed rather than engraved.

An admiral's or general's flag may be used on his invitations, and official seals and insignia in gold or color are often used on invitations for such occasions as inaugurations, dedications, ship christenings and commissionings, and graduation exercises. The family crest or coat of arms may be embossed without color at the top of wedding or other important invitations.

Note paper for formal use is about 6 by 7, or 5 by 8, inches in size, and is of fine quality in a glazed or kid (velvety) finish. The crest or insignia (if used) is engraved, and the paper is always white or cream color, with matching envelopes.

A double sheet with no crest is often used in answering formal invitations, such as weddings, dinners, receptions, etc. You write your reply on the first page only.

WORDING OF FORMAL INVITATIONS

The following general rules should be followed:

1. Abbreviations and initials are to be avoided, but there are some established exceptions:"Mr.," "Mrs.," "Dr.," "*R.s.v.p.*" (or *R.S.V.P.*), etc. When an initial is always used in place of a first or middle name, that initial may be used: "Lieutenant J. Marshall Jones."

2. Ranks, titles, and names are written in full: "Lieutenant, junior grade," "Lieutenant Commander," "Major General," "Lieutenant Colonel," "Rear Admiral," etc. The exception is that of "Second" and "First Lieutenant"; both are designated "Lieutenant" in the Army.

3. The date and hour are always spelled out, but only the day and month are capitalized: "Thursday, the seventh of January." "Half after eight o'clock" is preferable to "eight-thirty," although the latter is correct.

4. The person or persons issuing or acknowledging invitations refer to themselves by their full names: "Lieutenant and Mrs. John Jones, junior." (When your name is very long, "Jr." is correct.) But their guests or hosts are designated by their last names only: "Captain and Mrs. Brown."

5. Honor guests are designated by the phrases: "In honor of . . . ," which is used mainly for prominent persons, and "To meet . . . ," which is usually used for new arrivals and houseguests.

6. "White Tie" written or engraved in the lower right-hand corner of the invitation indicates a very formal function and means full evening dress, military or civilian.

7. "Black Tie" denotes the less formal occasion, and means the dinner dress uniform or tuxedo.

8. *R.s.v.p.* means a reply is mandatory.

9. *Regrets only* on less formal invitations, but never on wedding or very formal invitations, means that only those who cannot attend the function need reply. When many guests are invited, this keeps correspondence to a minimum. When a telephone number is added, you may answer in kind.

REPLIES TO FORMAL INVITATIONS

1. Answers should be written within 48 hours, preferably 24, hours, after you receive dinner or luncheon invitations. When you refuse early, a

hostess will have time to invite another guest without his feeling like a "fill in."

2. Replies are handwritten, in the third person, on the first page of folded white or cream-colored note paper.

3. However, when relatives or very close friends reply to a formal invitation, a personal hand-written reply in the first person is a correct and warm response.

4. An *acceptance* should include your own full title and name, the title and surname of the host and hostess, and the date and time; also the place, if not the host's address. The reason for this repetition is that the hostess may make corrections if the prospective guest has made a mistake.

5. A *regret* includes the same information, except that it makes no reference to the time or place.

6. Envelopes are addressed by hand to the host and hostess, or to an aide or social secretary if so indicated in the *R.s.v.p.* In civilian life it is customary to address the envelope to the hostess (or social secretary) even when the invitation was issued jointly with her husband.

7. A formal dinner or luncheon invitation to a married couple must be refused when either one or the other cannot accept. The rule here is: both or neither.

After accepting a formal invitation, you are committed to the occasion over all other occasions (other than duty), with the exception of your receiving a White House invitation, which takes precedence over any other invitation. In such a case, you will withdraw the previous acceptance. An invitation from the Chief of Mission takes precedence over all other invitations for service attachés, etc.

REPLY CARDS

Reply cards are usually enclosed with invitations to large official functions, such as a retirement ceremony, the luncheons following graduation exercises at the service academies and colleges, a ship's commissioning, parades and reviews, subscription dances, and balls. The purpose of the cards is to facilitate the check-off guest list.

The cards, with self-addressed envelopes, usually are the small fill-in type with specific information to be written by hand.

The reply card is fairly small and is engraved or printed in th same style as the invitation. It should be sent to a couple or individual, but it is best not to include a "number to attend" or the receiver may take for granted that they can bring extra people—children or houseguests.

Lieutenant Mary Doe

☐ **accepts**
☐ **regrets**

Saturday, May eighth
Army Navy Town Club

REPLIES AT THE SERVICE ACADEMIES

If you are a midshipman or cadet at the service or maritime academies, you reply to a formal invitation according to the general rules.

Remember to write by hand on the first page of folded note paper (white or cream-colored), in the third person. Answer promptly and include these steps in your *acceptance:*

1. Your title and full name, without abbreviations.
2. The title and last name of your host and/or hostess.
3. The occasion.
4. The date.
5. The time.
6. The place—if other than the host's address.

Midshipman John Ray Jones
accepts with pleasure
the kind invitation of
Admiral and Mrs. Lee
to dinner
on Saturday, the seventh of April
at seven-thirty o'clock

If you are requested to give the name of your date, his or her name is added as follows:

Midshipman John Ray Jones
Miss Mary Jane Smith
accept with pleasure
etc.

If you are requested to furnish the address as well as the name of your date, you write your formal acceptance without adding his or her name. Instead, you write the name and address on the aide's or flag lieutenant's *reply card* which is enclosed with the invitation.

A *regret* would be as follows:

Cadet Mary Anne Smith
regrets that because of official duties*
she will be unable to accept
the kind invitation of
General and Mrs. Williams
for Saturday, the twelfth of May

ADDRESSING THE ENVELOPE

After writing your reply, address the envelope to the person (or office) indicated in the lower left-hand corner of the invitation, or to the person (or office) whose name appears on the *reply card* enclosed in the invitation.

When you are replying to a formal invitation issued by an officer and his wife, such as a dinner to be held in their quarters, address the envelope to both the officer and his wife. For a less formal or an informal dinner, address the envelope to the hostess (the officer's wife). For example:

Mrs. John Levis Doe
Quarters 9
United States Military Academy
West Point, New York

INVITATIONS FOR MARRIED WOMEN OFFICERS

There are variations in addressing invitations for married women officers whose rank exceeds that of their officer husbands; for married women who have retained their maiden name; for commissioned officers who are married to noncommissioned officers; and for women officers who are married to civilian men.

There are differences in addressing invitations for official and non-official or social occasions. The important thing to remember is that the recognition is to the office, not to the individual, man or woman.

---

* Or—*because of illness, a previous engagement, etc.*

OFFICIAL INVITATIONS

When a woman officer and her husband are invited to an official occasion such as a reception, and her rank exceeds his, the invitation is addressed to her. On both the envelope and invitation his name will follow hers. For example, the envelope would be written in this way, with the second line indented three spaces:

> *Captain Jane Doe, U.S. Coast Guard Reserve*
> *Commander John Doe, U.S. Coast Guard*
> *Office of the Commandant*
> *U.S. Coast Guard*
> *Washington, D.C. 20590*

The handwritten wording for the invitation would be: Captain Doe and Commander Doe.

The invitation is sent to her office where an aide or junior officer takes care of the correspondence of a senior officer. When the invitation is addressed to a junior officer, it is sent to her quarters.

When a woman officer is married to a civilian or noncommissioned officer, his name with title or grade is on the second line of the envelope, and the invitation would read: "Lieutenant Doe and Dr. Doe," or "Lieutenant Doe and Sergeant Doe."

Should the married couple have the same rank and serve in the same service—and she has *not* retained her maiden name, the official invitation envelope could be addressed to "The Captains John Doe," and inside, "The Captains Doe."

When a married woman officer has *retained* her maiden name, the envelope could be addressed in this manner:

> *Captain Jane Smith, U.S. Coast Guard Reserve*
> *and Captain John Doe, U.S. Coast Guard (Retired)*
> *(her office address)*

Inside, the invitation would read: Captain Smith and Captain Doe.

SOCIAL INVITATIONS

Usually, a formal or informal (nonofficial) invitation is extended to a married couple in the same way as for everyone else—Lieutenant and Mrs. John Doe—regardless of the higher rank of the woman officer. If some women are touchy on the matter, then address the formal invitation as you would for the official occasion, but send it to the couple's home as you do the others.

Should the social occasion be held in the officers' club, the non-commissioned officer is as welcome as any senior guest. However, when the occasion is over, the noncommissioned spouse is not at liberty to visit the officers' club unless accompanied by his commissioned wife (or husband, as the case may be). An officers' club is officers' country.

RANKING CIVILIAN WOMEN

A civilian woman whose position and title are higher than that of her husband is addressed in the same way as the senior woman officer. A congresswoman or cabinet member is "The Honorable." Therefore, the envelope for the formal or official invitation would be addressed thus:

> *The Honorable Janet Doe*
> *Colonel John Doe, U.S. Army**
> *United States House of Representatives*
> *Washington, D.C. 20515*

Women in high positions in official Washington have an option in how their names are to appear on both official and social invitations. Most women use their husband's title on the social invitation: Mr. and Mrs. Doe; the official writing is: The Honorable Doe and Mr. Doe.

HANDWRITTEN INVITATIONS

The formal invitation does not have to be engraved but may be written by hand, on white or cream-colored note paper, in the third person. The wording and spacing follow the engraved form. The address or place of entertainment is usually centered underneath the line indicating the time, but may be written at the lower right-hand side.

> *Colonel and Mrs. John Smith*
> *request the pleasure of the company of*
> *Lieutenant Jones*
> *at dinner*
> *on Saturday, the ninth of January*
> *at eight o'clock*
> *Quarters 4311D*

R.s.v.p.   *Black Tie*

---

* A separate invitation may be sent to a person in a secondary but official position.

A sample acceptance would be:

Lieutenant Elizabeth Jones
accepts with pleasure
the kind invitation of
Colonel and Mrs. Smith
to dinner on Saturday, the ninth of January
at eight o'clock

A regret would say ". . . regrets that she will be unable to accept," or ". . . regrets that because of a previous engagement . . ." etc.

FORMAL EVENING RECEPTION

An invitation to a formal evening reception would be:

IN HONOR OF THE PRIME MINISTER OF PATRIA

AND

MRS. CAESAR

THE AMBASSADOR OF PATRIA AND MRS. LEGATE

REQUEST THE HONOR OF THE COMPANY OF

AT A RECEPTION

ON SATURDAY, THE FIFTH OF MAY

AT TEN O'CLOCK

R.S.V.P.   WHITE TIE
2698 CALIFORNIA STREET, N.W.   GRAND BALL ROOM, MAYFLOWER HOTEL

The acceptance would be something like this:

Major General and Mrs. James Smith
have the honor to accept
the kind invitation of
The Ambassador of Patria and Mrs. Legate
for Saturday, the fifth of May
at ten o'clock
Grand Ball Room, Mayflower Hotel

The regret would be:

Major General and Mrs. James Smith
regret that because of their absence from the city
they will be unable to have the honor of accepting
the kind invitation of
The Ambassador of Patria and Mrs. Legate
for Saturday, the fifth of May

SHIP-COMMISSIONING INVITATION AND RECEPTION CARD

THE COMMANDANT, FIRST NAVAL DISTRICT,
THE PROSPECTIVE COMMANDING OFFICER AND SHIP'S COMPANY
REQUEST THE HONOR OF YOUR PRESENCE
AT THE COMMISSIONING OF THE
USS JOHN SIDNEY MC CAIN (DL-3)
AT THE BOSTON NAVAL SHIPYARD, BOSTON, MASSACHUSETTS
ON MONDAY AFTERNOON, THE TWELFTH OF OCTOBER
NINETEEN HUNDRED AND FIFTY-THREE
AT TWO-THIRTY O'CLOCK

PLEASE PRESENT THIS CARD
AT THE HENLEY STREET GATE   CAMERAS NOT PERMITTED

THE COMMANDING OFFICER AND WARDROOM OFFICERS
OF THE USS JOHN SIDNEY MC CAIN (DL-3)
REQUEST THE PLEASURE OF YOUR COMPANY
AT A RECEPTION AT THE
COMMISSIONED OFFICERS' MESS
BUILDING 5, BOSTON NAVAL SHIPYARD
IMMEDIATELY FOLLOWING THE COMMISSIONING

R.S.V.P.

COMMANDER, BOSTON NAVAL SHIPYARD

UNIFORM CARD

A small card, stating the prescribed uniform, may be enclosed with an
official reception invitation. For example:

UNIFORM

White Dress

DANCE INVITATIONS

To a debutante ball:

THE COMMITTEE OF
THE CHARLESTON COTILLION
REQUEST THE HONOR OF THE PRESENCE OF
Cadet Richard Earl Doe
AT THE CHRISTMAS BALL
ON THURSDAY, THE TWENTY-SIXTH OF DECEMBER
AT HALF AFTER TEN O'CLOCK
THE FRANCIS MARION HOTEL

R.S.V.P.   WHITE TIE
387 KING STREET

Your acceptance would be:

Cadet Richard Earl Doe
accepts with pleasure
the kind invitation of
The Committee
of the Charleston Cotillion
for Thursday, the twenty-sixth of December
at half after ten o'clock
The Francis Marion Hotel

Your refusal could be:

Cadet Richard Earl Doe
*regrets that because of orderly duty**
he will be unable to accept
the kind invitation of
The Committee
of the Charleston Cotillion
for Thursday, the twenty-sixth of December

A less formal invitation may omit the name of the guest:

* Or: "regrets that he is unable to accept" etc.

COLONEL AND MRS. JOHN SMITH, JUNIOR
MISS MARY MARTHA SMITH
REQUEST THE PLEASURE OF YOUR COMPANY
at a small dance
on Saturday, the fifteenth of February
at ten o'clock
The Broadmoor

R.S.V.P.

DOGWOOD HILLS

ARLINGTON

In replying to invitations that carry the names of several persons on the invitation—such as co-hosts at a dinner or reception, or the names of the parents with that of their daughter written directly underneath, or the names of the sponsors of the event—these names also appear in your reply.

In answering an invitation to a "small dance," your reply should omit the word "small."

A FORMAL FILL-IN SERVICE ACADEMY INVITATION

The Class of Nineteen Hundred and Seventy-six
of the
United States Corps of Cadets
requests the pleasure of
the company of

Colonel and Mrs. Jones
at their Graduation Banquet and Hop
on Tuesday, the fourth of June
at eight o'clock in the evening

United States Military Academy

R.S.V.P.   Washington Hall

Cadet Hostess   Eisenhower Hall   Formal

2111 or 3104   white mess
or whites w/bow tie

THE USE OF TELEPHONE NUMBERS

At large commands where many invitations are issued, the Autovon is frequently used to verify a guest list and to replace immediately someone who cannot accept an invitation.

It is customary to place a telephone number under the *R.s.v.p.* or *Regrets only* on the invitation for the convenience of the guest in contacting the aide or social secretary who confirms the guest list. Such numbers are never placed on wedding or very formal social invitations, when handwritten replies are mandatory, but they are used on very important official and some formal invitations—such as those issued at the service academies.

TELEPHONE INVITATIONS

Telephone invitations are correct for formal functions, mainly for smaller affairs when the hostess makes the calls herself. The guest may accept at the moment, or if absent when the message was received, may reply by note or telephone.

An aide may call for his chief, or a secretary for a man or woman. In quarters, a maid may call for the hostess.

When the maid receives the call, the conversation may be somewhat as follows:

"Commander Smith's quarters."
"I'd like to speak to Mrs. Smith, please."
"May I ask who is calling, please?"
"I am calling for General and Mrs. Jones."
"I'm sorry, but Madam is not at home. May I take a message?"

"Would you please say that Mrs. Jones would like to know if Commander and Mrs. Smith could dine on Saturday, the fifth of March, at eight o'clock, at quarters 'M'?"
"To dine with General and Mrs. Jones on Saturday, the fifth of March at eight o'clock at quarters 'M' . . . very good. Thank you."
"Thank you."
Your reply is made in the same way: "Will you please tell General and Mrs. Jones that Commander and Mrs. Smith are happy to accept. . . ."

INVITATIONS BY TELEGRAM

A formal invitation sent by telegram might read:

GENERAL AND MRS. JAMES SMITH REQUEST THE PLEASURE OF COLONEL
AND MRS. RICHARD JONES COMPANY AT DINNER MAY FOURTH AT ARMY
NAVY CLUB EIGHT O'CLOCK

The reply could be stated thus:

COLONEL AND MRS. RICHARD JONES ACCEPT WITH PLEASURE GENERAL AND
MRS. SMITHS KIND INVITATION FOR FRIDAY MAY FOURTH ARMY NAVY CLUB
EIGHT O'CLOCK

POSTPONING OR ADVANCING INVITATIONS

If Colonel and Mrs. Smith must postpone the dance, the announcement
to that effect would follow the same form as the invitation:

COLONEL AND MRS. JOHN SMITH, JUNIOR

WISH TO ANNOUNCE

THAT THE DANCE IN HONOR OF THEIR DAUGHTER

MUST BE POSTPONED UNTIL

SATURDAY, THE TWENTY-SECOND OF FEBRUARY

PLEASE RESPOND TO

300 FIRST STREET

When it is necessary to postpone or advance the date of a formal
invitation, a notice is sent out similar to the original invitation, with
this information:

BECAUSE OF THE

IMMINENT DEPARTURE OF

THE CHIEF OF STAFF OF THE AIR FORCE

THE RECEPTION IN HONOR OF

GENERAL AND MRS. WARD

WILL BE ADVANCED FROM

THURSDAY EVENING, THE TWENTIETH OF JUNE

TO

FRIDAY EVENING, THE FOURTEENTH OF JUNE

AT NINE O'CLOCK

GRAND BALL ROOM, MAYFLOWER HOTEL

R.S.V.P.

The Citadel
Commemorating
The Bicentennial of the American Revolution
Requests the Honor of Your Presence
At a Lecture
by
Dr. James E. Doe
Director of Business History Studies
Indiana University
"Robert Morris and the Financing of the American Revolution"
Thursday, the sixth of November
at seven-thirty o'clock
Mark Clark Hall

Reception
Following the Lecture
at Alumni House

Please reply on the
enclosed card

FULLY PRINTED CARD FOR LECTURE AND
RECEPTION AT AN ROTC INSTITUTION

WHITE HOUSE INVITATIONS

An invitation to the White House must be answered promptly, no later
than twenty-four hours after its arrival. Should you be out of town, answer by Autovon (telephone) or by special delivery letter.

There are valid reasons why an invitation must be refused—illness,
official duty that takes you a distance from Washington, transfer of
duty, a death in the family. Otherwise you accept.

Do not be late for a White House function; rather, you should be
ten minutes or so early. Reception and dinner guests usually enter

through the Diplomatic Entrance, where your name is posted; then an usher will direct you to the room where all guests wait for the appearance of the President and his wife. For large receptions or parties of five hundred or more, the East Gate will be used by guests.

The President and his wife will greet and shake hands with each guest. You do not sit down until they do. You address the President and Vice President as "Mr. President" and "Mr. Vice President" and their wives as "Mrs. Doe." In prolonged conversation you address the President and other male dignitaries as "Sir."

Guests are seated according to protocol at a state dinner, with the nonranking husband or wife seated in accordance with their ranking or titled spouse.

At a reception, a military aide will make the presentations, with men preceding their wives in the line.

A reply to a formal White House invitation follows the regular form; it is sent to the office as indicated in the invitation's *R.s.v.p.* line. You reply to an informal invitation in the same way that it was extended—by phone or note, and it is addressed to the President's secretary, or his wife's secretary, or office, as indicated.

WITHDRAWING AN ACCEPTANCE

There are a few valid reasons for withdrawing the acceptance of an invitation: serious illness, a death in the family, prospective absence occasioned by a transfer of duty, official duty, or very important business elsewhere.

As mentioned earlier, an invitation from the White House or Chief of Mission takes precedence over all other invitations. In such cases, if you have already accepted an earlier invitation to a conflicting occasion, you would have to cancel your previous acceptance. For example:

Rear Admiral and Mrs. John Smith Hampton
regret that because of an invitation
to the White House
they must withdraw from
Captain and Mrs. Jones's dinner
on the third of May

RECALLING AN INVITATION

It is better to postpone than to cancel an invitation, once you have extended it, but a formal invitation may be recalled when unavoidable circumstances warrant. When the occasion was to have been small and the guests would know the reason for the withdrawing of the invitations—such as a bereavement or a serious accident—no reason need be stated:

THE INVITATIONS OF
GENERAL AND MRS. JOHN SMITH
FOR SATURDAY, THE FIFTEENTH OF MAY
ARE RECALLED

But when it is an official occasion involving guests who might not know the circumstances, the reason for recalling the invitation would be stated on printed forms, since engraving takes too long:

GENERAL AND MRS. JOHN SMITH
REGRET EXCEEDINGLY
THAT BECAUSE OF THE RECENT DEATH OF
FLEET ADMIRAL OWENS
THE INVITATIONS TO THE RECEPTION IN HONOR OF
THE SECRETARY OF DEFENSE
AND
MRS. WINGATE
MUST BE RECALLED

GUEST OF HONOR

It is contrary to custom to invite guests of higher rank than the honor guest at an official dinner or luncheon. However, when this is unavoidable, the following rules may be employed:

Ask the ranking guest to waive his or her right for the occasion in favor of the guest of honor.

Seat the guests according to precedence, even if it places the guest of honor well down the table. When ambassadors and very high-ranking guests are present, this plan must be followed.

Make the senior guest the co-host.

When the party or dinner is informal, you may have a guest of honor of lower rank than other guests. In extending the invitation to someone to be a guest of honor, you may say, "I would like so much to give a dinner for you,"—and when the person is married, ". . . for you and your wife (or husband)," for the invitation must include both. A letter may be written in this form:

Dear Mrs. Jones,

Will you and Senator Jones dine with us on either Thursday, the third of October, or Saturday, the twelfth at eight o'clock?
We want to ask some friends to meet you, and hope very much that we may be fortunate enough to find you free on one of those evenings.

Very sincerely,
Mary Smith

September seventoon

When invitations to guests are issued over the telephone, do not use the phrase "in honor of," as this phrase is used only on formal invitations. The hostess may say instead, "We are giving a dinner next Saturday, the tenth, for Senator and Mrs. Jones. . . ."

When invitation cards have been issued, reminder cards may be sent to the guest or guests of honor shortly before the occasion.

CHANGING YOUR ANSWER

When circumstances change after you have given a definite regret to an invitation, formal or informal, and you find that you can go to the occasion after all, immediately phone the host or hostess and explain your change of plans. If the occasion has a flexible guest list, such as a cocktail party, an at-home, or a reception, you will very likely be told to come ahead. But if the occasion is a seated luncheon or dinner, a theater party, or bridge luncheon, etc., another guest may have already been invited to take your place and one more would upset arrangements.

When you cannot attend an occasion after accepting, let your hosts know immediately. A matter of hours either way—accepting or refusing —can make all the difference to a hostess. Remember that hosts pay dearly for large or small catered affairs, whether guests show up or not.

SECTION V

Entertaining in the Home

CHAPTER 15

Entertaining at Dinner

TODAY'S SERVICE FAMILY is the forerunner in the new American custom of adapting the best of old European traditions to present-day needs on a modest income. With the modern service family living briefly in many states and various countries all over the world, it is only natural that the best of American as well as continental or Far Eastern customs are modified into everyday living.

The goal of any host and hostess is to serve the best food in the most pleasant surroundings to congenial guests. The service family combines the French tradition of good food with a Yankee minimum of time and expense. With the general lack of servants in the average household today, it is essential that modern entertaining fits today's needs—not yesterday's.

A young officer's household probably has little, if any, help. A higher-ranking officer's family may have a part-time maid—but household help is almost a vanished profession. The old rating of steward has also vanished, currently replaced by the mess management specialist (MS) in the Navy, airman aide in the Air Force, and enlisted aide in the Army. They are assigned only to the quarters of high-ranking officers, such as the Chief of Naval Operations, the Chiefs of Staff of the Army and Air Force, the Commandant of the Marine Corps, and the superintendents and presidents of the various academies and military schools.

When the occasion demands, waiters are available from a catering service or from an officers' club. Waitresses frequently serve at today's formal dinner—a procedure which once was considered incorrect.

In keeping with the times, less formal dinners are the order of the day, with the semiformal dinner or sit-down buffet the most favored. Buffet meals, with guests helping themselves, are popular from coast to coast.

The modern service family entertains more often, more casually, and has more fun entertaining, than ever before. The dining table may be in the dining room, in the family room, or on the patio. Men and women often exchange household duties that once were considered the duty of only one or the other.

It is gratifying to any host to know that friends come to his quarters because they want to—not have to. But it is not by chance that a dinner, large or small, is successful. The part that seems so easy is that way because it was planned to the last detail, long in advance, to avoid last-minute work.

However, officers and members of their families will attend many formal occasions through the years. As an officer, you will attend official, public, and state occasions, starting as a midshipman or cadet, and will continue to do so throughout your service career—and on into retired life.

But formal or informal, you should know exactly what to do as the guest—or the host—at any type of dinner.

CLASSIFICATIONS OF ENTERTAINING

There are three general classifications of entertaining:

Informal: There may be no servants, therefore no one serving at the table. The host and hostess serve two or three courses, probably buffet style.

Semiformal: There is service at the table, with the host and hostess helping somewhat (mostly before the meal); three or four courses are customary.

Formal: There is full service at the table, with no assistance from the host and hostess; waiters (or waitresses) serve four or five courses.

INFORMAL DINNERS

THE FAMILY DINNER

The family dinner is one that you will attend most often as a guest, or will most often give as the host. Since a dinner with a family is an intimate occasion, guests should consider it an honor to be invited into a home. It is customary for the hostess to extend the invitation by telephone or in person, or perhaps by a brief note (*See* Chapter 13, Informal Invitations and Replies.) As the host, you may extend the invitation in the name of the hostess: "Mary would like you to have supper with us on Saturday, at seven." If you are the only guest, and if there are children in the family, the dinner hour may be as early as six o'clock. Men wear conservative suits, or sports coats, if indicated, and women wear a daytime dress or pantsuits.

If you are a guest, the hostess should precede you into the dining room and tell you where to sit. And if you are the ranking or oldest male guest, you should be seated at the right of the hostess.

When a blessing, or grace, is said at the table, it is said before anything is touched—including the napkin. You may be asked to say the blessing. A blessing that is acceptable to all faiths is:

For what we are about to receive,
Lord, make us truly thankful.   Amen

The table may be simply set, with mats or a cloth, and a small bowl of flowers or a simple decoration the centerpiece. The food may already be on the table when you sit down, with the meat set in front of the host and the vegetables in front of the hostess.

If the hostess prefers, the platters and dishes of food—other than a very heavy dish such as a hot casserole—may be passed in one direction around the table, with each guest serving himself. The bread tray and jellies are also passed to each person. The water glasses should be filled before the family sits down, and each salad placed to the left of the forks.

Dessert may be served directly from the kitchen, after all plates and dishes have been removed from the table, with the dessert silver in place on the plate. When served at the table, the stack of plates along with the dessert, serving fork and/or spoon, are set directly in front of the hostess, and she serves each person. Sometimes the dessert silver is in place on the table before anyone is seated, parallel above each plate. The spoon is placed above the fork, with the handle of the spoon at the right, and the handle of the fork at the left.

Coffee is frequently served throughout the family dinner, in medium size cups (teacups), or it may be served with or after dessert. The coffee service may be placed on the sideboard or nearby table, with cups and saucers, sugar and cream. The coffee may be poured from there and placed to the right of each person at the table, with cream and sugar passed down the table.

At a family dinner—or any dinner—you may take second helpings *when offered,* or even a third if your hostess insists and if you really want the food. It is flattering to your host and hostess that you enjoy the meal, and you should say so. But if you do not care for a second helping, you need not feel any obligation to take it. When passing your plate for a second helping, leave your knife and fork on your plate, the knife above and parallel across the top or at the right of the plate, the fork placed below with tines up.

Wait for the hostess to begin eating before beginning yourself (unless she asks you not to wait for her), and wait until she rises from the table before doing so yourself. When something needs to be done during the meal, or afterwards, you may offer to assist—such as bringing in the coffee service, stack of plates, or clearing the table, but most hostesses prefer that guests do not help, or want their children to have this experience. When children are too small to help, she may appreciate your giving them a little time—which you should do anyway—engaging them in conversation or a game, while she does last-minute things. You should leave within an hour, when nothing has been planned after dinner such as a game of bridge.

PREPARING FOR GUESTS

In order to save time, money, and wear and tear, and when she has no help other than members of the family, a hostess should plan a dinner menu which requires very little last-minute preparation. The main dish should be something that can be placed in the oven before the arrival of the first guests, and that will finish cooking during the cocktail hour. Casseroles and roasts are favorite foods that can be prepared in advance. A frozen food compartment permits a variety of foods—from casseroles to desserts—to be prepared and stored days earlier.

All food should be purchased as far ahead as practical, all vegetables and fruits washed and ready to be used in salads or whatever dish is planned. The silver should be polished, the house cleaned, the flower arrangements assembled or purchased ahead of time. The dining table should be set early in the day. A detailed check-off list avoids a forgotten essential.

MENUS FOR INFORMAL DINNERS

Two or three courses are customary:

Two courses:

>   Main course (meat and vegetables), and dessert,
> or Casserole with, or without, salad; dessert (cool weather menu),
> or Seafood, chicken or turkey salad, etc., and dessert (summer menu),
> or Main course, salad and cheese (no dessert).

Three courses:

      Soup, main course, and dessert,

or Main course, salad, and dessert,

or First course (seafood, melon, etc.), entrée, and dessert,

or Casserole, salad, and dessert.

SERVING WITHOUT HELP

When the host and hostess serve the meal, the dinner plates may be placed directly in front of the host, with the meat placed above the plates, along with carving knife and fork. A portion of meat is placed by the host on each plate, which is then passed to the hostess for vegetables.

When a casserole is the main dish, it is placed on a hot pad above the stack of plates in front of the hostess. The serving fork is to the left and the serving spoon to the right of the casserole, and the hostess serves each guest. The filled salad plates would be to the left of the forks.

The hostess should indicate who is to receive the plate, with the first plate going to the woman at the right of the host. Should she not indicate to whom the plate will go, a male guest should pass it to the woman nearest him. All persons are served in the same way, with the hostess serving herself last. When the host serves, he serves himself last.

After the plates and dishes are cleared from the table—by the hostess or someone she may have asked to help—the dessert is served either from the kitchen, or when attractively prepared and easy to serve, from in front of her plate at the table. A torte is an example; some hostesses find that a simple but delicious dessert is a light sherbet placed in a large glass bowl over which frozen or fresh-cut fruits and their juices have been poured. Coffee is served with or after dessert, either at the table or in the living room.

INFORMAL DINNER, WITH HELP

When a maid serves eight or ten guests at a three-course dinner, where all the guests are seated, the hostess assists in serving at the table while the maid is busy in the kitchen. The first course of soup or fruit cup may be in place on the table when guests sit down. Upon the removal of the first course, the main course or entrée is brought in by the maid and placed in front of the hostess for serving.

The warmed plates are set directly in front of the hostess, and the hostess fills each plate. The maid sets the plate in front of each guest, serving from the left. The woman at the right of the host is served first, then the woman at the left of the host and on around the table. The hostess is served next to the last and the host last.

The hostess may prefer to pass each plate directly down the table, designating the plate for the woman at the right of the host, etc. This leaves the maid free to pass the rolls, or work in the kitchen.

The maid may serve the main course on a platter, with the vegetables placed by the meat. The platter is offered to the left of each guest.

After the main course is eaten, the maid removes the plates, the bread and butter plates, the relish dishes, salt and pepper shakers, bread tray, and serving platters. The dessert may be served from the kitchen, or the maid may place the dessert in front of the hostess for serving.

Coffee may be served at the table with the dessert, but it is usually served in the living room for all guests. The coffee service is placed on a low table. The hostess asks each person his preference for cream and sugar, and the cup is handed to the guest—who comes forward—or the

Dessert silver placed above the plate at informal dinner or luncheon, continental fashion. Cigarette trays are optional.

host or another guest hands the cups to the guests. The cream and sugar are passed on a small tray, with each guest helping himself.

BUFFET SUPPERS

The buffet supper is the favorite form of serving a large number of guests in a small space with, or without, help. A buffet supper or late supper is the best type of get-acquainted party.

At such a meal the table is placed in a space convenient for guests to move around it and serve themselves. The table is usually covered with a cloth, placed over a silence pad. There should be a centerpiece, not too large, and several sets of salt and pepper.

The stacks of plates, napkins, rows of silver, platters, and bowls of food should be placed in sequence around the table. Serving forks and spoons should be near the dishes they accompany. Dinner forks may be the only silver on the table, since a wise hostess does not serve foods difficult to cut, but knives are placed on the table if needed.

When there is no help, everything is placed in the dining room, for convenience in serving. A water pitcher and glasses, coffee service, and wine decanter and glasses may be on a sideboard or convenient table, if not on the dining table. Dessert and dessert plates and silver may also be on the sideboard, or they may be placed on the table or sideboard after the dishes for the main course have been taken away.

As a guest, you fill your plate and carry it into the living room, or any other room designated by the hostess. Small tables or folding tables are frequently provided by the hostess, but if not, you take any seat and balance your plate on your knees. At very large buffet meals, you will probably eat while standing up.

When you are through eating, you may place your plate on the sideboard or dining table, leaving the host or hostess, or the maid if there is one, to carry them into the kitchen. Or the maid may take the plates personally from each guest, removing two at a time. Guests may serve themselves dessert from the table or sideboard, and the coffee will be served later from a tray.

At buffet suppers, three courses are usually offered, as well as hot buttered rolls or biscuits. Although soup may be a first course, this is inconvenient to serve and is usually avoided by a busy hostess.

Buffet menus are varied, but may include:

Roast beef, turkey, or ham; salad, and dessert. All three roasts may be served at very large occasions.

or Main course of meat and vegetables, with or without salad, and dessert. The meat dish, such as chicken à la king, can usually be prepared well in advance.

or Any of the curries that are favored in the service set, with innumerable side dishes, plus salad, and dessert.

or A casserole, salad, and dessert.

SIT-DOWN BUFFET

The sit-down buffet table is set as it would be for dinner—with the exceptions of the plates and the main course, which are placed on the sideboard for guests to serve themselves. The napkins, silver, glasses, salt and pepper, and butter plates are all in place on the table.

Place mats are frequently used on the table, and there should be a centerpiece. If small tables—usually card tables—are used instead of the larger table, the centerpiece on such tables is small, to save space.

The dessert silver may be in place above the space for the plate, and butter plates are used as a matter of convenience. When dessert is served from the kitchen, the dessert silver will be brought on the dessert plate.

When there is a maid, soup may be the first course, and this is in place on the place plate when the guests sit down. The maid will remove used plates before guests serve themselves at the sideboard. Coffee is usually served at the table.

At very large buffet parties, the coffee service, water, wine, and glasses may be placed in convenient areas, with guests helping themselves.

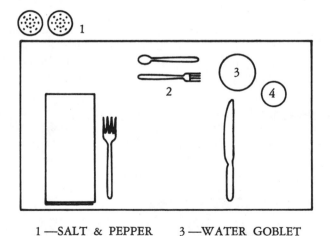

1—SALT & PEPPER   3—WATER GOBLET
2—DESSERT SILVER   4—WINEGLASS

The sit-down buffet.

FORMAL DINNERS

Today's formal dinner is what was termed semiformal in days when stewards or waiters were easily obtained. The main difference between today's formal—or semiformal—dinner and the truly formal dinner is in the service: fewer waiters will serve fewer courses to the same number of people, and black tie or its equivalent is usually worn by the men, with women in long dinner dresses.

The sit-down buffet is a favorite form of formal entertaining, because the very nicest appointments may be used, with the least service. Table decorations are as elaborate as any at the most formal table.

Place arrangement for a formal dinner.

From the left, the meat fork, salad fork, seafood cocktail in place plate, the salad knife (if needed), the meat knife, soup spoon (when needed), seafood fork. The water goblet stays throughout the dinner, but wine glasses are removed with their accompanying courses with the exception of the dessert wine glass which remains throughout the serving of demitasse. Only two wines, sherry and champagne, may be served. For the very formal table, fish forks and knives would be in place, and extra

wine glasses for the courses they accompany. Individual salts and peppers are placed above the place plate, or one set may be placed a little
below and to the right of the outer glass so that two guests may share
one set. It is optional to place cigarette trays on the formal table, but
when they are used, they are exchangeable with the placement of salts
and peppers.

A table cloth of linen, damask, or lace may be used, or mats of the
same materials. The silver will be sterling or an attractive substitute,
the glassware may be clear or jewel toned, and butter plates and ashtrays may be used. The first course of soup or seafood usually is in place
on the table when guests sit down, but it is preferable that hot soup be
served after guests are seated in order that it does not get cold.

Three or four courses are customarily served. A good sample for
such a meal is:

First course: soup, usually clear, or oysters or clams on the half shell,
    shrimp, melon, etc.
Second course: main course of meat and vegetables.
Third course: salad.
Fourth course: dessert, coffee.

You may smoke just before dessert, unless ashtrays are not provided—from which you may assume that your hostess does not wish you
to smoke at the table.

After-dinner coffee is served to both men and women in the living
room. The ranking woman guest will make the first gesture toward going
home around ten-thirty, when dancing or other entertainment has not
been provided.

VERY FORMAL DINNERS

A very formal dinner is always a dignified occasion, but it should not be a
cold and formidable affair. Although most very formal entertaining has
disappeared in the services, there are still official and state functions
which high-ranking officers must give and attend.

At such dinners the most delicious food is served, with the utmost
efficiency, at a table set with the most beautiful and correct appointments.
Full service, preferably by male waiters, is required at the truly formal
table.

Men wear black tie, unless white tie is indicated on the invitation,
and women wear formal attire. Place cards are used, and the hostess will
plan the seating arrangement, with due regard for the official status of
those present, for congeniality of guests, and the number to be invited.

When an equal number of men and women are at the table, care must be taken that men do not sit by other men or women by other women.

The formal table is customarily set with sterling silver, a damask, linen, or lace cloth, or mats, fine china, and crystal glassware. There should be a centerpiece of flowers flanked by silver candlesticks or candelabra. Customs have changed in recent years concerning the number of courses served, with four or five the usual number, but as many as seven or as few as three are occasionally served.

The high-ranking man is customarily seated to the right of the hostess, and the high-ranking woman to the right of the host. The host and hostess may be seated at opposite ends of the table, or they may sit opposite each other at the center of a very long or round table.

WHEN GUESTS ARRIVE

If you are a guest, you should arrive at the designated time—usually eight or half-past eight in the evening. Be on time. In quarters of officers of high rank, a mess management specialist (MS)—or the service equivalent—will open the door for you, and direct you to the coatroom. In homes of civilians with considerable means, a butler usually is at the door. Or a butler and other help will be hired for the occasion.

Male guests will find a small envelope in a tray on a hall table, with the name of their dinner partner enclosed. A table diagram will be conveniently displayed to enable the men to check the seating arrangement. At large dinners, a small folded card with the man's name on the outside and his partner's name on the inside on a small diagram, will show the seating positions at the table. Such cards are frequently used instead of the usual card and envelope.

Your hostess should stand just inside the living room door to greet guests, and the host should be nearby. Guests greet the hostess first, and then the host, before greeting other guests. A guest, or guests, of honor will be with the host and hostess. It is customary that when the guest of honor is a dignitary, an aide to the host will meet the guest at the gate of the station or base and escort the guest to the host's quarters. The host will be waiting in the hall to greet the honored guest, and to present other guests to him.

It is the duty of the host to see that each guest meets his or her dinner partner before going into the dining room. At large official dinners, aides introduce dinner partners when necessary; at other dinners, the host may ask a friend to make necessary introductions.

Your host, or an aide, introduces you into a group, then it is up to you to meet and talk with the other guests. A choice of one or two cocktails, as well as sherry and fruit or vegetable juice, will be offered before dinner. You usually take one, but no more than two cocktails before dinner.

ENTERING THE DINING ROOM

When dinner is announced, the hostess turns to the ranking male guest and says, "Shall we go in to dinner?" *But it is the host who offers his arm to the high-ranking woman guest and leads the way into the dining room.* When a guest is late—not counting the honor guest or guests—the general rule is to wait about 15 minutes after the cocktail hour before going in to dinner.

When the guest of honor is a man of *very* high position, or a dignitary of note, the hostess and guest of honor will enter the dining room first, with the host and ranking woman following. All other guests follow in pairs, in no order of precedence.

Place cards are usually laid flat on the napkin in the place plate, or ⁺hey will be standing at the head of each plate. Names are handwritten, ₩ith titles and last names only: "Mrs. Smith," "Captain Jones," "The Ambassador of Thailand," or "The Secretary of the Army." The last two are addressed as "Mr. Ambassador" and "Mr. Secretary." (*See* Chapter 18, Seating Plans and Precedence.)

SEATING

Women are usually seated as soon as they enter the dining room. They go to their chairs from the left and sit from the left, with the men at their right assisting with the chair. Men remain standing until the hostess takes her place, with the male guest of honor on her right seating her *after* he has first seated the woman to his right. If there is a butler he seats the hostess.

When seating a woman, the man steps behind her chair, draws it back carefully, then as she starts to sit down from the left, he slides the chair forward.

The number one waiter will be standing behind the hostess's chair, directing the service. As soon as all guests are seated, the first course is placed in the place plate, which is on the table when guests sit down. There will always be a plate before you until dessert is served.

The service customarily begins with the woman at the right of the host. (*See* Chapter 19, Rules of Serving at Table.) The number one waiter pours the wine as soon as the first course is sei ₋ed, and will serve other wines with the courses they accompany. If you do not care for wine, you may lightly touch the rim of the glass with your fingertips before the server starts to pour, or you may simply say, "No, thank you."

However, if there should be toasts, you would need the wine whether it is drunk or not.

At dinners held in homes, and at small formal dinners anywhere, you start eating as soon as the hostess begins (or the host, at a stag luncheon or dinner). At large formal dinners or banquets, you start eating as soon as those near you have been served.

Menus for formal dinners are varied. The following courses, with the wines that accompany each course, may be changed to three-, four-, or five-course menus by omitting certain courses. In this country, soup is traditionally the first course, although it may be preceded by seafood, such as oysters. In foreign countries, several more courses may be offered, and dinner may start at 9 or 9:30 P.M.

Sequence of Courses

Course	Accompanying Wine
Shrimp cocktail, oysters or clams on the half shell, fruit cup, or	white Burgundy
Soup (usually clear)	sherry
Fish, hot or cold	white Rhine
Main course of meat and vegetables, or	claret
Main course of game and vegetables	Burgundy
Salad	no new wine
Dessert (ice cream, sherbet, etc.), or	champagne
Fresh fruit (pears, grapes, etc.)	champagne

A *five-course dinner* could be: soup, fish, main course, salad, dessert.

A *four-course dinner* could be: soup, main course, salad, dessert.

A *three-course dinner* could be: soup, main course (with asparagus instead of salad), and dessert.

Rolls and after-dinner coffee are always served. Mints are frequently served after the final course, but not necessarily.

Although the use of butter plates is now condoned on the formal dinner table, their use depends upon the amount of space at the table since crowding is always to be avoided.

Cigarettes are offered at most formal dinners, but some hostesses prefer that there be no smoking at the table. Individual ashtrays may be placed above the plate, or between each two guests at the table. Urns or other containers of cigarettes may be placed on the table, and individual ashtrays offered each guest. Cigars and cigarettes may be served to the men after the women leave the table.

Demitasse and liqueurs may be served in the living room to the women, and at the table or in the library to the men, but usually are served in the living room to both men and women.

If dancing or games have not been planned for the evening, and if you are not going on to some other function, the guests will form naturally into conversational groups. The high-ranking woman guest should make the first move to leave when the time for departure comes—which usually is within an hour after the dinner is over.

Upon departure, you shake hands with your host and hostess and thank them for their hospitality. The hostess rises when guests rise to leave, but she does not leave the living room. The host, however, accompanies all guests to the door of the living room, and even walks to the front door or into the hall with high-ranking guests.

Although it is impossible to tell each guest good-bye at a large dinner, you should speak to your own dinner partner before leaving, as well as with others with whom you were just talking. The MS or butler will open the door for you and say, "Good night, Sir (or Madam)." You answer, "Good night and thank you."

THE LATE GUEST

When a guest is late, a hostess may delay serving dinner about 15 minutes, then she must proceed. The latecomer goes to his or her place upon arrival. The hostess remains seated—otherwise all gentlemen at the table would also have to rise. Only the man at the right of a late lady guest rises to seat her. The latecomer should briefly say, "I am very sorry to be late, it was unavoidable," then give an explanation to the hostess later.

RÉSUMÉ

INFORMAL DINNER RULES TO REMEMBER:

Invitations may be extended by telephone, in person, by note or by informal card. You may answer in the same manner.

The time is anywhere from 6 to 8 P.M., with 7 P.M. customary.

A man wears informal dress—usually a dark or light business suit, in season, or sports attire if indicated. Women wear afternoon or sports attire, or a long skirt, as indicated. The hostess may designate what to wear when the invitation is given, or a guest should feel free to ask.

Two or three courses are served, with the host and hostess serving.

The hostess is not served first by a servant unless she is the only woman at the table. When other women are at the table and the hostess serves, she serves herself last.

The table should be set simply but attractively, with a table cloth or mats, and a centerpiece.

One or two wines may be served, if desired. The bottle or decanter may be placed on the table, with guests serving themselves.

When nothing has been planned afterwards, such as bridge, you may leave within an hour after the dinner's conclusion.

Write a thank-you note to your hostess after being entertained, or telephone her. Regardless of the informality of the dinner, it's the hospitality of your hosts that you are thanking them for—not the expense.

FORMAL DINNER RULES:

Invitations may be extended by telephone, by handwritten note, or by the fill-in card. You should answer promptly and in the same manner, except that the fill-in invitation is answered by hand.

The time is usually 8 P.M., and men wear black tie. Women wear long dinner dress.

Three or four courses are customarily served.

The dinner may be a sit-down buffet.

Butter plates and ashtrays may be on the table.

Small tables seating four, six, or eight, are frequently used for seated dinners; tables for eight are popular, since they offer wider conversational range for guests.

Elaborate appointments, place mats or tablecloth, are used for formal as well as for very formal dinners.

Guests may leave about 10:30 P.M. when nothing is planned afterwards.

Remember to write a thank-you note, or telephone your hostess.

VERY FORMAL DINNER RULES:

Invitations are handwritten, engraved or printed, frequently the fill-in, in the third person, and you reply in the third person on white or cream-colored note paper. You should answer promptly. Invitations are also issued and replied to by telephone.

The time is usually 8 or 8:30 P.M., and you must be on time.

Men wear black tie or white tie (for state or very formal occasions) as indicated on the invitation. In telephoned invitations, the hostess, aide, or secretary will indicate which to wear. Women wear long evening dress.

A guest at any type of dinner greets the hostess first, the host next, and
then the other guests.

There is full service at the table, with from three to seven courses served
—customarily, four or five.

Butter plates are now used on the formal table.

"Turning the table" means co-operating with your hostess midway
through the meal by talking with the person at your left.

You do not leave until after the high-ranking guests leave, which may
be 30 minutes after the dinner is over, or usually within an hour.

The ranking lady makes the first move to leave—even when a man
present outranks her.

Courtesy requires that you write your hostess a note of thanks within two
or three days after being entertained. Or you may telephone.

CHAPTER 16

Luncheons & Lighter Repasts

OFFICIAL LUNCHEONS

Most luncheons that you, as an officer, will attend will be official occasions, frequently held in honor of a dignitary who may be a visitor to your base or station. These luncheons are often "stag," but when the guest of honor's wife and servicewomen attend, other women will be invited. Everyone should be on time.

The table arrangements and service for an official/formal luncheon are about the same as those for a less formal dinner. Three courses are customary, or four at the most. An informal luncheon may have only two courses, since the food served at noon time is lighter than that served at evening meals.

Place cards are a matter of convenience, and may be used for as few as eight or so guests. The table probably will be covered with a white cloth, but mats may be used. There should be a centerpiece, but no candles are used on luncheon tables. Cigarette trays and butter plates are usually in place, and the first course is on the table when everyone sits down. Each course is served by waiters or maids.

Cocktails are offered about 30 minutes before the meal is served. Sherry may be served at the table.

INFORMAL LUNCHEONS

When a hostess does not have help, a buffet luncheon is the easiest and most pleasant way to entertain a group of friends. The food may be arranged on a sideboard and the guests serve themselves and sit at card tables already set up in a given area, or anywhere convenient. After the soiled plates and dishes have been removed to the kitchen, the hostess places the dessert and coffee and tea on the sideboard for guests to help themselves, or she serves them directly from the kitchen to each guest.

In this calorie-counting day, menus are much simpler. A casserole or quiche, with salad, in winter would be sufficient; and salads and sandwiches in warm weather. Fruit is always a good dessert.

"Lunch" vs. "Luncheon"

When speaking of the noon meal, you refer to it as "lunch." You would say, "Yesterday I lunched with your classmate, Bob Smith." A hostess should say, "Luncheon is served" or "Shall we go in to lunch?"

TIME

Luncheons usually start at noon or 1 P.M., depending upon duty hours. You should stay about 30 to 45 minutes after luncheon, unless you must return to your station. You wear the uniform of the day at official luncheons. Nonmilitary women wear afternoon dress or suits. Luncheons may be longer when women attend. The high-ranking woman should properly start to leave no later than three o'clock.

INVITATIONS

Luncheon invitations may be given in person, by telephone, letter, "informals," personal cards, or the fill-in cards. You may answer in the same manner—except you always reply by handwritten note in answer to the formally written invitation, unless a telephone number is listed on official invitations.

GUEST OF HONOR

At a stag luncheon, the guest of honor or guest with the highest rank will be seated to the right of the host, with the second ranking guest to his left.

At a mixed luncheon, the guests are seated in the same way as at a dinner—the ranking lady at the right of the host and the ranking man at the right of the hostess.

At a women's luncheon, such as an officers' wives luncheon, the senior officer's wife is seated to the right of the hostess. When there is a guest of honor, such as a prominent speaker, the honored guest sits at the right of the hostess and the wife of the high-ranking officer to the left of the hostess.

MENUS

The menu for any luncheon is varied. A two-course summer luncheon could be: fruit or seafood salad, and dessert. A two-course winter luncheon could be: casserole with, or without, salad and dessert.

The customary three-course luncheon could be:

Soup, main course, dessert,
or Main course, salad, dessert,
or Fruit (melon or grapefruit), main course, dessert,
or Casserole, salad, dessert,
or Soufflé, salad, dessert.
Coffee or tea.

A formal luncheon consists of no more than four courses. For example: Soup, main course, salad, dessert.

Soup is usually in place on the table when guests sit down. A two-handled cup, with matching plate, is used. These cups are sometimes called "bouillon" cups, and after the bouillon or clear soup has cooled, the cup may be lifted with both hands, and the soup drunk. When soup is served at the informal table, the hostess may serve from a tureen placed in front of her.

Sherry is often served with the soup course, and may be the only wine served at luncheons. A white or red wine may be served, or both may be offered at formal meals. Iced tea is frequently in place on the summer table when guests sit down. The iced tea spoon may be at the right of the knives, or above the plate at an informal meal; it may also be placed on a coaster or small serving plate holding the iced tea glass. Hot tea may be served at the table, with the service the same as for coffee—except that the hostess always pours.

Second portions are not offered at a formal luncheon.

BREAKFAST

Breakfast is usually a simple meal, served informally except for such occasions as wedding breakfasts, hunt breakfasts, etc. A small bowl of flowers or fruit may be on the table, and the table is frequently bare. Mats of almost any gay material may be used.

The silver at each place is usually a fork, knife, and cereal spoon. A butter knife will be in place on the butter plate at a more formally set table. The coffee cup will be at the right of the knife, and the coffee spoon will be in place on the saucer at the right of the cup handle.

Jam is served in a dish set on a small plate, with the spoon in the plate. After you have served yourself, you leave the spoon in the dish. Fruit or fruit juice is usually in place on the breakfast plate, or the juice glass may be set at the right of the water glass—when water is on the table.

Plates may be arranged in the kitchen and brought in individually, or the food may be placed in dishes set on the table and passed around the table. Food is frequently kept hot on a hotplate set on the sideboard, along with the coffee and toast, with everyone serving himself.

At a family breakfast, the food is placed on the table for convenience in serving. When guests are present and time is not important, a leisurely breakfast may be served by the hostess. Then, fruit or fruit juice will be in place on the breakfast plate, with dry cereal placed above the plate on the table. The butter plate and knife will be set above the fork, and hot cereal and food will be served from the kitchen or from the sideboard.

WEDDING BREAKFAST (OR SUPPER)

Following a formal morning wedding, a breakfast is usually served for the guests. Wedding breakfast etiquette is discussed in Chapter 28, Wedding Receptions.

OTHER LIGHTER REPASTS

COFFEE

A "coffee" is an informal type of entertaining that is popular for wives of a unit, and usually is held on a weekday between 10 and 11:30 A.M. Dress is casual.

The menu is similar to that for a breakfast and usually consists of coffee, sweet rolls, biscuits, small sausages, etc.

BRUNCH

A brunch starts a little later than a "coffee," and is usually held between 11 A.M. and 1 P.M. It has a more elaborate menu than a "coffee," since it is a combination of breakfast and lunch. Hot muffins, scones, ham, sweet rolls, pastries, and fruit juice, as well as coffee may be served.

The brunch may be held in a home, on the patio or terrace, or in a club. Men as well as women are invited to a weekend brunch, or on a nonworking day. Attractive casual dress is worn.

Invitations to coffees and brunches are usually extended by telephone.

TEA

Teas, for a few or many guests, usually start at 4 P.M., and frequently are given to meet someone—a houseguest or a very special person. Guests should arrive no later than half an hour before the last hour indicated in the invitation.

In a home, a tea is usually held in the dining room and the table is always covered with a lace or elaborate cloth. The plates of food, the stacks of little tea plates, the napkins, cups and saucers, are arranged in a balanced pattern in relation to the floral centerpiece and to the two trays—one for the tea service and one for the coffee service—which are placed at opposite ends of the table. The cups and saucers are always placed close to the tea and coffee services.

The food served at a tea is varied, but always includes thin sandwiches and small cakes. The menu may include small rolls or biscuits filled with hot creamed chicken, small doughnuts, tarts, pastries, cake, nuts, and mints, as well as tea and coffee, with lemon and cream. The serving of tea may start as soon as the first guests arrive, with the hostess greeting each guest upon arrival. Close friends of the hostess are usually asked to pour.

Invitations are usually extended by telephone and replies are made in the same way.

When guests depart, the conventional remark is, "I must be going; thank you so much." The hostess may answer, "Good-bye, I'm so pleased you were able to come." The hostess may accompany a guest to the door of the living room, or a high-ranking guest or a much older guest to the front door.

Junior officers' wives, with limited budgets, frequently repay luncheon or dinner obligations with invitations to such brunches or teas. In the services (as elsewhere) obligations are repaid in keeping with one's budget.

RÉSUMÉ

LUNCHEON RULES TO REMEMBER

Invitations are extended by telephone, in person, by informal notes or
    personal cards, or by the fill-in cards for formal occasions. You an-
    swer in the same manner, but always by a handwritten note in an-
    swer to the more formal invitation.
The time is usually noon or 1 P.M. You are expected to be on time.
There are *no* luncheon partners when entering the dining room. You

walk into the room with whomever you were talking to when luncheon was announced. A man does *not* offer his arm to a woman when entering the dining room.

Butter plates and ashtrays may be in place on the formal as well as the informal table. If there are no ashtrays, do not smoke.

One wine is customarily served at the luncheon table, but two may be offered. Lighter wines are served at luncheons than at dinners.

CHAPTER 17

Setting the Table

THE BASIC RULE in setting any table, formal or informal, is that crowding must be avoided—there should be at least 24 inches of table space for each person—and everything on the table must balance. The centerpiece is in the middle of the table and is balanced by any other decorations placed around it—unless the table is placed against a wall, such as at a large buffet when space is needed; in that case, the centerpiece is placed closer to the wall.

The traditional table arrangements for six, eight, or eighteen guests shown here may be adapted for various numbers of guests:

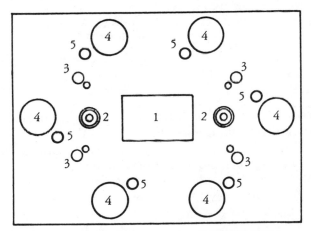

1—CENTERPIECE   2—CANDELABRA
3—SALTS & PEPPERS   4—PLATES
5—WATER GOBLETS

A table set for six.

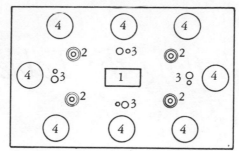

1 —CENTERPIECE   2 —CANDELSTICKS
3 —SALTS & PEPPERS   4 —PLATES

A table set for eight.

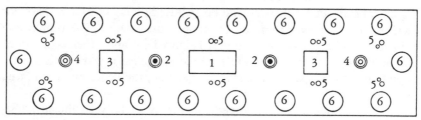

1 —CENTERPIECE   5 —SALTS AND PEPPERS
2 —TALL CANDELABRUM   6 —PLATES
3 —MATCHING FLOWERS OR FRUITS
4 —CANDELSTICK OR SMALL CANDELABRUM
A table set for eighteen.

THE MODERN TABLE

Although such things as table decorations—china, linens, and silver patterns—are usually confined to a "woman's world," it is a sharp young man who takes time to learn something about the furnishings of a household, since sooner or later most men get married.

In the present-day world of the midshipman, cadet, OCS, OTS, or bachelor officer (who may have no immediate thoughts of marriage), it is well to know what is correct in furnishings for the home since you will have the opportunity to buy beautiful articles at prices lower than at home, when you are on a practice cruise or overseas air cruise, and when you have duty abroad. Furthermore, such articles make excellent Christmas, wedding, birthday, or anniversary gifts, as well as hostess gifts when you have been a weekend guest in a home.

Today's modern table is one of utility as well as beauty. Mats have replaced the tablecloth on most tables—even the more formal table. Harmony in color and design, and balance of table appointments and decorations, are the main rules in setting any table, formal or informal.

The type of entertaining to be enjoyed usually determines the formality of the service. Table linens may be in every color of the artist's palette and in a wide range of fabrics.

Fine bone china, or any of the serviceable potteries or earthenwares, may be the choice of the hostess; glassware may be crystal—clear or colored, plain or etched. When possible, sterling silver is preferable for the more formal occasion, but stainless steel or silver plate is now acceptable on every table, and even preferred by many young couples, who either can't afford sterling or don't want the bother of polishing it. But sterling or silver plate, porcelain or pottery, fine table service is never mixed with coarse accessories any more than fine evening accessories would be mixed with sports attire.

There are a number of rules that are followed in setting the table:

TABLE LINEN

The traditional formal dinner table is covered with a white or ivory-colored damask tablecloth. However, the modern white or pastel-colored cloth of damask, lace, linen or polyester is more frequently used, as well as place mats of the same materials.

The tablecloth should never overhang the table by more than 18 inches, or less than 12 inches. A silence pad should fit the top of the table, with the tablecloth placed over the pad.

Matching napkins should be between 18 and 22 inches square—or 24 inches square for the very formal dinner table.

A lace or linen tablecloth for the formal luncheon or dinner table must not overhang the table, and mats are more frequently used.

Luncheon napkins are from 14 to 16 inches square, and are of matching materials.

Cocktail napkins are used before the luncheon or dinner, and are a third smaller than a luncheon napkin. They are of cloth or paper.

HOW TO FOLD NAPKINS

Large napkins are used at formal dinners or banquets. There are two customary ways of folding them: (1.) Fold the napkin once in each direction, then fold the square into thirds. Place on the place plate. (2.)

Fold the napkin into a square, then fold opposite corners together to form a three-sided shape. Place on place plate. When formal napkins are

Formal napkin folds.

monogrammed with three initials of equal size, their order is either in the order of the hostess's name (Mary Senn Fisher would read "MSF") or "mFs." A single initial is: "F."

Informal napkins are from 14 to 16 inches square, and are used for breakfast, luncheon, tea, or informal dinners, or buffet suppers. They are usually placed at the left of the forks. The open edges may be placed toward the plate and the table edge, or toward the left as illustrated.

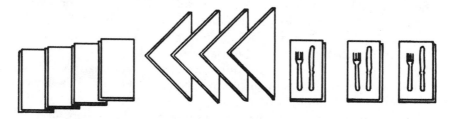

Informal napkin folds.

Napkins are customarily placed one inch from the edge of the table, on a line with the place plate and table silver. There are several ways to fold napkins at the informal table: (1.) Fold the napkin into a square, then fold it in half again. (2.) Fold a smaller napkin from corner to opposite corner to form a triangle, and place beside the plate with the triangle pointing *out* from the plate. (3.) Napkins for buffet suppers are folded in triangles or rectangles, and are placed near the stack of plates. Napkins may be placed in folded rectangles on the buffet table, with silver for each guest laid on each napkin. (4.) Napkins may be placed on the place plate when a first course is not on the plate.

TABLE CHINA

There are three main types of plates used daily: breakfast, luncheon, and dinner. In setting the table, the plate is placed an inch from the edge of the table, and the silver and napkin are also placed an inch from the table's edge.

Other pieces are also needed in daily living and for special occasions, including coffee and tea cups, serving dishes, and salts and peppers. Various-sized plates are needed for the soup cup or bowl, butter, seafood, etc. Place plates (or service plates) are the plates that are on the formal table when guests sit down.

Although all china used throughout the meal need not match, it is a rule that all plates used together at the same time should match; that is, all dinner plates used in the main course must be alike, all dessert plates alike, etc.

There are three sizes of cups most customarily used: the demitasse or small coffee cup used after formal and semiformal meals; the teacup or medium-sized coffee cup at luncheons and less formal meals; and the large coffee cup for breakfasts and informal meals.

The sizes of the main types of plates are:

The plate for the main course (the dinner plate): about 10 inches in diameter.
The luncheon plate: 9 inches.
The flat dessert or salad plate: about 8 inches.
The flat bread and butter plate is between 4 and 6 inches.
The soup plate, between 9 and 10 inches across, is a broad bowl about an inch deep with a broad flat rim; it is used at formal dinners. The handled cream soup or bouillion cup is used at luncheons and less formal dinners.

SERVING DISHES

A complete set of serving dishes is necessary to serve each six or eight guests. At a meal for 12 to 16 guests, a second set of serving dishes would be needed. Serving dishes may match the china service, or they may be silver. They should blend with the china service if they do not match exactly. There are many shapes and sizes, with oblong or oval dishes having broad flat bottoms and deep sides the most useful.

Two pairs of vegetable dishes are necessary, if you entertain often, with a smaller pair for everyday use and a larger pair for the serving of many persons. The customary sizes are:

Vegetables dishes, 12 to 14 inches, one or two pairs.

A bowl 5 or 6 inches deep, for soft foods, etc.

A shallow bowl, about 10 inches in diameter and 2 or 3 inches deep, for serving fruits, desserts, etc., or used as a centerpiece.

Bread tray or basket, of various sizes and materials. A silver tray may be used for serving asparagus, celery, carrot sticks, radishes, etc.

Sauceboat or gravy boat.

PLATTERS:

A small oval platter, 15 inches long, for meat or fish for a few persons.

A large oval platter, 18 inches long, for large roasts and cold meats; it is particularly useful at buffet meals.

A round platter, 12 inches in diameter, for serving pies, cakes, canapes, cookies, etc.

WATER AND WINE GLASSES

The stemmed water goblet is used on the more formal luncheon or dinner table, and is customarily placed above the knives. The goblets are usually filled with water before the guests sit down. Stemless water glasses are used at the less formal table, and after or between meals. Goblets and glasses come in a variety of sizes, shapes, and there are many different qualities of crystal or glass.

The smaller wine glasses are placed on the table in several ways—customarily to the right and forward of the water goblet. Wine glasses are placed in the order of their use, and are filled immediately after the course they accompany has been served. Sherry glasses are filled almost to the top, but wine glasses are filled no more than two-thirds.

Long-stemmed water and wine glasses are held by the thumb and first two fingers at the base of the bowl. Small stemmed glasses are held by the stems, and the tumblers are held near the base. Brandy snifters are held in the palms of both hands to warm the brandy.

When you hold a glass of chilled wine, hold it by the stem so that your fingers do not warm the glass, and thus the wine.

TABLE GLASSES

The most frequently used glasses on a table are the ones shown below. The dessert/champagne glass is interchangeable, and the iced beverage glass may be used for highballs.

From Left: Dessert/champagne glass, wine glass, water goblet, and iced beverage glass.

FLATWARE

Silver flatware is always placed on the table in the order of its use, starting from the outside and working in toward the plate. Although some of the following rules have been mentioned elsewhere, they are worth repeating in order to stay in your mind:

The silver, napkins, and plate are lined up *one inch* from the edge of the table.

Forks are placed at the left of the plate—with the exception of the seafood fork, which is placed at the right of the spoon, tines up.

There are never more than three forks in place on the table at any one time. If more forks are needed, they will be brought in with the course they accompany.

Knives and spoons are at the right of the plate, with the blade of the knife facing in toward the plate.

Teaspoons or place spoons are placed on the informal luncheon or dinner table, and are used for soup served in cups or for fruit. Teaspoons or cereal spoons are placed on the breakfast table and are used for grapefruits, cereals, etc.

Spoons for tea and coffee are placed on the saucers, at the right of the handles, before service.

Dessert spoons and/or forks are usually brought in on the dessert plate, with the fork at the left, the spoon at the right of the plate.

At informal meals, dessert spoons and/or forks may be placed on the
table above the plate. The spoon will be above, with the handle at
the right, and the fork will be directly below the spoon, with its
handle at the left. This is a European, not an American, custom.

The iced beverage spoon, used mainly at luncheons, may be placed on
the table at the right of the soup spoon, or it may be laid above the
plate, with the handle of the spoon at the right.

The individual butter knife is customarily placed across the top of the
butter plate, parallel with the edge of the table. The handle of the
knife is at the right, the blade facing toward the edge of the table.
The knife may be placed on the right side of the plate, parallel to
the other table silver. (See *illustration* page 264).

The steak knife is placed on the table in lieu of the regular knife.

TABLE DECORATIONS

The center of interest on the luncheon or dinner table is the centerpiece.
The size of the centerpiece depends upon the size and shape of the table,
but it should not be so tall or large that guests cannot see over it. When
candles are used, the flame must either be above or below eye level.

The basic formal table decoration is a centerpiece of a china, silver,
or porcelain bowl or tureen, filled with flowers, flanked by silver candelabra or four candlesticks. A long table will have matching replicas
of the centerpiece placed midway down each side of the table—and both
sides of the table must be alike.

In addition to the candelabra on the long table, four or more candlesticks with white or colored candles may be placed in rectangular fashion
around the centerpiece. When two candlesticks are shorter than the
others, they are placed at the ends of the table.

A single candelabrum, or a small bowl of flowers artistically arranged, may be used on the small formal or informal table. Flowers are
customarily used on any type of table, formal or informal, but modern
table settings include the use of almost any material or container in good
taste—fruit, vegetables, figurines, or driftwood. Modern or antique containers may be of silver, china, porcelain, or crystal for the most formal
table, and wood, pewter, glass, or pottery for the less formal table.

ASHTRAYS

Ashtrays are customarily placed on the most formal table today, but until
recent years smoking was not permitted at the table. Individual ashtrays
of sterling, china, or porcelain may be placed above the place plate, with

two cigarettes laid across the top of the tray, and a small book or box of matches laid in the lower part of the ashtray.

Larger urns or containers of china, porcelain, or sterling, may be placed on the table for cigarettes with individual ashtrays. At formal dinners, the guests may be offered cigarettes in silver boxes placed on a tray and served by a waiter just before dessert.

Ashtrays, either individual or for every two guests, are usually in place on the formal and informal table when the guests sit down.

CANDY DISHES

Candy is served at the table less frequently now than in former years. Candy dishes are considered a part of the table decorations, however, and may be placed between the candelabra and the place plates at each end of the formal table.

At a long table, the candy dishes would be spaced, at equal distances, midway down the sides. The candy may be passed by the hostess or served on a tray by a waiter.

FINGER BOWLS

Finger bowls may match the glass at the table, but not necessarily. The finger bowl is brought to the table in one of two ways:

On the dessert plate, with the dessert spoon at the right and the dessert fork at the left of the plate. The bowl is taken off the plate by the guest, who sets it on the table above and to the left of the plate. The guest places the dessert silver on the table, with the fork at the left and the spoon at the right of the plate. When a lace doily is under the finger bowl, this is also removed from the plate and is placed on the table under the finger bowl.

Or the finger bowl may be brought on the fruit plate, when fruit is the final course served. The finger bowl and fruit knife and fork are removed from the plate by the guest, and are placed on the table in the same manner as described above. When the finger bowl is brought in with no silver, the guest will know that no other course will be served.

Finger bowls may be brought in at any meal, but are most frequently offered at formal meals, or after the serving of lobsters or clams or any food that is greasy or that must be handled. The finger bowl is threequarters filled with cool water—or with warm water, when foods have been greasy to handle.

SALTS AND PEPPERS

One salt and pepper set may be placed on the informal table and passed around the table when needed. Antique condiment sets are frequently used on the informal table, and unusual or antique sets can add interest to a table.

On the formal table, an individual set may be placed directly above the place plate, or one set may be placed to the right of the line of glasses of a guest and used by the guest next to him as well. Sets are customarily placed in a rectangle around the centerpiece, with the pepper above and the salt below.

Open salts and peppers require a very small sterling or glass spoon.

TABLE LISTS

A young couple just starting out may begin the table service with a "starter set" for two. "Open-stock" china or silver or glassware means that extra pieces or sets are available for purchase at a later date. Established patterns are advisable, since replacements may be purchased whenever needed.

Sets of 4 or 8 are preferable for a young couple, with service for 12 the average in most households. When purchasing a service for 6, it is well to know that when the number of *dinner and salad plates* and *coffee cups* is doubled, the same list will take care of 12 guests at a two-course luncheon or dinner.

The average sizes in plates most frequently used are: dinner, 10½ inches; luncheon, 9 inches; dessert or salad, 8 inches. The place plates used at formal meals are approximately 9 or 10 inches in diameter.

In the average household, the medium-sized cup, or teacup, is used more often than any other cup; and the *place spoon* may be used for dessert, cereal, or soup—but not for cream soup.

A five-piece place setting includes the dinner plate, salad plate, bread and butter plate, teacup, and saucer. A service for six persons would include:

CHINA

    6 Dinner plates
    6 Bread and butter plates
    6 Salad or dessert plates
    6 Teacups and saucers
    2 Large coffee cups, family use
    1 Sugar bowl
    1 Cream pitcher
    6 Soup bowls

Extra pieces:
    6 Demitasse (after-dinner cups) and saucers
    6 Luncheon plates

Serving dishes:
    Platters, small, medium, or large
    Platter, round buffet
    Vegetable, open or closed
    Sauceboat

Useful pieces:
    Casserole
    Water pitcher of silver, glass, or pottery
    Salad bowl, wooden (preferable)
    Individual salad bowls
    Cereal bowls
    Butter dish, of china or silver
    Tea, coffee service: silver or china

Sets can be purchased or ordered at the nearest PX or Service Exchange at considerable savings.

GLASSWARE

Thin crystal, plain or etched, is used for formal and semiformal occasions. Modern glassware comes in all qualities, colors, and designs, and is used instead of crystal at less formal occasions. Water goblets and wine glasses may match, but not necessarily so. Glasses should harmonize in color, quality, and design for various occasions. A desirable list, which can be added to through the years, is:

- 6 Water goblets, stemmed, holding about 10 ounces (formal)
- 6 Water glasses for informal occasions
- 6 Wine glasses, stemmed, holding from 3 to 5 ounces
- 6 Sherry glasses, stemmed, 2 ounces
- 12 Cocktail glasses, 3 to 4 ounces (the cocktail and wine glasses may be interchanged if the wine glass is not too large; a large sherry glass may be used for cocktails)
- 12 Highball glasses, also used for iced tea or fruit juices, soft drinks, etc., 12 to 14 ounces, no stems
- 6 Fruit or vegetable juice glasses, no stems, 4 to 5 ounces
- 6 Liqueur glasses, stemmed
- 6 Finger bowls (usually for formal entertaining)
- 6 Champagne/dessert glasses.

SILVER FLATWARE

Your silver flatware pattern, when selected, should be for a lifetime. Since there is considerable difference in the cost of sterling, semi-sterling, silverplate, gold electroplate, pewter, and stainless steel, these differences are now discussed so that you may more easily make up your mind in selecting your pattern.

Sterling silver flatware not only is for a lifetime but is passed down through the generations. Sterling silver is a classic symbol of prestige and good taste; it is used for every occasion, and becomes more beautiful through the years.

Since pure silver is too soft to be used as flatware, copper is added for strength; by federal law the proportions are 925 parts pure silver and 75 parts copper. It is the most expensive.

Semi-sterling is a new kind of flatware designed for the modern way of living, that combines sterling silver handles with stainless steel knife blades, spoon bowls, and fork tines. It is almost care-free, being dishwasher proof. It costs about half the price of traditional sterling.

Silverplate is made by electroplating a layer of pure silver over a base metal, with an extra layer of silver at points of wear. You may be the only one who knows if it is sterling or not. It is dishwasher safe, and costs a fraction of the price of sterling.

Pewter flatware is fairly new on the market, although both the metal and patterns most popular today have a heritage that dates from the early days of this country. Pewter is an allow of lead-free blends of several metals, with a satin finish. It is nontarnishing and dishwasher-safe. It is completely safe for use with foods, unlike some of the early pewter which contained lead. The handles are pure pewter, the knife blades, spoon bowls, and fork tines of stainless steel. The price is moderate.

Gold electroplate flatware may be used for very special occasions since it is flatware electroplated with 24-karat gold; the finish is non-tarnish and is carefree. The price is in keeping with the gold karat.

Stainless steel flatware has come into its own in recent years, since the patterns are both very attractive and serviceable. It is low-care, dish-washer safe, and very reasonable in price. It is used for almost any occasion other than the most formal.

PLACE SETTINGS

The minimum place setting is the teaspoon, place knife, place fork, and salad or dessert fork. The next most needed pieces are the butter spreader and soup spoon.

The newer place spoon doubles for soup, cereal, and dessert. Other place setting pieces that are the most commonly used are the cocktail-seafood fork, demitasse spoon, iced beverage spoon, and individual steak knives.

Starter sets for four, or six place settings, may be increased to eight or twelve at your convenience and as needed. When you have place settings for four or six, you may want to add extra teaspoons, forks, and salad forks before some of the other pieces since these are the most used.

SERVING PIECES

A variety of multi-purpose serving pieces complement the place settings. Certain ones (indicated by*) are the essentials, the ones you'll need. The others are nice-to-have "extras" when convenient.

A salad serving fork and spoon are very nice to have in your silver pattern, and they may also be used for casseroles and larger dishes of vegetables or desserts. They may also be purchased in a variety of patterns of wood or glass that match the salad bowl. A carving set for slicing and

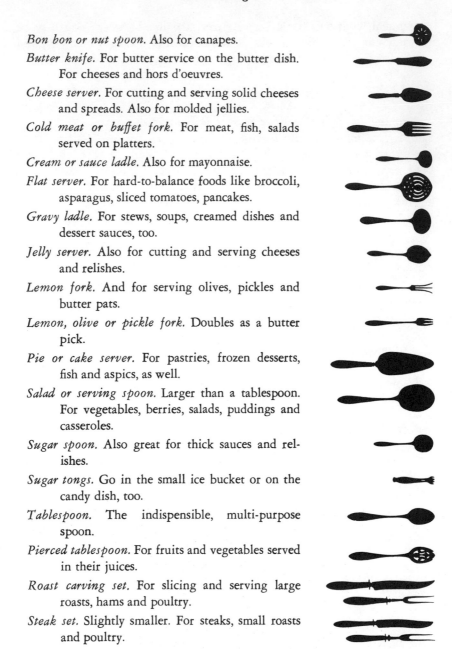

Bon bon or nut spoon. Also for canapes.

Butter knife. For butter service on the butter dish. For cheeses and hors d'oeuvres.

Cheese server. For cutting and serving solid cheeses and spreads. Also for molded jellies.

Cold meat or buffet fork. For meat, fish, salads served on platters.

Cream or sauce ladle. Also for mayonnaise.

Flat server. For hard-to-balance foods like broccoli, asparagus, sliced tomatoes, pancakes.

Gravy ladle. For stews, soups, creamed dishes and dessert sauces, too.

Jelly server. Also for cutting and serving cheeses and relishes.

Lemon fork. And for serving olives, pickles and butter pats.

Lemon, olive or pickle fork. Doubles as a butter pick.

Pie or cake server. For pastries, frozen desserts, fish and aspics, as well.

Salad or serving spoon. Larger than a tablespoon. For vegetables, berries, salads, puddings and casseroles.

Sugar spoon. Also great for thick sauces and relishes.

Sugar tongs. Go in the small ice bucket or on the candy dish, too.

Tablespoon. The indispensible, multi-purpose spoon.

Pierced tablespoon. For fruits and vegetables served in their juices.

Roast carving set. For slicing and serving large roasts, hams and poultry.

Steak set. Slightly smaller. For steaks, small roasts and poultry.

Courtesy of International Sterling

serving large roasts, hams and poultry, and/or a steak set for smaller roasts as well as for steaks will soon be on the needed list. Sugar tongs are a change from the regular sugar spoon.

TEA AND COFFEE SERVICE

A tea set includes a teapot (usually with an alcohol burner and stand), a cream pitcher, a sugar bowl, a tea caddy, and a bowl into which dregs of the teacups may be emptied. Sugar tongs or a spoon, a fork for serving lemon, and a strainer are needed, and all these should be placed on a tray.

A coffee set includes a coffeepot, a cream pitcher, and a sugar bowl, with sugar spoon, and all these should be placed on a tray. The tray should be large enough so that there is no crowding.

A tea and coffee set are usually combined, with the same sugar bowl and cream pitcher, sugar tongs, spoon, and tray useful for either service. There are three sizes of trays most useful in a household:

1. Eight-inch tray, used for serving one or two glasses of water or drinks.

2. Medium size 13-inch tray, for serving iced beverages, cocktails at small dinners and luncheons, or liqueurs at larger dinners, etc.

3. Large tray approximately 16 to 24 inches, for tea and coffee service. Useful for serving sandwiches, cakes, or at informal parties to place in a room with decanter and glasses or food for guests to serve themselves.

The coffee service usually is silver, with a matching teapot and accessories. However, many lovely teapots, sugars and creamers, are china, and both services may be of pewter, or the less expensive stainless steel.

CHAPTER 18

Seating Plans & Precedence

SEATING ARRANGEMENTS

It is customary at mixed dinners and luncheons that the high-ranking man sit at the right of the hostess, and his wife be seated at the right of the host. But at occasions governed by protocol, the high-ranking man is seated at the right of the hostess and the *high-ranking woman* is seated at the right of the host.

The high-ranking woman may be a Congresswoman or an admiral or general and not the wife of the high-ranking man. The second-ranking man is then seated to the left of the hostess and the second-ranking woman is to the host's left. The third-ranking woman sits at the right of the man of highest rank, the fourth woman is at the left of the man of second rank. Under this arrangement a hostess may find that a man would be seated alongside his wife, and since this is not done, it is the wife who is moved.

Unless they are officers or hold an official position of higher rank or title, women are seated according to the rank of their husbands.

Dinners for 6 or 10, 14 or 18, etc., are easily arranged, with the hosts sitting opposite each other and with married couples sitting by other guests. Women will not be sitting at the outside places, when such numbers of guests are at the table.

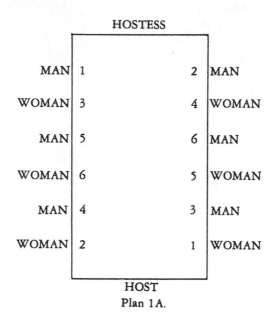

HOSTESS

MAN	1	2	MAN
WOMAN	3	4	WOMAN
MAN	5	6	MAN
WOMAN	6	5	WOMAN
MAN	4	3	MAN
WOMAN	2	1	WOMAN

HOST
Plan 1A.

The Traditional Arrangement

MULTIPLES OF FOUR

Any multiple of four—such as tables for 8, 12, 16, etc., means that the host and hostess cannot sit opposite each other without having to place two men or two women together when there is an equal number of each sex present. To avoid this, the hostess may relinquish her position at the end of the oblong or oval table and move one seat to the left, which places the male guest of honor opposite the host. When all couples are married, follow Plan 2A. When one couple is unmarried and they are seated together, use Plan 2B.

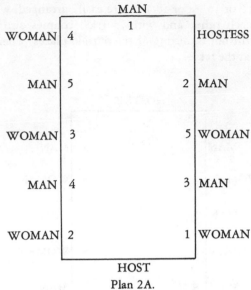

Plan 2A.

All couples married, seated apart.

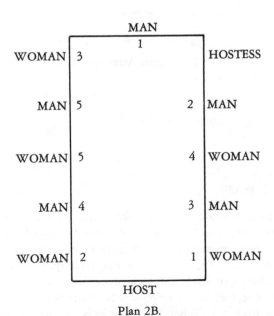

Plan 2B.

One couple unmarried, seated together.

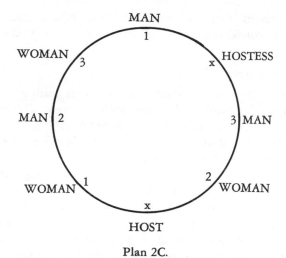

Plan 2C.

Round table for multiples of four, all couples married.

The round table is popular for both formal and informal luncheons and dinners. Although care must be exercised that women are not seated by each other at the more formal table, there is no problem about women having to sit at the ends of a table. There is a friendliness about a round table that appeals to young and old.

Hostesses have found that several round tables may be arranged for six or eight guests each, with the host at one table, the hostess at another, and co-hosts designated at any others. When protocol must be observed, some hostesses have ranking guests act as hosts at the various tables, thus strict protocol need not be followed.

Smaller round or oblong tables are usually set up in a banquet room, in addition to the head table for VIPs.

SEATING IN-LAWS

When the parents of a man or those of his wife are guests in their home, a man's mother or mother-in-law is seated to his right at the table, and his father or father-in-law is to the right of his wife.

When both sets of in-laws are on hand, his wife's mother is seated to his right, and his mother is seated to his left. His father is seated to his wife's right and her father is to her left. If many in-laws should be gathered together, such as at a holiday dinner, then the rule of seniority may be followed. When children are present, alternate them and the grandparents. Teen-agers may prefer to have a separate table.

If special guests have been invited to a dinner when both sets of parents are present, then the guests of honor take precedence—unless the parents are considered the guests of honor with the other guests invited to meet them.

SINGLE HOST OR HOSTESS

A single host or hostess may choose from several seating arrangements, depending upon the number of guests, their rank, etc. The high-ranking guests will be seated to the right of the host or hostess.

At a mixed luncheon or dinner, the host may ask a woman guest to act as hostess to balance the table when the number is not divided by four. In this case, Plan 1A may be followed, with the ranking male guest seated at the right of the guest-hostess.

The host may prefer to ask the ranking male guest to sit opposite him, when Plan 3A may be used. Plan 3B may be used when the ranking man and woman are not married to each other and the bachelor host does not want a hostess or co-host at a dinner divisible by four.

When a single woman entertains, the seating roles for women and men are exchanged in Plans 3A and 3B.

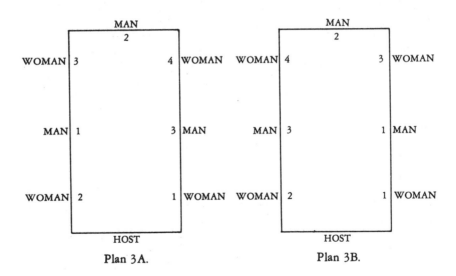

Plan 3A.   Plan 3B.

UNMARRIED WOMEN GUESTS

When a single man asks a young unmarried woman to be hostess or to assist at a luncheon or dinner party at his home or club, he should remember that this might be interpreted as a sign of intimacy of relationship when none is intended. When one particular young lady is asked to act as hostess, he should make certain that she leaves the party at the same time the other guests leave.

For a bachelor officer, the buffet style of entertaining is not only the easiest to plan and serve, but it also eliminates the necessity of a hostess at the table.

STAG DINNERS AND LUNCHEONS

A co-host is frequently appointed to assist the official host at a large stag dinner or luncheon. This is usually done in order to balance the rank at the official table.

CO-HOST

14.	10.	6.	2.		4.	8.	12.	16.
15.	11.	7.	3.		1.	5.	9.	13.

HOST

(Above) The co-host may be the next ranking guest after the guest of honor. If there are guests from foreign countries, as well as from the United States, the ranking United States guest could be appointed co-host. Foreign guests should be seated between guests of the host country.

Usually, the host and co-host sit opposite each other at the center of a long table. When there is no co-host, or when the dinner or luncheon is small, the host sits at the head of the table and the juniors at the foot.

SPEAKERS' TABLE

Tact and diplomacy are required in seating toastmaster and speakers at a banquet. The host or chairman will be seated at the center of the head table, with the guest of honor to his right and the second ranking guest to his left. The toastmaster is customarily at the left of the second ranking guest.

When very important nonmilitary guests are present, they may be seated in between the guests of official rank after the guest of honor and second official guest are seated.

When women attend and the speaker or guest of honor is a very

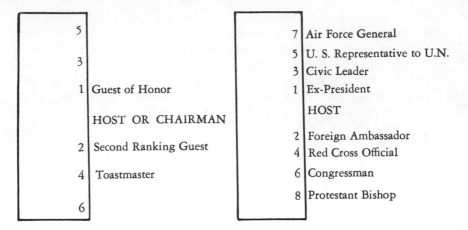

The customary banquet table.   The seating of distinguished guests.

important person, (number 1), the wife of the official host is seated in number 3 position, and the wife of the VIP is seated to the left of the official host in the number 2 chair. If the speaker is a lady, she is seated to the right of the official host or chairman, with the ranking lady to his left.

Should the main speaker or a guest of honor be outranked by others present, he need not be seated in seat 1, but it is correct to place him (or her) to the left of the official host in seat 2 or possibly seat 3.

Although guests are seated according to protocol at official/formal occasions, every effort must be made to place them according to congeniality. Juniors are customarily placed at the ends of the table, "with the salts and peppers."

CADET AND MIDSHIPMEN HOSTS

At the academies, when the cadets or midshipmen are the official hosts and high-ranking officers and their ladies are guests, there may be variations in seating arrangements. For example, at the formal ring banquet at West Point, where there always is a guest speaker, the chairman of the ring and crest committee (cadet) is host. To his right may be seated the superintendent's wife (1); the speaker (3); the dean's wife (5); the commandant (7). To his left are his date (2); the superintendent (4); the speaker's wife (6); the dean (8); the commandant's wife (9), and a nondating cadet member of the ring committee, which ensures no woman is seated at the end of the table. The number of guests at the table is increased or lessened as needed, but the multiple-of-four principle must be remembered.

It is desirable at all academies and colleges that young people learn how to be hosts. The Black, Gold, and Gray Room in Washington Hall at West Point is available to any group of cadets for organizational dinners, dining-ins, or special occasions. The round tables have chairs with academy crests, and table service includes silver flatware, Lenox china, and crystal wine and water goblets. The white plates have a black border centered with a gold emblem.

HORSESHOE TABLE

When horseshoe-shaped tables are used at large official banquets, the host and hostess will sit with their honor guests on the outside of the curving center. The other guests will sit down the sides.

When places are set both inside and outside the curving ends, the inside seats begin at the lower third section of the table, with the seats inside but nearer the host ranking those farther away on the outside. When the horseshoe has a prong, the *junior ranking guests* are seated on each side of it.

FORFEITURE OF POSITIONS

A host and hostess, with the exception of the President of the United States and the First Lady, relinquish their positions at the head and the end of their luncheon or dinner table is when their guest is a president or head of any country, a king or a queen.

Then, the reigning king or queen sits at the head of the table, and the wife or husband, respectively, at the other end of the table.

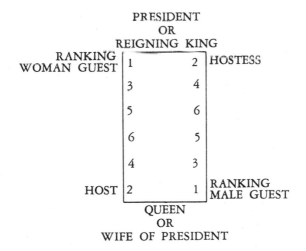

In order that they do not "give honor to themselves," the host and hostess sit to the *left* of the president or royalty, and their wives, respectively, with the high-ranking man and woman guests sitting at the *right* of the honored guests. This will place the high-ranking guests in the traditional guests of honor position.

At a men's or women's club luncheon or dinner, the ranking guests and club officers would be seated as follows:

x	Club officer
5	Guest
x	Club secretary
3	Guest
x	Honorary President
1	Guest
x	President
2	Guest
x	Club vice president
4	Guest
x	Club treasurer
6	Guest
x	Club officer

PLACE CARDS

Place cards are often used at the luncheon or dinner table, formal or informal, mainly as a matter of convenience in seating guests without confusion or according to protocol. Cards are of heavy plain white or cream-colored paper, with plain, gold, or silver beveled edges.

The cards are about 1½ by 2 inches, or 2 by 3 inches in size. The flag of an admiral or general, the seal of a ship or an embassy, or a family crest may be embossed or stamped in the top center or the upper left corner of the card.

The cards are customarily placed on top of the napkin in the place plate, or laid flat on the table above the plate.

Folded place cards are about 3 by 3¼ inches in size, and are folded in half, with the name written across the lower half of the card. They usually stand directly above the place plate.

Flat place card.   Standing or folded place card.

Names are written by hand on place cards, in black or dark blue ink. At formal occasions, names are usually written in script, such as "Mrs. Jones," "Colonel Smith," "The Ambassador of Norway," "The Secretary of the Army." At informal occasions first names are often used: "Marion," "Allan."

MENU CARDS

Menu cards may be used at official dinners, at state and public occasions, and occasionally in a home—such as for an anniversary dinner. A crest or coat of arms may be embossed at the top center of the card, which is of heavy white or cream-colored paper. An admiral's or general's flag or a seal is customarily used.

The card is about 4 by 5½ or 6 inches, with a gilded or silvered beveled edge. It is usually placed in a stand, or laid on the table. In homes, the cards may be placed in front of the host and hostess, and one for each three guests down each side of the formal table. They are placed about 6 inches above the plate.

The word "Menu" is written by hand in black ink beneath the crest, and one dish is written on each line centered directly underneath. The first letter on each line is capitalized and each course is separated by a space or asterisks.

Appetizers, bread, relishes, jellies, candy, and coffee are not written on the menu as they are on hotel menus. Menus for formal dinners are usually engraved in French, but on naval ships and in Army and Air Force messes—for instance at formal dinners in flag messes—they are printed, embossed, or handwritten in English.

Menus are frequently considered as souvenirs, such as those at the inaugural luncheon or at the Christmas dinners given annually at the academies.

PRECEDENCE IN ENTERTAINING

An officer of high rank, or one who serves with high-ranking officials, such as an attaché, must be well versed in local customs both at home and abroad. When serving abroad, consult the protocol section of the American Embassy. In Washington, you can get advice on problems of protocol in the foreign liaison section of the office of your service.

At nonofficial occasions, precedence at a dinner or luncheon is determined by the prominence of the guests, their age, and degree of friendship. In civilian life, age receives deference, as do professional and scholastic achievement.

In official life, strict protocol governs governmental, ecclesiastical, and diplomatic precedence, which has been established by international agreement. A younger official will precede an older official—if the office of the former is in a higher echelon.

When a person is the guest of honor at a dinner or luncheon, he or she may not be seated in the ranking position at the table—unless his or her rank justifies it, or if the higher-ranking guest concedes his position. When ambassadors and very high-ranking guests are present, guests are seated according to precedence—even though the guest of honor is seated down the table.

At times when you have to invite someone higher in rank than the guest of honor, you have these choices:

A. Ask the ranking guest to waive his or her right for the occasion in favor of the guest of honor.

B. Seat the guests according to precedence—although the guest or guests of honor are well down the table.

C. Have the senior guest co-host the party.

When nonranking guests are present at an official dinner or luncheon, their places at the table are determined by age, prominence, linguistic ability when foreigners are present, and congeniality. After the guests of honor and top officials have been seated, these nonranking guests are placed between those of official rank in the most congenial way for all concerned.

There are various ways in which a host and hostess may determine the equal seating of a number of high-ranking guests. For example, at a state dinner at the White House, three tables were arranged side by side with the President the host at one table, with the Chief Justice seated across from him; the First Lady was hostess at the second table, with the Speaker of the House beside her; and the Vice President was host at the third table.

MILITARY PRECEDENCE

Although the official governmental position of a man or woman is determined by election or appointment to the office, and the length of time served, in the military it is determined by promotion within the rank structure. Comparable rank and the date of its attainment is the basis for precedence among officers in all services, both here and in foreign countries.

A younger military officer precedes an older military officer—when the former's rank is higher.

A retired officer is ranked with but after an active-duty officer of the same grade.

Rank preempts the rule of "courtesy to the stranger." At an American dinner held in honor of a foreign officer, the latter would not sit in the guest of honor's chair when another foreign officer of higher rank is also a guest.

DIPLOMATIC PRECEDENCE

The precedence established in diplomatic life is the result of international agreement. The precedence of chiefs of missions depends upon the length of their service. An ambassador accredited in June precedes another appointed in October. An ambassador always precedes a minister who heads a legation.

Below the post of chargé d'affaires, the position of the mission is the base for precedence; in turn, this is determined by the ranking of its ambassador. A change of ambassador or minister of legation changes the relative positions of the entire staff.

Military (naval, air) attachés take precedence among themselves according to their respective grades and seniority of service. They rank after the counselors of embassy or legation; at a post where the Department of State has not assigned a counselor, they rank after the senior secretary. Assistant military attachés come after the lowest ranking second secretary.

PLANNING FOR THE VIP

The aide or officer who is designated to take care of local arrangements for the visit of a dignitary must carefully plan all details in advance. Sometimes a small detail is overlooked—to the consternation of all concerned. All plans should be made as early as possible. Information concerning the dignitary and his country, if he is a foreign VIP, should be studied, with reference notes close at hand.

The following suggestions should be followed:

1. Any reservations at hotels and restaurants should be in writing.

2. The dignitary should be met upon arrival and accompanied to his place of departure. A flag officer should be present at the arrival and departure of another flag officer.

3. Have a map of the area, and know the roads well. Make certain that all drivers of the official party are briefed on their schedules and know exactly where they are going, how to return, and just what to do should a car become separated from others in the party.

4. Allow time for any delays, such as travel to and from an airport, and baggage transfer.

5. Whenever possible, billeting should be provided for the local escort officer in the same building as that of the dignitary. Otherwise, he will need transportation.

6. If the schedule is a busy one, try to allow for breaks—such as sight-seeing, or time for a short rest.

7. Provide transportation, meals, and recreation for the aide or aides who accompany the dignitary. Usually they are officers of high rank, destined for future positions of authority in their country.

8. Aides are usually lodged in the BOQs, where room assignments should be made well in advance. The rooms should be in keeping with their standing as members of a dignitary's party.

9. When wives accompany the dignitaries, particularly foreign wives, advance plans must be made for their pleasure. There could be sightseeing trips, shopping, ladies' luncheons, teas, or brunches, which should be hosted by the wives of local dignitaries or officers of high rank, with other local or station wives attending.

ORDER OF RANK

The unofficial order of rank established by the White House and the Department of State for those in government service is as follows:

The President of the United States
The Vice-President of the United States
The Speaker of the House of Representatives
The Chief Justice of the United States
Former Presidents of the United States
The Secretary of State
Ambassadors of foreign powers
Widows of former Presidents of the United States

The Secretary-General of the United Nations
United States Representative to the United Nations
Ministers of foreign powers (chiefs of diplomatic missions)
Associate Justices of the Supreme Court of the United States and
     retired Associate Justices
The Secretary of the Treasury
The Secretary of Defense
The Attorney General
The Secretary of the Interior
The Secretary of Agriculture
The Secretary of Commerce
The Secretary of Labor
The Secretary of Health, Education, and Welfare
The Secretary of Housing and Urban Development
The Secretary of Transportation
Senators
*Governors of States
Acting heads of Executive Departments (in the absence of the Cabinet
     member)
Former Vice-Presidents of the United States
Members of the House of Representatives
Under Secretaries of State
Administrator, Agency of International Development
Director, United States Arms Control and Disarmament Agency
Chargés d'Affaires of foreign powers
Secretaries of the Army, the Navy, and the Air Force (ranked according
     to date of appointment)
Director, Bureau of the Budget
Chairman, Council of Economic Advisers
Chairman, Board of Governors, Federal Reserve
Under Secretaries of the Executive Department and Deputy Secretaries
Chairman, Joint Chiefs of Staff
Chiefs of Staff of the Army, the Navy, and the Air Force (ranked ac-
     cording to date of appointment)
Commandant of the Marine Corps
Five-Star Generals of the Army and Fleet Admirals
The Secretary-General, Organization of American States
Representatives to the Organization of American States
Director, Central Intelligence Agency

    * When in his own state the Governor of a state ranks directly under the
Vice President.

Administrator, General Services Administration
Director, United States Information Agency
Administrator, National Aeronautics and Space Administration
Chairman, the Atomic Energy Commission
Director, Defense Research and Engineering
Director, Office of Emergency Planning
Administrator, Federal Aviation Agency
Chairman, Civil Service Commission
Director, the Peace Corps
Special Assistants to the President
Deputy Under Secretaries of the Executive Departments
Assistant Secretaries of the Executive Departments
United States Chief of Protocol
Members of the Council of Economic Advisers
Active or Designate United States ambassadors and ministers (career
    rank, when in the United States)
Under Secretaries of the Army, the Navy, and the Air Force (ranked
    according to date of appointment)
Four-star generals and admirals
Assistant Secretaries of the Army, the Navy, and the Air Force (ranked
    according to date of appointment)
Lieutenant generals and vice admirals (three-star)
Ministers of foreign powers (serving in embassies, not accredited)
Deputy Assistant Secretaries of the Executive Departments
Counselors of embassies or legations of foreign powers
Major generals and rear admirals (two-star)
Brigadier generals and Commodores (one-star)
Assistant Chiefs of Protocol
The Secretary of the Senate

Since official posts and offices are frequently phased out or re-
organized with new titles, the above list is subject to change and the
foreign liaison section or the protocol section of your service should be
consulted for accuracy.

CHAPTER 19

Rules of Serving
at the Table

DUE TO THE general lack of help in the service household, the informal dinner is the most common and the formal seated dinner is more for senior officers and those who are attached to government agencies here or abroad. However, junior officers are promoted through the years, and someday may be host or hostess to a dignitary.

Today, four or five courses are served at the formal dinner; at the most elaborate, six courses are the maximum. Occasionally, when guests are going on to an official or social occasion such as a reception, lecture, or service ball, only three courses are served. When needed, food may be catered and waiters hired for the occasion.

For a formal dinner, two waiters are needed to serve 10 to 12 guests, not counting the cook in the kitchen. Two complete services (sets of serving dishes) are necessary. At a very formal dinner, one waiter serves each four guests. Almost twice the number of guests may be served with the same amount of help at a sit-down buffet, when the very nicest table appointments are used.

A waiter, or maid, can serve eight guests at a seated dinner of three courses in a home, but a hostess assists in serving at the table for a luncheon or dinner for 10 or 12, when there is help in the kitchen.

Many a versatile hostess serves a buffet supper for a dozen guests with no help, but this takes advance planning and food preparation, and an uncomplicated menu. No guest wants to see his hosts in a frenzied, exhausted condition—and no host wants to appear in such a condition. The hosts, too, should enjoy the party.

ESSENTIALS OF SERVICE

The service at the table must be efficient, quiet, and unobtrusive. Guests should not be rushed in eating, and there should be no long waits between courses.

Nothing is ever taken directly from the waiter's hand, or vice versa. Whatever it is, must be brought on a tray—a glass of water, etc.— with the tray held in the waiter's left hand, his right hand at his side.

Waiters, or a maid, address the host and male guests as "Sir" and the hostess and women guests as "Madam."

The waiter should wear a white coat, the maid a dark or conservative colored uniform with apron.

The woman at the right of the host is always served first and is always offered an untouched dish.

Everything is served at the very formal luncheon or dinner. Nothing is ever passed by the guest at the formal table.

RULES OF SERVICE

The rule of *informal* service is: Serve left, remove from the right. (An exception is the removal of the butter plate—from the left.)

The rule of *formal* service is: Serve left, remove from the left.

A waiter places one plate at a time at a formal luncheon or dinner. He places the plate in front of the guest, serving from the left, and he never reaches in front of a guest.

A waiter places two plates at a time at an informal dinner. He places one plate with his left hand to the left of the guest, then places the other plate with the right hand to the left of the next guest.

The serving dish is offered to the left of each guest at a comfortable level for serving. Dishes are offered with the waiter's left hand, with the right hand held close at his side or slightly behind his back. If the dish is very heavy it may be held with both hands.

The dish or platter rests on a folded napkin placed on the flat of the waiter's hand. At no time should he grasp the dish or platter by its rim.

A large serving spoon and fork are placed in each serving dish, face down, with the handles toward the guest.

At less formal meals, a waiter or maid may carry a serving dish in each hand, offering first the vegetable dish in his left hand, then the other vegetable dish in his right hand. The matching vegetable dishes may be placed on a tray and served to each guest, with the tray held on the left hand of the waiter. A vegetable (usually potatoes) may be placed on the meat platter.

Plates are removed after each course at luncheons or dinners when *all* guests have finished eating. Plates are removed at very large dinners or banquets after each guest has finished eating.

At a formal luncheon or dinner, the waiter holds the fresh-filled plate in his *right* hand while removing the used plate from the left of the guest with his left hand. The fresh plate is set down at the left of the guest.

At informal meals, to speed service, the waiter removes two plates at a time. After removing a used plate and a butter plate (or two used plates if butter plates are not used), he then brings back two fresh plates placing one with the right hand to the left of a guest and the other plate placed with the left hand to the left of the next guest.

Two waiters may work as a team in removing used plates, with the first waiter removing the used plate from the left, and placing it on the large tray carried by the second waiter. The first waiter takes a fresh plate from the tray, and places it before the guest, from the left side.

The table is cleared of crumbs before dessert, with the waiter holding a tray below the edge of the table, at the left of the guest. Crumbs, place cards, etc., are brushed into the tray with a folded napkin or table brush.

The order of removal at an informal luncheon or dinner is: plates, butter plates, serving dishes and platter, pepper, salt, bread tray, and crumbs.

ORDER OF SERVICE

At a dinner with *one service* (complete set of serving dishes) for six or eight guests, the woman at the right of the host is served first, then the host, then the woman at his left, and on clockwise around the table.

According to the placing of the table, and the location of the kitchen, the service may be counter-clockwise, always starting with the woman at the right of the host, then around the table, with the host served last.

At a dinner with *two services*, and from 12 to 16 guests, the *first* service should start with the woman at the right of the host and the *second* service with the woman seated to the right of the man at the right of the hostess.

When a very important man is guest of honor at the dinner, the second service may be started with the guest of honor at the right of the hostess.

When there are *three services*, and 18 to 22 guests, the *first* service goes to the woman at the right of the host, then clockwise; the *second* starts where the first leaves off (or after six servings), then the *third* takes up where the second leaves off. However, all services must be synchronized so that food is offered at about the same time.

At times it may be better to start one of the services (never the *first*) with a man. When there are 14 people, the man at the right of the hostess may be the first to be served at that end of the table, and when there are 20 persons, a service may start with the man at the left of the hostess.

A custom that is not practiced very often in this country, but that is observed in many foreign countries, including Latin America, is the serving of all women before the men. This is customary at very formal dinners and in most service messes. In this case, the woman on the right of the host is served first, then the woman on his left, and so on, ending with the hostess. Then the men are served in the same way, ending with the host. Men and women frequently leave the table together and go into the living room for demitasse.

COFFEE SERVICE

INFORMAL SERVICE

Coffee is served in several ways at informal luncheons and dinners. There are three main sizes of coffee cups: demitasse, or small cups used mainly after formal meals (but also after informal dinners); medium or teacup size for some less formal meals; and large cups for breakfast or family meals.

Coffee is frequently served at the informal table with, or following, dessert. At a family meal, with or without guests, coffee may be served throughout the meal. The coffee tray is usually prepared in advance, ready to be served by the hostess whenever needed. The tray may be placed on the sideboard, or the hostess may place the service on the table at her place, and serve each person. The cups may be passed down the table, after they are prepared with cream and sugar, or the cream and sugar may be passed around the table, with each person helping himself.

At informal luncheons or dinners, when there is a maid, she may place the coffee service before the hostess, who will pour and prepare each cup with cream and sugar. The cup may be passed around the table, or the maid may place it at each person's right.

The maid may place the coffeepot on a small tray, with an empty cup, sugar, and cream. She stands at each guest's right and asks his or her preference concerning sugar and cream, then places the cup at the right of the plate. Or the maid may stand at the left of each guest, with the guest helping himself to sugar and cream and placing the cup on the table himself. Additional cups will be on the sideboard convenient for serving.

The hostess may pour coffee in the living room, from a tray placed on a low table in front of her. She asks her guests their preference concerning cream and sugar, and hands each cup to the guests. The host may assist in handing the cups to the guests, or another woman guest may assist.

Before the coffee is served, the spoon is always placed on the saucer to the right of the cup handle.

FORMAL SERVICE

Demitasse is usually served in the living room to both men and women after formal luncheons, and after formal or informal dinners in a home.

Demitasse may be served in the living room to the women and at the dining table or in the library to the men, after formal dinners. There are a number of ways of doing this:

Two waiters work as a team, with the first waiter holding a small tray with a coffeepot, sugar and cream, and one cup. The second waiter follows with a large tray filled with cups and saucers. The first waiter asks each guest his preference for cream and sugar, then offers the cup on his small tray. Or the guest may help himself to cream and sugar.

The waiter has several cups on a tray, with cream and sugar, and stands before each guest who helps himself to cream and sugar.

At large occasions, the tray may be brought in with filled cups, cream, and sugar, with each guest helping himself.

TEA SERVICE

The serving of hot tea at the luncheon or informal table is similar to the service of coffee—except that the hostess invariably pours the tea. Although coffee is customarily served after luncheons and dinners, tea should be served to those who prefer it.

The maid may place the tea service in front of the hostess, or the hostess places the service on the table herself when there is no help. The hostess asks each guest his preference for lemon, cream, or sugar, then passes the cup down the table. The first cup goes to the woman at the right of the host.

When only one or two guests care for tea, the teapot, lemon, cream, and sugar would be placed on a tray and offered by a maid at the left of the guest, with the cup placed on the table at the guest's right.

When there is no help, the hostess may arrange a small tray and have the water hot before the meal, then quickly prepare the tea and serve it when neeeded.

Teaspoons are always placed on the saucer to the right of the cup handle before the tea is served.

COCKTAILS BEFORE MEALS

Cocktails may be offered before luncheons, and are customarily offered before dinner parties. Sherry, fruit juice, or tomato juice are usually offered on separate trays, the juice glasses being filled before brought into the living room.

There are several ways to serve cocktails before meals:

At formal or less formal occasions, the waiter may bring a large tray into the living room, with filled shakers and unfilled glasses. He will stand in front of each guest and ask if he wants a cocktail, then pour it. The guest takes the glass from the tray.

At more formal occasions, two waiters work as a team. The first waiter holds a tray with the shakers, and a second waiter follows with a tray with glasses for all drinks, and perhaps another shaker. The first waiter asks each guest what he wants, etc., and offers the drink on the small tray.

At large dinners, a tray of filled glasses is brought from the kitchen by the waiter, and offered to each guest.

When there is no help, the host may mix the cocktails in advance and place the tray with shakers and glasses in a convenient place in the living room before the guests arrive. The ice and the canapes (cocktail food) are brought in after the arrival of the first guests.

The host may prefer to place all ingredients on a large tray, and mix each drink upon the arrival of the guests.

SERVICE FOR WINES AND LIQUEURS

Wines are served at meals with the courses they accompany, with the first wine (usually sherry) poured after all guests have been seated and after some have been served. One wine is customary at an informal meal, but two may be offered. As many as four or five wines may be served at the very formal dinner, but two or three wines are customary. After the serving of sherry, champagne may be the only wine served throughout the formal dinner.

The waiter stands to the right of each person at the table, and pours the wine glass half or two-thirds full, according to the type of wine. An old custom is that a tablespoonful is poured first in the host's glass, in order that he determine the quality and clearness of the wine. Then the woman at the right of the host is served first, then the woman at the left of the host, and clockwise around the table. The glass of the host is filled last.

Wine glasses may remain on the table throughout the meal, except when three or four wines are to be served. In that case, the sherry glass is removed after the salad course. Wine glasses are refilled whenever empty.

Wines served at luncheons are lighter than those served at dinners. Sherry may be the only wine served at luncheons, or a white or red wine—sometimes both. Usually, red wines are decanted and the white wines are left in the bottle.

At informal meals, one bottle or decanter will serve each five or six guests, and a bottle or decanter may be placed at each end of the table for 10 or 12 guests. The host may fill the glass for the woman at his right, and at his left; then the bottle is passed around the table to his left.

Champagne may be served in the living room after a very formal dinner, or at a home wedding reception or dance. The bottles and empty glasses are placed on a tray, with a waiter pouring and serving each guest.

LIQUEURS

Liqueurs are customarily served after dinners, *not* luncheons. They are offered after formal and informal meals. They are customarily offered to both men and women in the living room, but may be served after a very formal dinner to the men at the table following the serving of coffee and cigars and cigarettes. Women are served in the living room.

The service for liqueurs is similar to that for cocktails at a formal dinner, with two waiters working as a team, with the first waiter holding a small tray and taking the liqueur and glass from a tray held by the second waiter.

At informal meals, the host or hostess serves liqueurs from a tray arranged beforehand with bottles and glasses.

CHAPTER 20

Duties of the Host
& Hostess

THE HOSTS

The "rule of thumb" at any party, formal or informal, is: good food, good conversation, and good company. The prime responsibility of the host and hostess is that guests enjoy the occasion. Not only must the food excel, but the guests must be congenial. An air of cold formality is to be avoided—even if the occasion is formal.

The host and hostess should be in the living room at least five or ten minutes before the luncheon or dinner hour, relaxed and ready to greet the guests. Each guest should be greeted warmly, but not effusively.

When incompatible personalities are brought together, a pleasant evening may be ruined. If it is unavoidable to have two such personalities at the same party, place them as far apart at a dining table as possible.

When a high-ranking person or dignitary is your guest, he must not be lionized to the extent that other guests feel neglected. Special respect is due guests in high position, but each guest must feel equally welcome.

As the host, you must talk with all guests during the course of the evening. You should move from group to group and make a special effort to introduce newcomers or a single or shy individual into small groups. Bring persons of less rank or position to meet the person of high rank, or the guest of honor.

A good host will "hear all and see all." You should notice when a guest is left out of a group, or when he or she seems bored. Come to the assistance of a guest who cannot gracefully move away from a bore. You should be careful of interrupting a group that is obviously congenial and enjoying themselves—but interrupt a group when the conversation has become controversial and particularly if the discussion is to the discredit of another guest or person.

A good host should try to anticipate his guests' needs, but never be over-anxious or too casual. A host should not insist that a guest have another drink or more food when he refuses. You may offer again, but allow a little time to elapse. Never urge a guest to have "just one more drink," and if a guest does not drink at all, never make a joke of it or point it out to other guests. Instead, offer any soft drinks that you have without comment.

When something goes wrong—when the food is burned, for instance, or when you run out of ginger ale—do not apologize profusely. Never apologize because your quarters are small and the food not elaborate. Don't discredit your hospitality by continually belittling it. Guests should not feel forced to reassure their host that the evening *is* wonderful and the food *is* superb.

At a buffet meal, when plates must be balanced in guests' laps, a wise hostess avoids serving food that must be cut with a knife. The hostess should always have a little food on her plate so that she can keep pace with the slowest eater.

Before the party, the host and hostess plan what guests will do following the meal. Bridge, charades, or dancing are frequently enjoyed, but many hosts prefer that guests continue in conversational groups.

THE GUESTS

As a guest, you owe it to your host and hostess to be congenial and to mix and talk with other guests at the luncheon or dinner party—or any social occasion. Upon arrival and departure, shake hands with your host and hostess.

At sometime during the party, large or small, you should talk with your hosts for a short time, but do not monopolize their time. A congenial guest moves from group to group, conversing with as many other guests as possible.

When your luncheon or dinner partner is a stranger to you, there are many agreeable subjects with which to start and maintain a conversation—current plays, a best seller, a TV program. If your partner is in one of the services, you can always discuss the merits of a recent duty station. However, each guest must carry his or her share of the conversation with some "small talk" which does not include business or "shop."

If it is your misfortune to be seated at the table alongside someone whom you do not particularly care for, you must conceal your personal feelings. You are expected to talk with your partner at your right, but do not forget the person at your left.

THE LATE GUEST

The hostess must decide how long to wait for a late dinner or luncheon guest. When something is being served that may be spoiled by waiting, she may not be able to wait. Also, the hosts may be planning on going to a lecture or dance, and it would be impossible to wait for the late guest. Usually, a hostess will hold serving no longer than 15 minutes past the set time.

THE OBNOXIOUS GUEST

Although you should do everything within reason to make your guests comfortable, your hospitality should not be taken advantage of by a rude or unthinking guest. It is always difficult for the host to handle a situation in which a guest makes himself undesirable by coarse conversation or by too much drink, or by becoming insulting to another guest. In consideration of the other guests, this cannot be tolerated. You may tactfully introduce another subject of conversation or suggest to the insulting guest that you show him something in another room, and thus draw him away from the group where he is not desired.

If necessary, you may have to help the unwise drinker into another room, or ask a trusted friend to assist you or to drive him home.

Since you are responsible for whatever happens within your home, no guest should be made to feel embarrassed about anything. You should not discuss any such unpleasant incident with others—but you might think twice about inviting such a guest into your home again.

As host, you may have to speed on his—or her—way the dinner guest who stays too long. You can sometimes accomplish this by mentioning an early morning golf game, the next day's heavy duty, or an important conference. And again you may have to disentangle yourself from the guest who opens a new—and lengthy—conversation at the door after he has already said good-bye.

Concerning the friend who habitually "drops in" around mealtime, the host and hostess should feel no obligation to ask him to stay for the meal at times when this is inconvenient. The hostess, or host, may say, "We have already made plans for the evening or I'd ask you to join us. . . . Perhaps some other time."

BREAKING AN ENGAGEMENT

A guest should not break an engagement for a luncheon or dinner party, unless an emergency arises such as illness or a change of orders. A sudden whim not to go because "you don't want to" or because a better invitation has been received, is no excuse at all after an invitation has been accepted.

An acceptance or refusal of an invitation should be made as soon as possible. Immediately check your calendar and make certain that you have no other commitment on that date. An early reply gives the hostess time to call another person without making him feel like a last-minute replacement, although a person should not mind being a replacement. When you refuse an invitation, give the reason for the refusal.

EXTENDING INVITATIONS

An invitation is *not* extended by saying, "You must come to dinner with us sometime . . .", but it *is* extended by setting the date.

Junior officers are not expected to repay the hospitality of their seniors in the same style, but in a way that they can afford. Hospitality is not weighed by the dollar.

DO'S AND DON'TS

Although some of the following tips have been mentioned elsewhere, they are considered important enough to state again in order that they are not overlooked.

A thoughtful guest will offer assistance to the host or hostess when assistance seems needed, particularly in a servantless house, but do not insist. If your offer is accepted, go about it quietly but efficiently. You must never "do the honors" in another man's house.

A thoughtless guest is one who asks the hostess at the last minute if a friend may come along—thus upsetting the seating plan at a more formal table.

No one wants to make an error in the use of silver at the table, but do not worry about it if you do. And when you spill something, do not overapologize and make everyone else uncomfortable.

But if you break something of value, try to replace it as soon as possible. If you break a coffee cup, do not buy one in another pattern—it will be of little use to the hostess and a waste of money. You may, instead, send flowers and a note of apology to the hostess. The note should be brief but sincere, with an expression of regret concerning the mishap.

A guest should accept no more than one or two cocktails before dinner, and no more than one or two liqueurs after dinner. The guest who overindulges in drink is a problem to a host—and a nuisance to everyone else.

Do not take a lighted cigarette to the dining table, and *never* use a saucer or plate as an ashtray. Although it is customary to have cigarettes and ashtrays on the most formal dinner table, a hostess may prefer no smoking at the table, and therefore smoking is not appropriate until after dinner—or not at all, should the hosts be allergic to smoke and not permit it in their home.

When you invite a single woman as your guest, and she comes and leaves by taxi, she is responsible for her own transportation and the fare. Should you live in the suburbs, where most people arrive by car, it is considerate of you to ask a person living in her area to offer a ride. But guests of all ages and numbers should take care of their own conveyance.

It goes without saying that you should never call attention to poor service or poor food that is served, or discuss such things with other guests.

Your Table Manners

CHAPTER 21

Good Table Manners

GOOD TABLE MANNERS in the services are good table manners anywhere. Customs may vary abroad and in various parts of the United States, but good fundamentals in eating are generally the same. The proper use of table silver should be as easy and as familiar to you as the proper use of any mechanical device you consider important to your career.

Mealtime is the time for enjoyment, not only of foods but also the company of others. Pleasant conversation, coupled with the relaxation that comes with knowing what to do, will mean pleasure in dining any place— in a luxurious hotel, in a home, or at an embassy.

Good manners are not turned on or off, in accordance with the importance of the occasion or the individual, yet neither do they mean rigid formality. The desirable attitude at even the most formal occasion is *relaxed politeness*, plus the ability to make interesting "small talk."

But it takes everyday practice before manners at the table become easy and automatic. Poor manners at home will invariably mean poor manners in the mess or the commandant's quarters.

TABLE TRADITIONS

The modern-day use of table silver goes back to A.D. 1100, when the wife of an Italian nobleman introduced the two-tined fork into table usage in Venice, because she did not like to pick up meat with her fingers.

261

The use of forks was not entirely satisfactory, and their use spread but slowly, even in Italy where they had the blessing of the nobility. Complete acceptance of the fork came only with the Renaissance, which also ushered in the use of the table knife to displace the common hunting knife which every freeman carried at all times on his belt and used at the table for cutting.

France and England were slower in accepting these customs, and it was not until the mid-1600's that English craftsmen commenced the manufacture of table knives and forks, and then spoons. These utensils were made of silver, and were considered a rarity.

As a result of the scarcity of table silver, it fell to the lot of the English gentry to formulate the table manners of the land. It is from them that Americans inherit their table manners, modified somewhat by native American thought and customs.

The first table napkins made their appearance in Reims, France, in the court of Charles VII. They were used exclusively in the palaces of kings and princes, and from the early part of the fifteenth century, they were lace trimmed and intricately embroidered.

Later, in the seventeenth century, napkins were an important decorative part in table setting. They were folded and pleated to represent flowers, birds, fans, etc. Ornate foldings are still used occasionally in Europe, and it is claimed that there are 400 ways of folding napkins. In this country, however, a few simple foldings are preferred

MEALS

Dinner is the main meal of the day in the United States, when it is the evening meal except for Sundays and holidays. Luncheon is the everyday noon meal, and a light or informal evening meal is usually called supper. (In certain sections of this country, dinner is the noon meal and supper the evening meal.)

Suppers are also held after formal occasions, such as weddings, dances, receptions, etc., and may be served very late. Buffet meals served in the evening are referred to as suppers, never dinners—even when guests are in evening attire.

When abroad, remember that dinners in many countries are not served until 9 or 9:30 in the evening.

EATING CUSTOMS

You may use the American or continental way of eating, but the favored American custom is to hold the dinner fork in your left hand to pin down the food for cutting, and then to transfer the fork, tines up, to the right hand for the purpose of eating. The continental, or European, custom of eating is to transfer the food to the mouth from the fork while it is still held in the left hand, tines down. Either fashion is correct.

In the United States, the *knife* is always held in the right hand, with the handle in your palm and your index finger along the back of the blade. After using the knife, never put it down on the table. Place the knife across the upper half of the plate, or on the right side of the plate, with the blade facing in.

The *fork* is held in the left hand while being used with the knife to cut food. The handle of the fork will rest in your palm, with your index finger extending along the back.

At all other times, the fork is preferably held in the right hand, tines up, with the handle controlled by your thumb and first two fingers in a manner similar to holding a pencil. The end of the handle should extend out between your thumb and index finger.

After the fork is used, put it on the plate below the knife, or at the left, and parallel to the knife, with the handle at the right, and the tines up.

The *spoon* is held in the right hand in the same manner as the fork. Correctly, the only spoon to appear on the table at the beginning of a meal is a soup spoon—except at breakfast. However, a modern hostess frequently places the teaspoon or place spoon at the right of the knife at an informal or family meal.

The most commonly used spoon is the teaspoon. It is used at informal meals for desserts, tea, coffee, cereals, grapefruit, etc. The multi-purpose *place spoon* is slightly larger than the teaspoon and is used for desserts and cereals as well as for soup served in a soup bowl or bouillon cup at less formal meals and luncheons.

The *coffee spoon* is laid on its saucer after being used. When coffee is served in a mug, and there is a tablecloth or mat that would stain, the bowl of the spoon may be rested, tip down, on the rim of your butter or dinner plate.

The place knife, place fork, and place spoon are the most frequently used today.

The individual *butter knife* (sometimes called a *butter spreader*) is usually laid across the top of the butter plate, with the handle at the right, the blade facing the edge of the table. The individual butter knife is used only to spread butter on a piece of bread. It is not used to take butter from the butter plate. A knife for that purpose is placed on the butter dish—when such a dish is used. The individual butter knife is much smaller than a dinner knife.

The *salad fork* is shorter than the luncheon or dinner fork, and may be used for either a salad or dessert course. The placing of the fork depends upon the time the salad course will be served. When the salad is served after the main course, the fork is placed next to the plate on the left-hand side, and inside the place fork. When served as a first course, the salad fork is placed outside the luncheon or dinner fork. When there is no separate salad course and the fork is to be used for dessert, the fork is usually placed on the dessert plate.

A *seafood fork*, usually called an oyster fork, is much shorter and slimmer than the salad fork, and is placed at the right or outside of the spoon. Sometimes the tines of the seafood fork rest in the bowl of the spoon, with the handle of the fork placed even with the handle of the spoon.

The *dessert spoon* is longer than a teaspoon and is placed on the dessert plate at formal meals as well as at most informal meals. But the place spoon, most frequently used for dessert, and/or fork, may be placed on the table at the beginning of an informal meal. (See *illustration* next page.)

The *iced beverage spoon* (called iced tea spoon) is a long-handled spoon, and after being used is laid on the small service plate or coaster which should be placed under the iced beverage glass. However, when no such plate or coaster has been provided, and if this is not a luncheon where you could rest the spoon on the rim of your butter or luncheon plate, as you would with a spoon for the coffee mug, then leave the spoon in the glass and drink with the handle held against the far side with your finger. Then leave the spoon in the glass. This is awkward—but correct.

Soup spoons are longer than the dessert spoon or teaspoon, and are oval-bowled. In using a soup spoon, dip the spoon *away* from you and avoid scraping the bottom of the soup bowl. After the spoon is used, it is placed on the soup plate on the right-hand side.

Demitasse (coffee) spoons are used with small cups of after-dinner, or after-luncheon, coffee. They are usually about four inches long, and are customarily placed on the saucer when coffee is served.

The *serving fork and spoon* are placed on the platter or in the vegetable dish. These pieces are larger than the regular fork and spoon.

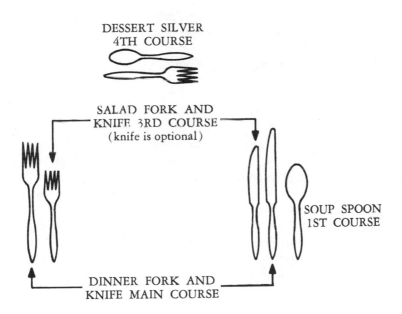

DESSERT SILVER
4TH COURSE

SALAD FORK AND
KNIFE 3RD COURSE
(knife is optional)

SOUP SPOON
1ST COURSE

DINNER FORK AND
KNIFE MAIN COURSE

In serving yourself, you hold these like other forks and spoons, with the fork in your left hand, the spoon in your right hand. Slip the spoon under a portion of food, and, while holding the food in place with the fork, transfer the food to your plate. Meats are usually portioned before serving, but if not, you cut the food with the spoon and transfer it to your plate with the fork and spoon. A pierced serving spoon permits liquids to drain from such vegetables as peas and corn.

Remember to use *table silver*, or *flatware* as it is called, beginning from the outside and working in toward the plate. There should never be more than three knives and three forks placed on the most formal table at any time. If more silver is needed, it should be brought in with the courses it accompanies.

A wide-rimmed *soup plate* is used at formal dinners, and *handled soup cups (bowls) or bouillon cups* at less formal meals and luncheons. The soup plate is placed on an underplate, with the rim of the under-plate showing about half an inch; you rest your soup spoon on this. You may use a soup (or place) spoon with the handled soup cup, and when cooled you may pick it up and drink from it.

Remember that *wines* are poured with the courses they accompany. It is correct to hold long-stemmed water goblets or wineglasses with the thumb and first two fingers at the base of the bowl. Small-stemmed glasses are held by the stems, and tumblers are held near the base. A brandy snifter is held in the palms of both hands to warm the liquor.

NAPKINS

Napkins are placed at the left of the forks at luncheons and informal meals, and on the place plate at formal meals. After you sit down at the table—and after grace has been said—place your napkin, half unfolded, in your lap as soon as your hostess takes up her napkin. To place the napkin smoothly, pick it up by the right top corners and spread in one motion across your lap.

At the end of the meal, replace the napkin *unfolded* at the left of your plate. At formal dinners, the napkin may be laid at the right of the plate. When paper napkins are used at informal meals, they are laid at the left of the plate, and when you are through with them, never crush them or roll them into a ball.

HOW TO EAT:

Artichokes are eaten by pulling off each leaf, with the base of the leaf dipped in a sauce and eaten. When down to the heart, you scrape or cut off the fuzz with a knife, then cut and eat the heart. Leaves are piled on the plate or butter plate.

Avocados, when halved, are eaten with a spoon. When peeled and served in a salad, they are eaten with a fork.

Bacon is eaten with a fork unless very crisp, then it is eaten with the fingers.

Cake is eaten with a fork when served as a dessert.

Caviar is served on small pieces of toast with cocktails, or in a bowl before dinner or at buffet suppers.

Cheese is frequently served at the table with the salad course. Cheese, fruit, and coffee are frequently served together as the final course, instead of dessert.

Chicken, broiled or fried, is held with the fork in the plate, while you strip the meat off the bones with your knife. Or, if not greasy, you may hold the chicken in your left hand against the plate, while you strip the meat off with the fork. At informal occasions, such as picnics, family meals, etc., fried chicken is eaten in the fingers.

Corn on the Cob is usually served only at informal meals, and may be held with the hands or by small spears inserted in each end. Salt, pepper, and butter are sometimes mixed in small pats or balls before the meal, or you can mix them yourself on the dinner plate before eating. Butter only a few rows of kernels at a time. Kernels may also be cut off the ear with the dinner knife.

Cream Puffs or Eclairs are eaten with a fork when served at the table.

Fish, unless served in pieces, is held in the plate with the fork while you slit it with the tip of the knife from head to tail. Insert the tip of the knife under the end of the backbone and lift out the skeleton. Lay the skeleton and bones on the side of the plate out of the way, or on plates provided by the host.

Frog Legs are eaten in the same manner as chicken.

Fresh Fruits (except citrus fruit) served at the table may be eaten either the American or continental way. Continental fashion is to skin the fruit, halve and stone it, then cut it into small pieces and eat these with the fork. The American way is to halve, quarter and stone the fruit with the knife and fork, but not skin it (except peaches); then you eat the quarters with your fingers or a fork. At a formal dinner, such fruit is always eaten with a fruit knife and fork. Fresh grapes and cherries are eaten whole. The pits are removed with the fingers and placed on the side of the plate.

Fruit compote (fruit cocktail), as any dessert fruit served in juice, is eaten with a spoon. Fruit served without juice, as in a salad, is eaten with a fork.

Grapefruit, or Oranges, are usually served in halves, and eaten with a
   fruit spoon or a teaspoon. Do no squeeze the fruit after eating.

Honey is taken by the spoonful. With a twisting motion of the serving
   spoon, catch any drops, then transfer the spoonful to the butter
   plate.

Ice Cream is served with a fork and/or spoon; the fork is for the solid
   part, the spoon for the softer. Ice cream is always eaten with a
   spoon when it is served in a sherbet glass.

Olives are held in the fingers while the flesh is eaten, and the stones are
   then placed on a butter plate. Small stuffed olives are eaten whole.

Oranges and Tangerines, served other than at the table, are peeled and
   held in the fingers, and segments eaten by hand; served at the
   table peeled in their juices, they are eaten with a spoon.

Onion Rings are eaten with a fork.

Pâté de Foie Gras, an imported paste made of goose livers, is frequently
   served on toast at cocktail parties, or with cocktails before dinner.
   Or you may find it placed in its own earthenware crock on a tray
   with a knife, and served at a buffet supper.

Pickles are held with the fingers and eaten when served with a sandwich,
   but are eaten with a fork when served with meat at a table.

Potato Chips are eaten with the fingers.

Potatoes, French fried, are eaten with the fork after being cut in shorter
   lengths, if necessary. Do not spear the potatoes with the fork, and
   then bite off pieces.

Radishes are placed on the side of the plate, or on the butter plate until
   you eat them.

Salad is cut and eaten with a fork. When iceberg lettuce is served, it may
   be cut with a knife and fork, then eaten with the fork.

Sandwiches are eaten by hand. The large or double-decker sandwiches
   may first be cut in half, then in quarter pieces, with a knife. They
   are then eaten by hand.

Seafoods are often eaten both with the fingers and with table silver, but
   usually with the latter.

Lobster and Hard-Shelled Crabs, boiled or broiled, demand dexterity.
   The major part of the meat is in the stomach cavity and the tail or
   claws. The claws of both the lobster and crabs demand careful—
   but similar—handling.

      For crabs, the general objective is the same as that for lob-
   sters. The best meat is in the large claws and the main body of the
   crab.

Oysters and Clams on the half shell are eaten raw, with an oyster fork.

They are lifted whole from the shell, sprinkled with lemon juice or dipped in cocktail sauce, and eaten in a single mouthful. When served as a first course, the half shells come to the table imbedded in cracked ice. Regardless of size, do not cut oysters or clams with your fork before eating them. Clams are usually served steamed, until the shell has opened. If not fully open, bend the shell back with fingers, then hold it in the left hand just over the dish and lift out the clam by its neck with your right hand. Pull the body of the clam out and discard the neck sheath. Hold the clam in your right hand, dip it whole in melted butter or broth, or both, and eat in one bite. You place the empty shells on the butter plate or on a dish especially provided for that purpose. Fried clams are eaten with a fork, since they are too greasy to hold. Clam broth is drunk in a separate bouillon cup or small bowl.

Shrimp, Oysters, Scallops, when fried, are eaten with a seafood fork. When shrimp are French fried, they may be held in the fingers by the tail, dipped in sauce, and eaten to the tail. Unshelled shrimp, which are never served with heads on, are held in the fingers, shelled, and eaten whole except for the end of the tail.

In shrimp cocktail, when the shrimp are very large and cannot be eaten one at a time, they may be cut in half with the side of the seafood fork. You would need to hold the stem of the glass with one hand while cutting the shrimp.

Spaghetti is twisted around the fork, cocoon fashion, and eaten from the fork tip. It is sometimes cut with the side of the fork before winding, but it is never bitten off.

Tortillas (thin Mexican corncakes) are laid flat on the left hand, or plate, and are filled with frijoles (kidney beans) or special sauce, as provided, then rolled and eaten from the end with the fingers.

Turkey (or poultry) is usually carved at the table by the host, and is eaten like chicken. There is an art in carving.

HOW TO CARVE

All men—and women too!—should know how to carve a roast or a turkey. Midshipmen, cadets, and junior officers should learn early how to carve—not knowing how is no excuse. The following illustrations should prove helpful.

Roast Beef may be carved at the table by the host, or it may be partially carved in the kitchen before being brought into the dining room. The carving of a rib roast is as follows:

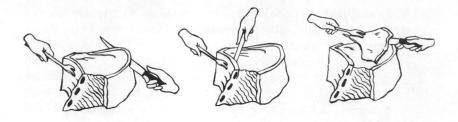

Turkey or Other Fowl:

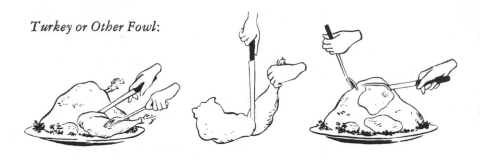

Ham:

Lamb:

How to Eat Lobster:

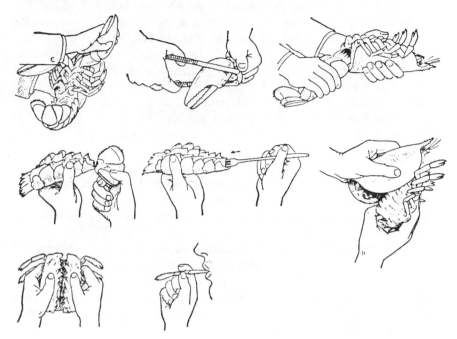

Courtesy State of Maine Department of Economic Development

EATING HABITS

There are many simple rules in eating that may seem elementary, but they are the rules by which you are judged. The difference between good or crude manners is the way you observe the following rules:

Do *not* talk with food in your mouth, make noises while eating or swallowing, chew food with your mouth open, or blow on hot liquids to cool them.

Avoid such unattractive eating habits as smacking your lips or taking too-large mouthfuls from food piled high on your fork. Use your napkin before drinking from a glass of water in order not to leave traces of food on the glass. Never lick your fingers after they have been in contact with food—use your napkin.

If something is out of reach at the table, do not rise out of your seat to obtain it, but ask for it to be passed. However, you may reach for anything you conveniently can without bothering your dinner partner.

Avoid curling your little finger on a cup handle—and be sure to remove the spoon from the cup after stirring and before drinking. Remember to place the spoon in the saucer, at the right of the cup handle, and not on the tablecloth. If the liquid seems hot, test it by sipping a spoonful—but do not continue drinking by spoonfuls.

You may tilt a soup plate away from you when almost empty, and you must remember to dip the spoon in the bowl *away* from you. Clear soup served in a cup or bowl with handles may be drunk. You must not place the bowl of the spoon in your mouth, but should sip somewhat from the side. Leave the spoon in the soup plate, *never* in the bouillon cup or cream soup bowl.

Bread and rolls are broken in half, and then into smaller pieces with the fingers. Do not cut breads with a knife. If butter is served, you butter each piece of bread before eating.

Jams and condiments go directly onto the butter plate, not onto the bread.

You must never place your elbows on the table while eating. Between courses, you may momentarily place your forearms on the table—if you do not turn your back on your dinner partner.

You should keep your elbows at your sides when cutting food; they move as easily up and down as sideways, and if held in, cannot hit your partner.

Do not slump at the table, but do not sit too rigidly or "at attention," either. Avoid twisting your feet around the chair legs or extending your legs under the table.

When finished eating, don't push back your plate—leave it where it was placed. Place your unfolded napkin at the left side of the plate—not in it.

Whenever you use your napkin, don't rub your lips—pat them.

TABLE TALK

Loud talk and laughter at the table are disturbing to others. The monopolized or too-intimate conversation between partners, to the exclusion of others, is equally impolite.

Be careful of controversial or unpleasant subjects, such as politics, religion, or death, and avoid talking "shop." Always remember not to discuss personal affairs or the opposite sex at the table, or before groups anywhere. Also, never criticize a senior in the mess or at any table.

Small talk—the pleasant, unofficial, interesting things in everyday living, such as plays or TV programs, bestsellers, the latest fashions, or your trip to Disney World—is always safe and noncontroversial.

DROPPED SILVERWARE

As a guest, when you drop a fork or spoon at the table, do not pick it up. When you obviously need another, ask the waiter for it, or the hostess—if she hasn't noticed your mishap. Do not apologize for the mistake. The less the incident is noticed, the better.

UNEXPECTED SITUATIONS

Common sense will dictate what to do in unexpected situations, such as uncontrolled coughing, choking, sneezing, blowing your nose, or when a foreign object is taken into your mouth.

When a sip of water does not help a fit of coughing, then leave the table. If you must sneeze, use your handkerchief, or your napkin.

Although it is better not to attend a dinner or any occasion when you have a cold, sometimes it is necessary that you attend unless you are quite ill, particularly at an official occasion. If you must use a handkerchief at the table, do so as unobtrusively as possible. If your cold is a serious one, it may be better to be excused from the table than to disturb the other guests.

Upon returning to the table, you need not apologize profusely, if at all. A murmured "sorry" may be said to the hostess, or in the general direction of the hostess at a long table. By apologizing or acting embarrassed over such a situation, you only draw attention to an incident that is best ignored.

Whenever possible, stay home and don't spread the germs.

CHOKING

When a person is choking on a piece of food, he needs help *immediately.* From the moment that something is lodged in the windpipe and cuts off oxygen, the victim has no more than four minutes to live. You do not have time to call a doctor. Such mishaps kill at least eight or nine Americans a day.

A choking victim while conscious—and he is conscious only a very short time—cannot speak and is in distress; he can nod his head when asked if he is choking. The beginnings of a heart attack are similar: the inability to breathe, growing pale, then turning blue, then unconsciousness.

The Heimlich Maneuver

A "bear hug" technique called the "Heimlich maneuver," named after the Cincinnati surgeon who devised it, has been endorsed by the American Medical Association. The following procedures should be memorized:

When the victim is standing or sitting: You stand behind him, wrap your arms around his waist, then make a fist with one of your hands and place it, thumb-side in, just above the victim's navel and just below the rib cage. You grasp the fist with your other hand and press into the victim's upper abdomen with a quick, upward thrust. Repeat several times, if necessary. Because there is always residual air trapped in the lungs, the sudden pressure forces the air upward and the obstruction is expelled.

When the victim is lying down: You place him face up and kneel astride his hips. With one of your hands on top of the other, place the heel of the bottom hand on the abdomen above the navel and below the rib cage. Press into the abdomen with a quick upward thrust.

When you are alone and choking: Press into a table or a sink—try anything that applies force just below your diaphragm. Or use your own fist.

If the maneuver costs a little internal damage or discomfort, it is nothing in comparison to saving a life—maybe your own.

CHAPTER 22

Dining in Public Places

SELECTING A RESTAURANT

Restaurants in the United States vary in as many ways as American ingenuity can express itself. They range from the milkshake-and-hamburger spots to expensive supper clubs. Hotel dining rooms and coffee shops cater to the most particular gourmet as well as the man who eats and runs.

There is an adage to the effect that experience is the best teacher. For the average man, it is good that experience has a few foundation stones on which to build. Mainly, you should remember that the more elaborate or formal the restaurant, the higher the bill and the slower the service.

You should learn something about the restaurant before entering its doors. In a strange city or in a foreign country, guide books will give such information. You can always ask a bell captain in a reputable hotel—regardless of whether you are staying there—about a good place to eat, and the approximate cost. You can mention the type of place you have in mind, inquire if there is music and dancing, and state that you like seafood or Italian food, etc. When money is an important consideration, you had better find out in advance whether or not a supper club has a cover charge. In order to ensure your getting a table at a well-patronized eating place, it is advisable that you make a reservation in advance.

When making a cross-country trip, quick information concerning good eating places can be found in excellent and inexpensive books or pamphlets which may be purchased in almost any drug store, or in travel guides put out by chain hotels or motels.

ENTERING THE RESTAURANT

You may check your coat and hat or a package at a restaurant, hotel, or supper club. Frequently, women prefer to wear their coats into the dining room and lay them across the backs of their chairs. Wait at the entrance of the dining room until the headwaiter comes up, and then ask, "Have you a table for two?"—or any desired number. You may tell the headwaiter where you would like to be seated, but when there is a crowd you may not get what you want.

Women precede the men and follow the headwaiter to the table. When there is no headwaiter or hostess, a man goes first to find a table. In a mixed group of several couples, the women are given the desirable seats, which usually are those facing the room at large or any view that is offered. Usually, the preferable seats are away from the aisle. At tables in an open space, women sit opposite each other; at banquettes or wall tables, they usually sit in the wall or inboard seats. As a small table for two, the man sits across from the woman, or by her at a banquette.

A man should help a woman with her coat by laying it over the chair back, or stand by while the waiter does this.

ORDERING

In most restaurants there are two methods of ordering a dinner: *table d'hôte* and *à la carte*. The first method means paying a single price for the complete meal as outlined on the menu. The second method involves paying a specific price for *each* item ordered. If a complete dinner is desired, it is more economical to order *table d'hôte*. Ordering *à la carte* is always more expensive, but also more selective; you get what you want.

The host will perhaps make suggestions to his guest or guests concerning the ordering of the dinner, such as "I understand that the chicken tetrazzini is excellent here. Do you care to try it?" or "Seafood is their specialty. Do you care for lobster?" Regardless of suggestions, the host always asks his guests, "What would you like?"

When a man takes a lady out to lunch or dinner, she may tell him what she wants, and then he places both orders. When you are host to a group, your guests will tell the waiter what they want, and sometimes how they wish certain dishes prepared—steaks well done, rare, etc. Dessert and coffee are usually ordered following the main course, when the waiter again brings menus for everyone to study.

Depending upon the part of the country you are in, the size of the city, and the type of restaurant involved, many different menus are encountered which may list local dishes, or menus entirely in French, or foods which are completely disguised. When you do not know what the dish may be, ask the waiter.

Most menus for a complete dinner include soup or tomato or fruit juice, or shrimp or fruit cocktail; a main course (or entrée) of meat and two vegetables, plus salad, dessert, and coffee. When a date accompanies a junior officer, it is to be hoped that she is aware of his financial status, but a young man should not ask someone to have dinner with him in an unknown restaurant *unless he is solvent.*

When you are host to a large group at dinner or luncheon, it is best to order the menu in advance. You may always telephone, but when you have time it is wise to talk with the headwaiter personally and make all plans in advance. The guests accept what is placed before them at such a dinner or luncheon, and there is little effort for a host and/or hostess.

WAITERS

A good waiter or waitress will give a couple or a group time to study the menu and determine what they care to order. But you should always remember that every waiter or waitress is a human being, and a little consideration toward them may prove the difference between good or indifferent service.

You address a waiter as "*Waiter*," not "*Hey you!*" or "*Boy*," and a waitress as "*Waitress*," or "*Miss*" (but you *never* address a waiter as "Sir.") In speaking to the waiter, a man refers to his guest as "the lady." When the waiter or waitress is busy, do not attract their attention by clapping your hands, drumming on the table with silverware, or hissing. When a waiter passes nearby, within hearing distance but fails to notice you, you may call "Waiter!" in a clear tone—but don't bark an order for attention.

The host should make any complaints concerning improperly prepared or served food, or when a mistake of any consequence has been made in the order. A very small error is not worth mentioning, but when anything of importance needs correcting, you do so quietly, but with firmness. Mistakes do happen, but they may not be the fault of the waiter who serves the food but does not prepare it.

If the waiter assigned to your table disappears continuously, or takes too long to serve you, this may be mentioned to the headwaiter. But do not lose your temper and shout or create a scene.

SHOULD YOU STAY?

After you have been seated at a table in a restaurant and you look at the menu and see that what you want is not listed or that you cannot afford the prices, you may get up and leave *if* you have not used any of the flatware or touched the water goblet or napkin or disarranged anything. Should the water goblet have been filled and bread or crackers placed on the table, you should leave a small tip and explain to the waiter why you are not staying, and go.

But if you have taken a sip of water or used the napkin, then order the least expensive item on the menu—and look more carefully next time, and be sure that you have enough money.

PAYING THE BILL

When it is time to leave, you quietly say to the waiter. "The check, please." The waiter may bring the check on a small tray, with the check face down, and set the tray by the host or whoever did the ordering. In a small eating place, the check may be laid on the table face down. The host or hostess will look at the bill long enough to see if it is correct, and then place the money on the tray.

The waiter will take the tray to the cashier and return any change; you usually leave this for the tip, deducting or adding to the sum as necessary. Or, in small eating places where the bill states, "Please pay the cashier," the host (or hostess) takes the check directly to the cashier and pays there. In this case, be sure you leave a suitable tip on the table for your waiter or waitress.

Tips customarily are 15 *percent* of the entire check. Pennies should not be left and it is better to avoid quantities of small change, like nickels and dimes.

If you should find an error in the check (other than a few cents), call this to the attention of your waiter. If he insists that the bill is correct—when you are certain that it is not—you may discuss this matter with the headwaiter, the cashier, or the manager. After all, it is your money that is involved.

When a stag or mixed group goes "Dutch treat," one person may be designated beforehand to pay the check, with others in the party settling up later. This avoids the clutter of paying at the dinner table, but it is inexcusable for anyone to forget to settle accounts immediately afterward with the one who paid.

If you are a guest at a dinner held in a hotel or restaurant, you should not offer to help your host or hostess pay the bill. Instead, repay such hospitality later with a dinner or similar social occasion of your own.

RESTAURANT MANNERS

Although a man should rise to his feet when a woman stops to chat at his table, this can be awkward to do, as well as inconsiderate of others at a crowded table. He need not rise completely to his feet under such crowded conditions, even when introductions are underway. A half-rise, or a brief attempt to rise, is acceptable. Ladies seated at the table may give a slight inclination of their heads, accompanied by a smile. Service-women do not rise when a senior stops by.

It is thoughtless of anyone to stop and talk at a table when hot or very cold food is before those eating. It is better just to nod or speak and then go on your way; later you can talk briefly with your friends during a lull in the service, or over coffee. When someone stops at your table, you need not ask him to sit down unless you and your guests so desire.

Do not rise when the restaurant hostess stops at the table to inquire about the service and the quality of your food. This is a courteous, business gesture—not social.

In any public eating place, you should never wipe the silver with your napkin; if it appears unclean, ask the waiter for fresh silver. When you drop a piece of silver or a napkin, leave it alone and ask for another. Do not write or chart a course on the tablecloth, and avoid cluttering up the floor space with your feet or bundles.

THE SINGLE WOMAN HOSTESS

In this day and age of equality between men and women, a man should not feel embarrassed when a woman invites him to dine with her in a restaurant—and makes it clear that *she* is the hostess and will pay the check.

If she knows him well, she might suggest giving him the money for the check before they enter the restaurant. He would, of course, return any money left over.

An easy way to pay for the dinner would be to use a credit card acceptable to the restaurant, say a Diner's Club Card. But if she prefers to pay cash, then she can find out how much the dinner will probably cost when she makes the reservation; at that time she could also make it clear to the person at the reservation desk that she will be the hostess and for the waiter to give her the check.

Should the check be paid for at the table, then she should have some large bills handy in her purse, and with a bit of adeptness place the money on the plate that the waiter places on the table.

When a single woman invites a married couple for dinner in a restaurant, again she must make it clearly understood beforehand that she is the hostess and they are her guests. Should the man insist upon paying the check (and this is very poor manners on his part since he knows who is hostess and he is making too much of the money angle) then she must be firm and point out that "This was my invitation and you are my guests."

When women dine together, it is best to "go Dutch" and ask the waiter for separate checks when ordering. This will save considerable time and confusion.

CHAPTER 23

Toasts

THE CUSTOM OF "TOASTING" goes back to ancient times when a piece of toast was placed in the goblet with the mead, or any alcoholic brew. When it became saturated the toast sank to the bottom of the goblet and after someone challenged "Toast!" it was necessary to drain the goblet in order to get to the toast.

Nowadays, one does not drain a glass of champagne or wine —the favorites for toasts. On the contrary, you take only a sip or two so there will be plenty of wine left for other toasts. Upon informal occasions, however, almost any liquid at hand may be used when making a toast: it is the occasion—the words of love or appreciation or respect which are shown the person toasted—that is important.

It is disrespectful for anyone not to participate in a toast. A teetotaler need only go through the motions of holding the glass to his lips.

Toasts are given upon various occasions—at wedding receptions, bachelor dinners, birthday parties, christenings, engagement parties, dinners, anniversaries, a dining-in, or a wetting-down party. A dining-in is a formal dinner given by a wing or unit or a military organization. A wetting-down is an informal party held in celebration of an advancement in rank in the services.

THE MECHANICS OF A TOAST

When you are the one receiving the toast at a table, you remain seated while everyone else stands and you do not sip your drink—or you will be drinking to yourself. After everyone else sits down, you may rise and thank them and offer a toast in return. A woman may respond with a toast or she may remain seated, smile at the person who toasted her and raise her glass in a gesture of "Thanks, and here's to you."

At formal occasions a toastmaster will propose the toasts. At a dining-in, it will be "Mr. Vice." A very high-ranking officer or a dignitary of church or state does not always return a toast; he may make a slight bow in recognition of the honor and remain seated while others stand. At less formal occasions anyone can propose a toast.

Toasts are generally given at the end of a meal, during or after dessert as soon as the wine or champagne is served and before any speeches are made.

When you are the one making the toasts at a formal occasion, you must be well prepared. You must have advance information about the person or persons to be toasted in order that your remarks are pertinent and related to the individual, and are accurate. If he or she is a close friend you may make a more personal remark.

When you tell an amusing story or joke, don't laugh at it yourself —allow your audience to appreciate it. Unless you are adept at dialects, avoid them.

Never tell a story or joke which may reflect adversely upon the person toasted, intentionally or otherwise. Anything that gibes another is out. Always, a toast must be brief. A toast is not a speech.

SAMPLE TOASTS

At an informal *engagement party*, given by the parents of the engaged girl (or a close member of her family if her parents are not living), the father proposes a toast to his daughter after all guests have arrived and have been served champagne or another wine. He calls for attention and raises his glass, saying words to this effect: "To my daughter, Susan, and my future son-in-law, William Smith. Let's drink to their happiness." Or, "I would like to have you join me in welcoming a new member to our family. To Susan and her fiancé, William Smith." The couple smile and, if seated, remain seated. Then the future bridegroom proposes a toast to his fiancée's family: "To Susan and her very wonderful parents."

At a *wedding reception*, the first toast is always offered by the best man and is always a toast to the bride and groom. For example: "I propose a toast to the bride and groom. Congratulations and best wishes." The couple may accept the toast by smiling and remaining seated.

When the bridegroom makes a toast to his bride he might say, "I want you to join me in this toast to Mary who has just made me the happiest man in the world."

At a reception where all guests are seated at tables, the third toast at the bride's table may be proposed by the groom to the bride's mother, with other toasts to the bridesmaids.

At a reception where everyone stands, the bride and groom cut the cake and eat the first piece; then everybody else has a piece of cake, and the toasts begin.

At a *bachelor dinner* given by a groom for his ushers (*See* Chapter 26, Military & Civilian Weddings), the groom's toast to the bride traditionally is, "To the bride." He will rise to his feet when giving the toast, and all others at the table will also rise to their feet.

At a *small dinner* a toast may be proposed by anyone as soon as the first wine has been served, and guests stand only if the person giving the toast stands. More than one toast may be drunk with the same glass of wine, and you may informally say, "To your health," or "Your health." You might say "Many happy returns" at a birthday party.

At a *child's baptism*, the toast to the child's health and prosperity is given during the reception, luncheon, or tea which usually follows the baptismal ceremony. The toast is proposed by the child's godfather.

ARMY TOAST

The traditional old Army toast "How" in drinking to one's health is equivalent to "Cheers." One story has it that during the Seminole War in Florida in 1841, Chief Coacoochee tried to imitate the officers' toasts by shouting "Hough!" Officers of the 8th Infantry and the 2nd Dragoons picked it up, and thus the custom spread throughout the Army.

CEREMONIAL TOASTS

All American officers should be familiar with the international customs observed when toasts are exchanged on board foreign ships or in foreign messes ashore, or at official dinners or luncheons given in honor of visiting dignitaries.

On these occasions, toward the end of the meal, the host—or the highest official of his country present—proposes a standing toast to the head of state (Sovereign or President) of the guest's country. This toast is customarily followed by the national anthem of the country concerned. The highest-ranking foreign guest then responds with a toast to the ruler of the host country, followed by its national anthem.

The preliminary ceremonial toasts may be succeeded by toasts to the countries or services represented. The order and subjects of all toasts should be previously agreed upon so that the host and guests will know what is expected of them. All present drink to a ruler or country, but they do not drink toasts proposed to themselves or to their own services.

When the guests represent more than one nation, the host proposes a collective toast to the heads of their several states, naming them in the order of the seniority of the representatives present.

To this collective toast the highest-ranking foreign officer present will respond on behalf of all guests by proposing the health of the head of state of the host.

Occasions and toasts typical of certain countries are given in the next few paragraphs.

BRITISH CUSTOMS

An an official dinner given by a British officer to an American officer, the British officer rises during or after dessert to toast the President of the United States, and then the orchestra plays "The Star-Spangled Banner." After the guests are seated, the American officer rises to toast "Her Majesty, Queen Elizabeth II," and the orchestra plays "God Save the Queen." These toasts are sometimes followed by short speeches and toasts to the services represented.

At regular mess dinners in the British armed services, the senior member of the mess proposes the toast, "The Queen," and all members in a low voice repeat "The Queen," and sip the toast. If an American officer should be a personal dinner guest in a mess where a toast to the Queen is drunk every night, the mess president might propose a toast to the corresponding U.S. service after the usual toast to the Queen.

The proper reply by the American officer then would be a toast to the corresponding British service. At official dinners, the British officer would toast "The President of the United States," and the senior American would reply with a toast "To Her Majesty, Queen Elizabeth II."

Officers of the Royal Navy have the unique and traditional privilege of remaining seated when toasting their sovereign at mess, although those serving in the royal yacht choose to rise.

FRENCH AND ITALIAN CUSTOMS

Officers of these services are more likely to begin a toast with the phrase, "I have the honor, etc." At a dinner for a senior American officer, the French host would probably say, "I have the honor to propose a toast to the President of the United States," and the American officer might reply with the toast, "It is my great honor to propose a toast to the President of the Republic of France."

SCANDINAVIAN CUSTOMS

In the Scandinavian countries ceremonial toasts are not customary, but instead the host "skoals" (toasts) each individual guest. No one drinks any wine at the table until after the host has made a general skoal welcoming all the guests. Then skoaling proceeds all during the meal, and women in particular must be on the alert to respond to individual skoals from the men.

Each man is supposed to skoal the woman sitting at his right at least once. The procedure is for him to raise his glass slightly from the table, and looking straight into his partner's eyes draw the glass down and toward his body, bow slightly, say "Skoal" and drink—not forgetting to salute again with his glass before putting it down. This skoal must be returned a few minutes later.

During the dinner the host and hostess are supposed to skoal everyone around the table, but it is incorrect for guests to toast them immediately. At the end of the meal, the guest of honor (seated at the left of the hostess in Scandinavian countries) makes a little speech of thanks, and skoals the host and hostess on behalf of all the guests, who join in this skoal.

JAPANESE CUSTOMS

At a Japanese dinner the customary procedure is all but reversed. The host, before dinner is begun, welcomes and toasts the guests from a seated position. The senior guest replies and thanks the host. Throughout the dinner, individual toasts are given. One person will pick up his cup, catch the eye of the one he is toasting, and both will drink but remain seated.

Toasts may be drunk with soft drinks, tea, sake, beer, etc. The important thing is to return the toast.

"TO YOUR HEALTH"

It is well to know the most simple form of toasting when abroad. The following examples mean "To Your Health":

French—A votre santé.
German—Prosit.
Spanish—Salud.
Swedish—Skoal.
Hebrew—L'Chaim (to life).
Greek—Is tin egian sou.

You should find out about the smoking customs in various countries, where there is much less smoking at meals than in this country. Or, allow the host or hostess to make the first move toward offering cigarettes at the table.

At a formal occasion, such as one held in England, there is no smoking before the "Queen's toast."

All About Weddings

CHAPTER 24

Planning the Wedding

THROUGHOUT THE COURSE of your service career you will be called upon to take part in weddings. You may be an usher or the best man, the maid or matron of honor. Perhaps the wedding will be your own. It is difficult, sometimes, for officers at sea or at some remote base, post, or station to obtain the correct and detailed information concerning wedding ceremonies, and what is expected of the ushers or bridesmaids.

The military wedding is like other weddings— except that the officers in the bridal party are in uniform, and the bride and groom usually leave the chapel or church under the traditional arch of swords (sabers). The groom's sword is used by the bride to cut the first piece of cake at the wedding reception.

The uniform worn should be in accordance with the kind of wedding planned—formal or informal—and with the season of the year. Evening dress uniform may be worn at the very formal wedding, and dinner or mess dress uniform at the less formal. Dress blues or whites are worn at informal weddings. Boutonnieres (or corsages) are never worn with uniforms.

The arch of swords takes place immediately following the ceremony—preferably when the couple leaves the chapel or church, on the steps or walk. The arch may be formed inside the chapel or church, upon leaving the chancel, *but this depends upon the religious convictions of the officiating chaplain or clergyman.* Ushers' swords (sabers) are un-buckled and left in a side room until after the religious ceremony, when they are buckled on in preparation for the arch of swords.

Since a church is a sanctuary, the arch is formed *with permission* inside chapels and churches. In case of bad weather, the arch may be formed in the vestibule.

ENGAGEMENT ANNOUNCEMENT

A formal engagement is announced by the bride-elect's parents, or closest relative, usually between six weeks and six months before the wedding date (the future groom's orders may determine the length of the engagement). Such an announcement is frequently made at a reception, tea, or some social occasion.

The parents of the bridegroom-elect should call on the family of the bride-to-be before the engagement is announced. If the family lives in a distant city, a note should be written or a phone call made to them. The bride-elect should, by note or voice, be cordially welcomed into the family.

In order to inform friends in a widespread area of the engagement —particularly service personnel who are in a constant state of transfer and whose new duty stations may not immediately be known—it is helpful to have the announcement published in a newspaper.

When the announcement is sent to a newspaper to be printed by a certain date—but not before that date—then state the date of release at the top left of the announcement, FOR RELEASE MONDAY, MARCH 15. The account should be signed by the mother or closest relative, for purposes of authenticity. For example:

Capt. John James Smith, USN (Ret.) and Mrs. Smith of Baltimore, Md., announce the engagement of their daughter, Mary Ann, to Ens. Donald James Adams, USN, son of Mr. and Mrs. William Claton Adams of St. Louis, Mo.

Miss Smith was graduated from Wellesley College, and made her debut at the Bachelors Cotillon in Baltimore. Ensign Adams attended Gilman School and was graduated from the U.S. Naval Academy, class of 1983. He is in flight training at Pensacola, Fla. The wedding will take place in December.

THE ENGAGEMENT RING

A man wants to give his prospective bride the nicest engagement ring that he can afford—but he should not go heavily in debt and take months to pay for it. A midshipman or cadet frequently gives his fiancée a miniature of his class ring, and ROTC college men give miniatures of their fraternity rings.

Frequently, a man will give a ring to his fiancée that has been in the family as a treasured keepsake, and this can be remounted if necessary. The girl wears the ring on her left hand, third finger. Following the wedding ceremony, the wedding ring is worn first.

ESSENTIALS OF A WEDDING

The essentials of planning a wedding are: (1) religious ceremony; (2) a father (brother, uncle, or any male relative of age) to give the bride away; (3) a best man for the groom; (4) an attendant for the bride; (5) a bouquet or corsage for the bride; (6) rings for the bride and groom (when he desires one); (7) a reception—if no more than a wedding cake and champagne or punch, tea, or coffee; (8) a wedding trip.

The most important thing to remember in planning a wedding is that the day belongs to the couple. The wedding should be what they truly desire, large or small, in a chapel or garden. Although the couple gives every consideration to the suggestions of the parents and others taking part in it, the decisions are primarily theirs.

The invitations should be ordered by the bride's family *six weeks* in advance of the wedding date, and they should be mailed out by the bride's family *three to four weeks* before the wedding day. Her family may send marriage announcements *after* the wedding takes place to those to whom invitations were not sent.

Usually, the bridegroom's parents and relatives have to travel to get to the wedding, and it is up to the bride's family to find lodging for them. Relatives and friends usually accommodate as many as possible; otherwise, rooms must be reserved in nearby motels or hotels.

It is up to the bridegroom's mother to let the bride's mother know how many will be arriving, and this should be done several weeks in advance. Unless they are financially hard up, those who use the rooms pay for them. Usually, luncheons and dinners are given by the bride's family and friends during the day or two the out-of-town guests are there.

THE CHAPLAIN

As in the case of all weddings, it is important that the engaged couple consult their chaplain (clergyman) before the wedding—as early as possible. When they are of mixed faith, or when the bride has been married previously, these facts must be brought to the attention of the chaplain or clergyman before the couple continue with their wedding plans.

He will advise you concerning such legal requirements as medical tests, obtaining the marriage license, and the signing of the Marriage Register.

Although chaplains prefer to officiate at ceremonies held in the chapel to which they are assigned, a clergyman from the couple's home church may assist at the ceremony—if this is acceptable to the chaplain and is so arranged beforehand. The officiating chaplain will be of the same faith as the couple. The chaplain, like the clergyman, is bound by his ordination vows to uphold the laws and regulations of his particular church regarding marriage.

Service chaplains are of many faiths, and as commissioned officers, they are subject to transfer. Therefore, customs change in the chapels and what is customary in one may not be in another.

Chaplains on active duty are paid by the service which they represent, and will not accept a fee. However, it is customary to offer any assisting civilian clergyman an honorarium, which the bridegroom pays. Since the amount varies, the prospective bridegroom should contact the office of the chaplain or clergyman to determine such fees, as well as those for an organist and soloist, if used.

CIVILIAN CLERGY

When a clergyman (minister, priest) assists the chaplain at a wedding, or when a clergyman officiates at a wedding in his own church, he receives a fee. This is handed to him by the best man in a sealed envelope before the ceremony, and is paid by the bridegroom or his or the bride's parents.

Fees vary throughout the country in accordance with local custom, the formality of the wedding, and the area. Fees usually are from $25 to $50, but in a large city may be $100. An assisting minister would receive less.

Other than chaplains, there are some faiths that do not permit their clergymen to accept fees, and this must be determined beforehand by the bridegroom. In such a case, remember that checks are written out to the church; otherwise when clergymen accept fees, they are written directly to them.

COUNSELING

The preparation for marriage includes much more than arranging for the ceremony. In uniform or in civilian life, a chaplain or clergyman will want to spend time in counseling the couple before the wedding takes place. Some denominations have special requirements related to preparation and counseling.

TIME OF THE WEDDING

The date and time of the wedding is decided by the couple and the bride's mother, but in the services the time is frequently a matter of convenience for the bridegroom. At the academies, June Week weddings are held according to the time chosen by drawings.

The most favored hour for a wedding differs in various sections of the country, with evening weddings perhaps held more frequently in the southern and southwestern states (probably due to the weather), and afternoon weddings often held at four, half-past four, or five o'clock, in northern and eastern states. High noon or half-past twelve is the favored hour for a morning wedding.

A formal wedding may be held in the daytime or in the evening— frequently at eight or half-past eight o'clock. The most formal wedding is one held in a church or chapel, but a formal wedding may also be held at home. Weddings—formal or informal—are held at almost any convenient hour of the day or evening.

Couples of various religious faiths should always discuss the time, day, and hour of their weddings with their chaplains or clergymen, priests, or rabbis, with particular concern for the Lenten season and holy days.

THE MILITARY CHAPEL

The chapel is reserved on a first-come, first-served basis. Permission for its use should be obtained as soon as possible, in order to secure the desired date and hour for your wedding. Whenever possible, applications should be made in writing to the chaplain's office months in advance of the event.

There is no charge for the use of the service chapel, but a donation to the chapel fund is expected. The fund is for the maintenance of candles, flowers, marriage books, music, and many other services provided by the chapel staff.

Although a chaplain never asks anyone to donate to the fund, it is their normal responsibility. The cost of the average wedding decorations in the academy chapels is forty dollars.

When the donation is made by check, it should be made out to the chapel or chapel fund, *not* to the chaplain. How much a bridegroom can give is determined by his circumstances.

JUNE WEEK WEDDINGS

Since June is the traditional month for weddings, it is advisable to make wedding dates earlier than usual for that month. June Week weddings are held in the chapels of all the service academies at scheduled times, for five days following graduation—on the hour in the main chapel and on the half-hour in the smaller chapels.

In order to schedule the many June Week weddings, forms are sent early in the year to all first classmen who plan marriage in the chapel, to be filled out and returned to the chaplain's office. Drawings are made for the scheduling.

The first wedding ceremony in the chapel will be performed early on the afternoon of graduation day. Ceremonies are also held in various churches in the academy communities. Photographers may take pictures after any chapel wedding, but never during the ceremony. Pictures are usually taken when the wedding party leaves the chapel under the arch of swords.

Rice and confetti are prohibited *inside* or *outside* the chapels. Wedding receptions are never held in the chapels—and no arrangements for them are ever made by the chapel staff.

Rooms for last-minute preparation are available for the bride and groom and their attendants, but there are no dressing rooms for either group.

ELIGIBILITY

To be eligible to be married in the chapel at any of the service academies, you should be a graduate, active or retired, or one of the following: a dependent; an officer or enlisted person assigned to the academy complex or your dependents; a faculty or staff member, active or retired, or your dependents who regularly attend chapel services.

CHURCHES OTHER THAN AT SERVICE ACADEMIES

Because of the many June weddings, it is also important to reserve time at *any* church as far in advance as possible.

THE MUSIC

Since traditional wedding ceremonies are religious ceremonies, the organist will play traditional wedding music and selections from the library of sacred music available in the chapel or church. The couple selects the music after consultation with the music director and chaplain.

It is customary but by no means obligatory for the bridal chorus from Wagner's *Lohengrin* and the wedding march from Mendelssohn's *Midsummer Night's Dream* to be played for the processional and recessional.

Less traditional music may be played in some churches, and a wide range is permitted in a few—but variations must be approved by the church organist or music director. No matter how modern the couple may be, some contemporary music is unsuitable for what should be a dignified occasion.

In the case of service weddings, when the organist is attached to the station, he receives no fee for his services. At other chapels, such as the Navy Chapel in Washington, D.C., the organist is a civilian and receives a fee for the wedding, and an additional fee when he attends the rehearsal. If the organist accompanies a soloist, there is an additional fee. Solos, if any, are always sung before the ceremony begins.

It is not necessary that the organist and soloist attend the wedding rehearsal, unless the couple so desires. The fees should be given to the organist and soloist at the rehearsal—or at some convenient time prior to the wedding. The bride's family pays for these fees.

FLOWERS AND DECORATIONS

Rules for decorating military chapels vary throughout the nation. At the academy chapels, flowers, candelabra, and white hangings are furnished by the Chapel Altar Guild and are the same for all weddings. Two vases of altar flowers are usually permitted. The altar flowers may be the only flowers used—where decorating the altar is permitted—at both informal and formal weddings. Sometimes the aisle posts or reserved pews are decorated, or greenery alone may be used in some churches and chapels.

Some chapels or churches do not furnish decorations, and if desired, they are arranged for by the bride's family. Any decorations which require alterations to the chapel or church (fastened to the pews or walls), will not be permitted without the chaplain's or clergyman's approval.

For chapel weddings held during holiday seasons, such as Christmas and Easter, flowers and decorations are furnished by the chaplain's office.

Flowers for the wedding party are the responsibility of the bride's parents, and should be delivered to the bride's room in the chapel in plenty of time for the ceremony. At a church wedding, they may be delivered either to the church or to the place where the bridal attendants are dressing.

WEDDING EXPENSES

A wedding and reception can cost anywhere from a few hundred to several thousand dollars. The cost depends upon the type of wedding, formal or informal; the number of guests and bridal attendants; the place of reception and the food and drinks; the invitations; photographer; bridal gown and parents' clothes; flowers; any fees for an organist, vocalist, or clergyman; any housing or transportation of guests.

The bride's family carries out the plans and main expenses of the wedding since they are responsible for their daughter up to the moment of her marriage. *But the groom should help decide the size and style of the wedding.*

No wedding should burden anyone—parents or participants. Therefore, no one should plan a wedding that they cannot afford and which might take months to pay for. A beautiful, meaningful wedding, formal or informal, can be one of simplicity but in good taste.

The expenses of a second wedding may or may not be paid for by the parents. If they gave a large first wedding and paid for an expensive reception, they are not committed to pay for the second—unless they want to. Or the expenses may be shared by the couple and her parents— or the couple may prefer to pay for all expenses themselves.

When an older couple marries, they pay for their own wedding and reception expenses.

EXPENSES OF THE BRIDE'S FAMILY

The bride's family pays for most of the expenses of the wedding—up to the moment she leaves their care. This includes the wedding invitations and/or announcements; wedding photographs before and during the event (at least one is given to the bridegroom's family; if they want more, they should offer to pay for them); trousseau; flowers for the church and reception and any other decorations not furnished by the chapel or church; fees for the organist, soloist, sexton, if any; bridesmaids' bouquets and presents for each bridesmaid (which are presented by the bride and are usually jewelry, such as a bracelet); the bridegroom's ring if he wants one; all reception expenses, and any car expenses to and from the wedding (and, frequently, the reception); also the hotel bills for out-of-town bridal attendants when they cannot be accommodated in the parents' home or the homes of relatives or friends. The bridal gown and all accessories are paid for by the bride's parents (but *not* the gowns of the bridal attendants), and they usually give the bride as nice a gift as possible for the new household.

THE DIVORCED FATHER'S RESPONSIBILITY

When parents are divorced, the question arises about the bride's father's responsibility—if any—toward the wedding expenses.

When the daughter and any other children live with the mother, the father almost always pays alimony and child support.

However, a father, when he is financially able, may want to help toward the wedding expenses and he should discuss with the bride what he might do. Perhaps he can pay for the wedding gown, or for the flowers, or for the reception. Otherwise, he might give the couple a special wedding present which they desire, or a check as large as he is able (or chooses) to give.

EXPENSES OF THE GROOM

The expenses of the groom and his family include the bride's engagement and wedding rings; marriage license; bride's bouquet (which she selects; the center of the bouquet may be removable and used for the going-away corsage); the corsages for both mothers; the ties and gloves for the best man and ushers, and mementos for each. Also, the clergyman's fee, if any—and, of course the wedding trip.

If the ushers and best man are in civilian dress, the groom pays for their boutonnieres, as well as boutonnieres for the fathers. But the ushers and best man pay for their own clothes (or rental charges), other than their ties and gloves, and for their transportation to and from the city or place of the wedding. The groom, or members of his or the bride's family, should try to find places for the groom's attendants to stay, otherwise the groom pays for any hotel bills incurred by his attendants.

The groom usually gives his bride a gift on, or just before, the wedding day. The gift is something lasting, usually jewelry. He pays for his bachelor dinner, if he has one, and it is held a few days before the wedding, but preferably *not* the night before. His gifts to his attendants are usually of gold or silver, such as cigarette cases or lighters, cuff links; they should all be alike.

A gift of substance is often given to the couple by his parents when possible.

THE WEDDING RING OR RINGS

When you are the prospective bridegroom, you and your fiancée should go to the jeweler in plenty of time to select and order the wedding ring —or rings, if you also want one. (This would be a good time to look at silver and china patterns and help select them.)

The modern wedding ring has little space for much engraving, so it is customary to inscribe only the initials and date, with the bride's initials coming first: "A.B.S. and M.W.J. 6 June 1977"; or the man's initials may be used first in this case: "M.W.J. to A.B.S.—"; or they may simply be inscribed: "A.B.S.-M.W.J." When the wedding band is wide and you desire an inscription, any personal phrase may be used.

After the ring is selected, the bride-elect does not see it again until the ring is placed on her finger during the ceremony. You pay for her ring, and it will be delivered to you.

When you also want a wedding ring (in the double ring ceremony), yours should be a little wider and heavier than a woman's wedding ring. You wear it on the third finger of your left hand, just as the bride does, and not on your little finger. Your ring is a gift from the bride. She pays for it, and it is engraved in a similar way to her own.

VARIANCES IN WEARING RINGS

A man or woman who has been married before never uses the wedding ring worn in the first wedding.

A woman does not have to have an engagement ring but legally she must have a wedding ring.

A *divorcée* usually removes the wedding ring, except when she has children—and nowadays she may remove it, regardless.

A *widow* wears her wedding ring until remarriage. If her first husband had a wedding ring, it is customarily interred with him.

THE ENGAGEMENT RING

In cases of a broken engagement the ring is returned to the man. In case of the death of the fiancé before marriage, the woman may keep the ring. If it is a family heirloom and treasured by the fiancé's family, it should be returned to them.

Usually the divorcée does not continue to wear her engagement ring, but will have it reset or redesigned into another piece of jewelry. Should she continue to wear it, it should not be worn on the traditional left-hand finger but may be worn on the little or middle finger of the left hand or on the right hand.

Upon remarriage, the widow or divorcée should no longer wear the engagement ring from the first marriage. She may wish to give the ring to an adult son or daughter, or have it restyled.

REHEARSAL AND REHEARSAL DINNER

In order that a wedding ceremony may proceed smoothly, it is customary that a rehearsal be held in the chapel or church at least a day or so in advance of the wedding, but it is a violation of good manners to hold such rehearsals immediately after a cocktail party.

Although it is a growing custom to schedule the rehearsal the night before the wedding, it is important that the rehearsal be held *before* the dinner for the bridal party.

The hour of rehearsal is set with the chaplain or clergyman at the convenience of all members of the bridal party *who are expected to attend.* No words of the ceremony are spoken during the rehearsal, but the chaplain or clergyman will indicate at what point each member takes his role. The actual wedding rings are not used, but the motion of placing the rings on the bride's and groom's fingers is practiced.

The rehearsal dinner usually is given by the groom's parents, otherwise by the bride's parents or an intimate friend or relative of either family. The guests should include the members of the bridal party, the chaplain or clergyman and his wife, and the wives and husbands of attendants. Other close relatives and friends of the couple may be invited if desired. At a large dinner, the fiancé or fiancée of a member of the bridal party may be included.

BRIDAL ATTENDANTS

The bride and groom may have only one attendant each: a best man and maid or matron of honor. Usually, there are a maid or matron of honor, a best man, and from two to six bridesmaids and ushers at the average wedding.

Usually the bride asks a sister or very close relative, or an intimate friend, to be her maid or matron of honor. The bridesmaids are close friends of the bride and usually include a sister or relative of the bridegroom.

Ushers and bridesmaids may be married or single. However, it is *not* necessary to ask both a husband and wife to be a member of the wedding party when only one is a close friend of the bride or groom. The husband or wife not included in the wedding party would be included in any prenuptial parties, but need not be invited to sit at the bridal table at the reception unless the bride and groom so desire.

At a very large wedding, there may be both a maid and matron of honor and as many as eight or ten bridesmaids and a corresponding number of ushers, or more, as well as junior bridesmaids (ten to fourteen years of age), flower girl (four to seven), pages, train bearers, and a ring bearer (four to five years old). The ring bearer wears a white or a dark suit and white shirt—never a miniature tux or tails.

Frequently, the bride gives a dinner for her bridesmaids on the night that the groom gives his bachelor dinner. When such a dinner is given, this is the time for the bride to give the bridesmaids their presents.

Several days before the wedding, preferably after they have all arrived, the bridesmaids and maid or matron of honor may give a joint shower or party for the bride-elect. Individual presents, or a joint present, or both, are given to her.

THE BEST MAN

The groom chooses his best man and ushers from among his closest friends and relatives. His best man may be a brother or intimate friend, and occasionally is his father.

The best man is the bridegroom's aide. It is his duty to carry on, regardless of what arises. In order to instill calmness in members of the bridal party, he must maintain it himself.

Before the ceremony, the best man checks on the groom's clothes, gloves (if worn), marriage license, wedding ring,—and if the ceremony is held in a church, he takes care of the clergyman's fee (furnished by the groom), which is enclosed in a sealed envelope. He checks to see what has to be signed, and if everything is in order. He notifies the ushers to be at the chapel or church at least twenty minutes before the ceremony, and he arrives with the groom to be sure that the latter is not late and that he is properly dressed. During the ceremony, he produces the ring at the chaplain's (clergyman's) request.

Following the couple's vows, the best man joins in the recessional, in which he customarily escorts the maid or matron of honor. Afterwards, he may wish to hurry on to the place of reception and check on details—such as stowing the bridal luggage in the going-away car. He does not stand in the receiving line at the reception, but is near to the groom to be of further help. His is the first toast to the bride and groom at the bridal table.

THE USHERS

The ushers represent not only the groom but the families of the bride and groom as well. They act as unofficial hosts, greeting the guests in a pleasant manner, and are escorts to the bridesmaids. Ushers give the couple individual gifts, or they may prefer to give a major gift together.

The number of ushers depends on the size of the wedding. An average-sized chapel wedding may be well handled by four to six ushers, with more serving at a large formal wedding. When the wedding is very small, no ushers may be needed. It is not necessary to have an equal number of ushers and bridesmaids. Usually, there are more ushers than bridesmaids since they have definite duties to perform.

The main duty of the ushers is to seat guests in the chapel, church, or home. In accordance with the chaplain's faith at a military wedding, ushers may—or may not—wear swords while ushering. If not, the swords are left at a place convenient for the arch of swords (sabers) ceremony. It is preferable that six ushers in uniform perform this ceremony, although more or fewer ushers may do it. Ushers may be in the uniform of one or more service.

When there are ushers who are nonmilitary and who are in civilian suits, they should be paired. During the arch of swords (sabers) ceremony, when held in the chancel area, the nonuniformed ushers may unobtrusively step to the side following the wedding vows, or they may step to the side following the recessional when the arch is held outdoors.

Ushers do not stand in the receiving line at the reception. They should make themselves useful in talking with the guests, and as dancing partners when dancing is held.

WHAT TO CALL IN-LAWS

Should a bride and groom call their new in-laws "Father" and "Mother" when this is what they call their own parents? This is a difficult question and must be answered by the individuals themselves. Perhaps the parents will suggest what their new daughter-or son-in-law call them: "Mom" and "Dad" or the use of their first names, "Ruth" and "Bill."

To end the worry, when nothing has been suggested, the young couple should ask their in-laws what they wish to be called. Until then, you may call them "Mr." and "Mrs." or "Colonel" and "Mrs.", both of which show respect, if not warmth.

WHAT TO WEAR

At a service wedding, officers wear the uniform in accordance with the formality of the wedding. *Evening dress uniform* conforms to civilian *white tie and tails*. *Dinner* or *mess dress uniform* is in accordance with *black tie*. *Service blues* or *whites* compare to a dark blue or conservative business suit or a cutaway. Any male member of the bridal party not in uniform dresses accordingly.

In service weddings, the uniforms of the groom, best man, and ushers are alike. In civilian ceremonies, the groom and best man should be dressed alike, but the ushers may be dressed like the groom and best man, or there may be slight differences in their shirts and ties. The fathers usually dress like the groom except that their ties need not match.

At service weddings, formal or informal, the groom and best man do not wear gloves because of the necessity of handling the ring, or rings. The ushers wear white gloves throughout the ceremony. At civilian weddings, the groom and best man carry gloves, if they so desire, but these need not be carried at informal weddings.

When you are a member of a civilian wedding party, you need to know the general dress for formal and informal, daytime or evening ceremonies:

VERY FORMAL DAYTIME (BEFORE 6 P.M.)

Bride: long white dress, train, veil, white shoes, gloves optional but are usually worn when the sleeves of the gown are short; a white bridal bouquet or white flowers on a white prayer book.

Bride's attendants: long dresses, headpiece, matching shoes, gloves optional; carry flowers.

Groom, his attendants, bride's father: cutaway, gray gloves, black shoes, ascots, and boutonnieres.

Mothers of couple: long dresses, small hat or head covering, gloves, corsage.

FORMAL DAYTIME (BEFORE 6 P.M.)

The same as for very formal daytime except that the groom and his attendants and the bride's father wear sack coats.

INFORMAL DAYTIME (BEFORE 6 P.M.)

Bride and her attendants: afternoon or cocktail style dress, or suit. Mothers of couple dress accordingly. Corsages.

Groom and his attendants: dark suits in winter; in summer, dark trousers and white or light-colored jacket or white trousers with charcoal or navy jacket; or in hot weather, white suit. Boutonnieres.

VERY FORMAL EVENING (AFTER 6 P.M.)

Bride and her attendants: same as for formal daytime; the bride's train may be longer.

Groom and his attendants: White tie—black tailcoat and starched shirt, wing collar, white tie, boutonnieres, black dress shoes and socks.

Mothers of couple: long evening or dinner dress with sleeves or jacket, small headdress, gloves optional, corsage.

FORMAL EVENING (AFTER 6 P.M.)

Dress is the same as for very formal evening except that men in the bridal party wear tuxedos (black tie); or summertime white jackets. Mothers of the couple wear long dresses.

INFORMAL EVENING (AFTER 6 P.M.)

Bride and her attendants: a simplified long white dress and short veil, small bouquet cocktail-style dress, or dressy suit.

Groom and his attendants: black tie, with white or dark jacket when bride wears long dress; dark suit when bride wears short dress or suit; black shoes and socks. Boutonnieres.

Mothers of the couple: short dresses or dressy suits, corsages.

The dress described is for the traditional wedding. There is considerable leeway in color and design for both men and women for the less formal and informal wedding. The fathers of the couple wear boutonnieres and the mothers wear corsages.

GUESTS

Officers wear service blues or whites at an informal wedding, or a dark blue or gray business suit or any conservative suit according to the season. The same type of business suit or dress blues or whites are worn at a formal daytime wedding, since cutaways are almost never worn now, except by the men in the most formal wedding party.

At a formal evening wedding, you wear the dinner or mess dress uniform or a dinner jacket, or evening dress uniform. Men may wear black tie at any formal evening wedding, and dark business suits at less formal or informal weddings.

Women wear long or short evening dresses with a jacket, or a dinner dress with sleeves for the formal evening wedding. For a less formal ceremony, you may wear a cocktail dress with a matching jacket or coat, and gloves are optional. An afternoon-style dress or a dressy suit is worn to a morning wedding and an afternoon dress or cocktail suit to an afternoon wedding. Children wear their best party clothes, but they do not attend the wedding unless their names have been included in the invitation.

SECOND MARRIAGES

A second marriage for a man does not affect the ceremony. When his bride has never been married, the wedding may be as formal as desired.

However, a second marriage for a woman means a small and informal wedding. She does *not* wear the traditional white wedding dress or veil, but usually wears a dress of pastel color (or white), long or short, with a small headdress, corsage, or a prayer book with a flower marker. The reception, however, may be large.

WOMAN OFFICER'S WEDDING

The wedding of a woman officer may be planned like that for any bride who will be wearing a traditional bridal gown, or she may be married in uniform. When the bridegroom is also an officer, he should dress in accordance with the type of gown or uniform his bride will be wearing. The formality of the wedding determines the uniform worn.

When the military bride-elect is serving at a station where she has many responsibilities and time is important, she must carefully weigh which type of wedding is best. If her home town is at a distance and the wedding will take place in the station chapel, her parents may not be able to help to any extent with the plans—they may not even be able to attend. In such a case she would have to make her own arrangements, which she may prefer to do; but even with the help of friends, a woman officer has less time than the average woman for the many necessities in planning a wedding.

A military wedding is usually scheduled during leave or at a time when a change of orders gives the couple an opportunity to drive to the new duty station or to have a longer wedding trip to some place of their choice. The date for the wedding can be made as soon as the leave is determined or the date of the change of orders, with the wedding probably held in the chapel and the reception in the officers' club.

When the bride chooses to wear the traditional wedding gown, she will save considerable time by making an appointment with a marriage consultant at any large reputable store who can coordinate her gown and those of the bridesmaids, with accessories.

As with the civilian career woman, the military woman can plan her wedding large or small, formal or informal, within her budget. But at any type of wedding, the commanding officers and their spouses and all or some of the staff officers in the couples' office or staff (and their wives or husbands)—depending upon the size of the station—should be invited.

OFFICIAL MARRIED STATUS

When a woman officer marries, it is mandatory that she notify the personnel department of her service concerning her married status. If she prefers, she may officially retain her maiden name, or she may use her married name. The following forms are applicable to any service with the exception of the head of office of the service to whom it is directed.

From: Lieutenant Janet J. DOE, USN, 123-45-6789/1100
To: Chief of Naval Personnel
Via: (Commanding Officer)

Subj: Marriage; notification of

Ref: (a) BUPERSMAN 5010240

Encl: (1) Photocopy of marriage certificate

1. In accordance with reference (a), the Chief of Naval Personnel is hereby notified of my marriage. Enclosure (1) is forwarded as proof of the marriage.

2. I do not desire to have my official records changed to indicate my married name.

JANET J. DOE

From: Lieutenant Janet J. DOE, USN, 123-45-6789/1100

To: Chief of Naval Personnel

Via: (Commanding Officer)

Subj: Change of name; request for

Ref: (a) BUPERSMAN 5010240

Encl: (1) Photocopy of marriage certificate

1. In accordance with reference (a), it is requested that my name be changed in the official records from Janet Joyce Doe to Janet Doe Jones due to my marriage. Enclosure (1) is forwarded as proof of the marriage.

JANET J. DOE*

PUBLISHED WEDDING ANNOUNCEMENT

Wedding accounts for publication in metropolitan newspapers should be sent to the society editor of the paper as soon as possible. When pictures are used, either candid or those taken by a professional photographer, glossy prints 8 by 10 inches in size are best.

* NOTE: New name cannot be used on any official forms until official change has been approved by the Chief of Naval Personnel (or the corresponding office of your service). The Chief of Naval Personnel acknowledges change of name in writing to officer concerned.

The account should include the pertinent information in the engagement announcement, as well as the date and time of the wedding, the name of the officiating chaplain (clergyman), the church or chapel, and the place of the reception. It is of interest to mention the new address of the couple or the duty station of the bridegroom. When either one is from a very old or distinguished family, such a fact may be included in the account. How much of the account will be used is determined by the policy of the paper.

A home-town paper will include additional information: the names and home-towns of the entire bridal party, as well as descriptions of the bridal gown and bouquet and, usually, that of the bridesmaids' and mothers' gowns and corsages as well.

When space permits, a newspaper may publish the names of distinguished or out-of-town guests, but a complete list of guests is never published. You may wish to send a brief notice to your alumni magazine or service paper, if such news is published.

MARRIAGE FINANCES

When you are the groom, you should have your financial house in order before marriage—with money to cover the wedding trip, regardless of how short or extended the trip may be. A wedding trip may be en route to a new duty station, and in this case motel or hotel reservations should be made in advance.

You also must have enough money to cover the costs of your new household, which may be in a town or at a base unfamiliar to you. A classmate or friend stationed there frequently is of assistance in helping you find temporary or permanent housing when you do not have assigned quarters.

Sometimes the family of the bride or the groom give the young couple a check as a wedding gift, and financial problems are of no immediate concern. But a young couple should work as a team in household finances, fully understanding the limitations of a paycheck.

Since an officer is subject to duty in remote areas, someone must handle the household and other financial obligations while he is gone. A young wife can contribute much to the success of a new marriage by her ability to handle these obligations. A household budget should be worked out and thoroughly understood by *both* of you, before the hour of departure.

CHAPTER 25

Wedding Invitations, Announcements, & Replies

TODAY, A BRIDE-ELECT has the choice of selecting contemporary wedding invitations (pastel colored paper, personal wordings) or the traditional invitations of white or ivory-colored paper with engraved lettering—a choice that was not possible just a few years ago within the realm of good taste. The traditional invitation is always beautiful, and always will be. Contemporary stylings can be beautiful when wordings are not faddish or eccentric and Halloween colors not used. Your good taste and the type of wedding you are having—formal or informal—should determine your selection.

TRADITIONAL WEDDING INVITATIONS

The traditional wedding invitation is engraved on white or ivory vellum or kid-finish paper. This may be a double sheet about 5½ by 7½ inches, that is folded and enclosed in the inner of one of two envelopes. A smaller invitation, about 4½ by 6 inches in size, is not folded and is placed sideways in the envelope.

In case of invitations using the double envelopes, the *inner* one has the guest's rank or title and last name written on it in black or dark blue ink, for example "Colonel and Mrs. Smith," with active or retired status *not* used. The tissue protecting the engraving on the invitation is not removed before placing in the envelope.

Although black engraving has been mandatory in past years—and is desirable—a good type of raised printing is available today, and is much less expensive. There are many lettering styles to choose from, but shaded Roman, antique Roman, and script are always in good taste.

As a general rule, abbreviations, initials, numerals, are to be avoided whenever possible, in wedding invitations. The hour is always written out in full. However, Roman numerals may denote a second or third generation: John Paul Truxtun II or III. The designation "Junior" applies to the next in direct line of descent. The numbers "II," etc., indicate the sequence in the use of the name. A man does not usually continue to add "Junior" or "Jr." after his name following the death of his father, but he may if his mother is still living.

SERVICE RANK

Commissioned officers of the rank of commander and up in the Navy and Coast Guard, and of captain and up in the Army, Air Force, and Marine Corps, should use their titles before their names on the invitation. The ranks of junior officers are placed beneath their names. The grades of second and first lieutenant, U.S. Army, are designated lieutenant.

Retired officers of the ranks of commander and lieutenant colonel and up, usually keep their titles in civilian life and use their titles on wedding invitations. When issuing a wedding invitation with his wife, the status of the retired officer is not used. But if he is a widower and issues the invitation in his own name, or if he is the bridegroom, then the word retired is used as follows:

Colonel John Doe
United States Air Force, Retired

Reserve officers on active duty only use their titles on wedding invitations or announcements. High-ranking officers who are retired but who keep their titles in civilian life use their titles.

Noncommissioned officers and enlisted men frequently use only their names with the branch of service immediately below.

The *rank designation is the same for active and retired officers and their wives.* The retired status is not used except by widowed or divorced officers. The wording is as shown on the following page:

Brigadier General and Mrs. John Henry Doe

request the honour of your presence

at the marriage of their daughter

Ann Carol

to

James Paul Smith

Lieutenant, United States Army*

on Thursday, the seventh of June

at half after four o'clock

Cadet Chapel

West Point, New York

* "Second" or "First" Lieutenant is designated in the Air Force and Marine Corps.

GUEST LIST

The groom sends a list of his friends' names and addresses to his mother, who in turn will send his list with her own to the mother of the bride. If his mother is dead, he will send the list to the bride's mother. If all guests are not to be invited to the reception or breakfast following the wedding, this should be designated on the list by an R for reception and C for ceremony. The bride's mother should keep an alphabetical check list for acceptances and regrets.

ISSUING INVITATIONS

Invitations are mailed by the bride's mother between three and four weeks before the event. She also sends invitations to the bridegroom's parents and to members of the bridal party, which are considered treasured mementos. If the parents of the bride are deceased, the invitations are issued by a close or older relative, a brother or grandparent. In the case of divorced parents, they would be issued in the name of the one with whom she has been living.

When a card is included in the invitation, inviting you to the reception or breakfast following the ceremony, the card customarily has an "R.S.V.P." and must be answered. A "regrets only" is *not* used. Invitations to some church weddings may not carry the "R.S.V.P." since they are all-inclusive of the congregation, and do not require an answer.

The home address of the bride's family is usually engraved on the reception or wedding breakfast card, so that replies will be sent to that address and *not* to the place of the wedding.

Nowadays, self-addressed and stamped (or unstamped) envelopes with reply cards are sometimes included with the invitations. Although it is preferable that replies are handwritten, the changing times have brought acceptance of this easy way to ensure replies. Still, when the bride's mother takes the time to send you, and possibly a hundred or so others a hand-addressed invitation to this all-important occasion, then you can take a few minutes of your time and properly answer it. Examples are in this chapter.

Wedding invitations are always sent to a married couple, even though you know only one or the other.

ADDRESSING ENVELOPES

A formal engraved wedding invitation or announcement usually has two envelopes: the *outside*, gummed, which bears the full name and address of the guest or guests, and the *inside* nongummed envelope which has only the rank or title, and the surname and encloses the invitation or announcement. The inside envelope is faced toward the back of the outside envelope when inserted, in order that the names will be face up when the envelope is opened.

All envelopes are addressed by hand, in black or dark blue ink. It is wise to order extra envelopes to allow for mistakes.

The *outside* envelope will be fully addressed without abbreviations, initials, or commas:

Major and Mrs. James Paul Doe
7618 Van Noy Court
Argonne Hills
Fort George G. Meade
Maryland 20755

The inner envelope is addressed: *Major and Mrs. Doe.*

Other adult members of the family, such as a grandmother or mother-in-law, should receive separate invitations. For a close relative, you may write *Grandmother*, etc., on the inner envelope.

You may write the name or names of teen-age children of the family directly under the parents' names on the outer envelope, and *Miss* or *Misses Doe* on the inner envelope. The outer envelope would be:

Major and Mrs. James Paul Doe
Miss Susan Doe
(address)

Or, when the children are under age, simply write: *Susan, Mary, and John* on the inside envelope under the parents' names, and the outer envelope could be addressed to: Major and Mrs. James Paul Doe and Family.

Invitations may be addressed to young brothers twelve years of age or younger as *The Messrs. Doe.* But Messrs. is used only for brothers, not for a father and son. A girl of any age may be addressed "Miss," and teen-age and high school-age boys are "Mr."

When a woman's service rank or civilian title exceeds that of her husband, for a social occasion such as a wedding her rank or title is not used on the invitation, and it is addressed to *Mr. and Mrs. John Earl Doe*, with the inside envelope addressed to *Mr. and Mrs. Doe.* (For official invitations her rank or title is used. See Chapter 14 *Formal Invitations and Replies.*)

The *inner envelope*, as stated elsewhere, has only the rank or title and surname of the invited guest or guests: *Major and Mrs. Doe.* An adult member of the family or other close relative would be addressed *Grandmother*, etc. A single person would be *Captain Jones* or *Mr. Smith.* In case of a married couple with the same rank and service, they would be the *Captains Doe.*

RETURN ADDRESS

It is sensible to have a legible return address on the wedding invitation envelope, and this should be determined at the time they are ordered. For years it has been a custom to have the return address embossed on the flap of the envelope, but too often it has been difficult or impossible to read.

It is important to have the return address in order for a person to know where to send a wedding gift. Should the person to whom the invitation is sent have moved without leaving an address, the invitation would be lost.

SERVICEWOMAN'S WEDDING INVITATION

When the bride is a member of the armed forces, she uses her title with the branches of service. (*See:* Service Rank, page 308.) For example:

LIEUTENANT GENERAL AND MRS. WILSON JOHN DOE
REQUEST THE HONOUR OF YOUR PRESENCE
AT THE MARRIAGE OF THEIR DAUGHTER
CAPTAIN ELIZABETH ANNE DOE
UNITED STATES MARINE CORPS
TO
MAJOR JAMES LEE SMITH
UNITED STATES ARMY
SATURDAY, THE FIFTH OF JANUARY
AT FOUR O'CLOCK
THE MARINE CORPS MEMORIAL CHAPEL
MARINE CORPS BASE
QUANTICO, VIRGINIA

When the wedding will be private and only close friends and relatives will be invited, or when the bride is a divorcée, but a large reception will be held, the wedding invitation could be oral or hand-written, and the *reception invitations* issued in this manner:

LIEUTENANT GENERAL AND MRS. WILSON JOHN DOE
REQUEST THE PLEASURE OF YOUR COMPANY
AT THE WEDDING RECEPTION
OF THEIR DAUGHTER
CAPTAIN ELIZABETH ANNE DOE
UNITED STATES MARINE CORPS
AND
MAJOR JAMES LEE SMITH
UNITED STATES ARMY
SATURDAY, THE FIFTH OF JANUARY
AT HALF AFTER FOUR O'CLOCK
QUARTERS ONE
MARINE CORPS BASE
QUANTICO, VIRGINIA

VARIATIONS IN WORDINGS

There are many variations in the wording of parts of the invitation:

1. When the bride's parents are deceased and a relative is sending the invitations:

MR. GEORGE OLIVER SMITH
REQUESTS THE HONOR OF YOUR PRESENCE
AT THE MARRIAGE OF HIS SISTER
MARY MARTHA
ETC.

2. When the bride's parents are divorced and the mother has not remarried, she uses her maiden surname with her former husband's name: Mrs. Brown Smith. When the divorce is "friendly," both names may be on the invitation and the mother's name appears first:

MRS. BROWN SMITH
AND
COMMANDER JOHN JAMES SMITH
UNITED STATES NAVY, RETIRED
REQUEST THE HONOR OF YOUR PRESENCE
AT THE MARRIAGE OF THEIR DAUGHTER
ETC.

3. When the bride's father is dead, or her parents are divorced, and her mother has remarried:

MR. AND MRS. PAUL LEWIS DORN
REQUEST THE HONOR OF YOUR PRESENCE
AT THE MARRIAGE OF HER* DAUGHTER
MARY MARTHA SMITH
ETC.

4. Or the invitations may be issued in the mother's name only:

MRS. PAUL LEWIS DORN
REQUESTS THE HONOR OF YOUR PRESENCE
AT THE MARRIAGE OF HER DAUGHTER
MARY MARTHA SMITH
ETC.

5. Or issued in the father's name only:

COLONEL PAUL LEWIS DORN
UNITED STATES AIR FORCE, RETIRED
REQUESTS THE HONOR OF YOUR PRESENCE
AT THE MARRIAGE OF HIS DAUGHTER
ETC.

6. If the bride's mother is dead and the father has married again, the form usually is:

COMMANDER AND MRS. JOHN JAMES SMITH
REQUEST THE HONOR OF YOUR PRESENCE
AT THE MARRIAGE OF HIS* DAUGHTER
MARY MARTHA
ETC.

This form applies to the bride's mother when she is a widow, or the bride's father when he is a widower, with the exception of the use of their single names and of the word "her" or "his," as appropriate, before the word "daughter."

7. When a young widow is married, the married name of the widow is given, and the form is:

---

* When the relationship is close, "their" would be used instead of "his" or "her" which would be inclusive of the stepmother or stepfather.

BRIGADIER GENERAL AND MRS. JOHN JAMES SMITH
REQUEST THE HONOR OF YOUR PRESENCE
AT THE MARRIAGE OF THEIR DAUGHTER
MARY MARTHA ADAMS
TO
JOHN DOE BLANK
SECOND LIEUTENANT, UNITED STATES AIR FORCE
ON SATURDAY, THE FIRST OF JUNE
AT SEVEN O'CLOCK
RANDOLPH AIR FORCE BASE CHAPEL
TEXAS

Or, when an older widow gives her own wedding, it is usually informal and handwritten invitations are sent. But when engraved or printed invitations are used, the form (in part) is:

THE HONOR OF YOUR PRESENCE
IS REQUESTED AT THE MARRIAGE OF
MRS. DONALD JAMES ADAMS
TO
JOHN DOE BLANK
ETC.

8. Engraved invitations to the wedding of a divorcée are infrequently sent. A divorcée's wedding is usually a small ceremony to which guests are invited by informal notes. But when invitations are sent, the above forms may be used with the divorcée's given name used with the last name of her former husband: "Martha Smith Adams," or for an older woman, "Mrs. Smith Adams."

9. When there are no close relatives or friends, or should she be an orphan, the bride may send out her own invitations, with the wording (in part) as follows:

THE HONOR OF YOUR PRESENCE
IS REQUESTED AT THE MARRIAGE OF
MISS MARY MARTHA SMITH
TO
DONALD JAMES ADAMS
ETC.

10. When sisters are married at a double wedding, the name of the older sister is given first:

COMMANDER AND MRS. JOHN JAMES SMITH
REQUEST THE HONOR OF YOUR PRESENCE
AT THE MARRIAGE OF THEIR DAUGHTERS
MARY MARTHA
TO
CAPTAIN DONALD JAMES ADAMS
UNITED STATES MARINE CORPS
AND
SARAH JANE
TO
FRED PERRY HAAS
ENSIGN, UNITED STATES COAST GUARD
ON MONDAY, THE FIRST OF JUNE
AT FOUR O'CLOCK
CHRIST EPISCOPAL CHURCH, GEORGETOWN
WASHINGTON, DISTRICT OF COLUMBIA

11. At a double wedding, when the brides and bridegrooms are very close friends, but are not related, the invitations may be written according to the rank of the fathers or bridegrooms, or in alphabetical order.

12. When the bride's parents are separated but not divorced, the fact of the separation is frequently ignored, and the invitations are engraved in the customary form.

13. When the bride-elect is adopted, there is no need to mention this fact. When her name is different and it is desirable to use it, both the engagement announcement and wedding invitation could use the words "adopted daughter."

CONTEMPORARY WORDINGS

Once, it was unheard of to change the wording of a formal wedding invitation. Although the traditional wedding is always in the best of taste and is unchanged for the truly formal wedding, there are variations today in less formal wordings that are meaningful and beautiful—freqeuntly in expressions of religious faith.

When personal wordings are preferred for informal invitations, caution must be observed or self-expressions become overly sentimental or extreme.

PAPER AND LETTERINGS

For less formal wedding invitations, pastel colors, new textures of paper, and a choice of lettering, such as regular or photo, are available at stationers. While white or ivory vellum are used for both the formal and informal invitations, there are such pastel colors as very pale yellow with brown lettering, blue, pink and green in soft hues.

Ivory deckle vellum and deckle white vellum are in good taste, along with a variety of textures and parchments.

LETTERING STYLES

Thermography is a very good substitute for engraving, when the expense of the invitations must be considered. The photo-letter techniques have script lettering and fine details usually associated with hand-engraving.

CONTEMPORARY WEDDING INVITATIONS

A COUPLE ISSUE THEIR OWN INVITATIONS:

MARY JANE SMITH
AND
WILLIAM HENRY DOE
INVITE YOU TO SHARE IN THE JOY
WHEN THEY EXCHANGE MARRIAGE VOWS
AND BEGIN THEIR NEW LIFE TOGETHER
SATURDAY, THE TWENTY-SIXTH OF MARCH
NINETEEN HUNDRED AND SEVENTY-SEVEN
AT TWO O'CLOCK
THE FIRST CHRISTIAN CHURCH
OKLAHOMA CITY, OKLAHOMA

THE TRADITIONAL WITH EXPRESSION OF FAITH:

DOCTOR AND MRS. JOHN JAMES SMITH
REQUEST THE HONOUR OF YOUR PRESENCE
TO WITNESS THE UNITING OF THEIR DAUGHTER
MARY JANE
AND
WILLIAM HENRY DOE
LIEUTENANT, UNITED STATES NAVAL RESERVE
TO BECOME ONE IN CHRIST
ON SATURDAY, THE TWENTY-FIFTH OF JUNE
AT HALF AFTER TWO O'CLOCK
EVANGELICAL PRESBYTERIAN CHURCH
RIDGELY AVENUE AND WILSON ROAD
ANNAPOLIS, MARYLAND

RECEPTION FOLLOWING
IN CHURCH HALL

THE FORMAL CONTEMPORARY INVITATION

Major General and Mrs. George Howard Doe

invite you to share in the joy

of the marriage uniting their daughter

Susan Jane

and

John Wayne Smith

Second Lieutenant, United States Air Force

on Saturday, the fifth of June

Nineteen hundred and seventy-six

at five o'clock in the afternoon

Cadet Chapel

United States Air Force Academy

Colorado

WHEN THE WEDDING IS GIVEN BY BOTH SETS OF PARENTS:

Less customary but becoming more frequent today is the informal or semiformal wedding that is given by both sets of parents. The wedding invitations are issued in the names of both sets of parents, and the reception is given jointly (and paid for jointly).

The parents of both the bride and groom would stand in the receiving line, or the fathers would be in the line briefly or not at all. In such a case the bridesmaids would be kept at a minimum, otherwise the line would be very long.

INVITATIONS FOR INFORMAL WEDDINGS

A small, informal wedding does not require engraved invitations. The mother of the bride may write short notes of invitation, or may telegraph or telephone the relatives and friends who are to be invited to the ceremony or to the reception, or to both.

The notes are written on conservative paper, white or cream color, giving the time and place of the ceremony. If the invitation is only for the reception, the time and place are all that is necessary. Informal invitations may be sent on short notice, but the usual two weeks in advance is customary.

The typical informal note would read something like this:

59 Southgate Avenue

Dear Mary,

Janet is being married here at home to Ensign John Jones, USN, who was graduated from the Naval Academy last week. The wedding will take place Monday, the eleventh of June, at four-thirty. We do hope you will be with us and will stay for a very small reception afterwards.

As ever,
Bess Smith

Answers to invitations to small weddings (even answers to invitations received by telegram) are made by letter—if you have time. A brief, sincere note on your personal paper would be correct.

RECEPTION INVITATIONS

There are several ways of extending an invitation for a wedding reception. If the wedding takes place in the morning or early afternoon, a *wedding breakfast* card is enclosed.

1. A small card about 3 by 4 inches, engraved on the same type paper as the wedding invitation, is included along with the invitation.

There is no crest or coat of arms on the card, and the protecting tissue (when provided) is not removed before mailing. The phrase "pleasure of your company" is used, since this is now a social occasion:

COLONEL AND MRS. JOHN JAMES SMITH
REQUEST THE PLEASURE OF YOUR COMPANY
AT THE WEDDING BREAKFAST
FOLLOWING THE CEREMONY
AT
DOGWOOD HILLS
ARLINGTON

R.S.V.P.

2. If the wedding is to be in the late afternoon or evening, a *reception invitation* card is enclosed with the wedding invitation:

Reception

immediately following the ceremony

Officers' Club, Bolling Air Force Base

The favour of a reply is requested
3909 Connecticut Avenue, Northwest
Washington, District of Columbia

3. When a wedding is very small, with *no* wedding invitations to be issued, but with a large reception planned afterwards, the *reception invitations* are engraved on paper about the same size as the traditional wedding invitation:

COLONEL AND MRS. JOHN JAMES SMITH
REQUEST THE PLEASURE OF YOUR COMPANY
AT THE WEDDING RECEPTION OF THEIR DAUGHTER
MARY MARTHA
AND
DONALD JAMES ADAMS
LIEUTENANT, UNITED STATES NAVAL RESERVE
ON MONDAY, THE FIRST OF JUNE
AT FOUR O'CLOCK
DOGWOOD HILLS
ARLINGTON, VIRGINIA

R.S.V.P.

4. The invitation to the reception may be included in the wedding invitation when all guests are invited to *both* the wedding and reception. The following information is added to the bottom of the wedding invitation, following the name and address of the church:

AND AFTERWARDS AT
DOGWOOD HILLS
ARLINGTON, VIRGINIA

R.S.V.P.

ACCEPTANCE AND REFUSALS

When you are invited to the ceremony and to the reception, or to the reception alone, the R.S.v.p. is usually requested and *must* be answered. Your reply will follow the form of the engraved invitation, or of the informal letter. You will write in longhand, on cream-colored or white note paper, and the form for the acceptance or regret is similar, except for the lines of acceptance or regret.

Your reply is addressed to the mother of the bride-elect —unless she is deceased; then you address it to the person who issued the invitation. If you received a reply card, just fill it in.

A simple but desirable form of answering the invitation to the wedding, to both the wedding and the reception, or to the reception only, is:

Lieutenant and Mrs. William Blank
accept with pleasure
the kind invitation of
Colonel and Mrs. Smith
for
Monday, the first of June
at four o'clock

The same general form is used to regret as to accept an invitation. You will remember that in all refusals of invitations, the hour of the occasion and the address are always omitted. When the refusal is for an invitation from a close friend, the reason why is frequently added in the second and third lines, such as: "regret that their absence from the city prevents their accepting."

A more detailed form for answering the invitation is shown in the following regret for a reception only:

Lieutenant and Mrs. William Blank
regret that they are unable to accept
the very kind invitation of
Colonel and Mrs. Smith
to the wedding reception of their daughter
Mary Martha
and
Donald James Adams
on Monday, the first of June

When either the husband or wife cannot accept the invitation, the person accepting may write the reply as follows:

Mrs. William Blank
accepts with pleasure
the kind invitation of
Colonel and Mrs. Smith
for
Monday, the first of June
at four o'clock
Lieutenant William Blank
regrets exceedingly
that he will be unable to accept

A reply to a small or informal wedding invitation is usually sent in the same form in which it was received. If by telephone or telegram, the answer may be sent in the same way to the sender of the invitation. If time is not short, it is preferable that you reply by a handwritten note. An acceptance could read:

Monday

Dear Mrs. Smith,

   I am very happy about your daughter's forthcoming marriage to my classmate, Dick Brown, and am pleased to be in the States and able to attend. I'll fly in and will be staying with friends.

Sincerely,
John Jones

MARRIAGE ANNOUNCEMENT

Engraved or printed marriage announcements are issued on the same type of paper used for wedding invitations, and are sent out *after* the marriage has been performed. The announcements are sent by the bride's parents or by a person designated to do this.

Wedding announcements are sent to less intimate friends and acquaintances who were not invited to the wedding, or to all friends and acquaintances following a ceremony when no guests were invited. The year is customarily written out:

CAPTAIN AND MRS. JOHN JONES SMITH
HAVE THE HONOR OF ANNOUNCING
THE MARRIAGE OF THEIR DAUGHTER
MARY ANN
TO
MR. GEORGE CARL WILSON
ON SATURDAY, THE SEVENTH OF JUNE
NINETEEN HUNDRED AND EIGHTY-THREE*
TREASURE ISLAND CHAPEL†
SAN FRANCISCO, CALIFORNIA

When the bride's parents do not approve the wedding, which may have been an elopement with a civil ceremony, or when the bride's parents are deceased and there are no close relatives, or when she is an orphan, the couple may announce their own marriage. When a civil ceremony was held, only the name of the city or town but not where it took place is mentioned:

MISS JANE ELLEN DOE
AND
WILLIAM JOHN SMITHFIELD
ENSIGN, UNITED STATES COAST GUARD
ANNOUNCE THEIR MARRIAGE
ON SATURDAY, THE FIFTH OF JUNE
ONE THOUSAND NINE HUNDRED AND EIGHTY-THREE
AT MYSTIC, CONNECTICUT

* A departure from the conventional wording of the wedding invitation is the use of the year, written out, in wedding announcements. In some cases, the year is not specified.

† The name of the church may, or may not, be added. The hour of the wedding is not specified.

RECALLING WEDDING INVITATIONS

Because of illness, change of orders—or a change of mind!—wedding invitations may have to be recalled, or postponed, after they have already been issued. Notices must then be sent to all those who received invitations. The best form for recalling a wedding invitation is:

DR. AND MRS. WILLIAM SMITH
ANNOUNCE THAT THE MARRIAGE OF THEIR DAUGHTER
MARY ELLEN
TO
ENSIGN JOHN LEE JONES
WILL NOT TAKE PLACE

When the wedding invitation is recalled because of a bereavement in the family, the engraved or printed card may state the reason:

DR. AND MRS.. WILLIAM SMITH
REGRET EXCEEDINGLY
THAT BECAUSE OF THE RECENT DEATH OF
THE FATHER OF ENSIGN JONES
THE INVITATIONS TO THE MARRIAGE OF THEIR DAUGHTER
MARY ELLEN
TO
ENSIGN JOHN LEE JONES
MUST BE RECALLED

Or:

MRS. WILLIAM SMITH
REGRETS THAT THE DEATH OF
DR. SMITH
OBLIGES HER TO RECALL THE INVITATIONS
TO THE WEDDING OF HER DAUGHTER

The recalling of the invitations in case of a death in the immediate families does not always mean that the wedding may not take place on the scheduled day. If the families agree, a very quiet ceremony may be held on the original day of the wedding, with perhaps only one attendant each for the bride and groom.

When members of the bridal party have already arrived, and some have come from a distance, or when the bridegroom is in the service and has only a few days' leave, or has a new duty that will take him some distance, the wedding may be held as scheduled, but with no guests other than members of the families and the bridal party.

POSTPONING INVITATIONS

When it is necessary to postpone a wedding, a form similar to this may be followed:

CAPTAIN AND MRS. JOHN JONES SMITH
ANNOUNCE THAT THE MARRIAGE OF THEIR DAUGHTER
MARY ANN
TO
MR. GEORGE CARL WILSON
HAS BEEN POSTPONED FROM
SATURDAY, THE FIRST OF JUNE
UNTIL
SATURDAY, THE TWENTY-SECOND OF JUNE
AT FOUR O'CLOCK
TREASURE ISLAND CHAPEL
SAN FRANCISCO, CALIFORNIA

"AT HOME" CARDS

When you want friends to know your new address, and when you know where you will be living long enough to make the cards worthwhile, "at home" cards are often enclosed in the same envelope with the wedding announcement.

The cards are similar to a large calling card—about 3 by 4 inches —and are the same color as the wedding announcement. One form is:

LIEUTENANT AND MRS. JOHN CARL SMITH

| | 9 COLUMBINE VISTA |
| AFTER THE FIRST OF JUNE | COLORADO SPRINGS, COLORADO |

Or a smaller card, about the size of the usual calling card, may be used:

AFTER JUNE 1ST
9 COLUMBINE VISTA
COLORADO SPRINGS, COLORADO

WEDDING ANNIVERSARIES

For announcements of wedding anniversaries, the year of the wedding and the year in which the invitation is issued are customarily stamped or engraved at the top of the anniversary invitation or announcement. The couple's initials or monogram, coat of arms, or a seal may be engraved in gold or silver, or in black or dark blue ink. Such invitations may be sent out by the couple (or by their children). An example in the first case would be:

1933   1983
MAJOR GENERAL AND MRS. JOHN JAMES SMITH
REQUEST THE PLEASURE OF
Colonel and Mrs. George Ballou's
COMPANY ON THE FIFTIETH ANNIVERSARY
OF THEIR MARRIAGE
ON FRIDAY EVENING, MAY THE THIRD
FROM SEVEN UNTIL NINE O'CLOCK
THE BROADMOOR
COLORADO SPRINGS, COLORADO

Or:

1933–1983
MAJOR GENERAL AND MRS. JOHN JAMES SMITH
AT HOME
FRIDAY, THE THIRD OF MAY
FROM FIVE UNTIL SEVEN O'CLOCK
237 MOUNTAIN VIEW ROAD
COLORADO SPRINGS, COLORADO

CHAPTER 26

Military & Civilian Weddings

ON TIME!

Everyone is expected to be on time at a wedding. The bride and her party should be in the chapel or church 30 minutes before the designated hour, and should go directly to the room made available for making final preparations. *It is inexcusable for the bridal party to be late.*

The groom, best man, and ushers should also arrive at the chapel (or church) at least 30 minutes before the time of the ceremony; ushers should have plenty of time to seat early arriving guests.

All guests should be seated before the exact time designated. When there is a soloist, guests should wait quietly at the rear of the chapel until the conclusion of the song.

CHAPEL OR CHURCH PEWS

When the center aisle of the chapel is banked by candelabra, two ushers will light the candles some 15 minutes before the hour of the ceremony. They proceed to the front of the chapel, with each usher lighting the candles on his side with the aid of tapers. The pews are frequently marked by ribbons or sprays of flowers at the pew ends.

Runners are infrequently used in service chapels. If they are used, two ushers march in step to the front of the chapel or church, where they grasp the runner, face the back, and walk until the runner is stretched as far as it will go.

Altar

Bride's side

Bride's family | Groom's family

Groom's side

friends | friends

Recessional

Processional

Chapel or Church with two aisles.

The center section may be divided by a white ribbon or rope, with the bride's family seated in the left side pews facing the altar, and the groom's family on the right. However, a warm and friendly way is not to use a dividing ribbon or rope, but for the families to sit in the first pews together but on "their" side. At a very large wedding, friends of the bride would sit at the far left, the groom's friends at the far right, as well as behind the families in the center section.

TWO AISLES

When the chapel or church does not have a single central aisle, but has two aisles, you may select one aisle and plan the wedding as though that were the only one. Or you may use one aisle for the processional, and the other aisle for the recessional. The bride's family would be seated in the front pews on the left side of the center section, and the bridegroom's family in the front right side pews.

USHERING

When guests arrive at the chapel (church or home), ushers ask if they wish to be seated on the bride's side or on the groom's side, or they may ask, "Are you a relative (or friend) of the bride or groom?" Guests are seated accordingly—on the *left* of the chapel facing the altar for the bride's friends, on the *right* for the groom's. An usher always offers his *right arm* to a lady when escorting her down the aisle.

However, when one side of the church is rapidly filling while the other side remains empty—as may happen when the groom's relatives and friends live at a distance—then the ushers may ask late-arriving guests to sit on the groom's side of the church.

A woman who arrives with her husband or other male guest is escorted to the proper pew, with the usher asking the man to follow. Children follow their parents. A man attending alone walks beside the usher—who does not offer his arm.

Nowadays, however, it is not unusual for an usher to escort both the husband and wife, walking together to a pew, rather than the husband (or male escort) trailing along behind.

Traditionally, each woman is escorted to a pew separately unless there are many guests waiting to be escorted. Then, the usher may offer the senior woman his right arm and ask the others in the party to follow. He may make appropriate remarks while escorting, but quietly, and in keeping with the dignity and reverence accorded a sanctuary. Guests should not be hurried to their seats, but the seating must be done with a minimum of delay; they are never seated during the rendition of a solo.

Guests who arrive first are given the choice aisle seats, and later arrivals take the inner seats. At a large wedding, the head usher may be given a typed alphabetical list of guests and the seating arrangement.

The commanding officer of the bride or groom, and his wife or her husband, may be invited to sit in the front pew if the parents are unable to attend. Where the parents are in attendance, the commanding officer's party may be accorded courteous recognition by being seated with the immediate family.

Flag and general officers, other commanding officers or dignitaries, may be seated in accordance with rank or station just behind the families of the couple, but rigid protocol is not adhered to at weddings.

The head ushers are so designated by the groom. One usher escorts the groom's mother to her pew on the right. Just before the ceremony is to start, the head usher escorts the bride's mother to her pew on the left— and she is the *last* person to be seated. The chapel doors are then closed, but if they are not locked the late-comer may seat himself in the back of the chapel. *But guests are not expected to be late.*

THE WEDDING CEREMONY

THE PROCESSIONAL

A wedding in an academy chapel follows the procedure explained here in detail. In general, this same procedure may be used in any chapel or church.

The procession forms upon the completion of the ushers' duties, with the ushers taking their places at the head of the procession in the vestibule.

The first note of the wedding march is the signal that the ceremony is about to begin. By this time, everything is in order, with everyone in his or her place. The order of procedure is:

A. The chaplain enters from a side door, faces the altar in a quiet moment of prayer, then turns left and advances toward the congregation.

B. The groom enters, followed at about two paces by the best man, and both are in the same marching step as paced by the chaplain. As they approach the altar area, they pause in a moment of prayer, then turn left and face the congregation and the direction from which the bride will enter.

C. Simultaneously with the appearance of the groom and best man, the first ushers start forward *in pairs*. The pairs of ushers are separated by *six pew spaces*. Ushers are paired so that the shorter ones precede the taller. (In other chapels and churches the ushers may walk singly.)

D. The ushers face the altar until all are in position, then they turn together and face the approaching bride.

E. The bridesmaids follow the ushers, walking *singly* in order that their loveliness may be observed by all guests. They are also *six pew spaces apart.* The bridesmaids face the altar until the arrival of the maid of honor. (The bridesmaids may also walk in pairs.)

F. The maid or matron of honor is *eight pew spaces* behind the

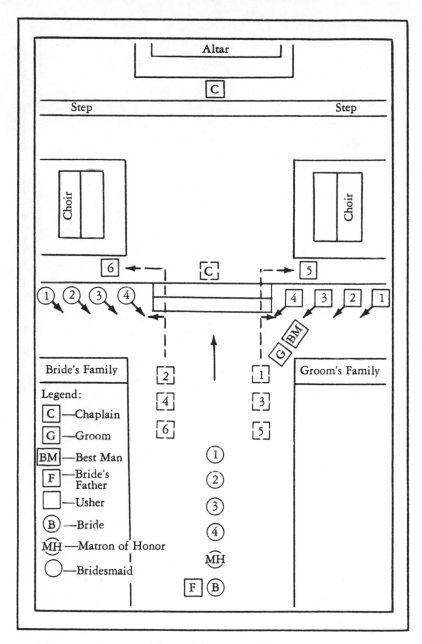

The wedding procession.

An alternate plan is for the bridesmaids and ushers to continue to the altar then take positions before the steps, to the left for the bridesmaids, to the right for the ushers.

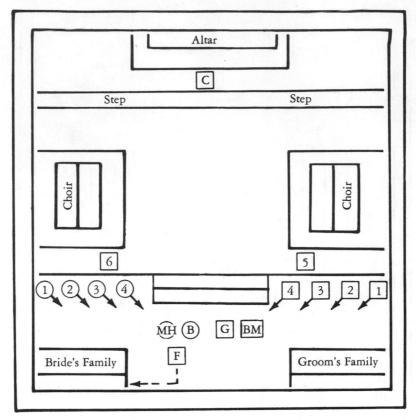

When the bridesmaids are in position, the chaplain
will advance toward the bride and groom.

bridesmaids. She also faces the altar, then she and the bridesmaids
together turn right and face the bride.

G. When there are a ring bearer and flower girl (in that order),
they walk *ten pew spaces* between the maid or matron of honor and the
bride—or, five pew spaces behind the maid or matron of honor, and five
pew spaces in front of the bride. (A ring bearer and/or flower girl may
walk singly or in pairs. They are not used as frequently as in former
years.)

H. The bride approaches on the *right* arm of her father.* The

* Although the bride customarily enters upon the right arm of her father,
it may be advisable that the bride approach the altar on the left arm of her

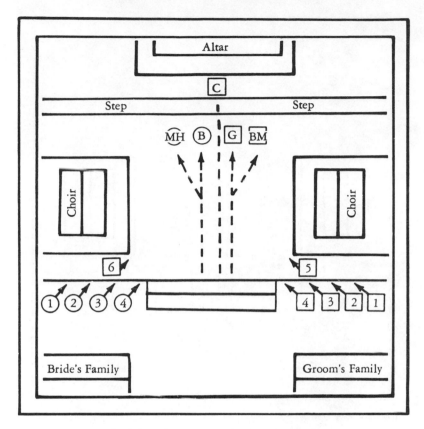

Positions for the ceremony at the altar.

father because; (a) it is less awkward at a certain point in the ceremony. When the father (or whoever gives the bride in marriage) is asked, "Who giveth this woman to be married to this man?" his answer, "I do" or "Her mother and I do," means that the bride is nearer the pew where the mother is seated. (b) At the time when the father places his daughter's right hand in the hand of the groom, if the daughter's right arm is in the father's left arm, this means that the passing of her hand to the hand of her husband-to-be is quite simple. (c) More- over, when the father is on the left side of his daughter, he then must make a choice of crossing in front of her and taking her right hand and placing it in the groom's, or going around her train and coming up between the bride and groom, taking her hand and crossing it over. (d) Since the bride's mother is sitting at the left side of the chapel or church, it is symbolic of the bride's de- votion to both parents that she pass between her mother and father on her way to the altar—which she cannot do when she is on the right arm of her father.

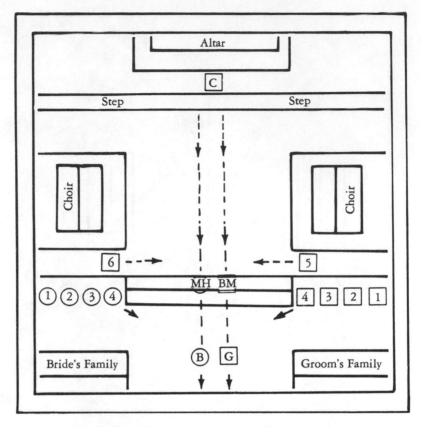

The bride and groom are the first to leave the chancel.
Plan A

members of the bridal party are now facing toward the chaplain, and the congregation is facing the altar.

I. When the bride reaches a point between the groom and the maid of honor, she pauses about three paces from the groom, the groom advances to meet her—at which time her father pauses, and she takes the *groom's* left arm.

J. Before the ceremony, the bride should tell the chaplain whether she would like the guests to be seated or to remain standing throughout the ceremony. When guests are to be seated, the chaplain says, "At the request of the bride, all guests will now be seated." The father of the bride then gives his daughter in marriage, and goes to his seat.

K. The chaplain leads the way to the altar and the wedding cere-

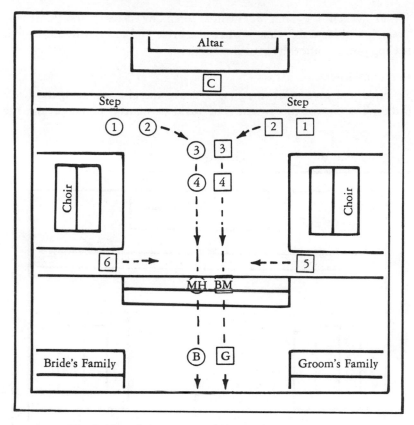

The bride and groom are the first to leave the chancel.
Alternate plan B

mony now takes place. Upon reaching the altar steps, the bride hands her bouquet or prayer book to the maid or matron of honor, and at the appropriate time the best man gives the groom the wedding ring. If the groom is also going to wear a wedding ring, the bride at the same time receives it from the maid or matron of honor.

When the bride and her parents so desire, at the point in the ceremony when the chaplain asks, "Who giveth this woman to be married?", her father may answer, "Her mother and I do."

L. At the conclusion of the ceremony, the bride and groom are congratulated by the chaplain, and the groom may now kiss his bride. She receives her bridal bouquet or prayer book from the maid or matron of honor, and holds it in her right arm ready for the recessional.

M. When the arch of swords ceremony takes place inside the chapel, it will be at this time—when the bride and groom rise from their kneeling position after the benediction.

THE RECESSIONAL

The bride and groom are the first to leave the chancel, with the bride on the *right arm* of the groom. The maid or matron of honor and the

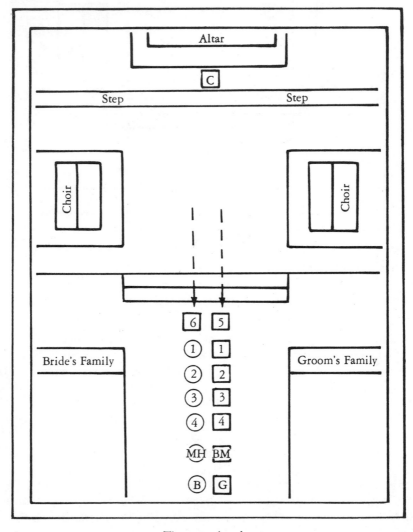

The recessional.

best man walk out together, followed by the bridesmaids and ushers in pairs. Ushers 5 and 6 escort the bride's and groom's mothers, followed by the chaplain, from the chapel before others leave.

When there are not two more ushers than bridesmaids, two head ushers will be designated to act as escorts to the bride's and groom's mothers who leave in that order.

There is no effort made to keep step with the music during the recessional, but everyone walks with a natural, smooth gait—neither hurried nor slow. Following the families' departure, the guests leave in no precedence of departure.

It is important when a wedding reception follows elsewhere, that the bride and groom go immediately to an anteroom, or any secluded area, after they reach the vestibule in order that they are not immediately extended congratulations and best wishes by the guests.

At a military ceremony, it is the duty of the ushers (in fair weather) to see that all guests go outdoors immediately after the wedding for the arch of swords ceremony. An usher may clearly—and courteously—request that guests "Please proceed to the chapel steps."

Members of the bridal party usually stand at either or both sides of the outer door of the chapel, with guests standing at any convenient place along the steps or walk.

When the ushers have taken their positions on the steps or walk, the best man will notify the bride and groom that the arch of swords ceremony can proceed.

ARCH OF SWORDS (SABERS) CEREMONY

Although the ushers usually act as sword bearers, other officers may be designated as sword bearers—which would accelerate the arch of swords ceremony following the wedding ceremony. It is customary that six or eight ushers (or designated sword bearers) take part in the ceremony. Although the chaplain's office will furnish swords (sabers) for the ceremony, it is customary, such as at West Point, for the cadets to furnish their own white belts, gloves, and breastplates.

If the ushers have removed their swords, they now hook them on. In an outdoor ceremony, they proceed down the steps of the chapel where they form, facing each other in equal numbers.

In the *naval services*, the head usher gives the command, "Officers, DRAW SWORDS," which is done in one continuous motion, tips touching. The bride and groom pass under the arch—*and only they may do so*—then they pause for a moment. The head usher gives the command, "Officers, RETURN (swords brought to the position of 'present arms') SWORDS."

Swords are returned to the scabbard for all but about *three or four inches* of their length. The final inches of travel are completed in unison, the swords returning home with a single click.

When permission is received from the chaplain to hold the arch of swords (sabers) ceremony indoors, it takes place just as the couple rises after receiving the blessing. All members of the bridal party wait until the ushers' swords are returned to their scabbards before the recessional proceeds.

In ths *Army* and *Air Force*, the *Arch of Sabers* is carried out in this way: when the bride and groom rise from their kneeling position after the benediction, the senior saber bearer gives the command, "CENTER FACE." This command moves the saber bearers into position facing each other. The next command is "ARCH SABERS," wherein each saber bearer raises his right arm with the saber, rotating it in a clockwise direction, so that the cutting edge of the saber will be on top, thus forming a true arch with his opposite across the aisle.

After the bride and groom pass under the arched sabers, the command is, "CARRY SABERS," followed almost immediately by "REAR FACE," with the saber bearers facing away from the altar, thus enabling them to march down the side aisle. They form again with arched sabers on the steps of the chapel.

CHAPTER 27

Special Weddings

A HOUSE WEDDING

A couple may be married at home if they so desire. A wedding at home can be as large and as elaborate as a church wedding.

The room farthest away from the door is usually the best place for the ceremony. A screen may be placed in front of a fireplace, and vases of white flowers may be effectively used. A long narrow table or altar can be placed in front of the screen, and this is where the bride and groom stand. The arrangement of the altar should be according to the direction of the chaplain or clergyman. The room should be emptied of as much heavy furniture as possible, with chairs and sofas placed along the walls. Other chairs should be placed in the room to form an aisle.

The immediate families of the bride and groom sit in the first rows of chairs placed to the left and right, respectively, of the aisle. The first chair at the left side of the aisle is for the bride's father, or whoever gives her away. There should be other chairs, but some—or most— guests will stand. The ushers do not have lists, but they stand near the front door and tell guests where they should go.

As soon as all the guests have arrived, the groom's mother goes up the aisle with her husband. The bride's mother is the last to be seated; she is escorted by a male relative or the head usher.

The chaplain or clergyman, the groom and best man, take their places as they would in church. The groom and best man stand near the altar, at the right side of the aisle, with the best man just behind and to the right of the groom. The bride's mother rises at the first note of the wedding march, and the procession follows the same form as in the chapel or church—except that ushers are *not* included.

The bridesmaids enter the room first, then the bride and her father. When the ceremony is over, the bride and groom usually stand at the altar, with guests coming up to extend their best wishes and congratulations. The groom kisses his bride at the altar—since he is always the first to kiss the bride after the ceremony.

The couple go directly to the room where the reception is to be held, with the guests following. There is usually no seated bride's table, and the reception may be as elaborate or simple as desired.

At a very small afternoon wedding at home, with only members of the immediate families and intimate friends attending, the bride may wear a long bridal gown or she may wear a pastel-colored or white afternoon dress or suit, with a corsage.

The bride and groom and their parents stand a little apart to greet guests. A buffet tea may be served, with a wedding cake centering the table. Punch, tea, and sandwiches should be placed in convenient sequence around the table. Invitations to such a small wedding may be handwritten, with wedding announcements sent out after the ceremony.

At a formal, evening, home wedding (usually held at eight o'clock or half after eight) the members of the bridal party may be in full evening dress, with men in dinner or mess dress or evening dress uniform, but more often in black tie. The bride wears the traditional long white bridal gown, and her attendants also wear long gowns. The mothers of the bride and groom, as well as the women guests, wear long dresses.

At less formal weddings, men wear business suits and women wear cocktail style or long dresses. The reception can be simple or elaborate.

THE DOUBLE WEDDING

At a *double wedding*, when two sisters are being married, the older takes precedence over the younger throughout the ceremony. The older sister walks up the aisle with her father, and the second sister walks with a brother, uncle, or other male relative or friend of the family. The father gives both daughters away—the older daughter first, then the younger.

The bridegrooms stand at the head of the aisle, with their best men behind them, the bridegroom of the older sister nearer the congregation. The older sister is at the left and the younger at the right during the ceremony, with the vows repeated separately. The older sister goes down the aisle *first* when the ceremony is over.

Usually, the sisters have the same bridesmaids, half of whom each sister selects. The ushers are also divided in this way, but each bride should have her own maid or matron of honor, and each groom should have his own best man. In the wedding procession, the maids or matrons of honor directly precede each bride, with the ushers, bridesmaids, etc., preceding the entire bridal party.

The family of both grooms may share the first pew at the right of the chapel or church, or the family of the groom of the older sister sit in the first pew, and the family of the groom of the second sister sit in the second pew.

At the wedding reception the older sister stands before the younger sister, with the traditional order followed thereon. The mother of the brides stands at the door to greet guests, with the mother of the older daughter's husband next to her, then the mother of the other groom beyond.

When the brides are not sisters at a double wedding, the older girl, or the higher-ranking of the brides' fathers, or the higher-ranking bridegroom may decide the question of which bride precedes the other. Sometimes the question is settled by alphabetical order of the brides' names. The same precedence follows at the reception.

VARIATIONS IN PROCEDURE

There are variations in the traditional wedding procedures—such as when the bride's parents are divorced, when one or the other of the parents has remarried, or when the bride's father or mother is dead. When the bride is a divorcée or a widow, the wedding is small but the reception may be as large and formal as desired.

When the *bride's parents are divorced*, the mother usually gives the wedding and the reception. The bride's father may give her in marriage, but he may—or may not—go to the wedding reception. On the day of the wedding, the father calls for the bride just before the ceremony.

At the chapel or church, he sits in the second pew during the ceremony; if he has remarried, he may sit in the third pew on the left with his present wife—if she attends. If the relationship is truly congenial, the father and his present wife attend the reception.

When the bride's mother has remarried, her present husband sits with her during the ceremony in the first pew at the left of the aisle. At the wedding reception, he acts as host. When the relationship with a stepfather has been a happy one, and the father of the bride is at a distance or cannot attend the ceremony, or when she prefers, the stepfather may give the bride in marriage.

When the *bride's father is deceased*, a brother, uncle, cousin, or a male relative of suitable age may give the bride away. Or a classmate of the father, or close friend, may be asked to give her in marriage. It is not improper but it is rather unusual for a mother to give her daughter in marriage; she may properly remain standing at the end of the first pew on the left and at the correct time say, "*I do.*"

When the *bride's mother is deceased,* and the father has remarried, the stepmother may be in charge of the wedding plans. If the bride prefers, an aunt, grandmother, or close friend of the family may act in this capacity.

When the *bride's parents are deceased*—or when they are living at a considerable distance from the place of the wedding, or when they cannot give the wedding for financial reasons, or will not for reasons of religious differences—the parents of the bridegroom may offer to give the wedding and/or the reception. The couple may prefer to marry quietly in the bride's parish, with members of the families and very close friends attending.

When a couple *elopes,* a civil marriage usually follows in a registrar's office or by a justice of the peace. When parents give their blessings, they may send out wedding announcements and give the couple a wedding reception with close friends and relatives attending. When the announcement is written or printed, only the name of the city or town appears and the fact that it was a civil ceremony does *not* appear.

SECOND MARRIAGES

There is little difference between the second marriage of a *mature* couple (often widows or widowers) and a couple one or both of whom have been *divorced.*

As with any less formal wedding—and a second wedding *is* less formal—invitations may be extended by word of mouth, by handwritten note, or they may be printed or engraved for the larger occasion.

The couple probably will have only two attendants, both contemporaries, or a daughter may be the maid or matron of honor and a son could be the best man. A younger couple could have daughters as junior attendants, or a small child as a flower girl or ring bearer. But whatever the age of the couple, their children, if any, are the most important guests at the wedding.

The *mature* bride should choose a pastel-colored dress (more flattering than white), whereas the younger bride may wear white, but neither the mature woman nor the divorcée wears the traditional wedding gown and veil, and the flowers should be either a corsage or a small bouquet. The groom should wear a business suit in keeping with the season.

The second wedding is customarily a small wedding with close friends and relatives attending, but the trend today seems to be toward larger weddings, since most couples want everyone who attends the ceremony to attend the reception also.

Although the weddings of a divorcée and a widow are similar, the widow usually waits a year before marrying again, partly out of respect for her deceased partner and partly to make certain she isn't marrying just to overcome loneliness, although this is no longer considered mandatory. The divorcée, however, can remarry as soon as her divorce becomes final. The same rules apply for the widower or divorced man.

CIVIL CEREMONY

When a couple cannot be married in a church (in cases of divorce) or when the couple has no religious affiliation or convictions, or when there is no time to plan a wedding—such as imminent orders for an officer—the wedding may be held in a judge's chambers or in a magistrate's office. There must be two witnesses—preferably close friends or relatives who will be maid or matron of honor and best man. Otherwise, the witnesses may be complete strangers to the couple but known to the officiating magistrate, probably members of the office staff.

The bridegroom should wear a business suit or service uniform and the bride a daytime dress, or suit, with a corsage. They may go on to a place of reception, most likely to a restaurant or club for luncheon or dinner. When reservations are made, this is the time to order a cake and champagne.

When there is no best man to take care of the fee, the bridegroom should do this at a convenient time before the wedding. The fee will be $25 or more, depending upon the place and the circumstances.

Should the wedding be held in a private home or a wedding chapel, the rules are about the same; except that in a home, should the officiating person be a high-ranking official who is a friend of the family, such as a judge of the Supreme Court or a mayor, you may consider sending a gift to him later, instead of a fee, with a note of thanks for his services.

Frequently, a couple who were married in a civil service without friends or relatives, or a couple who eloped, wish to remarry in a religious ceremony. When a reception was not held after the civil service, it can be planned like any other. If several years have elapsed after the civil ceremony, then only close friends and relatives should be invited, since the religious aspect in having the second marriage is being stressed. The bride should not wear a veil, but she may wear white.

RELIGIOUS DIFFERENCES

The various religious marriage ceremonies are essentially the same. There are differences in Protestant ceremonies; there are similarities between the Christian and Jewish ceremony; there are changes today in the Roman Catholic Church which permit interfaith marriages, and with the special consent of the bishop a nuptial mass may be solemnized between Catholics and nonCatholics who have been baptized.

In cases of interfaith marriages, or when one or the other of the couple has been married before, or divorced, and in any church or synagogue with strict procedural rules, these restrictions must be learned in advance and discussed with the officiating clergyman, rabbi, or priest. Prenuptial instruction is required by most churches.

In a *Roman Catholic* ceremony, weddings with a nuptial mass by custom are held in the morning between eight and noon, but today, nuptial mass may be held in the afternoon. Without a mass they may be held at almost any hour, with the couple taking communion together earlier in the day. A ceremony with a nuptial mass is longer than without it, and the bridal party is seated.

The father of the bride does not give her away. He escorts her up the aisle and at the moment he turns to enter his pew the bridegroom meets her and together they go to the altar. The ring may be received from the acolyte or the best man, and it is blessed by the priest before being handed to the groom.

Whether only the bride and groom enter the sanctuary for this blessing of the ring, or the couple and the best man and maid or matron-of-honor—or the entire bridal party—is determined by church custom.

A couple has a choice in the wording of vows: the traditional "To have and to hold," or a more modern version; repeating the vows after the priest, or reciting the vows to each other. The couple may choose selections from the Scriptures, from the Old or New Testament, or the Gospel.

In the *Jewish* faith, Orthodox (traditional), Conservative (moderate), or Reform (most lenient) weddings are not held between sundown Friday and sundown Saturday. Most weddings take place on late Saturday evenings or on Sunday. On holy days, and many days between the second day of Passover and the holidays of Shabuoth, weddings are not held.

Jewish weddings usually take place in synagogues, but both weddings and receptions may be held in clubs, halls, hotels. Before the ceremony, guests may be received by the bride and her attendants in a private room. Fathers do not "give their daughters away," but in the Reform ceremony the father escorts his daughter up the aisle to meet the groom, then he turns and sits in the pew.

In Orthodox and Conservative ceremonies, the fathers and mothers of both the bride and groom walk with them to the canopy at the altar. The ceremony is conducted under the canopy where the rabbi stands beside a table holding two glasses of wine. Although the parents may stand under the canopy with the bride and groom and maid or matron of honor and best man when there is room, they usually stand just on the outside. The service is in Aramaic, with the rabbi's address

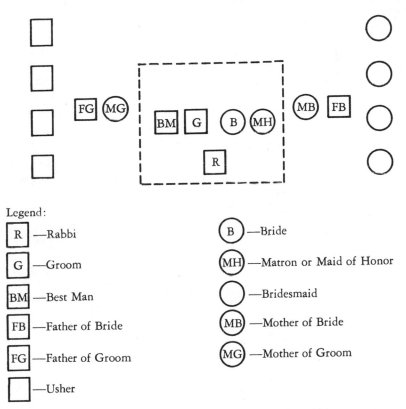

Legend:

R —Rabbi

G —Groom

BM —Best Man

FB —Father of Bride

FG —Father of Groom

—Usher

B —Bride

MH —Matron or Maid of Honor

—Bridesmaid

MB —Mother of Bride

MG —Mother of Groom

Orthodox Jewish Ceremony Under Canopy at Altar

to the couple in Hebrew or in the language of the couple or congregation. In a Reform wedding most of the service is in English.

All men wear yarmulkes—skull caps—or hats at Orthodox and Conservative ceremonies, and married women wear a hat or headdress. When male guests do not have a hat, skull caps are available in the vestibule. It is optional but desirable that single women wear a headdress. Men do not wear hats at a Reform service. Otherwise, dress is the same as for a Protestant wedding.

The Betrothal Benedictions open the Orothodox ceremony, followed by the ring ceremony, then the reading of the marriage contract—"Kesubah." After the wine is blessed, the rabbi hands one glass of wine to the groom, who takes a sip then passes it to his bride. The ritual in drinking the second glass of wine by both bride and groom is completed with the crushing of a glass under the shoe of the groom, which is an admonition that regardless of the happiness of this occasion the congregation should remember and work for the rebuilding of Zion.

In the Reform ceremony only one glass of wine is used, it is not crushed, and the canopy is not required.

The *Eastern Orthodox* ceremony is celebrated without mass, and is held in the afternoon or evening. The ceremony takes place at a table set near the front of the sanctuary but not at the altar. Guests and participants stand or kneel throughout the service. Vocal music is all that is permitted and the bride enters the room with wedding hymns sung by the choir. The bride is given in marriage by her father, who then returns to the side of his wife.

Prior to the wedding, the bride and groom fast, make confessions, and take communion. Although the ceremonial forms are similar to those of the Catholics, members of the church do not acknowledge the Pope as their spiritual leader. The Holy Trinity has deep significance, and after the final blessing the choir chants "Many Years" three times.

CHAPTER 28

Wedding Receptions

THE TYPE OF RECEPTION depends upon the type of wedding—formal or informal—as well as the number of guests to be invited, where it will be held, and the time of day or night the wedding will take place.

A wedding may be large or small, simple or elaborate, and the reception should be in keeping. A reception may be held in the home or garden, in an officers' or private club, at a hotel, or in the church parlors. When not held at home, reservations for the use of the reception room or rooms should be made well in advance of the wedding date.

RECEIVING LINE

At a comparatively large reception, such as one held at an officers' or private club, the mother of the bride customarily stands just inside the door, with the groom's mother standing next to her. The bride's mother greets the guests and introduces them to the groom's mother, then each guest moves on to greet each member of the bridal party, with the line formed a little apart from the mothers.

The fathers of the bride and groom may stand with the mothers for a time, but usually they prefer to be nearby and to mix with the guests. The best man and ushers never stand in the line; the best man should be near the groom, however, ready to help in any way possible, while the ushers act as unofficial hosts.

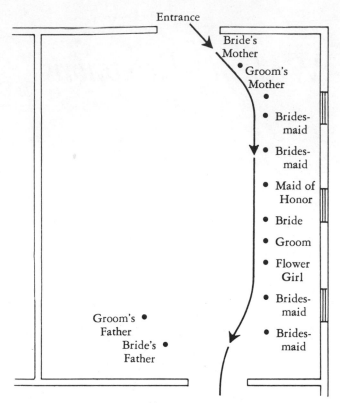

A version of the receiving line.

If the mother of the bride is not living, her father may receive the guests, or he may wish to ask a close relative, such as a grandmother or aunt, to receive with him. He stands just inside the door and introduces the guests in this manner, "This is Anne's grandmother, Mrs. Smith . . . Mother, Colonel James."

The bride and groom always stand together, and the bride is always on *the groom's right.* Next in order is the maid or matron of honor, then the bridesmaids. If a flower girl stands in the line for a while (she usually is seven or under), she should stand on the groom's left. Since she is very young she need not be in the line at all, or only for a short time. When sisters are bridesmaids, the older sister precedes the younger. The line remains intact until all guests have been greeted.

If you are a guest at a reception and there is no one to announce you as you approach the line, you announce yourself. You say to the bride's mother (who will extend her hand first), "I'm John Jones, Mrs. Smith. Such a lovely wedding." You shake hands briefly, but do not linger in the line even though you may be a longtime friend.

When you greet the bridal party, you offer *best wishes to the bride* and *congratulations to the bridegroom*. You *never* congratulate the bride. You may say a few words to the groom about how lovely his bride is, and he may answer, "Thank you so much," and agree that she is lovely as he passes you along. Usually, you have little more time than to say, "How do you do."

The simplest form of reception is one where the bride's mother and father greet the guests and introduce them to the groom's parents, with the guests going over to the bride and groom standing together and wishing them well.

At a small reception, the mothers of the bride and groom may stand in a continuous line with the bride and groom and the maid or matron of honor.

At a large reception, the receiving line may be in this order: half the bridesmaids, the maid or matron of honor, the bride, the groom, the flower girl, and the rest of the bridesmaids. The mothers of the bride and groom stand in the customary position near the door to the reception room. At some weddings the bridesmaids do not stand in the line—which speeds up the flow of guests. The line does not disband until all guests have been received, with the mother of the bride making the move to leave.

Women in the receiving line may wear gloves, but take them off as soon as the line is disbanded. However, when the bride's gown has long sleeves, she does not wear gloves. It is optional for women guests to wear gloves when going through the line, then remove them.

RECEIVING LINE AT THE CHAPEL OR CHURCH

When a small reception is planned, to which it is impossible to invite all the guests who may come to the wedding, a receiving line may be held in the foyer of the chapel or church immediately after the recessional, but confirmation must first be obtained from the chaplain.

This type of receiving line is a friendly and thoughtful way of receiving the congratulations of the congregation. Guests who may have come from a distance and at some personal inconvenience will thus have the opportunity to speak to the bride and groom and to wish them happiness.

When such a receiving line is formed at the chapel, the same procedure is followed as at the reception. The bride stands on the groom's right and the maid or matron of honor at the right of the bride. The bridesmaids usually stand at the right of the maid of honor.

The bride's mother customarily receives alone at the door, but she may be accompanied by the groom's mother. The fathers of the bride and groom stand beside their wives, if they choose, or they may walk about among the guests. The ushers and best man are *not* in the receiving line.

VARIATIONS

When the bride's parents are *divorced* and the daughter has been living with her mother, it is the mother who customarily gives the wedding and the reception. Then, she is the hostess and will stand first in the receiving line.

When the father gives the wedding and the reception, and he has remarried, his *present* wife acts as hostess; if his first wife (the bride's mother) attends, she attends as an important guest.

If the father and mother have not remarried and have a friendly relationship, he may ask her to stand in the receiving line with him at the reception—but he will be first in line since he is the host. Although this procedure has been frowned on in past years, the bride is *their* daughter; when she wants very much for them all to be together on this important day, then this variance is acceptable. Also, the growing increase in divorces in this country has necessitated many changes in social customs.

When the father has not remarried and the mother has, he may receive guests by himself, or he may ask his mother or sister or an older daughter to assist.

When the bride's mother has remarried, she alone or she and the stepfather will receive guests. When the bride has not had a very friendly relationship with her stepfather, it is better that he not stand in the line but mingle with the guests.

Sometimes the mother gives the wedding and the father gives the reception, or vice versa. The one who gives the reception is considered the host.

When divorced parents are not on good terms, it is better that the one who does not give the wedding and reception stay away from the reception.

When the *bride's parents are deceased*—or when they are ill or are living at a distance and cannot attend the wedding, or when the wedding is in the home town of the bridegroom's parents—then the bridegroom's parents may offer to give the wedding and/or the reception.

When the parents are deceased or incapacitated, the bride may ask a grandmother, aunt, older sister, godmother, or very close older friend, or the bridegroom's mother, to receive guests.

At a *double wedding reception* the older sister and her husband stand in line before the younger sister and her bridegroom; when bridal attendants serve both brides, the usual procedure is followed. When both brides have their own attendants, then there could be two lines, with the mother of the older bride receiving in the first line with the bridegroom's mother, and the mother of the bridegroom of the younger daughter receiving in the second line.

RECEPTION FOOD

There are three main types of food served at wedding receptions: a light buffet tea at small and informal receptions, with more elaborate food at the formal afternoon reception; a wedding breakfast, which follows morning or noon weddings; a buffet supper following evening ceremonies.

The type of drinks served depends upon the wishes of the bride and groom—or sometimes the area where the couple is married. At large weddings in most cities, an open bar is usual; in some communities liquor is not served. Usually, no matter where, champagne is offered along with fruit punch for nondrinkers. On a cold day coffee and tea are welcome.

At a very small reception, a wedding cake and punch with which to toast the bride are all that need be offered. It is customary at an afternoon reception, however, that a buffet include tea and coffee, thin sandwiches, small cakes, and fruit punch or champagne. At any type of reception, however, there is always a wedding cake.

At a late afternoon reception, the menu could be a seafood salad (shrimp, lobster, crab), ice cream molds, tea, coffee, and cakes. The menu could also be cold turkey or chicken, salad, ice cream or sherbet, tea, coffee, and cakes. By adding a hot soup and omitting the tea, either menu could be used for a buffet breakfast.

The menu for the wedding breakfast could be breast of chicken, tomato aspic, biscuits, ice cream or sherbet, wedding cake, and champagne or punch. Creamed sweetbreads and peas, or baked ham and salads, little cakes ("petits fours") demitasse, champagne and/or punch are frequently served.

A menu often served to guests who eat standing up is: creamed chicken in pastry shells, and peas, salad, ice cream molds or meringues, cakes, coffee, and champagne or punch. This is good for afternoon or evening receptions.

The buffet menu may be seafood, roast turkey, ham, or beef—or all of them, if the reception is very large. Any wedding breakfast, luncheon, or supper may be served to guests seated at tables, but customarily it is served buffet style, with the food, plates, and other accessories in place on a long table or tables, with guests serving themselves and eating standing up.

Food for a large reception held at home is usually catered.

SEATING ARRANGEMENTS

At a seated wedding breakfast or supper, there are usually two tables, one for the bride and groom and bridal party, the other for the parents and their intimate friends. The bride's table is always covered with a white cloth, and the wedding cake is placed in the center of the table. At a large table white flowers may be placed on either side of the cake.

The bride and groom sit together at one end or at the center of the table, with the bride on the groom's right. The best man sits to the right of the bride, and the maid or matron of honor sits to the left of the groom. The bridesmaids and ushers alternate around the table.

The parents' table is set with a white cloth and flowers, and the parents of the bride sit across from each other as they would in their own home.

The father of the groom sits at the right of the bride's mother, and the chaplain or clergyman sits at her left. The mother of the groom sits at the right of the bride's father, and the wife of the chaplain or clergyman sits at his left. Members of both immediate families, with intimate friends, sit at the table. All other guests may be seated at small tables for four or six each, or they may not be served at tables but eat standing up.

At smaller weddings, the bride's table and the parents' table are combined. Such an arrangement could be:

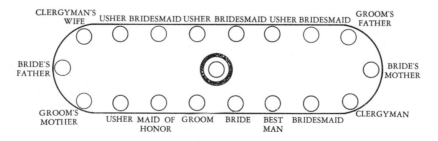

Bride's and parents' table combined.

At a buffet table, the food is placed in convenient sequence together with stacks of plates, rows of silver, and napkins, with guests serving themselves at the table. The cake may be the centerpiece, or it may be placed on a smaller table, with guests coming to the table for a serving.

Champagne or punch is always placed on a table by itself except at a very small wedding, when it may be set on the main buffet table. There is usually a nonalcoholic drink served in addition to champagne or punch.

At the bridal table at a military wedding, the groom unsheathes his sword and hands it to the bride, who stands to his right, and she cuts the first piece of cake with his hand over hers. At a civilian wedding, the bride and groom cut the wedding cake in the same manner, with a silver knife usually decorated with a white ribbon. Whether or not there is a seated bride's table, the first toast is always proposed by the best man to the bride and groom. Other toasts may be to the bride's mother, proposed by the groom; then toasts to the bridesmaids, etc. (*See* Chapter 23, Toasts.)

When dancing follows, the bride and groom have the first dance together, usually a waltz. Then the father of the bride dances with the groom's mother, and the bride's mother with the groom's father. After the first dance, the bride dances with her father-in-law and the groom dances with his mother-in-law; then the bride dances with her father, the best man, and the ushers, while the groom dances with his mother, the maid or matron of honor, and the bridesmaids. When the attendants join in, other guests also participate. The dancing may continue for an hour or so. Music is usually provided by a trio, unless the wedding is very large, when more musicians would be needed.

GOING AWAY

It is a tradition that the bride throw her bouquet to her bridesmaids standing in a group, either from the stairs or in a doorway, near the closing hour of the reception. The bride and groom then change into traveling clothes, while the guests wait to see the couple off.

The parents tell the bride and groom good-bye in private, then the couple go outdoors to a car that is waiting while the guests traditionally throw confetti or rice or rose petals on the couple. The destination of the wedding trip, and its duration, are strictly up to the couple—and the length of time the groom may have on leave, between duty stations, or from his job.

Gifts For Weddings, Anniversaries, & Showers

WHEN YOU RECEIVE an invitation to a wedding and reception, and accept, you send a gift. When you receive an invitation to the wedding only, or when you receive a wedding announcement, you are not obligated to send a gift, but may if you so choose. When you are invited to a double wedding but know only one of the couples, you need only send a gift to that one couple.

Following an elopement or a civil marriage, when there was no reception, you send a gift when you know the couple well and want to. Usually, the ones who do not have a reception, perhaps because they cannot afford it, are the ones who most appreciate a gift.

Although most gifts are sent to the bride-elect before the wedding, there are times when they must be sent afterwards—then they are addressed to the couple at their new address.

When mailed, make certain that the package is wrapped carefully and insured against breakage or being crushed. Should this happen, the bride must save the wrapping showing the insurance stamp, for proof of mishandling and for the insurance claim.

WHAT TO GIVE

When you buy a gift, the old rule of "getting something that you would like for yourself" rarely holds true. The other person's taste may be completely different from yours, and the bride may be hoping to fill in a set of china or bed linens with a different color and design than the one you had in mind. Pictures in good taste are not given too often, and are always needed.

Don't buy more than you can afford to give. Some of the loveliest and most treasured gifts are those that a person makes or has handed down in the family—a patchwork quilt or crocheted bedspread, a piece of needlepoint, a wild-flower picture, an old Spode dish.

What you give is a wedding present that you know the couple needs or wants. It may be beautiful, something to be cherished through the years, or it may be practical and used every day. It is always better to give something small but choice rather than a large showy present. One or two cups and saucers or plates in the bride's china pattern, a single piece of sterling flatware, or a crystal goblet are always appreciated.

Sterling silver, which constantly increases in value, will last the couple's lifetime and can be passed down to future generations. Good linens are another item of beauty and durability, but sizes of bed sheets, blankets, and bedspreads, and the kind of tablecloth must be learned beforehand. No-iron bed and table linens are a must for a bride. Place mats are used for all types of entertaining.

Brides will list their silver, crystal, and china patterns at stores which have gift registers; sometimes they list only one, silver. Service-oriented brides know that crystal and china may be purchased when officers have foreign duty or cruises, and prefer to have less expensive china and glassware during their frequent-moving years when things are easily broken. And sterling is very expensive. Brides often select brightly colored or patterned china to use with plain-colored mats—or the reverse.

Many brides prefer practical gifts for everyday living, such as a vacuum cleaner, ironing board and iron, electric fry pan, crock pot, casseroles, a set of stainless steel kitchen utensils (skillet, pots, pans), a set of stainless steel flatware, carving set and steak knives, a set of graduated knives, a spice rack, cannister set, mixing bowls and spatulas; no-stick roasting pan, cookie sheets, pie and cake pans, salad bowl set, salt and pepper mills, small electrical appliances such as a hand mixer, blender, can opener, toaster; bathroom scales, matching bathmat and towel sets and shower curtain; a pair of pillows—the choice seems limitless for both wedding and shower presents. Many of the smaller, less expensive articles mentioned make excellent shower gifts.

Before making certain selections—those with color and size particularly—ask the bride's mother what her daughter could use and prefers. In case of duplication, a bride should always feel free to exchange any present.

GIFTS TO EACH OTHER

The bride and groom exchange gifts with each other just before the wedding day—and these should be meaningful. The officer's parents may have a piece of jewelry that they would like his bride to have; or he may have found something on a cruise or foreign duty that would please her. A string of pearls from Japan—cultured or any grade within his financial circumstances—makes a desirable gift.

In turn, the bride selects something that he does not have and would enjoy through the years—possibly her bridal picture in a silver frame, small enough that he could take it with him, later on. Perhaps it would be a fitted leather traveling case, or monogrammed gold or silver cuff links. Or she may knit him a sweater or compile a photo album which he will enjoy through the years.

MONEY GIFTS

Many young couples starting out on a shoestring need money more than a present. Before the wedding, a check could be sent to the bride's address, written in her name or in the name of both. Afterwards, the check should be made out to them as a couple: "Lieutenant and Mrs. John E. Doe," or "Mary and John Doe."

Bonds or stocks are also a welcome gift. When saved, the dividends are helpful.

ETHNIC GROUPS

It is customary for certain ethnic groups to give money as a wedding gift. A number of Jewish and Italian people retain this tradition.

The money should be in the form of a check, made out to the bride-elect or to her and her fiancé, and it is often handed to one or the other of them in the receiving line at the reception. Otherwise, the check may be mailed to the bride-elect at her home or delivered in person by the giver, or sent to the couple after the wedding.

SECOND MARRIAGE GIFTS

When you are invited to the wedding and reception of a couple, one or both of whom have been married before, and if you are a close friend or relative, you will probably want to send a present, but you are not obligated to.

GIFTS FOR ELOPERS

Your affection for the bride and groom, and their families, will determine whether or not you send the couple a gift—after their return home, or after a marriage announcement has been sent out.

SHOWER GIFTS

Friends of the bride-elect—but not immediate members of her family—usually give her a shower or two before the wedding. It is customary for the bridesmaids and maid or matron of honor to give a joint shower within the week of the wedding, after any out-of-towners have arrived.

Shower presents are taken, not delivered by a store, to the home of the hostess, and each one is opened by the bride-to-be who thanks the giver then and there. It is not necessary for her to write thank-you notes except to the hostess and anyone who sent a gift but could not attend. Always enclose a gift card.

The hostess should ask someone to keep a record of who gave what, and gifts should be in accordance with the type of shower stated in the invitation—linen, miscellaneous, kitchen. The latter can be very original as well as useful, such as a sturdy wastepaper basket filled with canned foods, spices, or small kitchen appliances.

MUSTS FOR THE BRIDE

It takes time to write the many thank-you notes, which all brides must do when they receive wedding presents. They are handwritten, with a mention of the gift, not just "thank you for the lovely present. . . ."

Such a note might read:

Dear Mrs. Smith,

It was thoughtful of you and Colonel Smith to send us such a needed picture. The temple rubbing is now hanging over our fireplace mantel, and it is beautiful.

Thank you very much.

Very sincerely,
Jane Doe

For a belated present you might write:

Dear Grandmother,

John and I are delighted with your check, it will make all the difference in our being able to decorate our new quarters as we really want to.

We plan to buy an oil painting of the Rampart Range which we have long admired, and when you feel better we hope that you will come and see it. We are sure that you will like it, too. Thank you.

With love,
Jane

As many thank-you notes as possible should be written before the wedding. Afterward, you will have about two months to get them off. If you wait longer than three or four months, the sender will wonder if the gift was received; it is embarrassing to hear from someone who asks if it arrived safely—when it has.

A *gift-register* book is the best way to keep a list of the gifts as they arrive. Such books are available at stationery or other stores, or you may use a lined notebook and make the headings yourself. This book can be a memento of the wedding but it is essential to keep a clear account of who gave what.

The headings might be:

No.	Sent By	Article	Sender's Address	Date Rec'd	Thanks Sent
14	Dr. and Mrs. G. W. Doe	Silver spoons (2)	1130 Conn. Ave. D.C.	8/5	8/7

There will be sheets of numbered stickers with the book that you buy—or you can make your own—and one sticker is placed on the bottom of each gift, or a set or pair, after it is opened. The corresponding number is written in the book, and this cross-check will insure that the gift does not get mixed up.

DISPLAYING THE GIFTS

This not only gives the bride-elect pleasure but shows appreciation for them. A room in your home should be set aside, with tables set up and covered with white tablecloths or sheets. Unnecessary furniture is moved out of the room, to enable people to walk around easily. Gifts are never displayed at a club or hotel where the reception is held. Out-of-town guests especially should be invited to drop by at a time convenient for all.

Gifts should be displayed to their best advantage. Sometimes silver is placed on one table, china on another; but sterling and silver-plate or pewter might show up to better advantage separated but not "hidden." The donor's cards usually are placed with the gifts, but not necessarily so. When checks are displayed, arrange them so that the amounts are concealed but not the signatures.

RETURNING PRESENTS

When a wedding is cancelled or annulled, gifts are returned. When an engagement is broken, gifts are also returned. But when a marriage breaks up almost immediately, gifts are not returned but are divided between the ex-partners.

The briefest of notes should be included with the returned gift, stating that the engagement or marriage is over but not giving the reason why.

WEDDING ANNIVERSARY GIFTS

Any happy couple wants to observe their wedding anniversary, maybe with a small party for close friends, perhaps a dinner together in a special restaurant, or when years have gone by, with a more formal party, dinner, or at-home.

When a couple observes their twenty-fifth or fiftieth anniversary, they may want to make a special occasion of it and send out invitations engraved or printed in silver or gold. Sometimes they will request that no gifts be given, which, of course, should be honored.

Sometimes a money-tree is given in lieu of unwanted presents when someone other than they themselves gives the party. Then, the "tree," which may be a real branch, is sprayed with white, silver, or gold paint and the dollar bills taped to it. No one gives more than a few.

Since an older couple may be a little touchy about receiving money, even though they need it, a little tact can be employed and the invitation, either oral or written (but never in a newspaper account), could state "Gifts for a Money Tree are welcome."

But when gifts are not wanted, the invitation should so state.

The following list shows the types of gifts suitable for the various anniversaries:

	Traditional	Modern
First	Paper	Clocks
Second	Cotton	China
Third	Leather	Crystal, glass
Fourth	Fruit, flowers	Appliances
Fifth	Wood	Silverware
Sixth	Iron, candy	Wood
Seventh	Wool, copper	Desk sets
Eighth	Bronze	Linen, laces
Ninth	Pottery	Leather
Tenth	Tin, aluminum	Diamond jewelry
Eleventh	Steel	Costume jewelry
Twelfth	Silk, linen	Pearls
Thirteenth	Lace	Furs, textiles
Fourteenth	Ivory	Gold jewelry
Fifteenth	Crystal, glass	Watch
Twentieth	China	Platinum
Twenty-fifth	Silver	Silver, pewter
Thirtieth	Pearl	Diamond
Thirty-fifth	Coral	Jade
Fortieth	Ruby	Ruby
Forty-fifth	Sapphire	Sapphire
Fiftieth	Gold	Gold
Fifty-fifth	Emerald	Emerald
Sixtieth	Diamond	Diamond

RULES TO REMEMBER

When you have been invited to a wedding, you should be aware of the customary rules for giving presents. These are as follows:

Send presents to friends and relatives when they are close to you—but you are not obligated to send a present to everyone who sends you a wedding invitation or announcement.

When you receive an invitation to a wedding reception, send a gift if you accept, but you need not if you regret.

Do not send more than you can afford—and always remember that quality is superior to quantity.

When you receive many invitations (such as the innumerable Graduation Week weddings at the service academies), send presents only to those classmates or friends close to you, whether you attend the ceremony or not.

When you are invited to the wedding but not the reception, you are not obligated to send a present—but you may, if you so desire.

When there are no invitations or announcements nor any reception after a civil ceremony, you send a present to the couple according to your friendship with them. Every young couple enjoys a wedding present, and will always treasure it. If you prefer, you may take or send the couple a house-warming present.

In case of a broken engagement, cancelled or annulled marriage, the woman returns the gifts to the sender with a brief but tactful note. There is no need to explain why.

When a marriage is dissolved shortly after it has taken place, presents need not be returned. Meaningful ones should be retained by each ex-partner, particularly those given by relatives and close friends.

SECTION VIII

On The Go

CHAPTER 30

The Traveler

SERVICE PEOPLE are traveling people, and for those making their own plans for a leave for the first time, or for a trip for their children, the following suggestions should prove helpful. Obviously, when being transferred to a new station or post, whether in the United States or abroad, all the necessary information will be made available to them.

First, there are the basics to attend to, such as making your reservations early enough so that you will get what you want when you want it; passports when going abroad, and visas and vaccinations as needed in certain countries. Your doctor will give you the necessary shots, and health certificates for retired people and civilians usually are available at the county health department. Passports should be applied for early, with summer months being the busiest time for travel thus the slowest in getting your passport processed. You will need three small pictures and your birth certificate if it is your first passport, so have them ready. You can ask at any post office concerning passports.

It is wise to read up on the foreign countries to be visited, and learn what to expect in the way of climate and what clothing will be needed. A good language booklet and guidebook are helpful; your travel agent frequently can help you, or information can be found in the library. You should carefully consider purchasing travel insurance before departure. A tour group will be offered a package deal.

Have a check-off list of all the things that must be done before departure. In order to secure a house, make certain that all lights are turned off, water taps closed, newspaper and mail delivery stopped, pets taken to a kennel, and plans made for having the grass cut and house-plants watered. Should you be leaving small children at home while you are away, be absolutely certain that the person in charge is reliable. Always leave a copy of your itinerary with a member of the family.

By departure time, everything should be in order: traveler's checks purchased, small change available, passport, and such necessities as your eye glasses, medicines, aspirin. Also your toothbrush and toothpaste, comb, brush, and kleenex; although these can be purchased in any air-port or almost anyplace, it is a nuisance to have to do so. Should you be bothered with travel sickness, take a motion-sickness tablet half-an-hour before departure and carry a supply of them with you throughout the trip. Have everything laid out or hanging in a section of the clothes closet where nothing will be overlooked; then the night preceding an early-morning departure pack the bag (preferably, only one plus a tote). Fold everything carefully, placing the heavier things in the bottom of the bag. Then re-check your passport folder, tickets, wallet, or handbag.

An experienced traveler will take extra money, and medicine and eyeglasses, if needed, "just in case." But *never* pack valuables, passports, traveler's checks or all your medicine in your luggage. Carry them with you.

LUGGAGE

Travel light! And this includes your luggage as well as what is inside it. You need strong but not heavy luggage. The new carry-on luggage comes in two or three sizes and is designed to be carried on board the larger planes where it is stowed. Then you can carry it off with no further delay other than at the customs area.

The regular size carry-on has staggered hangars, large flat pockets for holding shirts, blouses, and underwear. It will hold up to three suits or six dresses; six shirts or blouses; six sets of underwear and socks or stockings. There is room for your dress shoes (you should wear your walking shoes) and for a nonbulky robe and houseslippers.

Your razor or cosmetic kit will fit into this suitcase, or you may prefer to have the smaller carry-under bag which fits under the plane seat; women may prefer the tote bag with shoulder strap. When you take either of these smaller bags, your kit, folding umbrella, camera, film, scarf, and other small items, or purchases will fit into it.

When traveling abroad, you will need an adapter for electrical appliances, such as razors, hair-dryers, and heating pads, since the voltage is different from that in this country. Adapters can be purchased in a hardware store, and some better European hotels have them for rent, with the money refunded upon departure; but you cannot count on this.

Another "must" to put in the carry-under or tote bag is a small box or plastic bag of soap granules for washing your drip-dry clothes. Cleaning and laundry services are both slow and expensive abroad as well as in this country; something washed out during the evening is usually dry by morning.

WEIGHT

The weight limitation for your luggage on an overseas flight is variable, with two pieces allowed to be checked through and one carry-on. If you have more, you pay for it. What you carry with you, such as an all-purpose coat and camera, are not weighed. Security in airports requires that your things be x-rayed before you are permitted on board a plane, including your handbag. A special envelope has been designed for the protection of film, which is frequently destroyed.

FARES

First-class seats cost more than the economy-class seats, and charter (tour) groups are the least expensive of all—but the latter are made at certain times for a definite length of time, with a set date for return. Meals and soft drinks are included in all fares on a long trip. Economy class and charter groups pay for their own cocktails.

First-class fare offers a little more comfort, the seats are roomier, and cocktails are free. But you pay for it. Out-of-season trips are much less expensive than those taken during a regular season, as far as fares and hotel accommodations are concerned.

WHAT TO TAKE

What clothing to take depends upon where you are going. A wise traveler will take dacrons and polyesters or any kind of drip-dry material that can be laundered and worn time and again; thus fewer things need be taken. In the old days when trips—particularly those aboard ship—demanded formal dress (which had to be dry-cleaned) for many occasions, traveling was much more difficult with the many pieces of luggage involved. Keep a checklist of what to pack.

Today, pantsuits are worn by women all over the civilized world—including the Ginza in Tokyo where older generation Japanese women in their kimonos and obis walk side by side with the younger generation in jeans, slacks, and pantsuits. For any kind of travel, pantsuits are the most popular attire for women of all ages because they are the most comfortable.

Generally, women will need an extra pair of slacks and a blouse or two; an afternoon dress or costume (jacket) dress which can be worn just about anywhere; possibly a long skirt, not fancy, but noncrushable, and a blouse or top to go with it. A pair of dress shoes, a scarf, an all-purpose coat—or in a warm climate, a lightweight sweater, a raincoat or folding umbrella, a few underthings—and that is about it.

A man needs one good basic suit, either dark or a little lighter in color according to the destination; slacks and shirts, a pair of dress shoes —these are the basics. If business is being combined with pleasure, the basic dark suit is a must. Slacks and a sport jacket or a suit are the usual attire on the flight. In cooler climates, you may need an all-purpose coat—otherwise forget it. It's easily lost and a bother to carry, and a sweater is much easier to pack.

TEMPERATURES

Some like it hot, some like it cold, but everyone wants to know what sort of weather to expect in the area to be visited. Weather can be tempermental and the opposite of what is predicted, but in general the average temperatures both day and night in these cities are as follows:

AT HOME

U.S. Eastern Cities

(Day-Night)

	JAN FEB	MAR APR	MAY JUNE	JULY AUG	SEP OCT	NOV DEC
Boston	36 20	49 33	70 53	92 62	66 50	44 30
New York	38 24	50 36	70 57	86 66	69 54	46 33
Philadelphia	40 25	52 38	75 58	86 67	71 53	48 34
Wash., D.C.	42 27	58 39	79 59	85 67	73 53	50 33
Miami	75 61	79 65	85 73	86 76	85 73	77 64

U.S. Central Cities

(Day-Night)

	JAN FEB	MAR APR	MAY JUNE	JULY AUG	SEP OCT	NOV DEC
Chicago	33 19	49 35	70 55	80 66	67 53	42 29
Cleveland	35 23	57 38	76 54	87 67	71 51	41 26
Detroit	33 19	50 32	75 52	83 62	68 48	40 27
Kansas City	41 23	60 40	80 61	90 70	84 55	48 30
Pittsburgh	37 21	60 37	74 53	85 65	70 49	41 26
St. Louis	41 25	59 41	80 62	87 70	74 56	48 32

For these cities, your basic city wardrobe—tailored suits, several knits and dinner dresses. Chicago will probably live up to its windy-city nickname in the winter, so be prepared with slim skirts, hats you can anchor firmly, and a really warm coat. In summer, it gets hot, so bring silks and cottons.

U.S. Western Cities

(Day-Night)

	JAN FEB	MAR APR	MAY JUNE	JULY AUG	SEP OCT	NOV DEC
Denver	44 20	55 31	75 49	85 56	71 44	49 24
Las Vegas	58 36	73 46	93 69	104 75	89 60	63 37
Los Angeles	65 47	69 50	74 55	82 60	78 57	70 50
Phoenix	67 41	78 50	96 64	102 77	91 62	70 44
San Francisco	57 46	61 49	65 52	65 58	68 59	60 49

ABROAD

Europe

(Day-Night)

	JAN FEB	MAR APR	MAY JUNE	JULY AUG	SEP OCT	NOV DEC
Athens	55 42	64 49	81 64	90 72	79 63	61 49
Berlin	36 27	49 34	68 50	73 55	62 46	40 32
Copenhagen	35 29	43 34	61 49	67 56	56 48	41 26
Dublin	47 35	51 36	61 45	66 51	59 44	49 37
Frankfurt	37 27	45 34	69 49	73 55	61 45	41 32
Geneva	34 28	48 36	64 54	70 60	58 47	39 32
Lisbon	55 47	61 53	72 61	76 66	66 61	60 50
London	44 35	52 38	65 48	71 54	61 47	47 38
Madrid	50 34	60 40	76 53	87 62	71 51	51 38
Milan	44 34	55 42	70 56	78 63	66 52	48 38
Paris	44 33	55 38	70 49	76 55	65 47	47 36
Rome	54 39	63 47	77 58	87 66	75 58	57 43
Zurich	34 28	48 36	64 54	70 60	58 47	39 32

Near East and Africa

(Day-Night)

	JAN FEB	MAR APR	MAY JUNE	JULY AUG	SEP OCT	NOV DEC
Addis Ababa	76 45	77 49	76 49	69 50	74 47	73 42
Cairo	69 46	80 54	92 65	95 71	87 65	74 53
Capetown	79 60	75 55	66 47	64 45	68 50	75 56
Dar es Salaam	88 77	87 74	85 69	83 66	84 68	87 73
Johannesburg	78 58	74 52	64 41	66 41	75 50	78 56
Kampala/Entebbe	80 64	79 65	77 64	77 62	79 62	79 63
Nairobi	78 54	76 57	71 54	70 51	76 53	74 55
Tel Aviv	64 47	71 50	81 59	85 69	84 61	76 50
Tunis	60 43	68 49	80 59	91 68	82 62	64 47
Tripoli	62 48	70 54	79 64	86 71	83 68	69 53

Far East

(Day-Night)

	JAN FEB	MAR APR	MAY JUNE	JULY AUG	SEP OCT	NOV DEC
Bangkok	93 68	96 74	94 76	92 76	91 75	89 69
Bombay	93 56	98 64	97 73	94 72	93 71	94 60
Hong Kong	64 55	70 63	83 75	87 78	83 75	70 61
Tokyo	47 30	58 41	73 58	84 70	76 60	55 38

Courtesy of TWA.

SHIP TRAVEL

On a transatlantic liner crossing, which is almost a thing of the past, more evening clothes are usually necessary than in a cruise ship. However, dress is modified nowadays for first-class passengers, who may wear evening dress (once considered a necessity) or with men in dark or light suits, according to the season, and women in cocktail dresses. In any case, evening dress is not worn on the first and last nights aboard ship, due to the hustle and bustle. Tourist class passengers are much more relaxed in dress.

Customarily, the captain will host a cocktail party for first-class passengers, and another for the tourist class. He usually gives smaller parties for VIPs on board, to which you may be invited; or you may be asked to have dinner at the captain's table. You should accept.

Slacks, pantsuits, bathing suits—with capes or kaftans when out of the water—are worn throughout the day, when shuffleboard and other games are enjoyed, as well as swimming.

Although the number of bags that you take on board ship, and their weight, is no problem while at sea, you must think about their handling when going ashore. Then, your luggage leaves the ship when you do.

CRUISE SHIP

Dress on board a cruise ship is always casual, other than the night of the captain's party when guests are a little dressier or there may be a costume party. You wear leisure clothes befitting the climate. Colorful but simple daytime or cocktail dresses are worn in the evening by the ladies, and men wear lightweight suits in the evening and leisure suits, slacks, or shorts during the day. Everyone wears sandals, and dark glasses are a necessity. Even in warm climates the nights may turn cool so it is wise to take along a lightweight sweater.

It is always best to travel light, although your luggage is left on board while you are in port.

BON VOYAGE PARTY

A bon voyage party is one when your friends see you off on your trip. They will know your sailing time and you should set up the party at least an hour before departure. They may bring champagne as a going-away gift, but you should arrange with the steward for soft drinks and hors d'oeuvres. You must bring your own liquor on board if you plan to serve it, since it cannot be served by the steward or purchased at the bar until the ship sails.

Regardless of the fact that the party is in your honor, you should pay for the food or whatever is ordered during the party.

YOUTH TRIPS

Many high schools throughout the country organize trips for students to various foreign countries in the early spring (when rates are low), usually for a week or ten days. Teachers or possibly parents act as leaders, with at least two for a group of twenty. Reservations are usually made in second-class hotels that are clean and adequate, but probably have only one bathroom for several rooms.

Students are asked to travel light (one piece plus a tote), since they will have to handle their own luggage most of the time. They should take along enough underclothing for the trip since it may not always be possible to wash out their things. Parents should make certain that some soap granules are included in their luggage to be used whenever possible.

Slacks and jeans, shirts and tops, a jacket, are worn by both boys and girls. Mix and match clothing is desirable for a girl who can interchange a blouse with a skirt or slacks.

High school and college students and young people of all such ages frequently set off for a summer's travel abroad, with knapsacks on their backs and no place in particular to stay, other than a list of inexpensive youth hostels that exist all over Europe. Whenever possible, a list of hostels should be left at home with their parents, in case of emergency.

These students and young people should have confirmed return reservations and tickets with a reputable airline before leaving home, since reservations are hard to come by in the tourist season. Otherwise they might not be able to return home when they want to—usually when their money runs out.

SPENDING MONEY

All students should be advised by their leaders and parents not to spend too much money on souvenirs or "junk" gifts, but to save some for one or two nicer presents. It is up to the leaders to see that the most interesting museums and tourist attractions are visited, and not to leave the students "on their own" too much, since it is sometimes difficult for them to find their way to these places alone.

THE WC

All travelers should be aware of some of the differences in customs in other countries, particularly those who speak only English. Fortunately, English is spoken by someone almost everyplace you go. In any language, WC stands for water closet or toilet. There may be a separate WC for men and women, with a drawing of a man or woman above each, or marked for men or women in the language of the country. Or only one WC may be provided for everyone. Public water closets usually have a small charge.

First-class hotels in any country are about the same as those at home. In small hotels in Europe and various countries, one bathroom may be used by occupants of several rooms, or the whole floor, with a washbasin or a pitcher of water and a bowl provided.

PUSH-BUTTON SERVICE

In some European hotels, particularly in older ones, there may be no telephone in the room. Instead, there may be a panel with a system of push-buttons, with a figure of a maid or waiter or valet above each indicating which button is to be pushed for service.

CHAPTER 31

Hotel & Motel Manners

UNLESS YOU ARE an experienced traveler, there may be a moment of uneasiness when you step up to the desk clerk in a hotel or motel to register. A newly married man may wonder about the best way to sign his name—and his wife's—and how much, and whom, he should tip.

Before you start your trip, however, you may wonder where you can obtain the best information concerning hotels and motels in general. There are a number of reliable sources of information concerning places to stay in each state, such as the AAA, Tour Aids, or any local travel agent.

When you know where and when you will be arriving, you should write or phone the selected hotel or motel for a reservation, and if time permits you should ask that the reservation be confirmed. You should specify the price of the room that you want, the number of people who will be occupying the room or rooms, what type of accommodations you need, and the expected length of your stay. Nowadays, all large motel chains have a service whereby you can have your reservation made instantaneously.

When your request is confirmed, be sure that you do not lose the confirmation slip; this little piece of paper can be very important when a busy clerk has bungled your reservation.

HOTELS

Any good hotel in any city in any country has a doorman who greets guests upon their arrival. When you are a guest and are arriving by car, tell the doorman that you would like a porter to come for your bags—unless you are smart enough to travel light and can carry your bag yourself.

If you plan to use the hotel's garage, tell the doorman and he will arrange to have your car taken there. If you are not using the hotel garage, ask the doorman where you can park your car. Unless he does some special service for you, it is not necessary to tip him at this time. If you should arrive at the hotel by taxi, the doorman will open the taxi door, but no tip is required.

When you do not travel light and the porter has taken your bags to the lobby, he will direct you to the desk. The usual tip is 50 cents for a heavy bag, or one dollar for a heavy load with several pieces of luggage. Give the desk clerk your name and say that you have a reservation.

When you do not have a reservation, tell the clerk what you would like and ask if such a room is available.

You will undoubtedly want to know what the price of the room will be, so ask. If the price is more than you can pay, ask the clerk if he has something less expensive. When there is nothing else—you stay or you leave.

REGISTERING

If the price of the room is satisfactory, you sign the register. It is necessary in all states and in all countries that you sign the hotel or motel register, writing your name and your home town, or your ship or station. Usually, the desk clerk asks for a street address, and at a motel, your car license number.

When you sign the register, you write, "Lieutenant John Smith, Washington, D.C." In the case of married couples, you sign the register, "Lieutenant and Mrs. John Smith, Washington, D.C."; *never* "Lieutenant John Smith and wife." A divorcée is "Mrs. Jones Smith" or "Mrs. Jane Smith."

After you have registered, the bellboy will precede you to your room with the key. After he has deposited your luggage, turned on the lights, and asked if there is anything else that you need, you are expected to tip him a quarter for opening the room and 25 cents for each bag that he carried—or more if it was very heavy. Your tip may be more at an expensive hotel, but the maximum should be a dollar.

SPECIAL SERVICES

All hotels offer many personal services, and these services are usually spelled out somewhere in the room, along with the prices. In a big hotel, it is often perplexing to know to whom you should make your request. The easiest way is to pick up the phone and ask for room service, and tell them what it is that you want. Sometimes you will be referred to the valet (pronounced "val-lay"), in which case you ask for valet service. Large hotels will have one number for all services and will tell you whom to call, or else will take your order directly.

For any special services, you can pay at the time they are received, or you can have the charge put on your bill by signing the check that accompanied the service. Should you need extra towels or blankets, call the housekeeper. She will have a maid bring you the necessary items, but you must be specific in what you need. If you need one blanket and three towels, say so. In most hotels, the housekeeper also is in charge of lost and found articles.

Should the luxury of having breakfast in bed appeal to you, remember that food served in the room is always subject to a substantial extra service charge. If you must be economical, the coffee shop to be found in most hotels will have the fastest service at about half the cost.

ROOMS WITH—OR WITHOUT MEALS

European plan means that the price of the room does not include any meals. Some hotels furnish instant coffee and cream which you prepare, along with croissants or sweet rolls for breakfast. *American plan* means that the price of the room includes all meals. The latter plan is usually found in resort hotels, and has one disadvantage. You must take all your meals at the hotel or else you will be losing money. If you want to take your meals when and where the fancy strikes you, it is best that you select a hotel that does not operate under the American plan.

There is also a *modified American plan* at many resort hotels, where you have breakfast and either lunch or dinner at the hotel but are free to take the other meal anywhere you choose. These very popular plans vary a great deal in different areas, so it is wise to be doubly sure of what is included in the price.

When you prefer the American plan, you will find that you are usually given a specific table in the hotel dining room which you will occupy at each meal—if the table meets with your approval—during your entire stay. In Europe, this same system is practiced at some small hotels under the title of *pension*. When you register at a resort hotel, it is well that you inquire into the practice of serving meals.

HOTEL MANNERS

As a guest, you must be considerate of employees in a hotel, but you should always be impersonal. An important rule to follow in addressing employees in a hotel is to look at them, know what you are going to say, and speak distinctly.

When a guest appears uncertain or ill at ease, some hotel employees become careless with that guest's requests. A guest should be calm but firm when making requests—and, equally, should make no requests that are not reasonable.

You should tip in accordance with your income, the hotel's reputation, and the service rendered. If the service has been poor, you tip accordingly. While you may not want to under-tip, it is just as bad taste to over-tip—particularly when you cannot afford it.

MOTELS

Motels are a boon to those traveling by car. The average motel differs basically from a hotel in that there are almost no services provided, no garage problems, and almost no tipping. There is little fuss and bother; you arrive and leave without delay.

However, a motor lodge may be a large several-storied complex with coffee shops and restaurants, and offer services similar to a hotel. In such a place you tip for services—when used—as you would in a hotel, such as when the bellhop opens the room or carries in your luggage. But of course you may carry your own luggage.

Before you register or pay out any money at a motel, you may ask the motel operator to show you the room that you expect to occupy. The first-hand inspection gives you the opportunity to make sure that the room is clean, in order, and that it meets your standards. If not, you may ask to see another room—or not accept it at all, and go on your way.

Accredited motels are approved by various qualified organizations and inspected at regular intervals. You will soon learn to recognize these motels, for all motels are anxious to advertise the fact that they are accredited.

Most motels require that you pay in advance in order to facilitate early morning checkouts, so be ready to pay promptly upon registering. When you are driving cross-country and know where you will be the following day or night, it is advisable to make advance reservations. In the summer months and in resort areas, motels should be reserved well in advance. When you find a motel chain that you like, it is well to stay with it on your whole trip. The various managers will make advance reservations free of charge, in a matter of minutes.

MOTEL MANNERS

Although you are paying for the motel room, you should treat it with the same respect that you would the belongings of another person. Before taking ashtrays and towels as souvenirs, stop and consider how much it would cost you if guests in *your* home carried off ashtrays and towels.

For tipping customs in hotels and motels, *see* Chapter 32 Tipping.

Tipping

IN AMERICA

It's easy to trip over tips, particularly since tipping varies in certain sections of this country, as well as abroad. Like death, poverty, and taxes, tipping is always with us.

Originally, tips were given to individuals for services better or beyond those expected. Nowadays, tips are expected for almost any kind of service, but you should never tip a person for inefficient or discourteous service; neither should you allow yourself to be bullied into too large a tip by a scornful attendant.

Never over-tip; that is considered flashy. But neither should you be cheap and under-tip. Learn at the start what a fair tip is—and then stick to your system.

If a crafty waiter brings you only large coins or folding money, don't allow yourself to be intimidated; just ask him courteously to bring you some smaller change.

When you do tip, be pleasant about it. You should glance at the person you are tipping, and for good service you should say, "Thank you."

It is a wise person who always carries a quantity of small change for small tips.

WHEN NOT TO TIP

While it is important to know when to tip, it is equally important to know when not to tip. If you make a mistake and offer a tip to someone who should not be tipped, you will discover your error when your tip is waved away. In such a case you simply re-pocket your money.

You do not tip professional people, including nurses, ship's officers, government employees, lawyers, doctors, stenographers, department store workers, or owners or managers of places of business.

You don't tip ushers in theaters. You may give presents at Christmas time to any delivery person, such as your postman, a newspaper boy, garage attendant, or garbage collector. They may prefer a present of folding money—a dollar or two—or a carton of cigarettes, cigars, a tie, candy, or fruit.

Do not tip nurses or doctors, but you may tip maids and attendants at a hospital for special services. In a private or semi-private room, you may give a dollar to each attendant; you do not tip in wards.

If you would like to give something to your nurse upon departure, or at Christmas time, fruit, candy, or a box of cookies are acceptable. When leaving the gift for the nurse at the hospital, there should be enough for all the staff who cared for the patient, and this should be left at the desk nearest the patient's room. A note could state that, "This is for the staff on Wing A who have been so nice to my son."

Tipping Chart (Subject to constant change.)

Wine and Dine

 In a restaurant:

  WAITER—15% of the bill.

  HEADWAITER (maitre d'hotel or captain)—no tip unless he made arrangements, then $2 to $5.

  WINE STEWARD—when he serves, 15% of the wine bill.

  CHECKROOM ATTENDANT—25¢ for each coat

  PARKING ATTENDANT—50¢ when he both parks and gets your car.

  BUSBOY—no tip.

  AT A COUNTER—15% of your check. No tip for only coffee or soft drink. Follow "No Tipping" sign.

  CAFETERIA—no tip.

 In a nightclub: (Generally the same as in a restaurant; but—)

  ENTERTAINERS—do not tip; you may buy the star a drink.

  CIGARETTE GIRL—25¢ plus the cost of cigarettes.

  HAT CHECK GIRL—25¢.

AT A BAR—bartender 15% of check (do not tip manager or owner).

LADIES-ROOM ATTENDANT—25¢ for services; otherwise no tip.

Hotels and Motels
At a hotel:

BELLBOYS—25¢ for opening room; 25¢ to 50¢ a bag depending on size and weight, maximum tip $1. 25¢ for room deliveries.

DOORMAN—25¢ for helping with luggage; none for hailing a taxi, unless there is difficulty in finding one.

ROOM WAITERS—15% of bill for each meal.

CHAMBERMAIDS—no tip for one-night stay; for longer stay, $1 up, depending on service.

VALETS—no tip, since they are concessionaires and not employees.

ROOM CLERKS, MANAGERS, STAFF—no tips.

At a motel: Customarily, no tips. Bellboys, waiters in coffee shop, same as a hotel.

At a resort: (Generally the same as for hotels, plus)

HEADWAITER—usually tipped at the end of your stay, or every two weeks.

BOATMEN, GUIDES—$1 to $5, according to service, for a one- or two-week stay in a resort. (This is in addition to their regular wages.)

CADDIE—25¢ for a fee of $2 or less; 50¢ for a fee over $2.

Transportation
In a Taxi:

DRIVER—15% of higher fare. Or: fare 50¢ to $1.50, tip 25¢; from $1.50 to $2 tip 30¢ to 35¢; from $2 to $3, tip 40¢ to 50¢; up to $5, tip 75¢ to $1.

On a Train:

PULLMAN PORTER (day trip)—$1 a night.

CONDUCTOR—no tips except for special services, $1 and up.

DINING CAR WAITER—15 % of bill; not less than 25¢.

STATION REDCAPS—rates differ, usually 25¢ to 50¢ a bag.

On a Plane: ((No tipping of stewards, stewardesses, pilots, reservation clerks, limousine drivers, or anyone in airline uniform.)

AIRCAP (not employed by airlines)—25¢ a bag.

On a Cruise Ship:

SHIP'S OFFICERS (including doctor, purser, and chief steward) not tipped. Ten % to 15% of the cost of your passage is distributed between the service crew: cabin and dining-room stewards, one half; the remainder is divided between the other stewards in proportion to their services. Some cruise lines charge for "gratuities" in the fare, thus tips are not given except for special services.

On a luxury liner: (five days to a week's transatlantic crossing)

CABIN STEWARD OR STEWARDESS—$10, first class; $7 cabin class; $5, tourist.

DINING ROOM STEWARD—same.

HEAD DINING STEWARD—$5, first class; $3, cabin class, $2 tourist.

DECK STEWARD—$3, first class; $2, cabin class, $1, tourist.

STEVEDORES—$2 to $5 for large trunks; suitcases, 50¢ each.

CABIN BOY—25¢ for each errand.

LOUNGE AND BAR STEWARD—15% of bill at time of service; no less than 25¢.

On a tour bus:

GUIDES-DRIVERS—It is not obligatory for passengers on a tour in a sightseeing bus to tip the guides or driver-guides, but on a long tour they usually "pass around the hat—or envelope—" on their behalf. This amount is about 25¢ to 50¢ per person; more in Europe. On a regular charter or sightseeing bus there is no tipping.

Grooming

Barbershop:

HAIRCUT—about 50¢ in small city, 50¢ or more in large. If a "styling," 15% of bill.

SHAVE, SHAMPOO, MANICURE—50¢ to $2 for one or all.

SHOPOWNER—usually no tip, but a Christmas remembrance by regular customer. But some may prefer a tip.

Beauty Parlor:

SHAMPOO, HAIRSET—15% of bill.

PERMANENT—15% of bill.

MANICURIST—50¢ to 75¢.

The owner-operator, in the past, did not want tips; but like the barbershop owner, many prefer tips to Christmas gifts. If he or she says "no thank you" when you offer a tip, don't take offense. When they accept, about 10% of the bill is customary.

Private Clubs (No tips to any employee at a private or country club or officers' club other than those mentioned below, but Christmas presents are given to employees by members who chip in.)

CADDIE—15% of regular club charge of 18 holes; 15 or 20% for 9 holes.

GOLF PRO—no tip.

LOCKER ROOM ATTENDANT—$1, by a guest; $1 to $2 a month by a member.

GROOM—50¢ for hired horse. $1 to stable boy of host's stable.

WAITERS—15% of drink bill.

Special Sports

SKIING PRO—no tip. (Tips are usually included in the cost of the lodge; otherwise, tip as you would in a hotel.)

SHOOTING—$2 for general helper. $4 to $5 for guide for the day. This is in addition to the guide's wages. (Take your own ammunition when you are a guest at a lodge.)

FISHING—Prices vary in all sorts of fishing, including charter boat fishing. Dutch treat is customary in group fishing, and the tips above fees may be:

CAPTAIN—frequently the catch but no tip.

MATES—$2 to $5 each.

GUIDES—$2 a day (in addition to their wages).

House Guest (You usually do not tip servants unless you have spent several nights in a home. You tip just before your departure, preferably not in front of your hosts. You may give presents instead of tips.

MAID OR COOK—$3; couple $5.

Apartment: (Depending on area and type of building, for Christmas giving)

JANITORS—$3 to $5, according to service.

ELEVATOR HELP—$5.

DOORMAN—$5 or up.

ABROAD

No matter where you go when abroad, do not tip in American money. Make certain that you have sufficient quantities of small foreign change for tips. Before leaving the U.S. you should obtain about ten dollars worth of the currencies for the first country on your itinerary. Large banks and money exchanges can obtain the money for you; then cash travelel's checks as needed. Of course, you can always get your traveler's checks exchanged in the airport—but this takes time, or at your hotel upon arrival.

It is helpful to carry a currency converter with you until you become familiar with the currency of the country. Then you can tell at a glance that 100 lire is about 16 cents and 15 pesetas is 26 cents.

Wallet or purse-size booklets are available at airport newstands or at travel agencies.

In the better hotels throughout Europe, and in countries such as Japan, there will be a 15 percent service charge which is prorated and added to your bill instead of tipping. Extra tips are for such services as shoeshining and the carrying of luggage. When there is no service charge you prorate the customary 15 per cent among those who help you, in accordance with custom and services rendered.

Some working people depend on tips to make ends meet; they receive little or no wages and must rely on tips. The washroom attendant, for example, counts on the 10 cents, or equivalent, that you will pay. And remember that in Europe and the British Isles, "W.C." means water closet—the lavatory—with signs posted in public places and on doors. You tip the attendant at bath houses in the Orient and at the saunas in the Scandinavian countries. You bathe in private or public bath houses or saunas in these countries.

Guides are always tipped in Europe. If there is no fixed fee for the guide, then your tip will depend on the length of the tour. If there is a fixed fee, tip 15 percent of that amount. The gas station attendant—especially in Germany, Italy, and France—should receive a small tip when he does more than fill the gas tank. And the porter who shines the shoes you leave outside the door of your hotel room should receive a small tip.

	Waiters	Chamber-maids	Bellhops & Baggage Porters	Doorman
Great Britain	10% to 15% of check.	10 pence (21¢) a day, or 40-50 pence (84¢ to $1.00) a week.	10 pence (21¢) a bag.	10 pence (21¢) for calling a cab.
France	12% to 15% service charge usually included on check.	2 francs (45¢) a day, 10 francs ($2.27) a week.	3-5 francs (68¢-$1.14) for a load of luggage, 2 francs (45¢) a bag or a service.	2 francs (45¢) for calling a cab.
West Germany	5% of check over usual service charge.	1 mark (39¢) for 1 night's stay, 5 marks ($1.94) a week.	1 mark (39¢) a bag or a service.	1 mark (39¢) for calling a cab.
Italy	10% of check over service charge.	100 lire (15¢) a day, 500 lire (75¢) a week.	100-150 lire (15¢-22¢) a bag or a service.	100 lire (15¢) for calling a cab.
Switzerland	service charge included by law, leave small change in addition.	Included in hotel service charge. Tip 2 Sw. Fr. (75¢) for a special service.	1 Sw. Fr. (37¢) per bag or minimum of 2 Sw. Frs. (75¢).	1 Sw. Fr. (37¢) for calling a cab.
Spain	25 pesetas minimum (43¢) over 15% service charge; 5% to 10% over check.	10 pesetas (17¢) a day, 50 pesetas (78¢) a week.	25 pesetas (43¢) a bag, or a service in room; 10 pesetas to bellhops.	5-10 pesetas (9-17¢) for calling a cab.
Portugal	10% to 15% service charge included on check; leave 5% more.	50 escudos ($1.92) a week.	5 escudos (19¢) a bag. 2.50 escudos (10¢) a service.	5 escudos (19¢) for calling a cab.

Concierge	Taxicab Driver	Station Porter	Ladies' Room Attendant	Hairdresser	Theatre Usher
50 pence ($1.06) for special service.	10p (21¢) on fares up to 50p; 15 pence on fares up to 75p; 10%-15% if higher.	10 pence (21¢) a bag.	10 pence (21¢).	20% of the bill.	Nothing.
2 francs (45¢) a service, 10 francs ($2.27) a week, even if no services are performed.	10% to 15% of the meter.	Railroad station 2 francs (45¢) a bag. Airport 2 francs (45¢) a bag.	1 franc (23¢).	15% to 20% of the bill, if not included.	1 franc (23¢) at a cinema, up to 2 francs (45¢) for orchestra seats at a play or concert.
1-2 marks (39-77¢) a special service.	10% of the meter.	Fixed rates.	50 pfennigs (19¢).	15% of bill.	Nothing.
10% of his bill for cables, phone calls, etc.	10% of the meter. Average, 100 to 150 lire. (15-22¢).	200 lire (30¢) a bag.	50 to 100 lire (7¢-15¢).	300 lire (45¢).	100 lire (15¢).
2-5 Sw. frs. (75¢-$1.87) for special service, given on departure.	12% to 15% of the meter.	Local tariff plus 10%.	1 Sw. fr. (37¢).	15% of the bill.	1 Sw. fr. (37¢) if program given.
No tip if not much service; 25 pesetas (43¢) a day or more, depending on service performed, if by hotel.	5 pesetas (9¢), if fare is under 50 pesetas, 10% if higher.	Min. of 30 pesetas for up to 2 bags (52¢) and 15 pesetas (26¢) for each addl. bag.	5 pesetas (9¢).	10 pesetas (17¢) or 10% of the bill.	5 pesetas (9¢) per person (bullfights, football matches, etc.).
10 escudos (38¢) a service.	15% of the price registered.	5 escudos (19¢) a bag.	2.50 escudos (10¢).	10 escudos (38¢).	5 escudos (19¢).

	Waiters	*Chamber-maids*	*Bellhops & Baggage Porters*	*Doorman*
Greece	10% to 15% service charge included on check; leave 5% to 10% more.	100 drachmas ($3.23) for a week.	10 drachmas (32¢); for a lot of luggage, 20 drachmas (65¢).	10 drachmas (32¢) for calling a cab.
Austria	5% over usual service charge.	5 schillings a day (27¢), 20 schillings a week ($1.10).	5 schillings (27¢).	5 schillings (27¢).
Ireland	10% to 15% of check. 10% where service included.	10 pence a day (21¢) or 40-50 pence a week (84¢ to $1.06).	10 pence a bag (21¢).	20 pence (42¢) for calling a cab.
Egypt	10% over the 10% service charge.	50 piasters per week ($1.15).	25 piasters (40¢).	10 piasters (16¢).

* Chart courtesy of Mary Gordon, Travel Advisor, TWA.

Concierge	Taxicab Driver	Station Porter	Ladies' Room Attendant	Hairdresser	Theatre Usher
20 drachmas for special service (65¢).	4 drachmas (13¢) or less	5 drachmas (16¢) a bag.	5 drachmas (16¢)	30 drachmas (97¢).	5 drachmas (16¢).
10-20 schillings (55¢ to $1.10).	10% of meter.	Fixed rate 5 schillings (27¢).	1-2 schillings (5¢ to 11¢).	5-10 schillings (27¢ to 55¢).	Nothing.
25-45 pence for special service (50¢ to 95¢).	15 pence on fares up to 50 pence (32¢).	10 pence (21¢) a bag.	5 pence (11¢).	15%-20% of the bill (32¢ to 42¢).	Nothing.
50 piasters for a special service (81¢).	10% of the meter.	10 piasters per bag but not less than 20 piasters (10¢ to 32¢).	10 piasters (16¢).	25 piasters (40¢).	5 piasters (8¢).

CHAPTER 33

Places of Entertainment & Private Clubs

MOVIES

Without taking a poll, it is safe to say that just about everybody has attended a movie. Yet, there is sometimes a lack of common everyday courtesy among movie-goers—including the peanut and popcorn eater, the paper rattler, the loud whisperer. There is the person who passes back and forth in front of you and the character who lolls in his seat and overflows on the arms of your seat.

Your manners at a movie or theater ought to be the same whether you go alone, in a group, or with a date. Common courtesy should be observed at all times.

If you are a man escorting a woman, take her into the lobby where she can wait while you buy the tickets. If the line is long and the weather pleasant, she may prefer to stand outside in line and talk with you.

After you have bought your tickets, take off your overcoat in the lobby. Your guest may also take off her coat, but women usually prefer to leave their coats on until after they sit down.

Before going down the aisle, ask your guest where she would like to sit—in front, near the center, etc.—then walk *ahead* of her and look for suitable seats. After you have found them, step aside and allow her to go ahead of you into the row.

If your seats are in the center of a section, be careful of the people you are passing. You should pass facing the screen, as quickly as possible, and say "Excuse me" or "Thank you" in a low tone. Watch out for the coat you are carrying, for it often sweeps the heads of people in the row in front of you.

Once you are in your seats, you should assist your guest with her coat, and do this without blocking the view of those seated behind you. The best place for your own coat and hat is in your lap, or both coats may be placed over the backs of your seats and your hat balanced on your knees or placed in the rack under your seat, when one is provided.

There is little reason for conversation at the movies or theater, but if you *must* talk, then by all means whisper softly. If you are also one who cannot get through a movie without a little snack, then get something that doesn't crackle when the wrapper is removed or when you are eating it. And try not to engage in demonstrations of affection. If for no other reason, remember that you paid good money to *see* the show—not *give* it. After the movie is over, do not put your coat on until you reach the lobby.

When you attend a movie in a large group, or when you are the host to such a group, see if it is possible to get seats together. Then precede your guests to the seats and see that they are seated in mixed order.

PAYING FOR TICKETS

When you are the host or hostess at a theater or movie party, or when you invite just one guest, you pay for the tickets. When you are a guest, do not insist on paying, or helping to pay for them.

When a woman is hostess at a movie or theater party and asks a man to buy the tickets in advance and gives him the money for them, he should *not* offer to pay or feel any hesitancy in taking the money.

If a group decides on the spur of the moment to attend a performance, then couples go "Dutch treat." Usully the men pay for their dates' tickets, but nowadays (due to Women's Lib!) the women may want to pay for their own—particularly if their dates are academy or college-age students on a small allowance.

THEATER

At the legitimate theater, you are expected to be on time, with curtain time usually 8:30 P.M. for an evening performance. You may check your hats and coats for a quarter, or you may take them to your seats.

You may buy a program before taking your seats, but this is not necessary since the theater management issues a plain but sufficient playbill. If you want a more detailed program, one is enough for two or more persons.

There are always ushers at theaters, and you should wait for one to show you to your seats. During intermission, you may want to go to the lobby to smoke. If your guest is a woman and does not care to smoke, you may excuse yourself and go ahead. If only she wants to smoke, you should accompany her to the lobby and wait with her.

When the lights in the lobby are dimmed, or when a bell rings, the management is signaling that the next act is about to begin and you should return to your seats immediately. Don't linger and then be forced to stumble over someone's feet in a darkened theater.

If for some very good reason you are late at curtain time, you should stand in the back of the theater until the first intermission.

OPERAS, CONCERTS, AND THE BALLET

Operas, concerts, and the ballet are other forms of entertainment that you will encounter through the years. Frequently, you will be invited to attend such functions as a guest. Although the opera once was a full-dress affair, you will see only a few men in white tie or black tie—most men are in dark business suits. Your hostess will indicate what you should wear; otherwise you should ask her. Frequently, a formal dinner will precede the theater and formal dress is worn.

If your hostess is a patron of the arts, she may have a box, although many of the newer theaters do not have them. Each box contains chairs which are arranged in pairs from the front of the box—where the most desirable seats are—to the rear. It is customary for the hostess to sit in the first row, on the chair farthest from the stage, with the ranking woman guest seated by the hostess in the seat closest to the stage. The ranking man is seated directly behind the hostess, with the host seated behind the ranking woman. Unless your hostess especially assigns you a seat, you should take the rear seat farthest from the stage.

At concerts, the conductor of a symphony orchestra will turn around and face the audience at the end of a number—and you should not begin applauding until he does so. At a piano recital, do not applaud between the movements of a sonata, or a similar piece of work, even though the pianist momentarily stops playing.

If you should have the misfortune to develop a coughing or sneezing fit, leave the room or auditorium, since any noise is disturbing to an artist, but intermissions are plainly marked on the program, and that is the only time you should leave the auditorium, if at all possible.

Encore numbers are often played or sung after the artist has received a number of curtain calls, or after much applause. He will indicate that there will be an encore, and this cue stops further applause.

If the music at an opera or concert is too classical for your uneducated ear, or the ballet is beyond your appreciation, never fidget or show signs of boredom. The other people there will be enjoying themselves and it is discourteous to interrupt their pleasure.

By attending as many performances in the fine arts as possible, your untrained ear may be keenly sharpened and your boredom turned to enjoyment.

PRIVATE CLUBS

Private clubs, in one form or another, exist all over the country. The types most familiar are the country clubs, the fraternities and sororities at colleges and universities, and the officers' clubs at military installations.

A country club usually has a club house, golf course, swimming pool, tennis courts, etc. The membership is by invitation and there probably will be a large initiation fee and sizable monthly club dues. A club member should pay his bills on time. Failure to pay what you owe may lead to expulsion from the club. If you cannot afford to stay in a club, resign before your debts accumulate.

When you are invited to be a guest at such a club, you should look upon the invitation in somewhat the same manner as being asked into a home, and take part in whatever the activity for which you were invited. On the golf course, you are not expected to pay for anything other than your caddy fee, if you use one, although if you are invited by the same member more than once, you should offer to pay your greens fee. And it is always a mark of politeness to offer to pay your host's caddy fee as well as your own.

As a guest, you must remember that your host has accepted the responsibility of introducing you into his club and to his friends, and you naturally do not want to turn this responsibility into a liability. In brief, do not embarrass your host. A man should not barge up to a good-looking girl and say he is Bill Jones's guest—Bill Jones may not know her either! And if he does know her, he will make the proper introduction—just as he would at home.

Sometimes, when you are stationed in an area where friends of your family or friends of your own are members of a private club, you may be given a guest card for a limited time. The card will be given to you by your friend, or it may be mailed to you by the club. This card must be handled with discretion.

A guest card means that you enjoy the privileges of the club, and that you pay for these privileges—such as food, drinks, and any small fee for the use of the swimming pool or golf course. Sometimes these fees are printed on the card, but if not, inquire at the club's business office concerning such fees. You should realize that there is usually a moderate charge to the member for each guest card which he requests.

When you accept the guest membership, take the card to the office, where your name is placed on the guest list. Leave your address where bills are to be sent, and, upon receiving the bill, pay it *immediately*. When you don't pay, your bill is placed on the account of your sponsor —and you may lose a friend. Guest cards do not give you the right to nominate *anyone else* for guest cards in the club. Customarily, a guest card does not give you the privilege of taking guests to the club for meals, etc.

Private clubs, other than country clubs, are usually located in the city proper, and generally have rooms for entertaining. There usually are dining rooms, a library, lounge, and bar, besides bedrooms where members live, or rooms where out-of-town members may stay briefly. Some intown clubs have indoor athletic facilities as well. The atmosphere of such clubs is more home-like than at a country club, and there will be fewer members. These members are usually friends of long standing and as a guest, your behavior must be circumspect.

The problem of money is the same here as at the country club— you cannot pay for privileges. If you are given guest privileges for a limited period of time, you are charged for these privileges as at the country club. Although the private town club is more intimate, you yourself must not presume to intimacy with the members.

Many older members of private clubs have many little privileges; certain chairs in certain parts of a room may be "theirs." A table by a window at one side of the dining room may always be occupied by a certain man or group at a given hour. It is well to respect these privileges.

Before or just after leaving the area, be sure to write a note to whoever extended you guest privileges—to the member (if this was the case), *and* to the club president, mentioning any individual who showed you special courtesies.

Most private clubs—including country clubs—do not permit tipping of club personnel. However, the locker-room attendant at the country club or town club may be tipped when he has done some special service for you. Ask your host what is the usual tip for such services in his club.

COLLEGE FRATERNITIES AND SORORITIES

Men's social fraternities and women's sororities have their own houses on or near the campuses of colleges and universities throughout the country. Anywhere from forty to one hundred members make these houses their homes during the academic year, and a housemother is assigned to each.

Membership is by invitation, and the houses are governed by strict rules of manners and conduct. Infractions of rules cause the member to be fined, and a serious infraction may result in the failure of a pledge to be accepted or the expulsion of one who is already a member.

As a guest, you must observe the fraternity's house rules—particularly those concerning drinking and gambling. At many colleges and universities, drinking and gambling have as heavy a penalty as at a service academy.

A national social fraternity is a closed organization with private weekly meetings, and a guest should not ask questions concerning these meetings. Questions concerning the history or membership of a fraternity are in order, but not its business.

Lastly, a guest should endeavor to follow any custom of the fraternity or sorority, such as singing the fraternity song at the table, and standing while singing it.

At a sorority house, the housemother is more in evidence than at a fraternity house and respect is always shown her. Most sororities have a curfew, and a man must be careful to get his date back to her house on time. You will not be permitted to stay on at the house after curfew, so don't try. As a rule, most sorority houses do not have male guests for casual meals, but you will probably be invited for more formal dinners.

CIVIC ORGANIZATIONS

Retired as well as active-duty officers are frequently asked to join a civic or service organization that has a large membership, with its goal civic improvement and national and international good will. Such organizations are the Rotary, the Chamber of Commerce, and the Military Order of World Wars (MOWW).

Although an active-duty officer has little time for such membership, he joins whenever possible; later, upon retirement, he will have a nucleus of friends almost anywhere he chooses to live. Frequently, the active-duty officer is invited to attend a meeting as guest speaker on military matters. Such a member or guest speaker is an ambassador of his service.

OFFICERS' CLUBS

Officers' clubs will become the most familiar type of club life that you will experience in your own professional life. Stations and posts, both in the United States and overseas, have an officers' club to which you will automatically be extended the privilege of joining. Some of these clubs have monthly dues and others do not, but every officer should join the club of his station and give it wholehearted support.

The majority of these clubs are located on the station or post, and have a dining room, several lounges, and a bar. Each club has its own house rules, and you should be quick to discover what they are. Always take pride in your club, and treat it with the same respect and thoughtfulness that you would your own home.

Some clubs use the chit system, whereby all services must be paid for with chits from a coupon book that you buy from the office. Others are on a cash basis only, and still others have members sign their orders on chits provided for that purpose. When the club is on the latter system, you will be billed at the end of the month, and, as with all other bills, you should pay your club bill promptly. If you do not—and the last date for payment is usually made known to you by the house rules —you may be placed in the unfortunate position of having your name posted in some prominent place as a delinquent member.

As a member, you may have as many guests as you wish—but you must remember that on the chit system the bill is *yours*. If you are with a group who are not in the service, you may settle the bill between yourselves later.

Your conduct in any officers' club should be beyond reproach. There may be many senior officers present, who, though not in your party, may be visiting the club; and loud, boisterous behavior may attract unwanted attention your way. Remember, this is an *officers'* club, not a boys' or girls' hangout.

Although the question of rank does not assert itself as such at an officers' club, you should show the same courtesies to senior officers there that you would anywhere else. Respect to age and rank will prompt you into the correct approach when greeting and speaking with seniors.

When an officer, man or women, is married to a noncommissioned officer and the noncom accompanies the officer to the club, he or she is as welcome as anyone else. However, the officers' club is for officers only and should not be used by the noncom unless accompanied by his or her spouse.

Dress in all clubs is prescribed by the house rules; some clubs permit sports attire until 6 P.M., other clubs are more formal. When you visit a club at another station—or a club of a different service—it is wise to find out in advance if there are any big differences in club regulations.

You will find through the years that your officers' club is an integral part of your service life, and as a member, it is up to you to help keep the club standards high.

CHAPTER 34

The Houseguest

THROUGHOUT YOUR LIFE, you will frequently extend or receive invitations to visit. As the guest, you may be invited to stay with a friend when you are passing through his city. A midshipman or cadet is often asked to spend the holidays with a roommate, for example, or to attend a house party. Usually, your friends are in about the same circumstances as you are, and you should act in their home as you would in your own. As the host, you expect a houseguest to be congenial and courteous.

THE WEEKEND GUEST

The weekend guest is probably the most frequent type of guest. The invitation is extended in person, by telephone, letter, or telegram. As the guest, you should answer immediately, and your reply must be definite.

When accepting the invitation, make it clear when you expect to arrive and how. In some cases, you may need to be met, thus your time of arrival is important. When refusing the invitation, you should always say *why*.

The host will usually give you some information concerning the weekend so that you will know what to bring. When something special is planned—a formal dance, a boating trip, golf, tennis, etc.—the host should suggest the necessary clothes or sports equipment needed. If the hosts do not mention anything in particular, you may take it for granted that the weekend is informal—but it is better to *ask* than to be caught unprepared.

A guest is always concerned about how much luggage to take. Most guests bring too much luggage rather than too little, which is cumbersome to all hands. The proper amount is frequently decided by the method of travel, but a carry-all that holds everything including a shaving or cosmetic kit should take care of an average weekend. Although luggage is expensive, you will need it for the rest of your life, since you will be traveling a great deal in the service. It is wise to invest in good quality luggage as soon as you can afford it.

HOUSE PARTIES

As a member of a house party, you can expect to share a room with other guests. You may never have met some of them before, and it is important that you get all names straight at the beginning of the visit. It is a compliment to a stranger that you remember his or her name. At any house party, the hosts should always try to have guests who will be congenial with each other.

WHAT TO TAKE

In this day of drip-dry clothing, you can take less clothing—and pack it more easily—than ever before. What you will need depends upon where you will visit—the climate, type of community, (a summer colony or a city apartment), but no matter where you go, travel light.

Usually, a man needs a dark or conservative suit, dress shoes, a sport jacket and slacks—which he will probably wear on the trip—and an extra pair of slacks; one pair of pajamas, two changes of shirts a day, socks, changes of underwear, and house slippers (soft and crushable ones that will take little room in a bag). For an informal weekend, he may need more sport shirts, a sweater, Bermuda shorts, an extra pair of slacks, and swimming trunks, rather than dress clothes.

A woman should wear a pantsuit and walking shoes on the trip, and take a cocktail dress if a party or dinner is planned; a daytime dress for luncheon or casual wear; sports clothes for whatever activities her hosts told her about; and dress shoes; or more casual clothes for a summer weekend. A robe, pajamas, house slippers are also needed.

When your hosts plan a special occasion—such as deep-sea fishing, you need not worry about fishing gear, since your hosts will undoubtedly have all the necessary equipment or they would not plan such an occasion.

When formal entertaining is planned, a man will need his dinner jacket. If you do not own one, take your blue dress uniform (or service equivalent) with the black bow tie, or your summer whites or blues. A service woman would probably prefer a long dress to her uniform.

After you have packed everything you need, recheck your luggage. Persons who travel on short notice should have a check list taped on the inside of the shaving or cosmetic kit, or some other convenient spot. You should include in your list such items as toothpaste, aspirin, cigarettes, medicines, comb and brush.

DUTIES OF GUESTS

The duty of any guest is to be congenial at all times. If you are the guest, then you should not be hard to please, or one who contributes little to the pleasure of others. When you take part in a game, try to join in the fun. When you truly can't participate in the activity, then give a valid reason.

In a servantless household, you should not be a burden to your hosts. It is important that you be on time for meals. Your hostess usually tells you at what time meals will be served—so be there. The matter of being on time holds for any activity in which you may engage —a boat trip, a golf game, or any planned event. If anything, be a little ahead of time.

The breakfast hour may be a minor problem in a household; the host may go to work early, the family may be early or late risers, the children may get off to school in the usual early morning confusion. A hostess may find it easier to send a tray to your room when you want to sleep late. If you do not care for breakfast, or eat lightly, say so and relieve your hostess of extra work.

A considerate guest will be alert to the household routine, particularly in small quarters. If you sleep on the sofa in the living room, that part of the house cannot be occupied until you are dressed, and it is helpful if you make your own bed. On the day of departure, take off the sheets, place them in the clothes hamper, then smooth the spread over the bed, unless your hostess tells you not to bother.

When a bathroom is shared by the family and guests, you should be careful not to overstay your fair time or use all the hot water. Try to leave the bathroom as neat as when you entered it. Don't leave damp towels on the floor, or a razor in the wash basin. Always hang up your clothes in your room, and do not leave your clothes lying around on the living room furniture.

You should offer to help your hosts when there are no servants, but do not insist if your hostess says "no." Try to be helpful, but don't get in the way.

A thoughtful guest will take a small gift to his or her hostess. Nowadays the old standby of a box of candy may not be appreciated by a diet-conscious hostess. It is a wise traveler who buys many small and inexpensive gifts while in foreign countries—gifts that cost a few dollars there, but more in this country—to use as hostess gifts.

A guest may choose to take a small gift to each of the children in the family, rather than a gift to the hostess. In this case, candy or inexpensive toys are a good choice. When a guest does not take gifts to his hostess or the children, he may send something after his departure. Upon any occasion, flowers are always in good taste. The rule of thumb concerning gifts is: they should never be expensive, but must always be of *good quality*.

THE HOST'S RESPONSIBILITY

When you have houseguests, can you accept an invitation to another party? Not often. The problem is that in mentioning to the prospective hosts that you have guests, they may feel impelled to invite them also. When they are not invited, should you stay home when you really want to go?

Such questions are worrisome.

For certain kinds of parties—cocktails, receptions, or a club dance, another guest or two may not make any difference; but a seated dinner or luncheon would, and you should not expect your houseguests to be invited—although they may be.

When your houseguests are with you for an extended visit, you should occasionally feel free to accept another party—certainly an official affair such as one given by your commanding officer. Then you would explain to your guests why you need to go but that you are not at liberty to take guests, and make plans for their comfort and pleasure during the time that you are gone.

OVERSTEPPING HOSPITALITY

When you are visiting in a town or community where you have other friends, you must be careful not to use the house where you are staying as a springboard for renewing these other acquaintances. Your hosts may urge you to have your friends visit you in their home, and you are free to do so, but you must guard against overstepping your host's hospitality. It might be better to visit your friends at times when your hosts have other obligations—or to save such visits until your stay in your host's home is over.

When you are the guest, you must also remember not to talk endlessly on the telephone and to pay for all toll charges, including tax.

The houseguest does not arbitrarily bring along a classmate or friend "because he had room in the car" or "because Joe used to live here and wants to see the place." No one should bring along an un-expected guest, be he relative or friend, unless he or she first inquires of his host if this is convenient. And discretion must be used as to whether the question should be raised at all.

PETS

Everyone loves his own cat, dog, or bird, and sometimes the other fellow's, but when visiting or going on leave the question of what to do with the family pet arises.

You can take the pet with you, leave it with a friend, or take it to the vet—for a fee. But if you can afford a vacation trip, you should be able to afford the fee.

When you are to be a houseguest, you must make absolutely cer-tain that your hosts are willing for you to bring your pet. Otherwise, they may not only object to your bringing it but also they may have no place or provisions for it. Remember, too, that some people are allergic to animals. And some people just plain don't like them.

Sometimes friends have an agreement to exchange pet-sitting. But never force your pet on anyone. If a person asks to keep him, fine. But there are a few people who have a hard time saying "no" and seethe over their accepting such a responsibility—in which case you might lose a friend.

For an overnight, a responsible neighborhood youngster can feed and water your pet and check on its welfare for a reasonable amount. On the road, when staying in motels, you should check beforehand as to their provision for pets.

When traveling by car and taking the cat or dog with you, keep the pet on a leash when he needs to run. Otherwise he might take off and not be able to find his way back to you.

And *never* leave a pet in a locked car with windows closed in hot weather; he can suffocate or die from the heat in a very short time.

ACCIDENTS IN HOMES

When something unexpected happens—such as your breaking a valu-able object, or becoming suddenly ill—common sense will tell you what to do. In case you broke something which you can replace, you should do so at your earliest convenience. If you cannot replace it, send a gift which you feel your hostess will enjoy, such as flowers or a nice potted plant which can give pleasure for some time.

Say how sorry you are for such a mishap at the time of the accident, and after your departure briefly state on your personal card, enclosed with the replacement or flowers, that you regret the incident.

If you should become ill while on your visit, let your hosts know— and call a doctor. Any host would be distressed to learn that his guest was ill, but foolishly said nothing about it. Of course, the guest should pay for all doctor fees or medicines especially bought for him.

DEPARTURE

When you leave after a visit, be sure that you have not forgotten anything. A check list is handy in preventing this. It is a bother for your host to wrap and mail your eyeglasses or some other object, so don't leave anything behind.

When you have said that you plan to leave at a given time—do so. Don't be persuaded to take a later bus; your hosts may be sincere when they urge you to stay longer, but usually a family has other plans or obligations. In any case, it's *time to leave*!

Also, be sure to let your hosts know well ahead of time when you expect to leave. It is not good manners to bring your packed bag abruptly into the living room and say *thanks* and *goodbye*, and then leave. This is inconsiderate, because your hosts will probably think you are hurt or angry to leave so suddenly.

When there is a servant in the home, you should give her or him something. Some homes have the family cook who is an integral part of the family and whom you undoubtedly have met during your visit. Before you leave, stop in the kitchen and give her a dollar or so, depending upon the length of your stay. Do not hand the money to your hostess and ask her to give it to the cook—*you* hand it to her in person. And add something complimentary, such as "Yours is the best spoon-bread I've ever eaten!"

In a large home, unless your hostess asks you not to give the servants a tip, you should give them something if they performed any services for you. Usually a dollar or so is sufficient, but this is also determined by the length of your stay.

As soon as you are back at home or at your station, write a note of thanks to both your host and hostess, addressed to the hostess (*See* Chapter 12, Social & Personal Correspondence.) Express your sincere appreciation for their hospitality, and mention some special incident if possible. Your letter should be on its way within two days after your visit.

UNEXPECTED GUESTS

Service people are in a constant state of change, due to new duty stations. Therefore, they frequently are "on the road." Although it is pleasant and convenient for long-time friends to stay overnight or a few days with classmates while en route to new stations, do not take advantage of your friends or descend on near-strangers.

You should always telephone a would-be host (or write when you have time), either at his office or home, before going to his home—regardless of how well you know him. Then you will know if it is convenient for you to stop by, either for a meal or overnight. There may be illness in the family, they may have other guests, or they may have made other plans for the very time you would be stopping there.

It is no excuse that you need to stay with someone because you are short of funds. Other than an emergency trip, you know in advance when you will be leaving your station, and an *adult* saves for emergencies.

VISITS TO CIVILIAN COLLEGES

In visiting a civilian college, a midshipman or cadet should not be too surprised at the differences he or she will find—particularly the lack of regimentation of the students. Every college campus has its rules, regulations, and conventions, however, and you will discover that these actually differ but little in spirit from those to which you are accustomed.

Informality of dress is the rule at colleges, just as regulation of dress is stressed at the academies. You will further find that there are a few special rules by which the college community lives, and by learning them, you will establish yourself in a congenial friendship with people whose purposes in life are surprisingly similar to your own.

You may be a guest on a college campus, either as a member of an athletic team or as a social guest for the weekend. In either case, your academy will be judged by your actions. A midshipman or cadet member of an athletic squad should follow the special instructions of the officer sport representative and the coach during his or her stay on campus.

As a social guest, the normal rules for a weekend guest apply here. You must be alert to observe the local ground rules, and follow them conscientiously. At all times, be congenial.

The rules for a man visiting a girl's college may be a little more strict, but the weekend has been planned for your entertainment, and you will have a good time if you are a good sport and observe certain regulations—such as:

Do not violate rules concerning drinking on or off campus.

Get the arrangements straight concerning the time of your arrival, departure, transportation, clothes, etc. (You will be facing the same problem every date faces when she comes to your academy or college.)

Remember that you have a hostess—your date—and do not play wolf to the entire campus.

Your hostess may reserve and pay for your room during your stay—and sometimes your meals and tips. But you should pay for taxis, flowers, refreshments, snacks, and all other such supplementary expenses.

For suggestions for the hop weekend and graduation week at the service academies, *see* Chapter 4, The Hop Weekend.

CHAPTER 35

Good Sportsmanship

GOOD MANNERS at sports contests are synonymous with good sportsmanship. Every officer has taken part in athletics at some time in his or her past, either as a player in the game or as an observer, and undoubtedly will do so many times in the future.

In the world of sports, there is a saying to the effect that, "If you want to find out what kind of man he is, play golf with him when he is off his game, or go fishing with him when they aren't biting."

Good sportsmanship embodies the ideals of fairness, self-control, support of the team, and performing to the best of one's ability and honor. Qualities of this nature are expected of anyone, anywhere, at any age—and it is best to learn them early.

It is good sportsmanship for midshipmen and cadets to cheer when it is announced that another service academy is winning a game. You want the other academy to win every game—except, of course, the one they are playing against your own team!

Although no one likes to lose, a good loser will compliment the winner on his skill, and a good winner will commiserate with the loser's ill luck.

There are many ways to show good sportsmanship, other than on the golf greens or at a sports contest. A good sport is the person who can take the various setbacks of life, and not complain about them.

OFFICIALS

The spectator is always very much a part of any game. The player reacts to the roar of the crowd as much as the fan thrills to the exploits of the player. The officials of the contest are also aware of the spectators and must always be on the lookout for the person who attempts to interfere with the rules of the game, or who tries to intimidate the official by heckling him.

An official is empowered to remove a player from a team for unsportsmanlike conduct as well as for the infraction of a rule. And he is empowered to eject from the stands anyone who abuses the rules of the game, and he may stop the contest when discourteous actions continue after due warnings. Thus, a penalty may be invoked on a team, or, when the infraction is serious, the game may be forfeited—which means that one or more spectators can be responsible for the loss of the game by their favorite team.

Officials of amateur or professional contests are selected after passing rigid examinations in a particular sport. The rules of the contest which they enforce have been adopted after intensive study by national sports associations, and they spell out the conduct of play that will ensure fair play for all concerned.

The decisions of officials are matters of judgment made according to vantage point and interpretation of rules. When a spectator becomes enraged over a ruling, he should realize that officials are calling the rule as they see it. Whether he agrees or not, he must abide by the decisions of the official in charge of the contest.

BOOING

The American baseball fan is a peculiar brand of individual of intense loyalty to the home team and at the same time its severest critic. He knows better than the manager when to bunt, hit, and run. The "bum" of the previous inning may become the hero of the day by a timely hit. The fan seems to be a maze of contradictions, and is consistent only in his inconsistencies.

The baiting of officials at any sports contest is very poor manners. And throwing debris on the field or at the players and officials, running onto the field of play, or using abusive or profane language, are most flagrant displays of bad manners.

While enthusiastic cheering for your favorite athlete or team is expected, booing a decision or play which goes against your team is not only childish, but also unsportsmanlike.

SPORTSMANSHIP

The most common breaches of good manners at sports events are excessive noises made by spectators or players in an effort to divert the opponent. This interference includes shouting, whistling, clapping of hands, dropping of objects, sudden movements of the arms or legs, or any other distraction.

The sports program at the service academies covers the proper behavior of midshipmen and cadets at all sports events, from both the participant and spectator viewpoint. At least twenty sports have team competition. Among the rules of courtesy are those of keeping quiet when an opponent or a member of your own team is attempting a free throw in basketball, a putt in golf, a strike in bowling, or a rally in tennis. Any game of skill demands concentration by the player.

Displays of temper, such as obscene language or fighting, defeat the purpose of the game. Spectators should conduct themselves in such a manner that they do not reflect discredit upon their academy or college. This includes conduct during liberty periods following the game as well as at the game itself, and is particularly important for uniformed personnel, as the entire service may be judged as rowdy by the isolated indiscretions of a few individuals.

Since many football games are played during inclement weather, there is a problem of personal comfort versus good manners. An umbrella may keep the rain from your head—but it may also block the view of someone behind you. Also, jumping up with an umbrella during an exciting play is not without its hazards for those sitting nearby.

Football games are frequently played in weather that is uncomfortably cold for the spectator. A number of persons use this as an excuse for consuming alcoholic beverages in the stands. This is not only illegal in many stadiums, but is a reflection upon the individual. Uniformed members of the armed forces have a special responsibility to conduct themselves as ladies and gentlemen.

In golf matches, no one should move, talk, or stand close to or directly behind the ball or hole when a player is making a stroke. Attention should be paid to the casting of shadows between the hole and a ball about to be played. Players should leave the putting green immediately upon determining the result of a hole.

When a ball is lost, or when your twosome or foursome is taking excessive time to play, you should signal other players behind you to go through you and wait until this second group has played past you and is out of range before continuing play.

A woman is responsible for her own golf bag. Presumably, she is in good health and able to care for her own bag or she wouldn't be on the course.

The fast-moving game of tennis requires good manners by the spectators in that players are distracted by moving objects in their range of vision. A tennis ball in flight moves with great speed and any unexpected movement in the neighborhood can throw a player off his game. Any movement at the opposite end of the court, especially, should be held to an absolute minimum.

If you should be sitting in a stand that faces more than one court, you should not move from one match to another until play is over except on the odd games when the players change courts. You do not applaud during a rally, but you may when the point has been played out. Errors such as a shot that goes out of court or into the net should not be applauded even if it gives the point to your favorite player. Only express approval for *good* strokes.

A number of specific sports have not been mentioned—not because they are less important, but because the good manners at other sports are similar to those already discussed. The basis of the rules in any sport is the spirit of fair play. The line between the rules and good manners is a fine one. The distinction might be set in this manner: the rules prescribe penalties to be invoked when there is a violation, whereas there generally is no penalty for a break of good sportsmanship *except* the censure of your neighbors or the public.

YOUR ALMA MATER

Every academy or college man or woman is proud to hear the song of their alma mater played or sung. Midshipmen and cadets stand at attention when their own alma mater is played or sung; therefore, it is good manners to stand when the opponent's alma mater is played or sung.

PAYING A WOMAN'S WAY

It was once considered gentlemanly for a man to offer to pay for a woman's expenses, no matter what. Today, when a single woman is included in a group that is going on a fishing trip, a ski weekend, a hunting trip, or a sports event of some kind, she should pay for her transportation and her share of the expenses involved; unless, of course, she has been specifically invited as a guest. In either case, it should be clearly understood in advance what she should or should not pay for.

When young people find themselves traveling together to the

same destination, by chance or by pre-arrangement, there is no need for a man to pay a woman's expenses, other than for small trifles if he wishes.

Older men, whose wives have never worked or earned their own money, are often uncomfortable when women insist on paying their own way. Although the man should drop the subject, still a woman's discretion should guide the decision.

PAYING YOUR OWN WAY

A good sport pays for his or her share of any casual entertainment when a group gets together on the golf course, at a theater party, or for drinks in the officers' club. It is a custom for a person or couple to go no-host or "Dutch treat," with expenses evenly divided.

When you go sailing with friends, you may volunteer to split the expenses or to bring drinks and some food. There must be an understanding beforehand, however; otherwise you might show up with a lot of provisions that merely duplicate your host's preparations.

When fishing, the host always offers to divide the catch regardless of who caught the fish. In the case of an accident, you replace any lost tackle as soon as possible.

Deep-sea fishing is luxury fishing at its best, and is expensive. The no-host situation is customary, with a small group chartering a boat and splitting expenses. Prices vary for charter boats at different ports, with three or four persons going out at a time. In party-boat fishing, when many people go out for a day or a half-day, expenses are much less.

The problems encountered with a skiing party are slightly akin to those of a safari—you usually travel a distance to get to your destination, and stay a weekend at least. When unmarried women are in the group, dormitory-style lodging is customary, and they usually pay for their own lodging. Tipping is similar to that in any hotel.

On a hunting trip, guests are expected to bring their own clothing, guns, and ammunition—unless the host has specifically said that he has equipment for all hands.

When you are a guest at a private game preserve or hunting camp, you may be assigned a guide. You tip the guide depending upon the length of your stay and the services you received. This tip is in addition to the share of the guide's wages which courtesy or custom would assign to you.

When you are invited as a guest to play on the golf course at a country club, you should pay your own way whenever you can. Usually, your invitation is a privilege extended to you by a member, and you should be prepared to pay all other costs—or as many as your host will permit. Such expenses include greens fees, caddies, food and drink.

However, you should find out first if the club runs on a cash or a chit basis. When everything is paid for in cash, the guest has no problem; when the member host signs you in, have your greens fee ready. If your host insists that he take care of the fees, accept and thank him. When he pays for the greens fee, you should pay for both caddies, if you use them. When everything is by chit service, then you should return your host's hospitality by inviting him to your ship or station, or to some other function of comparable degree.

The Military Family

CHAPTER 36

The Distaff Side

EVERYONE WANTS to lead a happy, worthwhile life. To achieve this goal—which must be earned—it is important that wives of servicemen understand the customs of the service in everyday living. A bride who has always lived in a civilian community may at first be bewildered by the regulations and traditions of the service.

In many ways there is no difference in living on a post or base — or living in Little Rock. You have friends in for pot-luck supper, you probably are a member of the church and PTA, have joined a garden club, and play golf or some other sport. There are churches and garden clubs and golf greens just about everywhere—at the base or post or in Little Rock. Wherever you live there are certain things expected of you: congeniality, friendship, a sharing of your time and effort by participating in community affairs.

One of the main differences between service and civilian life is that a service family is always on the go. Every few years—or less—a change of orders means a change in friendships, schools, and activities which may give the distaff side a sense of shallow roots. The good thing about it is the opportunity to widen your scope of friends and to extend your knowledge through travel in various areas of this country as well as overseas.

WIVES' INFORMATION PROGRAM

As a way of getting better acquainted with everyday service life, a wives' information program has been established at many posts and stations throughout the country. New brides, financées, and wives of all ages new to the station are invited to attend the free classes by the commanding officer of the station.

For example, at the Naval Base, Charleston, South Carolina, morning classes are held twice a week, with coffee breaks and free nursery service provided.

Speakers talk on almost any subject pertaining to service life, from five minutes to half an hour, with a question and answer period. Subjects range from the steps in a husband's career, the rank and rate structure, the various benefits such as health and retirement programs, financial and legal counseling that are available, and pay and allowance.

The CO sends out a letter to the wives stating where the classes will be held, the dates, and the hours. A "Welcome Aboard" folder is given to each woman attending. This folder includes maps and charts of the base or post as well as of the surrounding areas, including historic places of interest and good eating places. There are telephone lists of the most used facilities, the civic, fraternal, and service clubs in the area, schools and their entrance requirements, where to apply for your driver's license, and information about the base nursery, thrift shops, and housing referral office.

THE PX

You will need your ID card whenever you shop in the commissary or post exchange (PX) or in other government-run stores. Your ID card bears your photograph and signature. If you should have the misfortune to lose the card, report it to the station officials immediately and it will be replaced.

A service wife can save money at the commissary, where groceries are purchased, and in the post exchange where you can buy anything from clothing to bicycles. There are discounts on gas and other services at the filling station and garage. Each PX operates within the Armed Services Exchange Regulations, and it is illegal to sell to unauthorized persons—so it behooves you or any dependent to make purchases only for your own use or as a bona fide gift. There are also commissaries and exchanges overseas. Members of one service, and their dependents, are permitted to make purchases in the post exchange and commissary of any other service.

NEWCOMERS

A first for any newcomer to a station (base or post) is to get acquainted with others as soon as possible. The commanding officer (CO) of the station customarily gives a "newcomers reception" each year which is informal—no hats, gloves, or calling cards. For a daytime reception you should wear a pretty but not elaborate afternoon dress and your husband should wear the uniform designated in the invitation, or a business suit. There will be others new to the station—you will not be alone. Since formal social calls are a thing of the past, most commanding officers consider such receptions as "calls made and paid."

Frequently, the CO's wife or the president of the women's club affiliated with the station will give a brunch, coffee, or tea for the wives. This is a pleasant way to meet others. Since most women's clubs have a number of activities which meet separately, you will have the opportunity to join a group with the same interests as yours, which might be antiques, needlepoint, drama, gourmet cooking—or whatever.

Although formal social calls are no longer customary (there simply isn't time for them on large or busy stations), there is nothing friendlier than a telephone call that welcomes you to the station. Or an invitation to join a bowling group. Or a person who asks when it will be convenient to stop by and say "hello."

And after a year or so, when you are the old-timer and newcomers arrive at the station, *you* should remember to extend the welcome.

VOLUNTEERS

There are a number of organizations connected with the station which need volunteer help. The hospital, chapel guild, thrift and gift shops, nursery, youth organizations, Young Life, Boy and Girl Scouts, the Red Cross—all need volunteers. Your time—as much as you can give—is important to their success. A station newsletter will print information about such volunteer work, and the officer in charge of station activities is always helpful.

The widespread work of the Relief and Aid Societies of each service augments that of the Red Cross. In Washington, D.C. where the headquarters of the Military Wives Association, Inc. is located, wives from all services work actively for the legislative well-being of the military family, both active and retired. They are particularly concerned for the service widow and the benefits to which she is entitled.

If you have small children, many wives get together for babysitting and car pools, taking turns in caring for others' children as well as their own, and in driving to meetings.

HOUSING PROBLEMS

The Armed Forces Hostess Association, located in the Pentagon, Washington, D.C., has an extensive file on world-wide housing for service personnel. The office is staffed by volunteer workers who are wives or members of the family of armed forces personnel in the area.

In addition to the housing files, information is also available on clothing needs, travel tips, schools, churches, commissaries, climate, etc. When you write for information, make certain that your questions are specific. You should give your full name and grade; service; base, post, or station; and include a self-addressed and stamped return envelope.

The Armed Forces Housing office in the Pentagon handles housing requests for service personnel transferred to the Washington area. Staff members will help you in renting or buying a house, and will advise you on the location of schools, shopping areas, and transportation systems. There is no charge for these services.

SERVICE AID SOCIETIES

There are a number of service organizations that give immediate financial assistance to people in the services and their families. Each organization has auxiliaries, sections, or branches throughout the United States, as well as in other areas of the world. They are not connected with the American Red Cross, but work in cooperation with that organization.

Financial assistance is given for such needs as nonreceipt of pay or family allowances; expenses incidental to emergency leave; medical, dental, and hospital expenses; funeral expenses; emergency food supplies; unpaid rent with eviction notices; the training of dependents in order to make them self-supporting; assistance with educational or vocational training for service children above the high school level.

These various organizations include the *Army Emergency Relief* (AER), the *Navy Relief Society*, which includes the Marine Corps and the Coast Guard; and the *Air Force Aid Society*. All have headquarters in Washington, D.C.

These organizations raise funds by membership dues and fund-raising campaigns by such groups as officers' and NCO clubs and service women's clubs, as well as by the proceeds from balls, special shows, and sports events.

TIPS FOR HOUSEWIVES

Chances are that the personal grooming regulations for servicewomen will last a lifetime. In the services it becomes a habit to stand straight, to be neat and well groomed.

All too often in the busy daily routine of being a housewife and mother—and a woman should be *proud* of these titles which are the most demanding of all—it is easy when at home to "let yourself go." Sometimes these daily habits carry over into public life. For these busy, but sometimes careless women, here are some tips:

Do not comb or fuss with your hair in public places—particularly not in restaurants, or at any meal or when you are around food.

While preparing food, be careful that your hair is not loose and blowsy in order to keep it out of the food. Wear a net or lightweight scarf.

Don't wear hair curlers in public. If you must go to the commissary after shampooing, wear a scarf over those pink sausages.

Avoid making a performance of putting on lipstick in public. When necessary, take a quick look in a small mirror and do a touch-up. In a restaurant, for more extensive repair you should excuse yourself and go to the restroom.

Be careful of sitting awkwardly in a chair, knees apart. Older women especially are guilty of this careless habit.

ALONE AND LONELY

When an officer has overseas duty or goes to sea and the family remains at home, a problem sometimes arises for the wife: loneliness. Too often loneliness leads to depression or to a drinking problem. On the bright side, a wife alone now has the time to accomplish something that she may have longed to do: continue her education, pursue a hobby, do volunteer work. If they have children, most wives keep very busy with them and the housework.

When there are no children or if they are in school, a part- or full-time job not only will take your mind off yourself but give you extra spending money. A savings account will allow you and your husband, when he returns, the opportunity to finance something that otherwise you could not afford—perhaps a second honeymoon!

PROTECTING YOURSELF

If you are living alone, or must drive through isolated areas or for some distance, you must take safety precautions. Nine times out of ten, nothing will happen—but you must think about that tenth time that could prove harmful. Even in the daytime you should keep the doors of your house locked, with a chain on. The wrong sort of person is on the alert for an empty house or apartment, or one without a man in it.

Automatic night lights which can be set to go on and off at

definite times are helpful when you are gone overnight or for any length of time. When you will be gone from your house for a night or two, a neighbor's children can be asked to pick up the mail and newspaper, and a quarter or two or a small gift will make them happy.

If you plan to be gone a longer length of time, have the newspaper delivery stopped until your return and the post office will hold your mail, when requested, for a stated time. And hire someone to cut the grass during your absence.

Always lock car doors after parking a car and avoid poorly lighted or isolated parking lots. Should you forget to lock the car, look behind the driver's seat where an intruder might hide before getting in. Make certain that the tires are not low, and always check the gas gauge before starting out.

ASSAULT

In case of assault or attempted assault, scream. Fight with anything at hand, and with your fists and feet. If you have time—should this be a drunken or retarded person, try and talk him out of it. No one wants to be fatally injured and a lethal weapon in the intruder's hand precludes much resistance, but statistics prove that when women resist, less than 5 percent are killed.

Authorities say that there are ways that a woman can help herself, that some women submit in fear of their lives, or become hypnotized with fear. When you can, fight. Yell "Fire!" People will come running when the dreaded word fire is shouted—but too few people will intercede otherwise, either thinking this is a family fight—or simply not wanting to get involved.

A woman can carry a small but useful object with her in a lonely or crime-ridden area, in her purse or on the car seat. Car doors should be kept locked. A shrill whistle can scare off a wrong-doer. A simple object is a plastic lemon which can be purchased in any grocery store; remove the lemon juice and replace it with ammonia which can be quickly squirted at the attacker's eyes. But whatever the object, it must be reached instantly.

There are a few basic rules that a woman should follow: keep out of lonely areas day or night, but particularly after dark in parking lots. Keep the chain on your door at home. Have your house key in your hand and ready for use when returning home so that you do not waste time hunting for it—time that gives an assaulter the chance to grab it and force himself inside the house. Do not permit your children to hitch-hike—boy or girl, and never pick up hitchhikers yourself.

Officials* in crime detection and prevention state most assaults are planned; that only a few are spur-of-the-moment acts. The individual may be a person you know, or someone who has seen you somewhere. When an assault takes place, this should be reported to authorities in person or anonymously. You need not press charges, but in order to prevent such attacks on others, a description of the attacker must be given. Such information is kept confidential.

Some women take karate lessons to learn how to help protect themselves. There are classes given by various organizations, such as the YWCA, which will instruct you in self-defense. For example, it is well to know that the heel of your shoe can be a handy weapon, or that your thumbs pushed into an assaulter's eyes or your sharply raised knee to the groin or stomach can gain you valuable time.

YOUR CHILDREN

A wife is father, mother, and the protector of the family when her husband is away. Children should be given a set of rules to go by—in the house as well as out. Small children must be told never to accept goodies from a stranger, or to get into his car, or to talk with any unknown adult either on the school ground or on the sidewalk. A mother should always know where the children are—and they should know where she is. There is nothing more disturbing to most children than to return to an empty or unlighted house.

Teenagers can be almost as unsuspecting of a wrong-doer's intentions because teens are in a questioning and learning stage of life. Their mother should know about their friends—without seeming to be inquisitive. She needs patience and understanding—even when it runs thin. Rules should be made for hours to come home, household chores, allowances. But a teenager should have time for privacy.

FAMILY SECURITY

As soon as a man learns that he will have duty where his family will not be going, he should get his household affairs in order long before departure. He should talk over with his wife what is to be done in his absence, how this is to be carried out, and what to do in case of emergency.

After moving out of quarters and into a house or apartment, she

* The Sex Offense Squad and the Rape Crisis Center in Washington, D.C.

will be making the decisions: paying the bills, balancing the budget, keeping the car in condition, and disciplining the children.

A wife must have ready access to the important family records—and she must understand them. A young wife may have had little experience in handling financial affairs before marriage, so a little time and patience should be shown by the husband in explaining their importance. However, a young officer may have had little financial experience himself; in this case, it would be wise to seek outside advice.

Records are usually kept in a safety deposit box in a bank or trust company. These records should include a copy of the officer's service record and insurance premiums for car, house, and life. He may choose to have such premiums paid out of his monthly paycheck but this must be arranged beforehand by his writing to the Finance Center of his service—Cleveland for the Navy, Indianapolis for the Army, Denver for the Air Force, and Kansas City for the Marines—giving detailed information. Since it takes about eight weeks for the Center to set the wheels in motion, this must be done as soon as possible.

Other records should include: medical benefits; an up-to-date will (the station legal officer can help with this); marriage and birth certificates; bank and savings accounts; investments such as stocks and bonds; real estate, and an estimate of its present value; a power of attorney; family death records, and burial site information.

Also included should be the names, addresses, and telephone numbers of persons to be contacted in case of emergency: his commanding officer and duty station; the Aid or Relief Society of his service; the national headquarters or local chapter of the American Red Cross; the legal assistance officer; the nearest military hospital, and the chaplain or minister in your area.

BASE PAY

One of the first financial lessons a bride learns about is the monthly paycheck which is mailed to her husband from the Finance Center of his service.

The *base pay* of all members of the armed forces is determined by Congress, based on rank; it is the same in all services for officers of the same rank. The pay is subject to federal income tax. Since 1968 Congress has authorized annual pay raises, which are semiautomatic.

There is *hazardous duty pay* for aviators, submariners, and those serving in parachute, demolition, and diving details. There is *hostile fire pay* for the time a man spends in a combat zone, and *career incentive pay* for medical and dental officers.

ALLOWANCES

Extra allowances make things a little easier for service men and women. Every active-duty officer receives a *subsistence allowance* each month, which is not taxable. For officers who are not assigned government-furnished quarters on base but must find housing in a nearby town or community, a *basic allowance for quarters* is issued to him each month, with a little more for those with dependents.

When an officer goes overseas or has sea duty, there is *family separation allowance* and *travel allowance*. When you move, you will have professional packers and movers—all you need to do is have things clean and ready to pack, guard the inventory list, and keep your children, your pets, and yourself out of the way.

ALLOTMENTS

An allotment is that portion of your husband's paycheck which he allots to you, or any individual, business, or agent during his absence. This is accomplished by his writing to his Finance Center, directing how much of his check is to be sent, and where.

The allotment may be changed by the officer at any time, in writing. Otherwise it will stay in effect until an emergency decrees a change (when a man is known to be a prisoner of war or missing in action and the family needs financial aid), or until his death.

A wife's allotment will be mailed to her each month from the Finance Center. The amount must be discussed fully before his departure.

When authorized by the officer in writing (it is his paycheck), the Finance Center will purchase government bonds and hold them in safe-keeping until his return, or will withhold a designated amount from his paycheck during the time that he is gone, which will accrue and earn good interest.

LEAVE

Leave is the authorized absence of a serviceman or servicewoman from his or her duty station. In the civilian world, it is vacation time. However, leave is chargeable against his or her leave account, with 30 days granted each year. This amounts to about two-and-a-half days for each month of duty.

You can take your leave all at one time, or a few days or a week or so at a time. Or you may not take your leave at all. When it accumulates as "earned leave" to 60 days—you take it or lose it. Men in combat areas, however, have 90 days of earned leave.

For the good of all concerned, the officer should talk with his CO about the best time to take his leave, and do it early.

Then there is *sick leave*, given for those under medical care, and *emergency leave* when death or disaster occurs in a family. The Red Cross verifies these emergencies. Up to 45 days of *advance leave* may be granted for an emergency, with immediate military transportation to the place of emergency. When disaster strikes, there is no cut in pay or allowance, and the best government hospital and medical services are tendered the ill or injured.

PROMOTIONS

A wife new to service life will soon learn that the system of her husband's promotion is based on his years of experience and qualifications. Second lieutenants in the Army, Air Force, and Marines and ensigns in the Navy and Coast Guard are automatically promoted to the next grade. But after that their records are scrutinized by members of the selection board where promotions are being considered. The board of about six senior officers meets annually to pass on the records of all officers in the promotion zone.

As rank increases, selections become tighter. Each officer's record or "jacket" includes his fitness report which has been sent in by his commanding officer each year or whenever he is transferred. This report includes his performance of duty, any disciplinary action, and the CO's overall evaluation.

A spot promotion, as it sounds, is made when an officer serves with exceptional ability and his commanding officer promotes him on the spot.

The deep selection of an officer is made out of his zone—before his regular time for being promoted. This usually occurs when his specialities (outstanding) are needed in a specific command.

Since Congress sets the numerical strength of the armed forces, the need for officers in each service changes constantly. In times of war the number of men is greatly enlarged; in times of peace the number is sharply reduced.

It is important that a wife be aware of the many facets of service life, and the roadblocks which may curtail her husband's career. When he fails to be promoted or is retired early in his career for physical disability, she may be called upon for more sympathy and moral support than at any other time in their married life.

PASSED OVER

There is no greater trauma for a dedicated young officer than to be "passed over." Too often he has a deep sense of rejection: *Why me?*

When a large number of officers are being considered and only a few can be picked up, it may be the man with only a slightly higher "number" than another. For example, a service academy graduate has a permanent number based on his academic standing and aptitude; when two officers have equal ability and only one can be chosen, the number may be the deciding factor. Every serviceman and servicewoman has a lineal number; upon retirement his name is placed on the retired list, and upon death it is removed.

When an officer of junior rank—first lieutenant, captain, and major in the Army, Air Force, and Marines, or lieutenant or lieutenant commander in the Navy and Coast Guard—has *twice* failed to be promoted, he is "passed over."

This means mandatory retirement, with severance pay equal to two months' base pay but not over $15,000, and no benefits. Reserve officers with at least five years' active duty receive similar pay.

Once an officer attains the permanent rank of major in the Army, Air Force, and Marines, and lieutenant commander in the Navy and Coast Guard, he may remain on active duty for 20 years. The higher the rank the longer the officer stays in. A captain in the Navy who is not selected for rear admiral, or the Army brigadier general who does not make major general must retire after completing 30 years of active duty.

SEPARATED

An officer of any rank may be separated involuntarily from the service due to a court-martial, misconduct, mismanagement of personnel or government affairs, financial irresponsibility, or when he is considered temperamentally unsuitable to the service. The officer has the right to be heard before a Board of Inquiry where he may state his side of the case.

RESIGNATION

When an officer resigns his commission he receives no retirement pay or other benefits; he will be unable to use the commissaries, post exchanges, or officers' clubs. A resignation is a voluntary act by the officer and is considered an "unqualified resignation."

A "qualified resignation" is given a member of the armed forces for several reasons—for a violation of honor, or for "the good of the service"—a serious charge.

RETIREMENT

Many officers retire after 20 years of service. Some stay in for 30 or so years and achieve flag rank. A handful become three-star admirals and three- or four-star generals and retire in accordance with government regulations around the age of 62.

Upon retiring, an officer will receive a retirement check for life. The amount of the check is based on his or her rank at the time of retirement and the number of years served. He (or she) will be entitled to many benefits: medical, travel (space available), use of the commissary and exchange, and the many facilities of the officers' club.

Very important is his opportunity to enter into a low-cost Survivor Benefit Plan (SBP) for military retirees which will give his family financial protection in case of his death—when the retirement check stops. The Uniformed Services Health Benefits Program (USHBP), including the Civilian Health and Medical Program of the Uniformed Services (CHAMPUS), offers service families care or assistance at a civilian hospital or facility at government expense. For more about an officer's retirement, *see* Chapter 45, When You Retire.

MIA AND POW

In times of war a man is declared missing in action (MIA) when his fate is not known during or after his assigned duty. He will remain on the missing-in-action list until he is found or officially declared dead. Since the officer is the one who receives pay, his paycheck will continue but is held and credited to his account until his status is legally determined.

Allowances and allotments will continue as set up. If an allotment was not made, his wife or next of kin may request through his service that such an allotment be set up for reasons of financial need.

When a man is known to have been captured by the enemy, he is officially declared a prisoner of war (POW). Whether MIA or POW, his next of kin will be immediately notified by his commanding officer and the bureau or department of his service.

A family assistance program aids the families of war prisoners and those missing in action. Various forms of benefits and programs have been established to help the families, and these can be learned from your chaplain or legal officer.

DEATH

When your husband dies on active duty, his commanding officer or his representative will notify you immediately. His death is then verified by a telegram from his service bureau or department.

Should he die at home or on leave, his commanding officer or the nearest military station should be notified at once. A Red Cross representative or the station chaplain will help in every possible way.

When the officer dies on active duty, his survivors will immediately receive a sum amounting up to $3,000. The deceased may be buried in any national cemetery (space available) at government expense, or in the cemetery of the family's choice with provision made for expenses. Transportation is furnished.

Within a year of death, transportation is also furnished for families to move to another house, in another state if necessary, or the household goods may be stored up to six months. If you are in quarters you will be given time to move out, but quarters are soon needed for others reporting in.

There is Dependency and Indemnity Compensation (DIC) for the widow, with payments based on the pay grade of the deceased and the number and age of children in the family. If the widow remarries, the payments stop but will continue for the children unless they are adopted by the new husband.

PERSONAL HELP

When an emergency or serious problem arises, you should seek the advice of the station legal officer. Your problem, no matter how grave, will be held in confidence. However, the legal officer cannot represent service personnel in civilian courts, but he or she can give you names and addresses of civilian counsel.

When a person needs help on such problems as alcoholism, child abuse, depression, or serious mental disturbances with possible threats of suicide or drug addiction, help is obtainable from trained medical professionals who have been commissioned in the services. The earlier you seek help, the sooner the symptoms of the problem can be detected and corrected.

There are many sources of help, depending upon the nature of your trouble. The base or station chaplain is always ready to talk with you about any emotional or personal problem; a trained psychiatrist is available for the disturbed.

IN CASE OF ACCIDENT

In case of an accident or sudden illness, call the doctor and/or take the person stricken to the emergency room of the nearest hospital. The name, telephone number, and address of your doctor and hospital should be in your wallet or handbag. When you know that a member of your family—

or you yourself—has a history of heart attacks, diabetes, or cannot take penicillin, it is vital that such information is kept with that person at all times, particularly when traveling.

There should be a first-aid kit in the car and in the home, safe from the children but in a place with easy access, and it is the wise parent who is well-versed in first-aid procedures and has a *First Aid Guide*.

THE WIDOW

At first, a widow may not care to go to large or gay social affairs, and she should not be urged to do so. There is no set time for mourning as in former years. Black or somber dress is rarely worn, other than to the funeral services, although a widow usually wears more subdued dress for as long as she likes.

A psychiatrist has stated that loneliness is the mother of depression. When a bereaved person grieves to the extent that she becomes a recluse from friends and family, when self-pity overwhelms her, these are signs of depression. Her friends are the ones who can help the most during this time of stress.

HELP YOURSELF

In time, you, the bereaved, must help yourself. At first you may want to talk about your loss, to reminisce about the happy times in your married life. And your friends should be sympathetic listeners.

But to dwell on one's unhappiness too long, to wear a mournful face, to lose emotional control too often will eventually drive even the best friend away—at least for awhile. The sooner you mix with others, have a few friends in for dinner or a drink, take a trip, or play golf, the better off you will be.

The best therapy of all may be a part- or full-time job or volunteer work.

FINANCIAL HELP

The legal assistance officer at any station will help you, the widow, in the preparation of the necessary papers for Social Security, indemnity compensation, and any other benefits to which you are entitled. In a civilian community, consult a lawyer.

There are several agencies which can assist in obtaining a loan or grant for study or training. The Aid or Relief Societies of your husband's service can help, and information may be obtained from the Military Wives Association, Inc., in Washington, D.C.

If your husband was a member of the Mutual Aid Association, you will have no need to worry about ready cash, because a check will be sent to you immediately.

Service widows are given priority in Civil Service positions, when qualified. For more information, *see* Chapter 45, When You Retire, and Chapter 39, Emergency & Death.

CHAPTER 37

The Family

YOUR CHILDREN

Children are people. *Little* people with big feelings that can be hurt just like your own. Some parents constantly scold small children in an effort to make them be polite or kiss someone they don't want to kiss.

Of course parents want their children to shake hands politely, to smile, and say "hello." But a shy child, a constantly goaded child, will balk. When a child holds back, or cries, or hides his head, he needs a little special understanding—not nagging or shaking. In his own good time, he will surprise you by smiling and saying "hello."

It is desirable that children use the word "Sir" when speaking to a senior, but the word—like seasoning—should not be overused. And a little girl's curtsy is outmoded.

It is desirable that parents do not permit—or insist—that their children call them by their given names: "Bob" and "Mary." Given names are for equality.

GODPARENTS

Following the birth of a child, parents sometimes choose godparents from among close friends or relatives who usually are of the same religion and who will keep in contact with the child throughout the years.

When the child is christened, the godparents attend whenever possible, but they can accept by proxy if unable to attend.

Godparents should give the child a christening present, sometimes a silver cup with the baby's name engraved on it, or older godparents may want to start a college fund with a savings account, or give a bond in the child's name. You accept the honor of being a godparent whenever possible, but not when you feel that the responsibility is too great.

TABLE MANNERS

When your child joins the family table, he should learn a few everyday manners—slowly—so that they become a habit: to be clean when he (or she) comes to the table, especially his hands; to close his mouth when he chews food, and to talk only after the food is swallowed. He shouldn't play with his food, dangle it on his fork, or smack his lips. Eventually he must learn not to interrupt others, but this takes time because children talk spontaneously.

A child must learn to ask for food, not grab for it. When he finishes eating, he should ask if he may be excused to leave the table when others are still eating.

WHEN SMALL CHILDREN STAY HOME

It's fun to take your children along whenever you can. But there are times when they should stay home, for everyone's sake, including theirs. At a wedding, for instance, young children tire quickly, are keyed up after the splendor of the wedding—and become noisy, bothersome, or weary at the reception—or all three!

Children should not be taken with you to any social affair unless specifically invited. Your friends know that you have children, so when they are not included in an invitation, parents should not take them along.

Should you be the hosts and others ask if they may bring their children when it is inconvenient for you, then be frank. You know which of your friends are apt to do this; so when extending the invitation say, "I'm not having any children this time, and I want to give you plenty of time to get a sitter." To offset the possibility of any problem, try to suggest the name of a trusted sitter.

OLDER CHILDREN

Good manners for young people do not come about suddenly with approaching adulthood—they are acquired as small children. The child taught to say "thank you" or "excuse me" will automatically be able to express thanks or any other amenity when he is older.

Teenagers need to be told *why* they cannot do something that seems logical to them, but not to their parents. In order to make a house regulation hold, explain why they can or cannot do what Tom, Dick, and Mary are doing. Don't arbitrarily say, "Because I say so, that's why."

It takes patience for parents to pull through the teen years, but the pattern of their children's lives may be set during these years. Parents often do not understand teenagers very well because the teens don't understand themselves too well. This is a growing, a learning stage of life. And they have dream times, to the exclusion of everyone else.

Teens need friends as everyone does, and wise parents will make certain that through the years their children's friends are welcome in the home. Letting them have a hand in planning and carrying out their own informal parties or special occasions is always a good idea.

It is easy for parents to become too involved with their children, or to expect too much from them in family participation at certain ages. The youngster who had a wonderful time on the family trip last summer may flatly refuse to go this summer; he or she may want to stay home and cut grass, deliver papers, baby sit, or go to the swimming pool.

Teen-age sloppiness seems endless; therefore, house rules should be established as to their keeping their room in order, taking baths, and shampooing—habits that should be established early in life.

The matter of allowances is something that parents and children have to work out together, depending on the needs of the youngsters and how they carry out their household chores, as well as the financial status of the parents. But regardless of the parents' financial status, it is better for a teenager to have too little than too much, to earn some money of his own and find out that it can be hard to come by. Otherwise he might have trouble later on in dealing with the school of hard knocks.

THE BABYSITTER

When you leave your children with a babysitter, or should your daughter be the babysitter, a little advance planning of what should or shouldn't be done will be helpful for all concerned.

First, you should tell the children ahead of time that a sitter will be staying with them and who that person is. Ask a new sitter to come ten or fifteen minutes early so that you can show them around the house and they can get acquainted with the children.

Second, explain all rules for the children: their bedtime hour; TV programs to be seen or not seen, and how long they may watch; what, if any, snacks are permitted before bedtime; the "specials" that a small child finds necessary for contentment such as a particular blanket or teddybear.

Third, leave your telephone number and the name of the person or place where you can be reached; also, should an emergency arise, the telephone number of the doctor, close neighbor, or friend whom they can call for help.

Fourth, explain all do's and don'ts: that the doors are to be kept locked and that no one is to be admitted—not even persons who claim to be friends or relatives; that the sitter is not to have a guest unless you give permission; that a small child is never to be left alone in a bathtub— not even when the phone rings; that small children are not left un- attended while the sitter watches TV or does homework; that the TV or radio must be set at low volume in order to hear the cry of a child.

IN-LAWS

Relatives should be friends. You can't choose your relatives like your friends, but you should try to get along together in harmony regardless of differences in age and opinions.

In-laws should be your very best friends. Often, parents-in-law and a young couple immediately develop a warm relationship that lasts a lifetime. Other times, there are almost immediate problems. In-law problems, according to marriage counselors, rank almost even with finan- cial woes for young couples.

In-laws should not interfere. They should not give advice, unless asked for, and refrain from giving more than asked for.

Whenever possible, parents and their married children should not live together. Should it be necessary, and the parents are living in the younger couple's home, the parents should have a room of their own and stay in it at certain times in order to give the younger couple privacy and time to talk things over and make plans together. But they should not be expected to stay in their room for long periods of time, or shushed up like small children—this is unkind. Of course, the same holds true for single parents living with their children and married children living with their parents.

Too often a possessive parent looks upon a child as a possession— my house, my car, my son. Parents should realize that a child is on loan to them only until adulthood, then he or she is on his own.

When parents realize this, they can make plans of their own— travel, do volunteer work or part-time work, develop a hobby or new interest—in addition to their grandchildren. Too often, young people ignore an older parent, frequently out of thoughtlessness, but sometimes deliberately. When there is friendship between in-laws and their children, annoying or troublesome problems can be aired and talked over. Then, hard feelings are not apt to occur.

THE ELDERLY

All too often, the elderly are the overlooked in one's busy struggle with life. When a person is old and infirm, they appreciate a little attention more than anyone else—other than small children. Usually, they are the last to get it.

When you know that someone is confined to their home, or a nursing home or hospital, a few minutes of your time will give them more pleasure than any gift that you can offer. When the aged cannot get out, it is very important who comes in.

If distance or time does not permit a visit, then a brief phone call— a receiver grows heavy in a weak hand—a pleasant newsy note, or an anniversary card help to brighten a long day.

When an elderly person feels like getting out, it is thoughtful of you to invite them for a ride on a nice day, or to take them to lunch in a tearoom.

Should you ever have to make the decision to place someone in a nursing home, make absolutely certain that it is well recommended, clean, the attendants and nursing staff efficient and kind, and that a qualified doctor is in attendance. Do not stop in the entrance lobby when you check it out, but visit the kitchen and the dining and recreation areas as well.

THE UNMARRIED COUPLE

The changing attitudes in today's liberated social world have raised a number of questions that once were never mentioned or were no more than Victorian "back street" whisperings.

Be as it may, some people live together outside the marriage vows and are accepted in a number of social patterns of life—more frequently in larger cities and on some college campuses. Within families, there may be heartbreak, embarrassment, a strain on the family ties. Therefore, it is not as simple as a person "living his own life and not hurting anyone else."

To ward off some of these ill feelings within a family, the unmarried couple cannot expect parents (or other relatives or friends, usually seniors) to accept their way of life and let them share a room in the parents' home. When someone wants to bring home their roommate for the weekend, and that roomate is of the opposite sex, their relationship should first be explained if they expect to stay together in the same room. Otherwise, when they know that a parent or parents (relatives or friends) would object, they should agree to stay in separate rooms.

This is not old-fashioned of the parents or friends; it is the difference in social mores, in moral standards, and religious convictions of individuals.

When introducing an unmarried couple who may be visiting in your home—or anywhere—simple say, "This is Mary Smith (or just 'Mary' if she is a relative), "and John Doe."

GIVING GIFTS

Everyone likes a present, but a conscientious person does not want gifts from those he or she does not know well—or too many gifts from a friend or relative. Many young people with little to spend for gifts make a rule—and announce it early to friends and relatives (with the probable exception of parents and children), that they wish to give presents once a year (at Christmas or birthdays) and that cards and notes will be sent upon other occasions. They also request that others do likewise in regard to them.

When you consider that the average person (and double this for married couples) has parents, grandparents, sisters, brothers, aunts, uncles, nieces, nephews, as well as in-laws, godparents, and close friends to remember—the gift list can become endless as well as expensive.

In selecting a present, it is better to give a thoughtful though inexpensive gift in excellent taste rather than a showy though costly one. Something you make yourself may be the most treasured.

GIFTS FOR OLDER PEOPLE

Many older people can buy whatever they want within reason—or already have it—and care little for presents. They might rather have a phone call or a long newsy letter if they live at a distance.

For those who live with you or nearby, gifts can be a problem. When they have only a small income, however, there is no problem. Usable things are always best—but try to find out first if they want what you plan to give. A transistor radio gives pleasure throughout a sleepless night; and for the bedridden, comfortable house shoes and/or a robe will keep them warm.

One of the nicest gifts for anyone is fruit. Oranges, grapefruit, pears, and apples are shipped from a number of reliable growers in this country directly to one's door, at a time specified in the purchase. This is also easy for the donor—no packing, no wrapping, no mailing. For those who entertain or have friends drop in frequently, cheese, smoked ham or turkey, nuts, jellies, cookies, candy, flowers, or a potted plant give much more pleasure than another tie or a fancy nylon nightgown that will never be worn.

GIFTS FOR YOUNG PEOPLE

It is difficult sometimes for an older person to find the right gift for a young person—child, teenager, or married. Styles change rapidly, fads come and go; and when possible, it is better to find out ahead of time what is needed or wanted, and the exact size or color if clothing is indicated. When in doubt, send a check.

SENDING MONEY

Although a check may not be as much fun to send, there comes a time when shopping in crowds—or shopping at all—becomes a chore, or you may not have a clue as to what to send. Then a check is in order.

Quite often a check is a blessing and is the nicest gift of all. Then, the child can choose her own cuddly robe, the teenager can afford something the sender never heard of, and the college student or graduate has a little nest egg. It's a lovely feeling to have some money to spend exactly as you please.

JOINT PRESENTS

There are times when a joint present is much more desirable than individual ones. An office staff or an organization may contribute to a single expensive present which an engaged or newly married couple might not otherwise be able to have. For example, a starter set of sterling flatware; or if the couple wishes something of a practical nature, a stainless steel set of kitchen utensils or a vacuum cleaner. A few dollars given by each person to the office "kitty" goes a long way toward a gift that will last a lifetime.

A joint gift is often given to a retiring or detached officer upon his or her departure, or to someone who is promoted in rank and honored at a wetting-down party. A new baby is the recipient of a unit's joint gift, and a group of office workers often go in on a shower gift together. Children may all chip in for a single lovely present for their parents' wedding anniversary.

NO GIFTS

When an invitation states "No gifts," please honor it. When you go ahead and show up at a party bearing a gift, everyone feels uncomfortable, including the recipient.

If you are a close friend of the guest of honor at a no-gift party, you could take or send a gift to him or her at home beforehand. Flowers are always acceptable for special occasions.

WEDDING PRESENTS

Probably the most meaningful gift of all is a wedding present. The gift should be selected with care, with consideration given to the needs and desires of the couple receiving it. The gift should be as nice as you can afford to give since it will be used and enjoyed for the duration of the marriage. Frequently a very nice gift is something that the couple might not be able to afford for a long time, if ever. Therefore, it is cherished. (For more information, *see* Chapter 26.)

ACKNOWLEDGING GIFTS

It is mandatory that all gifts are acknowledged by the receiver, young or old. If a person can spend time and money to send you a gift, you can take the time to say "thank you." A note (or sometimes a phone call) should be written within a day or two of receiving the gift.

ON FOREIGN DUTY

Service personnel have a golden opportunity to buy unusual and beautiful gifts while serving on foreign duty. Although prices are higher than in former years, and the dollar has depreciated in some countries, a good shopper can find many a bargain and gifts of lasting interest.

Each country has some specialty, something uniquely its own. A wise man or woman will learn everything possible about the country before arriving, then you can save your money by comparative shopping after you reach the station or port. Small objects that can be easily mailed or packed and later used for gifts should be an important part of your shopping.

SECTION X

The Serious Side of Life

CHAPTER 38

Your Religion

THE RELIGIOUS BELIEFS of men have much in common, regardless of formal religious affiliations. Notwithstanding the many different religious denominations and the great variety of individual attitudes toward religion, the student of theology is generally impressed by the similarities, rather than the differences, in the basic teachings of all religions.

When you understand these similarities, it becomes apparent how ill-mannered and foolish it is for any person to make light of another's beliefs, or to make derogatory remarks about the faith of another. A person who does so is violating a basic fundamental of both his own and the other's religion—*to love thy neighbor.*

It is not enough for an officer simply to understand and respect the beliefs of another. In the social observances of religious ceremonials there are many occasions in which individuals of different religions are brought together in a common participation. It is necessary that you know the proper behavior and procedures to be followed on such occasions, since they will become a part of your everyday living.

As you go about your daily social and official life, you will be called upon to take part in numerous religious ceremonies, in either an active or impassive role. In most cases, you will do no more than stand quietly, uncovered, and with bowed head, until the ceremony is concluded.

There are other occasions when you will be asked to take an active part in a religious ceremony, such as at funerals, weddings, baptisms, and services of thanksgiving. Simple benedictions by a chaplain in an outdoor ceremony mean that you uncover and follow the motions of the chaplain.

Ceremonies in a church or chapel require specific knowledge of procedure. A member of a wedding party or a funeral cortege needs to learn everything possible about his responsibilities before the ceremony, and it is advisable that you find out ahead of time from the rabbi, chaplain, or clergyman of that particular faith, what you are to do.

BLESSINGS AT THE TABLE

As a guest at a meal, you may be called upon to take part in a simple family observance of religious custom. These expressions of thanksgiving may help you:

Catholic: "Bless us, O Lord, and these, Thy gifts, which we are about to receive from Thy bounty. Through Christ our Lord. Amen."

Jewish: "Lift up your hands toward the sanctuary and bless the Lord. Blessed art Thou, O Lord our God, King of the universe, who bringest forth bread from the earth. Amen."

Protestant: "Bless, O Lord, this food to our use, and us to Thy service, and make us ever mindful of the needs of others, in Jesus' name. Amen."

When you are a guest in a home of another religious affiliation, do not attempt to use a blessing of the host's religion unless you are familiar with it. Instead, use your own favorite grace and say it in your own sincere way.

CHILD'S BAPTISM

The baptism of an infant is usually held in a chapel or church. A Protestant child should be baptized within the first year of its life, preferably when two to six months old. The baptism frequently follows the regular Sunday morning service.

A Catholic infant is baptized at an age of two weeks to one month, and the ceremony is frequently held at an early hour on Sunday afternoon.

In the Jewish faith, a ceremony for male infants is held in a synagogue, home, or hospital eight days after birth. The naming of female infants takes place the week following birth, during services at the synagogue.

The parents issue invitations by note or telephone, with a reception, tea, or luncheon following the religious ceremony. The party is usually held at the home of the parents, and guests are close friends and relatives of the families.

A white cake and wine, or fruit punch, may be served at the reception. Toasts to the child's health and prosperity are proposed by a godfather, if there is one, when dessert is served at a luncheon, or later on at the reception or tea.

Officers of the parent's immediate service unit usually present the child with a gift, such as a silver christening cup, which may be engraved with the child's name, date of christening, and the title of the service unit of the donors.

RELIGION IN THE ARMED FORCES

Military personnel have the opportunity to attend church services since armed forces regulations require that all commanding officers permit limited duty on Sundays for this purpose. Services may be attended on weekdays by those whose faiths call for services during the week.

Protestant, Catholic, and Jewish services are held at all major installations, and usually one or two are held at the smallest base or post. Those of other faiths are provided services whenever possible, either in nearby houses of worship or by visiting clergy.

Chaplains hold military rank and are in uniform. They have been trained at seminaries and ordained as are all other clergymen before entering the service. There are chaplain's assistants and lay leaders who may conduct services under chaplain's supervision.

Cadets and midshipmen attend church services on a voluntary basis in their academy chapels or in a church in the community. Each academy has one or more chapels. All academies have Bible study classes and prayer groups, which are also attended on a voluntary basis. There are such organizations as the Fellowship of Christian Athletes, a nondenominational fellowship for Bible study that invites outstanding athletes as speakers, and the Officers' Christian Fellowship that was founded at the Military Academy. The cadets and midshipmen assist the chaplains in various ways: as ushers at church services and choir programs, and they teach Sunday School classes for family members of service personnel.

As a member of a given church, the chaplain must follow his denomination's teachings. Therefore he works within the boundaries of his denomination: answers first to the church.

When a chaplain tells a couple that they must be counseled before their wedding, or that he cannot marry non-members of the church, or a divorced person, they should not be offended: he cannot, due to his conscience and his church.

CHAPTER 39

Emergency & Death

WHEN THERE HAS BEEN a serious accident or the death of an active-duty officer, while on leave or en route to a base, post, or station, this information is telephoned as soon as possible to the commanding officer of the nearest armed forces activity. The following information should be given:

The officer's full name, rank, and service number; where the death, accident, or illness, took place; the extent of the injury and present condition, if living; the name, address, and telephone number of the physician in charge, and of the hospital or place where the patient or deceased is at that time; where the person—you or whoever—giving the information can be reached.

A military officer will be assigned to check on the accident or illness, and to assist in every way possible. In case of an automobile accident, it is necessary to have verification that the accident was not the fault of the deceased or injured, and that no negligence or carelessness was involved—otherwise the family may not receive all forthcoming benefits.

Service personnel, whether officer or enlisted, receive emergency medical treatment at any government hospital or, when none is available, at a civilian hospital at government expense. A survivor assistance officer of the armed forces activity and its chaplain will aid the deceased or injured officer's or enlisted man's family.

DEATH

You will need help at this most devastating of times—the death of a loved one. A relative or close friend, a member of the Relief or Aid

Society of your service or the Red Cross, are some of the people who can help with the details such as: contacting the funeral director in a non-military area, or the survivor assistance officer of the nearest military installation; notifying the newspapers in which the obituary notice will be published and compiling accurate information; phoning the chaplain or clergyman and relatives or friends who live at a distance. If the officer was retired and in a second career, his or her employer must be notified.

Arrangements must be made for the funeral: the money for a private or civilian interment; clothing to be sent to the funeral director; clothing to be worn by the family; flowers to be sent by the family for the service; transportation for other than active-duty personnel.

Then, there will be legal business that must be attended to: the reading of the will; the accounting of personal property, taxes, insurance, benefits. The retirement plan that was taken—or not taken—may determine the survivor's new way of life. There are many informative books available about probating wills, and how to avoid probate, that a wise person should have read before death, so that his heirs have as little difficulty and expense as possible at this time.

Many widows are shocked to learn that unless the checking or savings account was in both names—a joint account—that she will be unable to draw funds until legal matters are determined—and this may take time. A widow whose husband was on active duty will receive a check amounting to at least $3,000—depending upon the length of time that her husband was in the service. But the retirement check for a retired officer stops immediately after death. When the family car was registered only in the name of the deceased, in most states the car can be driven by the widow or next of kin upon showing the death certificate.

OFFICIAL NOTIFICATION OF DEATH

A notification of death must be sent to certain military departments. Using the form shown on the following page, you enclose a copy of the death certificate with each form. Retired and reserve officers' widows (or next of kin) should promptly notify these departments in order to set in motion the annuities that will be payable to the family.

When a member of the family of a serviceperson dies, this information must first be given to the local Red Cross. In turn they must notify the Red Cross on the military base or post, which verifies his or her emergency leave.

NOTIFICATION OF DEATH OF RETIRED MEMBER

From:_____

(Full name of widow, next of kin or executor)

_____

(Mailing address—street)

_____

(City, state, zip code)

_____

(Date)

To:

1. This is to inform you that _____

(Last name) (First Name) (Middle Name)

_____,_____,| | | | | | | | died on _____.

(Grade) (Service No.) (Soc. Sec. No.)   (Date)

2. Copy of death certificate is enclosed.

3. I am the ☐ widow, ☐ child, ☐ executor or ☐ other (explain)

_____

4. My Social Security number is | | | | | | | | .

Sincerely,

Enclosure

_____

(Signature)

Please enclose copy
of death certificate.

One form is sent to the pertinent service:

Army

The Adjutant General, Department of the Army, Attn: DAAG, Alexandria, Va. 22332

Navy

Chief of Naval Personnel, Department of the Navy, Attn: PERS-732, Washington, D.C. 20370

Air Force

U.S. Air Force Military Personnel Center, Attn: Casualty Reporting & Survivor Assistance Branch, Randolph Air Force Base, Tex. 78148

Marine Corps

Commandant, United States Marine Corps, Attn: MC-DNA, Washington, D.C. 20380

Coast Guard

Commandant (G-PS-1/62), United States Coast Guard, 400 7th Street, S.W., Washington, D.C. 20590

Public Health Service

Chief, Employment, Operations Branch, USPHS—Room 4-35, Parklawn Blvd., Rockville, Md. 20852

NOAA*

Chief, Commissioned Personnel Division, 6010 Executive Blvd., Rockville, Md. 20852

However, the Army and Navy require three separate letters; the Air Force and Marine Corps two; and the Coast Guard, Public Health Service, and NOAA only one.

The other letters go to the following:

Army

U.S. Army Finance and Accounting Center, Retired Pay Division, Indianapolis, Ind. 46249

Navy

Navy Finance Center, Retired Pay Department, Anthony J. Celebrezze Federal Building, Cleveland, Ohio 44199

Air Force

Air Force Accounting & Finance Center, 3800 York Street, Attn: Retired Pay Division, Denver, Colo. 80205

---

* National Oceanic and Atmospheric Administration.

Marine Corps
> Marine Corps Finance Center, Retired Pay Division, Kansas City, Mo. 64197

And copies are sent to:

Army
> Commanding General, U.S. Army Reserve Components and Administration Center, 9700 Page Blvd., St. Louis, Mo. 63132

Navy
> Commanding Officer, Naval Reserve Personnel Center, New Orleans, La. 70146

INTERMENT IN NATIONAL CEMETERY

Active and retired members of the armed forces and their dependents are entitled to burial in a national cemetery, space available. Application is made by contacting the superintendent of the cemetery either where the deceased wanted to be interred, or that of the family's choice. No grave sites are reserved in advance in a national cemetery. All states have national cemeteries, and the majority have space. But space is not always available at Arlington National Cemetery. Eligibility at all national cemeteries must be verified.

A headstone or grave marker (or urn) and an American flag are automatically provided at a national cemetery. Military honors are not part of their program, but the superintendent will assist you with details. Usually, honors are rendered by the nearest military installation or local veterans organization.

In the naval services, arrangements for burial at sea are made through the Naval District Commandant, with written instructions for this event. Availability of this service depends upon ships schedules.

EXPENSES

The active-duty serviceman or servicewoman who dies is entitled not only to interment in a national cemetery, with transportation costs for his family, but his household furnishings may be stored up to six months then moved to any place within a year. The next of kin receives a death gratuity equivalent to six months' base pay to a maximum of $3,000 which is for immediate expenditures.

The Veterans Administration pays $250 when burial of a retired serviceman or servicewoman is in a national cemetery in a nonservice-connected death, or $400 when burial is in a private cemetery in a nonservice-connected death. When the cause of death was service connected, $800 is paid for burial in either a national or private cemetery.

CREMATION

The services for those cremated are the same as that for a burial. Since a minister includes the burial prayers in the funeral service, the family need not go to the crematorium. When they wish to do so, a very brief service will be held there.

The ashes will later be delivered to the family who may dispose of them in any legal way. The urn is usually deposited in a section of the churchyard or cemetery set aside for this purpose.

MEMORIAL SERVICE

A memorial service may be held for a number of reasons, frequently at the previous request of the deceased. Such a service is held when it is necessary to wait a length of time after the death occurred, such as at a distance, or upon verification of the death, or when a serviceman or servicewoman was lost at sea or in battle and never recovered, or following cremation.

The mourners meet in a chapel or church and a brief eulogy is given by the chaplain or clergyman or a close friend. There usually is a period of meditation, a hymn, or organ music. There will be altar flowers, but friends attending should not send flowers.

NONMILITARY EXPENSES

When interment will not be held in a national cemetery, the cemetery plot can be purchased at any time and the deed placed with your will.

There are rules offered by the Federal Trade Commission which can save you time and money. They state that the cost of an average funeral is from $1,200 to $2,000, but that the cost can be cut by several hundred dollars by following these suggestions:

In negotiating with a funeral home, take along a third party to help— someone not closely involved in the loss, a friend or religious counselor.

Don't hesitate to consult with several establishments to compare costs and services since there is a wide range of prices among funeral homes.

Most funeral homes offer what is called a "complete" service—embalming, casket, use of chapel and vehicles. But ask about extras.

You can expect to pay an additional $500 to $1,000 for a cemetery plot, a protective vault for the grave, and sales taxes.

A standard service is frequently offered, with the price of the casket the only variable. Although you purchase an inexpensive casket, you may still get the same range of services as with a more expensive one.

Be aware of merchandising techniques when selecting a casket. Some lower-priced models are placed among the more expensive ones, where they appear at a disadvantage.

If cremation is chosen, embalming is not required in most states; expenses are between $150 and $300.

Should you want more information about funeral planning, write to the Federal Trade Commission, Regional Office, 2840 Federal Building, 915 Second Avenue, Seattle, Washington 98174. Or to the National Funeral Directors Association, 135 West Wells Street, Milwaukee, Wisconsin 53203. The Continental Association of Funeral and Memorial Societies is located at 1828 L Street, N.W., Washington, D.C. 20036.

PRIVATE SERVICES

When the funeral is private, you go to the services only when notified to do so. Only the family and closest friends go to the grave site. When the announcement states *services and interment private*, you do not go to either, unless notified. When a published account does not mention "private" you may go to the services but not to the grave site.

An out-of-town relative or friend should find their own place to stay overnight and take meals—unless the family tells them otherwise. This is no time to add an extra burden to the family, particularly if the bereaved is elderly or ill. Should there be room in the house or quarters, or in the home of a friend, the family will tell you so.

CIVILIAN FUNERALS

The services may be held in a church, chapel, home, or in a funeral home. More services are being held in the funeral home than in past years, with the funeral director in charge of arrangements and all possible responsibilities.

IN A CHURCH

The family sits in the first few pews of the church, on the right side of a center aisle when the waiting room is on that side, with the pallbearers on the left. The casket is usually covered with a blanket or spray of flowers from the family, and is closed by Catholic or Jewish custom and by the wishes of Protestant families.

Those attending the services sit wherever they choose; women wear street dress, not necessarily dark. Older women in the family usually wear black, with hats optional; younger women wear dark or subdued dress, and young children wear Sunday School dress which may be white or any light, but not bright, color. Men in the family wear dark suits, others wear conservative suits.

Frequently, there is no processional, with the family entering through a door nearest the pews where they will be sitting. If there is a processional, it forms in the vestibule. The clergyman and choir, if any, enter from the rear, then the honorary pallbearers in pairs; then the casket, followed by the family. The widow or widower walks with a member of the family, the widow escorted by the eldest male relative, a son, brother, or uncle; the widower walks with his oldest daughter. Other members of the family walk in pairs directly behind.

The procession leaves in the same order as it entered, except that the choir stays in place. The family follows the hearse to the cemetery in the first car or cars, with the pallbearers, ushers, clergyman, and close friends going to the graveside.

AT THE HOUSE

In a house, the living room or the largest room would be used, with the casket resting on a stand furnished by the funeral director, who also furnishes extra chairs. The service may be a little simpler, with a little more privacy offered for those who need or desire it.

FUNERAL HOMES

In a funeral home (parlor) where the casket remains until the day of the funeral, members of the family often receive friends at specified times before the service. Such hours are stated in a published obituary; if they are not so published, no receiving hours are planned.

There will be a register furnished by the funeral parlor in which friends attending write their names. This will later be given to the family. You need stay only a brief time after extending your sympathy, and the bereaved need only say, "Thank you for coming," or make some more personal remark. Do not smoke in the room where friends are received.

Services held in the funeral home chapel are the same as those held in a church. The clergyman is paid a fee (usually $10 or $25, or more at a very large service), which is handed to him by a member of the family in an envelope before the services.

The flowers sent by friends will be placed throughout the room or rooms, then taken to the grave site.

DIVORCED PARTNERS

A divorced man or woman may want to pay respect to the former wife or husband. The divorced person may go to the funeral parlor for a short time, but he or she should not sit with the bereaved family at the services or go to the cemetery—unless invited by the family to do so.

When there has been unpleasantness after the divorce, the ex-spouse may prefer to send flowers or a charity contribution with a brief note of condolence and not go to the funeral parlor or attend the services.

A divorced man or woman is *never* a widower or widow.

AFTER THE FUNERAL

It is wise to find out beforehand if the bereaved want relatives and guests to be with them after the funeral, or not. Some people want to get their minds off their sorrow for awhile and find it beneficial to be with others. Some prefer to be quietly alone.

In many areas of the country, it is customary for friends and neighbors, or members of a church group or organization, to prepare food and have it on the table, buffet style, when the family returns from the services wtih their friends.

In this way, people from out of town who may not have seen the family for some time will have the opportunity, though briefly, to talk with them.

MESSAGES OF CONDOLENCE

Whether or not you are able to attend the funeral, it is important that you send a message of condolence. The purpose of the message is to express your sympathy to the closest member, or members, of the deceased person's family. The brief note, letter, telegram, or telephone call should be taken care of immediately upon your learning of the death.

You may find a letter of condolence difficult to write—many persons do. But it is very important for the bereaved person or persons to receive a message of sympathy, *to know that you care*, and you should do this immediately.

When writing the message, address it to the nearest living relative, whether you know him or her, or not. On the death of a male friend, send the message to his wife, if he was married, or to his parents, if he was single. If there are no surviving parents the message should be addressed to a brother or sister, or any near relative.

Letters of condolence are always written by hand, usually on plain white paper of the more formal type. Your letter should be short and simple—but sincere. Since you desire to express comfort to the bereaved, do not dwell on the illness or manner of death. (For the form of a letter of condolence, and its reply, *see* Chapter 12, Social & Personal Correspondence.)

FLORAL OFFERING OR CONTRIBUTIONS TO CHARITY

When sending flowers to a funeral, *never send them in the name of the deceased.* If the services are to be held in a home, the flowers should be sent to the nearest relative. When services are to be held in a chapel, church, or funeral home, the florist will send them there, addressed to "The funeral of Mr. Smith Jones." Write your full name on the plain white card enclosed with the flowers. If the relationship with the bereaved was a close one, then sign your name "John Doe" or "Ann and John Doe." Do not write "Ann and John" since there may be many Anns and Johns. You may sign "Captain and Mrs. John Doe" or enclose your personal card or joint card.

When the obituary notice states "Please omit flowers," then omit them. If the notice states that contributions may be sent to a charity in lieu of flowers, you may send a check to the charity with a note stating that the check is in memory of the deceased.

You may send your personal card to the family saying that you have done this, but never mention the amount sent to the charity. The charity should notify the bereaved family upon the receipt of the contribution.

Later, the widow or widower or a member of the family (or in case of illness, a close friend) will acknowledge the flowers, contributions to charity, telegrams or letters of condolence, in brief handwritten notes. A note of appreciation should be sent to the chaplain (or officiating clergyman) thanking him for his help.

CALLS ON THE BEREAVED

When you live near the bereaved person or persons, you will want to call on him or her—if they are close friends or relatives. The purpose of such a call is to give comfort and sympathy to the bereaved. When speaking to them, you may say, "I'm so sorry," and briefly but warmly press their hand. You do not ply them with questions; if they want to talk to you, you should listen and answer sympathetically.

Whether you can be of assistance or are invading a family's privacy depends upon how well you know the bereaved. Your own good sense should give you the answer. When you cannot be of assistance, all calls should be brief.

In some cases, a family may urgently need assistance—as well as sympathy—whether you know them well or not. Such a case may follow an accident and death, which are always a shock to a family. Then, you may be able to help out with thoughtfulness, and consideration of feelings.

Of great help is the care of any children in the bereaved family for a day or two. Perhaps you can best help by wiring or telephoning friends of the family who are at a distance. Someone is usually needed in a bereaved house to answer telephone calls or to do whatever is generally necessary. A casserole—any food—may be urgently needed.

You should never take offense if you should call on a bereaved family and whoever answers the door says that the family is not receiving visitors. (Such calls, of course, are never returned.) You may leave your personal card with the phrase, "Deepest sympathy," written across it.

When calls are received at the funeral chapel, a member of the family or its representative should be present during the afternoon or evening when calls are expected to be made.

When signing the register in a funeral home, a married couple signs on one line, "Lieutenant and Mrs. John Doe." Should they visit the funeral home at different times, they would sign separately as "Mrs. John Doe" and "Lieutenant John Doe." A single person signs his or her name in full, such as "Major James Smith" or "Captain Mary Ann Brown."

When making a call, try not to become over-emotional, for such actions will only be adding to the bereaveds' distress rather than comforting them. Friends less close to the bereaved family may call at the funeral home, rather than at the house.

IN MOURNING

In recent years, there have been many changes made in the conventions of mourning—particularly in the matter of dress. Most people feel that grief is a private thing, and that the public appearance of an individual *after the funeral* is not determined by set rules but by necessity and personal feelings.

Members of the family wear mourning at the funeral, with women customarily dressed in all black or white, according to the season. Navy blue and other dark shades are sometimes worn. Servicemen wear the prescribed uniform, with retired officers and civilian men wearing dark suits and ties. It is no longer customary for men to wear black arm bands or mourning badges, although you may do so, if desired, or when required by uniform regulations.

It is not necessary to wear mourning clothes for any length of time following the funeral, or at all. However, customs vary throughout the nation, and conventional mourning is observed in certain sections.

How long a person should stay in social seclusion following a bereavement is a personal matter. It is proper that the bereaved attend the theater, concert, movies, and small quiet gatherings not too long after the loss. It is desirable that a bereaved person does not stay in seclusion.

Wedding invitations may be sent to those in mourning, and it is correct for the bereaved to accept such an invitation if he or she so chooses. Small weddings for members of the immediate families may continue, after being scheduled, during a time of mourning.

Generally, the gaiety of the occasion will determine whether a bereaved person attends a social function within a few weeks or months after a death in the immediate family. Men usually do not resume their social life for at least two months afterwards, and a widow usually does not go to certain functions—such as dances, balls, etc.—for several months.

DONATING YOUR BODY

Should you want to donate your body, or parts of it, after death for scientific research—such as for kidney or eye transplants, you should notify any specific hospital or research institution to this effect, or you may sign an organ donor card that gives a right to an institution for this purpose.

First, you should explain this wish to your family, then inform your doctor; after death, a transplant must be done immediately.

Some states provide an opportunity for any person 18 years of age or over to designate on his or her driver's license that upon death he wishes to donate his body for purpose of transplantation, therapy, medical research, or education. Other states, in a legalized anatomical gift act, furnish cards which are signed before witnesses and should be carried in your wallet, handbag, or car.

CHAPTER 40

The Military Funeral

THE MILITARY FUNERAL CEREMONY is based on customs and traditions that have developed through the years. The ceremony demonstrates the nation's recognition of the debt it owes for the services and sacrifices of the members of the armed forces.

The casket is covered with the American flag. It is usually transported to the cemetery on a caisson, and is carried from the caisson to the grave by six military body bearers. In addition to the body bearers, honorary pallbearers are usually designated who march to the cemetery alongside the caisson or ride ahead of the chaplain.

At the cemetery, the casket is placed over the grave and the body bearers hold the flag-pall waist high over the casket. After the committal service is read by the chaplain, a firing party fires three volleys. A bugler sounds "Taps," and the military funeral is completed. The body bearers then fold the flag and it is presented to the next of kin.

These basic elements are the foundation of all military funerals, whether last rites are being conducted for a private or seaman, or final honors are being paid at the grave of an admiral or general.

GENERAL INFORMATION

1. Military funerals are divided into the three following classes:

With chapel service, followed by the march to the grave or place of local disposition with the prescribed escort.

Without chapel service, the funeral procession forming at the entrance
(or at a point within reasonable distance) of the cemetery.
With graveside services only.

2. A military funeral with full honors includes the following elements:

Band
Escort as appropriate, including firing squad and bugler
Colors
Clergy
Caisson and body bearers
Honorary pallbearers.

3. The services of a chaplain are provided unless the family of the
deceased requests another clergyman to officiate. If a civilian clergyman
officiates, he should follow the same general procedures as the chaplain.
The desires of the family are given the fullest consideration possible in
the selection of the elements, but the funeral is conducted as prescribed
in appropriate service regulations.

4. The commanding officer or his representative assists in making
the funeral arrangements and supervises the conduct of the funeral.

5. When honorary pallbearers are desired, they are selected by the
family of the deceased or their representative, or when so requested, by
the commanding officer.

6. All persons attending the military funeral in uniform face the
casket and execute the hand salute at any time the casket is being moved,
during the firing of the volley, and while "Taps" is being sounded.
Honorary pallbearers in uniform conform to the above rules when not in
motion. Military personnel in civilian clothes and civilian men stand at
attention, uncovered, and hold the headdress over the left breast.

7. The word "chapel" is interpreted to include the church, home,
or other place where services are held, exclusive of the service at the
grave.

8. The word "casket" is interpreted to include a receptacle containing the cremated remains of the deceased.

9. When any serviceman or servicewoman dies on active duty, his
or her remains are transported to the place of interment and interred at
government expense. When he or she dies on overseas duty or at a
distance, the remains are flown to the Air Force facility, the Military
Airlift Command (MAC) at Dover, Delaware, then to the place of interment.

10. The remains of retired personnel are transported by commercial

means at the family's expense, with some assistance from such organizations as the Veterans Administration (when eligible), but not at government expense. They are interred at government expense.

FUNERAL WITH CHAPEL SERVICE

Before the service begins, the funeral escort is formed in line facing the chapel. The band forms on the flank toward the direction of march.

Members of the immediate family, relatives, and friends of the deceased should be seated in the chapel before the casket is taken in. Chapel ushers should ensure that a sufficient number of front seats on the right side of the chapel facing the altar are reserved for the immediate family. The two front pews on the left are reserved for the honorary pallbearers. If body bearers are used to carry the casket into position inside the chapel, seats are reserved for them in the rear of the chapel.

The conveyance bearing the remains to the chapel should arrive a few moments before the time set for the service. Since the casket normally is covered with the national colors, the escort is called to attention and the escort commander salutes as the conveyance arrives.

When all is in readiness to move the casket into the chapel, the escort commander brings the escort to *present arms.* At this command, the band renders honors, if appropriate, followed by a hymn. At the first note of the hymn, the casket is removed from the conveyance by the body bearers and carried between the ranks of the honorary pallbearers, if any, into the chapel. As soon as the casket enters the chapel, the band ceases to play. The escort is then brought to order and given *at ease.*

When honorary pallbearers are present, they are formed in two ranks, facing each other, thus forming an aisle from the conveyance to the entrance to the chapel. At the first note of the music, and while the casket is being carried between them, the honorary pallbearers uncover or salute as appropriate. They will then follow the casket in a column of twos into the chapel and sit in the pews to the left front.

The funeral director—or in his absence, the chaplain's assistant—moves the bier as previously prescribed by the chaplain. If there is no bier, the body bearers carry the casket as instructed by the chaplain beforehand.

At the conclusion of the chapel service, the body bearers follow the honorary pallbearers, or if there are none, they follow the chaplain in a column of twos as the casket is moved to the entrance of the chapel. When honorary pallbearers are present, they form an aisle from the entrance of the chapel to the conveyance (caisson or hearse) and uncover or salute as prescribed.

When the casket appears at the entrance of the chapel at the conclusion of the service, the funeral escort and band repeat the procedures as prescribed for entering the chapel. The band ceases playing and the escort is brought to order when the casket has been secured to the caisson or in the hearse.

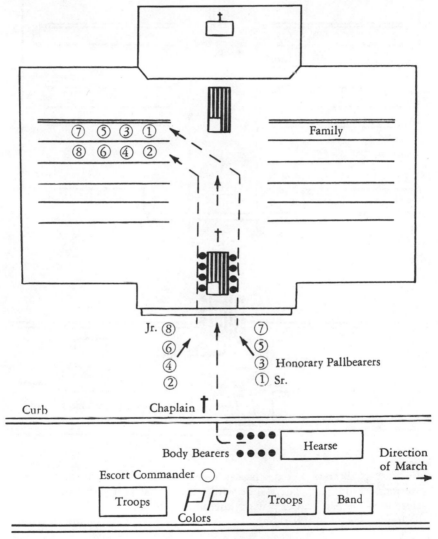

Entering the Chapel

Honorary pallbearers salute while honors are being rendered; then they fall in behind the casket to enter the chapel.

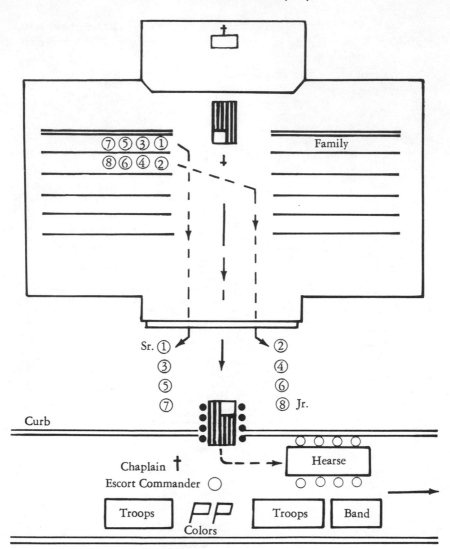

Leaving the Chapel

Honorary pallbearers precede the casket out of the chapel and take reverse positions, as indicated. They salute while escort renders honors and hold the salute until the band ceases playing; then they take positions on either side of the hearse or caisson. (If riding, they proceed to cars ahead of the chaplain's car.)

After the casket has been placed on the caisson or in the hearse, the honorary pallbearers enter their cars, or if marching, form a column on each side of the caisson or hearse with the leading member of each column even with the front wheels of the conveyance. When they ride, it is the body bearers who form columns on each side of the conveyance.

The family group follows the casket out of the chapel and remains at the chapel entrance until the honorary pallbearers have broken ranks to take their position. The ushers then escort the family to their conveyance, with all other mourners proceeding to their own cars.

The procession to the grave site is formed in the order of march shown on the facing page.

The escort commander puts the band and escort in *march*, and the procession marches slowly to solemn music. If there is a considerable distance from the chapel to the grave, the escort—after leaving the chapel area—may march *at ease* in quick time, with no band music. The escort is brought to attention in the vicinity of the grave.

As the procession nears the grave, the marching elements move to their predesignated positions. The band and military escorts are formed in a line behind and facing the foot of the grave, with other marching elements placed as near as practicable. The firing squad takes position so that it will not fire directly over the mourners.

When the caisson or hearse comes to a halt, the honorary pallbearers again form in two ranks with an aisle extending from the conveyance toward the graveside. If the grave is too near the road to permit this formation, they should take their positions at the graveside before the removal of the casket from the caisson or hearse.

When all is in readiness to remove the casket from the conveyance, the escort commander commands, "Present, ARMS." At this command, the band renders honors if appropriate, followed by a hymn. At the first note of the hymn, the body bearers remove the casket from the caisson or hearse.

Preceded by the chaplain, the body bearers carry the casket between the ranks of honorary pallbearers to the grave and place it on the lowering device. They remain in position facing the casket; then, they raise the flag from the casket and hold it in a horizontal position waist high until the conclusion of "Taps."

As soon as the casket has passed between them, the honorary pallbearers face toward the grave and follow the casket in a column of twos to their position at the grave. The family proceeds to their designated places.

When the casket has been placed over the grave, the band ceases playing and the escort is brought to the order. The escort commander

☐	Police Escort
◯	Escort Commander
☐	Band
☐	Troops
◿	Colors
⌐¬	Honorary Pallbearers (when riding)
⊞	Chaplain
◿	Personal Flag
☐	Hearse or Caisson (Honorary Pallbearers, when marching)
⠿	Body Bearers (alongside hearse or caisson if no pallbearers)
☐	Family
☐	Enlisted Men from Command of Deceased
☐	Officers from Command of Deceased
☐	Delegations
☐	Societies
☐	Citizens

Procession to the Grave Site

The escort commander makes all turns at road intersections and he should turn about occasionally to make certain that the escort is in correct formation. A police escort precedes the escort commander to keep traffic clear en route to the grave site.

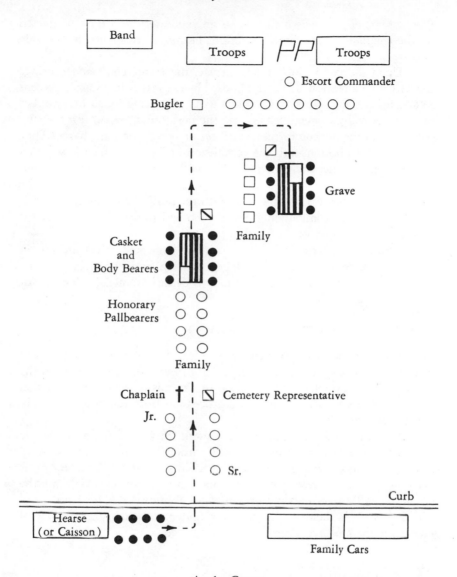

At the Grave

Honorary pallbearers salute while the casket is being removed from the hearse or caisson and hold the salute until the casket has passed between them. They salute at the grave during volleys and "Taps."

then commands, "Parade, REST." The graveside service is now conducted by the chaplain. After the benediction, he moves two steps to the side or rear.

Upon the conclusion of the service, the escort commander brings the escort to attention. He commands, "Escort less firing squad, present ARMS: firing squad, FIRE THREE VOLLEYS." The firing squad fires volleys of blank cartridges; then, they assume the position of *present arms* on the command of the noncommissioned officer or petty officer in charge. They remain in this position until the conclusion of "Taps," which is sounded by the bugler immediately after the last volley. The entire escort is then brought to order.

The body bearers box the flag, with the senior body bearer giving it to the chaplain or commanding officer who will present it to the next of kin or a representative of the family.

After the presentation of the flag, the band and escort are put in *march* by the escort commander. When retiring from the vicinity of the grave site, care should be exercised not to detract from the solemnity of the occasion.

FUNERAL WITHOUT CHAPEL SERVICE

When the funeral is without chapel service, the escort usually forms at or near the entrance to the cemetery. The officer in charge supervises the transfer of the casket from the hearse to the caisson or makes provision for the hearse to be included in the procession from the point of origin to the grave site.

When honorary pallbearers are present, they are formed in a single line facing the caisson or hearse. Their order of march is the same as already described. While the casket is being transferred, the escort is brought to *present arms*, the band plays an appropriate air, and the honorary pallbearers uncover or salute as appropriate. The family and friends remain in their cars during the transfer of the casket. The funeral procession then forms and proceeds as prescribed.

GRAVESIDE SERVICE

The military elements (chaplain, body bearers, firing squad, and bugler) participating in a graveside service are in position before the arrival of the remains. The procedure is the same as already described.

The leader of the firing squad gives the appropriate orders for the firing of three volleys and the bugler sounds "Taps" immediately upon completion of the last volley. The senior body bearer gives the order to march off after the flag has been presented to the next of kin.

CREMATION

For all phases of the funeral where the receptacle containing the cremated remains is carried by hand, one body bearer will be designated to do so. Four men detailed as flagbearers will follow the receptacle when it is carried from the conveyance into the chapel, from the chapel to the conveyance, or from the conveyance to the grave. The flag is folded and is carried by the leading flagbearer on the right.

When the receptacle has been placed on a stand before the chancel of the chapel or in the conveyance, the folded flag is placed beside the receptacle. If the caisson is equipped with a casket container for the receptacle, the open flag is laid upon the container as prescribed for a casket.

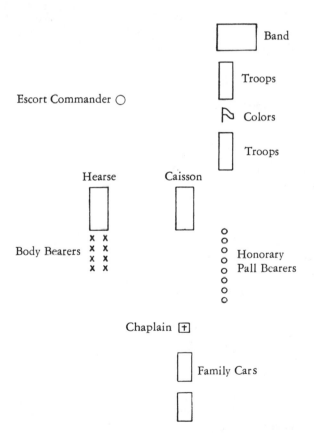

Receiving the Remains at the Gate

In cases where the remains are conducted to a crematory and the ashes are to be interred with military honors at a later time, the ceremony consists only of the escort to the crematory. Arms are presented as the remains are carried inside, and the firing of volleys and the sounding of "Taps" are omitted.

When the ceremony is held at the crematory, with no further military honors, volleys are fired and "Taps" is sounded at the discretion of the commanding officer.

CANNON SALUTE

The funeral of a flag or general officer (active or retired), which takes place at or near a military installation, will be marked with minute guns equal to the number to which the officer was entitled and will be fired at noon on the day of the funeral.

The cannon salute corresponding to the grade of the deceased will be fired immediately atfer the benediction, followed by three volleys of artillery, guns firing simultaneously, or three volleys of musketry.

AVIATION PARTICIPATION

When there is aviation participation in a military funeral, it is timed so that the airplanes appear over the procession while the remains are being taken to the grave.

When the funeral is that of an aviator, it is customary for the airplanes to fly in a normal tactical formation less one aircraft, indicating the vacancy resulting from the loss of the deceased.

FRATERNAL OR PATRIOTIC ORGANIZATIONS

A fraternal or military organization of which the deceased was a member may take part in the funeral service with the consent of the immediate family of the deceased.

When the ritual is military or semi-military, the rites begin immediately upon the conclusion of the military religious service. If the ritual contains the firing of three volleys and the sounding of "Taps," the military firing bugler is used at the appropriate time.

SPECIAL MILITARY FUNERAL

A special military funeral is held for the following dignitaries:

Secretary of Defense.
Deputy and former Secretary of Defense.
Secretaries of the Army, Navy, and Air Force.

Chairman, Joint Chiefs of Staff.
Five-Star generals and admirals.
Chief of Staff, U.S. Army.
Chief of Staff, U.S. Air Force.
Chief of Naval Operations.
Commandant, U.S. Marine Corps.
Commandant, U.S. Coast Guard.
Other personages specifically designated by the Secretary of Defense.
Foreign military personnel when designated by the President.

In each service, the commanding officer of the military or naval command or district in which the death occurs is the designated representative of the Secretary of Defense to make the necessary arrangements for the special funeral. He handles the following details:

1. Issues invitations and pertinent information to invited guests.

2. Includes with the invitations appropriate parking stickers for automobiles, and seating tickets for the Amphitheater when interment is to be in Arlington National Cemetery.

3. Appoints and notifies an officer for liaison with the family of the deceased.

4. Provides press releases and coverage.

5. Notifies persons selected as escort commander, honorary pall-bearers, and special honor guard (for arrival ceremony).

Upon request, the Commandant, U.S. Marine Corps or the Commandant of the U.S. Coast Guard will perform these functions for deceased personnel of their services.

When the death of a dignitary occurs in Washington, D.C., the remains are moved to a selected place of repose where they are attended by a Guard of Honor composed of members of all the armed services. When death occurs outside the immediate area, the remains are transported to Washington for final honors where they will be met at the point of arrival by a reception party and escorted to the place of repose.

After three days, the remains are then escorted from the place of repose to the Amphitheater, Washington Cathedral, or the church where the funeral service will be held.

When burial is to be outside of Washington, the remains are escorted from the place of repose to the point of departure where honors are accorded.

BOXING THE FLAG

The flag that covers the casket symbolizes the service of the deceased in the armed forces of the United States. The three volleys that are fired, according to ancient belief, are to scare away evil spirits. The playing of "Taps" over the grave marks the beginning of the last sleep and expresses confidence in an ultimate reveille to come.

The flag is folded immediately after the sounding of "Taps." The body bearers hold the flag at the pall over the grave and fold the flag in the accustomed manner. The senior body bearer hands it to the chaplain or the officer in charge, who in turn presents it to the next of kin or a representative of the family.

DUTIES OF PALLBEARERS

Active pallbearers, called body bearers, are six to eight men who carry the casket whenever necessary. At a military funeral, they are service personnel appointed by the command.

Honorary pallbearers are persons who have no duties to perform other than rendering appropriate honors to the deceased. They may be few, or more, in number, but never more than twelve. They are appointed by the family of the deceased, usually from among the close friends or honored acquaintances of the deceased, or at the request of the family, they may be appointed by the commanding officer.

The officer in charge of the funeral arrangements should give detailed information to the active and honorary pallbearers in advance of the funeral, including the uniform to be worn, mourning sleeve bands, etc.

CHECK LIST

The officer in charge of a military funeral must have specific information in order to carry out the arrangements. To ensure accurate information, a check list should include the following:

1. *General Information*
   a. The name, grade, and serial number of the deceased.
   b. Religious faith.
   c. Name and address of funeral director.
   d. Name and address of next of kin.
2. *Personnel*
   a. Chaplain of appropriate faith; name, grade, and serial number.
   b. Appropriate escort.
   c. Band, color guard (4 men), body bearers (6 or 8), honorary pallbearers (usually 6 to 10), firing squad (8), bugler.
3. *Equipment*
   a. Aerial escort.
   b. Caisson.

    c. Blank cartridges for funeral volleys.

    d. Interment flag for civilian funeral director.

4. *Next of Kin*

    a. What type of service is desired: time, date, location.

    b. The name, rank, serial number, address of service chaplain, or the name and address of civilian clergyman.

    c. Type of funeral procession, if desired.

    d. Honorary pallbearers, selected by family or command; their names, addresses, telephone numbers.

    e. The type of graveside ceremony: with volleys? "Taps?"

    f. Ceremonies by fraternal or patriotic organizations.

    g. Approximate number of relatives and friends attending services.

    h. Music: any particular compositions?

5. *Civilian Funeral Director*

    a. Name and location of cemetery, exact location of grave site.

    b. Time and date of interment services.

    c. Will he transport flowers from chapel to grave? Collect cards from flowers to be given to next of kin?

6. *Miscellaneous*

    a. Determine routes of march, positions, etc.

    b. Arrange for traffic control.

    c. Make certain equipment is ready at the right time and place.

    d. Ensure that each person taking part in the funeral ceremony knows his duties.

MISCELLANEOUS RULES

1. The casket is always carried foot first, except that of a clergyman which is carried head first.

2. When the flag is draped over the casket, the blue field is over the left shoulder of the deceased.

3. The cap and sword of the deceased are never displayed on the flag-draped casket, but may be placed under it.

4. The bearer of the personal flag of a deceased general or flag officer marches in front of the hearse or caisson.

5. Mourning Flag: The colors are hoisted to the peak of the flagpole or staff, and then they are lowered halfway. When the flag is removed, it is again raised to the peak before being lowered. Where flags cannot be flown at half-staff, they should have a black streamer from the spearhead halfway down the flag. Flags hung horizontally or perpendicularly should bear a black bunting border of appropriate width.

6. The national ensign is never dipped at a funeral, but a unit or battalion flag is dipped when appropriate.

7. The word "pall" denotes the flag at the waist level, stretched taut, and kept even at all points while being held.

8. Military funerals are rarely postponed on account of bad weather.

9. The distinction between grave site and graveside is: grave site is the section of the cemetery where the funeral will take place; graveside is the lot in which the burial takes place.

10. At a military funeral, service personnel wear the prescribed uniform with mourning sleeve bands. At a nonmilitary funeral, men wear dark business suits; mourning bands are no longer customary.

11. A chaplain at a military post or base is never given a fee for his services, but a note of appreciation for his help should be written by a member of the family.

12. A fee of twenty-five dollars for an average funeral is given to a civilian clergyman. The fee may be enclosed in a letter of appreciation and handed to him before the services.

SECTION XI

Strictly Service

CHAPTER 41

Salutes

VARIOUS CUSTOMS concerning salutes are covered in the regulations of each service, as well as in specific regulations of the service academies, and the reserve and officer-training programs.

All servicemen and servicewomen should know the regulations not only of his or her own service, but of all services. The rules for military etiquette are founded on custom and tradition, and their strict observance forms an important factor in the maintenance of discipline which must be observed equally by all officers and enlisted personnel. The responsibility is a mutual one in which the junior accepts the role of initiating the act of courtesy.

ORIGIN OF THE SALUTE

There are various schools of thought on the origin of the salute, one tracing the custom to the days of chivalry when knights in mail raised their visors to friends for the purpose of identification. The junior was required to make the first gesture, in keeping with gradations of rank.

Another possible origin of the salute goes back to the days of the Borgias, when assassinations by dagger were not uncommon, and it was customary for men to approach each other with raised hand, palm to the front, to prove that no dagger was concealed.

However, from the earliest days of military organization, the junior

471

uncovered when meeting or addressing a senior; gradually, the act of uncovering was simplified into touching the cap and, finally, into the present-day salute which means: "I greet you."

THE HAND SALUTE

The hand salute is required on naval and military installations both on and off duty. At other places and times, it may be suspended by regulations or local order.

You always salute the commanding officer (or any flag or general officer) any time you meet him or her during the day. You should salute your other seniors the first time you meet them each day. Remember "Precept and Example"; those of less rank than you will imitate you, for better or for worse.

MANNER OF SALUTING

The hand salute is executed by raising your right hand smartly until the tip of your forefinger touches the lower part of your headgear, slightly to the right of your right eye.

The upper arm is parallel to the ground, thumb and fingers are extended and joined, the palm is down, and there is a straight line from the tip of the middle finger to the elbow.

The salute is concluded by dropping your hand down to your side in one clean motion. Avoid slapping your leg as you do so.

In the Army and Air Force, when uncovered you touch your right eyebrow.

It is important that you keep your head and eyes turned toward the saluted person.

SALUTING DISTANCE

Saluting distance is that distance at which recognition is easy. Usually it does not exceed *thirty paces*. The first position of the hand salute is rendered when the person to be saluted is *six paces* distant, or at the nearest point of approach if it is apparent that he or she is not going to approach to within six paces. Twenty-five paces is not considered excessive. Hold the first position of the salute until the person saluted has passed or the salute is returned, then execute the second movement of the hand salute.

A salute is rendered only at a halt or a walk. If running, a person comes to a walk before saluting.

When overtaking a senior, whom the junior must pass, the salute shall be given when the junior is abreast of the senior and the junior should ask, "By your leave, Sir?"

It is customary in the Air Force that, when a senior officer on foot approaches a junior, the junior render the salute *at or within twelve paces*. Should the junior be at double-time when he or she encounters the senior, the junior slows his pace to quick-time, renders the salute, then resumes double-time. Should the senior wish to speak to the junior, the junior salutes as the senior approaches and again when the conversation is terminated.

Salutes are usually accompanied by an exchange of greetings, depending upon the time of day, such as: "Good morning, Sir" or "Ma'am," or "Good evening, Colonel Blank."
From early morning until noon: "Good morning—."
From noon to evening meal: "Good afternoon—."
From evening meal until turning in: "Good evening—."

COVERED—AND UNCOVERED

In the *Army* and *Air Force*, you salute when covered or uncovered.

In the *naval services*, protocol does not call for saluting when uncovered except for the return of uncovered salutes rendered first by Army or Air Force personnel. The exception in this case follows the general rule that *"Social customs or military courtesy should always be interpreted so as to prevent awkward situations."* Therefore, the Navy establishes an exception whereby any uncovered salute may be returned. When uncovered, the Navy initiates salutes by coming to a position of attention.

Individuals *under arms* uncover only when:

Seated as a member of or in attendance on a court or board
Entering places of worship
Indoors and not on duty
In attendance at an official reception
Entering messing facilities during meal hours.

In certain public places, such as a church, theater, or hotel dining room, servicewomen sometimes wear their hats or caps when men do not. In such instances, women are technically "uncovered" and do not salute.

WHEN TO SALUTE

The salute is rendered but *once* if the senior remains in the immediate vicinity and no conversation takes place. If a conversation does take place, the junior again salutes the senior on departing or when the senior leaves.

In making reports, the person making the report salutes first, regardless of rank; for example, a regimental commander making a report to the brigade adjutant during a ceremony or a head of department commander making a report to an officer of the deck lieutenant.

When men or women officers are of the same rank, they may salute simultaneously, but usually they merely exchange greetings.

The saluting requirement varies upon certain occasions, such as:

If you, the senior, are in the company of a junior or company grade officer and a field grade officer approaches, the salute will be initiated by the field grade officer who salutes you, the ranking officer. When you return the salute, the junior or company grade officer will salute simultaneously with you.

If you are conversing with a senior officer and a junior approaches, you salute at the same time as the senior. If the senior is unaware of the junior's salute, do not interrupt him by rendering your salute to the junior.

Customarily, you will salute with your right hand. If an injury prevents your doing so, render a left-hand salute.

REPORTING TO AN OFFICER

The salute is always rendered by the junior on reporting to a senior. Juniors are expected to rise and stand at attention whenever a senior officer enters their room or office, and remain standing until the senior gives permission to *carry on* or *at ease.*

A junior stands at attention when addressed by a senior. If covered, the junior salutes when first addressed and again upon the conclusion of the conversation. If uncovered, the junior stands at attention throughout the conversation unless otherwise directed.

Midshipmen, cadets, and other officer candidates are subject to local regulations which generally require that when addressing an officer, during the salute, and before entering upon any conversation, they give their names; for instance, "Midshipman Doe, Sir," or "Sir, Cadet Thomas reports to Captain Brown." The salute is held throughout the report and until it is returned by the officer.

It is customary to relax this procedure as officer candidates approach graduation and as they become known to their senior officers. This is a matter for the officer candidate's own good judgment. The word "Sir" shall always be added to statements by the very junior; thus, "I report for duty, Sir." The "Sir" or "Ma'am" is a military expression which is always used in connection with "yes" or "no," whenever conversing with senior men and women officers.

Reporting indoors unarmed: When reporting to an officer in his or her office, a junior not wearing arms removes his hat or cap (and any outer garments such as an overcoat, raincoat, or overshoes), knocks, and enters when told to do so. Upon entering he should approach to within about two paces from the officer and stand at attention. While standing, a salutation such as "Good morning, Sir, I wish to make the daily magazine report," should be given. When the business has been terminated, he should leave promptly.

On shipboard, the salutation and the manner of conducting the following business ordinarily follows prescribed lines of official informality as befits working shipboard life. Too rigid formality must be avoided. The respect due the senior officer is a most important factor of the situation and as long as this is shown in a sincere manner, proper shipboard procedure will not be a problem.

Reporting indoors, under arms: Ordinarily, in the services reports are not made indoors under arms except in rare cases. In carrying a rifle, a junior enters with the rifle at the trail, halts, and renders the rifle salute at *order arms.* When wearing sidearms or duty belt, the hand salute is given and the hat is kept on.

Reporting outdoors: The procedure outdoors is the same as described in the foregoing two paragraphs. The hat is never removed outdoors, and the junior armed with the rifle may, in approaching the senior, carry it at the trail or at right shoulder arms. He executes the rifle salute at the order or at right shoulder arms.

It is improper to change the rifle position when addressing or being addressed by a senior except during a formal inspection. For example, if at right shoulder arms upon approaching or being approached by a senior, you render the salute at the position held. This avoids awkwardness which would result if the junior approached the senior at right shoulder arms, then came to the order—and then rendered the salute.

The term "outdoors" is construed to include such buildings as armories, gymnasiums, and other huge-roofed enclosures used for drills. Theater canopies, covered walks, and other shelters open on the sides to the weather, are also considered outdoors.

"Indoors" includes offices, corridors, etc. The expression "under arms" means carrying the arms, or having them attached to the person by sling, holster, or other means. In the absence of arms, it refers to the equipment pertaining directly to the arms, such as cartridge belt, pistol holder, sword belt, or automatic rifle belt.

SALUTING IN GROUPS

In formation: Individuals in formation do not salute or return salutes except at the command, "PRESENT ARMS." The individual in charge will salute and acknowledge salutes for the whole formation. Commanders of organizations or detachments which are not a part of a larger formation salute officers of higher grades by bringing the organization or detachment to attention before saluting.

An individual in formation *at ease* or *at rest* comes to attention when addressed by a person superior to him in rank. The group will remain at attention until directed by the senior, "CARRY ON," or "AT EASE," but will continue to be aware of the senior's presence during the time he is in conversation with members of the group, or whatever his business may be.

Not in formation: On the approach of an officer of higher rank, a group of individuals not in formation is called to attention by the first person noticing the senior officer, and all in the group come to attention and salute. Individuals participating in games, and members of details at work, do not salute. The individual in charge of a work detail—if not actively engaged—salutes or acknowledges salutes for the whole detail. A unit resting alongside a road does not come to attention upon the approach of an officer.

However, if the officer addresses an individual or group, they come to attention and remain at attention (unless otherwise ordered) until the termination of the conversation, at which time they salute the officer.

SALUTING IN AUTOMOBILES

A senior officer passing in an automobile is entitled to a salute, which will be returned when conditions permit. If driving, he will not return a salute when safety is involved.

In some cases, it may be awkward for the senior officer to return the salute properly. He may then make recognition by a modified salute or a slight nod of the head.

In case a detail is riding in an automobile, the individual in charge renders the hand salute for the entire detail.

Juniors must be alert to notice the passing of automobiles from which the flag of a high-ranking dignitary is displayed and, when such is observed, be punctilious in saluting the occupant of the car. These salutes should be rendered at all times, day or night, on all occasions, whether the flag officer or high-ranking dignitary is covered or not.

You should remember that officers of high rank, civilian leaders of the state and federal governments, and foreign dignitaries will have the insignia of the highest ranking passenger displayed on the automobile in either flag or plate form.

COURTESIES TO INDIVIDUALS

When an officer enters a room, midshipmen, cadets, and other juniors present will uncover (if unarmed) and stand at attention until the officer directs otherwise or leaves the room. When more than one person is present, the first to see the officer commands "Attention!" in a sufficiently loud and clear tone.

When an officer enters a room used as an office, workshop, or recreation room, those at work or play therein are not required to come to attention unless addressed by him. A junior, when addressed by a senior, comes to attention—except in the transaction of routine business between individuals at work.

A junior shall always answer "Sir" or "Ma'am" when his name is called by an officer. However, it is preferable for the junior to call the senior by his or her title and name, such as "Captain Jones," rather than by the impersonal "Sir" or "Ma'am." Women officers are addressed as "Ma'am" or by rank, and are accorded the same courtesies as for men.

Junior male officers escorting young ladies will, on meeting their senior officers, render the customary salute. If seated, they should rise and salute. It is customary for the lady being escorted to remain seated. However, on both occasions, it is considered good form for her to look at the officer being saluted, during the period of the salute, and to that extent she joins in the recognition of the senior officer.

Civilians may be saluted by persons in uniform, but the uniform hat or cap is not raised as a form of salutation. In turn, the civilian gentleman will tip or raise his hat.

Midshipmen or cadets are expected to salute their contemporaries on duty when addressed by or addressing them officially, and they salute the professors at the various academies and colleges.

All officers must remember that personal likes and dislikes have nothing to do with salutes. Therefore, you salute whenever necessary, without discrimination.

WHOM TO SALUTE

As a member of a service you salute all individuals who are senior to you in rank in any of the armed forces of the United States or of friendly foreign governments, and also officers of the Coast and Geodetic Survey and of the Public Health Service who are serving with the armed forces of the United States.

In addition, there are certain appointed or elected civilian members of both our national and state governments who are so honored. Among those you customarily salute are the following:

President of the United States
Vice President of the United States
State governors

Secretary of Defense
Deputy Secretary of Defense
Secretaries of the Army, Navy, and Air Force.

Among the members of friendly foreign governments whom you salute are:

Heads of State
Ambassadors
Ministers of Defense or other civilian leaders of defense establishments and their assistants at or above the level of the Assistant Secretary of the Army, Navy, and Air Force.
Officers, male or female, in any of the armed forces.

WHEN NOT TO SALUTE

In some situations, the salute is not appropriate. In general, do *not* salute when:

Engaged in routine work if the salute would interfere.
Indoors, except when reporting to a senior or when on duty as a sentinel or guard.
Carrying articles with both hands or being otherwise so occupied as to make saluting impracticable.
The rendition of the salute is obviously inappropriate.
A prisoner (the guard does the saluting for the prisoner).
Working as a member of a detail, or engaged in sports or social functions.
You are the driver of a moving automobile. However, whenever practicable, you should return the salutes of others.
In places of public assemblage such as theaters or churches, and in public conveyances.
You are in the ranks of a formation. However, if at ease in a formation, you come to attention when addressed by a senior.

CHAPTER 42

Flag Etiquette

A MILITARY MAN (or woman) is expected to be something of an expert upon the national flag, including its history, its etiquette, and the customs and conventions which govern its display and handling. But regardless of whether one is in military or civilian life, every loyal American citizen should know the history of his country's flag, and what you should do when the flag passes in parade, when you are passing by in a car, and what is expected of you should you be asked to review a parade.

HISTORY

With the onset of the American Revolution each of the 13 colonies created its own flag, frequently several of them. They were symbolic of the country and the struggle for independence and carried a tree, anchor, rattlesnake, or beaver and a motto such as "HOPE," "LIBERTY," or "AN APPEAL TO HEAVEN." A noted one bore a coiled rattlesnake and the motto "DON'T TREAD ON ME." Each regiment had its own colors, and the naval vessels and privateers fitted out by each colony flew distinctive flags.

Standardization became necessary and on 2 December 1775, the Continental Congress approved the design of a flag which was first hoisted aboard the *Alfred* by Lieutenant John Paul Jones. It consisted of 13 red and white stripes and, on a canton, the British Union Jack with its crosses of St. George and St. Andrew.

On 1 January 1776, identical flags were displayed in the lines of the colonial forces besieging Boston, the same day that the new Continental Army came into being. This famous flag has been called the Continental flag and, later, the Grand Union flag. After the Declaration of Independence, continued use of the British Union Jack became inappropriate, and a new flag was created. The first Act of Congress establishing the Stars and Stripes, 14 June 1777, ordained the present arrangement of stripes but merely stated that the 13 white stars would represent "a new constellation" on a union of blue.

The Continental Army adopted a design in which the 13 stars were arranged in a circle so that no colony should take precedence. The first Navy version of the Stars and Stripes had the stars arranged in a staggered formation of alternate lines and rows of threes and twos, on a blue field. Variations in the stripes continued, and privateers continued to use the superseded flag with its British Union Jack. But eventually order emerged from what must have been a chaotic condition.

Both stars and stripes continued to be added; after the admission of Kentucky and Vermont, a resolution, which provided for the addition of a stripe and a star for each new state, was adopted by Congress on 1 May 1795, giving the flag 15 stars and 15 stripes. This flag flew over Fort Mc-Henry on the occasion of its bombardment by a British fleet and inspired Francis Scott Key to write "The Star-Spangled Banner," later to become our national anthem.

Realizing that the flag would soon become unwieldly, Captain Samuel C. Reid, U.S. Navy, who commanded the *General Armstrong* during the War of 1812, suggested to Congress that the stripes be fixed at 13 in number to represent the original 13 colonies that had struggled to found the nation and had become its first states, and that a star be added to the blue field for every state coming into the Union. This suggestion became the text of a resolution by Congress, effective 18 April 1818, whereby the flag should contain 13 alternate red and white stripes representing the 13 original states, with a new star added for each new state on the July 4th following its admission. The flag next ordered had 20 stars.

During the Mexican War the Stars and Stripes had 28 and 29 stars; during the Civil War it had from 33 to 35, no stars being removed because of the states which had seceded. In the Spanish-American War it had 45 stars. During the first and second World Wars and the Korean conflict it had the familiar 48 stars. With the admission of Alaska as a state on 3 January 1959, and Hawaii on 21 August 1959, the 49th and 50th stars were added.

The *jack*, a nautical flag, corresponds in design to the blue field and its stars. It is flown from the jackstaff (in the bow) on government vessels while at anchor, provided that the national flag is being displayed. Another American flag frequently seen is the yachting ensign, displayed by privately owned craft, which consists of the 13 red and white stripes and a blue field with 13 stars arranged in a circle about a white foul anchor.

HOW TO DISPLAY THE FLAG

The national flag should be raised and lowered by hand. It should be displayed only from sunrise to sunset, or between such hours as may be designated by proper authority. Do not raise the flag while it is furled. Unfurl it, then hoist it quickly to the top of the staff. In lowering it, however, lower it slowly and with dignity. Place no objects on or over the flag. For instance, various articles are sometimes placed on a speaker's table covered with the flag. This practice should be avoided.

When displayed in the chancel or on a platform in a church, the flag should be placed on a staff at the clergyman's right, and all other flags at his left. If displayed in the body of the church, the flag should be at the congregation's right as they face the clergyman.

Other miscellaneous rules are:

When displayed over the middle of the street, the flag should be suspended vertically, with the union to the north in an east-west street, or to the east in a north-south street.

When displayed with another flag, from crossed staffs, the flag of the United States of America should be on the right (the flag's own right) and its staff should be in front of the staff of the other flag.

When the flag is to be flown at half-mast, it should be hoisted to the peak for an instant, and then lowered to the half-mast position; but before being lowered for the day, it should again be raised to the peak. "Half-mast" means hauling down the flag to one-half the distance between the top and the bottom of the staff. On Memorial Day the flag is displayed at half-mast until noon only, then it is hoisted to the top of the staff for the rest of the day.

When flags of states or cities or pennants of societies are displayed on separate halyards, but from the same pole on which the flag of the United States of America is being flown, the latter should always be hoisted first and lowered last.

When the flag is suspended over a sidewalk from a rope, extending from house to pole at the edge of the sidewalk, the flag should be hoisted out from the building, toward the pole, union first.

When the flag is displayed from a staff projecting horizontally or at any angle from the window sill, balcony, or front of a building, the union of the flag should go clear to the peak of the staff (unless the flag is to be displayed at half-mast).

When the flag is used to cover a casket at funerals or ceremonies honoring a person deceased, it should be so placed that the union is at the head and over the left shoulder. The flag should not be lowered into the grave or allowed to touch the ground.

When the flag is displayed in a manner other than by being flown from a staff, it should be flat, whether indoors or out. When displayed either horizontally or vertically against a wall, the union should be uppermost and to the flag's own right; that is, to the observer's left. When displayed in a window, it should be in the same manner; that is, with the union or blue field to the left of the observer in the street. When festoons, rosettes, or drapings in the national colors are desired, bunting of blue, white, and red should be used, but never the flag itself.

In this country or in any parade of U. S. troops, when carried in a procession with another flag or flags, the Stars and Stripes should have the place of honor at the right; or, when there is a line of other flags, our national flag may be *in front* of the center of that line.

International usage forbids the display of the flag of one nation above that of another nation in time of peace.

When the flags of two or more nations are displayed, they should be flown from separate staffs of the same height, and the flags should be of approximately equal size.

A federal law provides that a trademark cannot be registered which consists of, or comprises, among other things, "the flag, coat-of-arms, or other insignia of the United States, or any simulation thereof."

At all times, every precaution should be taken to prevent the flag from becoming soiled. It should not be allowed to touch the ground or floor, or to brush against objects.

When the flag is used at the unveiling of a statue or monument, it should not be used as a covering of the object to be unveiled. If it is displayed on such occasions, it should not be allowed to fall to the ground, but should be hung aloft to form a feature of the ceremony.

The pledge to the flag is as follows: "I pledge allegiance to the flag of the United States of America and to the Republic for which it stands, one Nation, under God, indivisible, with Liberty and Justice for all."

APPROVED FLAG CUSTOMS

Laws have been written to govern the use of the flag and to ensure a proper respect for the Stars and Stripes. Custom has decreed certain other observances in regard to its use.

All services have precise regulations regarding the display of the national flag—when, where, and how it shall be hoisted or lowered. When naval vessels are at anchor, the national ensign and the Union Jack are flown from the flagstaff and the jackstaff, respectively, from 8 A.M. to sunset. When other vessels are entering or leaving port, the flag is flown prior to 8 A.M. and after sunset.

When the ship is getting under way or coming to anchor, cruising near land, falling in with other ships, or engaged in battle, the national ensign is flown during daylight from the gaff, or as directed.

It is the custom at all bases, posts, and stations to raise the flag every morning at 8 o'clock, and it remains flying until sunset or retreat.

Only one flag may be flown above the Stars and Stripes, and that is the Church Pennant, a dark blue cross on a white background. Code signal books of the Navy, which date back to the early 1860's, state: "The Church Pennant will be hoisted immediately above the ensign at the peak or flagstaff at the time of commencing and kept hoisted during the continuance of divine service on board all vessels of the Navy."

A chaplain's flag may be displayed at the place of divine worship or in his office, and it may be flown from the chaplain's car.

Civilian dignitaries of the federal and state governments, as well as flag and general officers, are entitled to individual flags which indicate their title or grade. They also have automobile flags which are attached to a staff on official cars.

The national flag may be displayed on all days when the weather permits, but it should especially be displayed on New Year's Day; Inauguration Day, January 20; Lincoln's Birthday; Washington's Birthday; Armed Forces Day, third Saturday in May; Memorial Day (half-staff until noon); Flag Day, June 14; Independence Day, July 4; Labor Day, first Monday in September; Columbus Day; Veterans Day; Thanksgiving Day, third or fourth Thursday in November; Christmas Day, December 25; and such other days as may be proclaimed national holidays by the President of the United States, as well as on the birthdays of states (the dates of their admission into the Union), and on state holidays. By state and national law, the dates of some of these holidays vary; therefore, no dates are given for them.

FOR FUNERALS

If a serviceman or servicewoman dies while on active duty, the flag for the funeral ceremonies is provided by the service to which he or she belonged. However, if he—or she—dies as an honorably discharged veteran, the flag is provided by the Veterans Administration, Washington, D.C., and may be procured from the nearest post office.

In filling out the application, the person signing for the flag must state whether he is the next of kin or other kinship. The flag must be presented to the next of kin at the proper time during the burial service. If there is no relative of the deceased or, if one cannot be located, the flag must be returned to the Veterans Administration in the franked container provided for that purpose.

Postmasters require proof of honorable discharge of a deceased service member before issuing the flag for use at funeral ceremonies, but flags are issued promptly upon proper evidence being presented.

When the national flag is worn out, it should be disposed of with due reverence. According to an approved custom, the union is first cut from the flag; and then the two pieces, which now no longer form a flag, are cremated.

UNITED NATIONS FLAG REGULATIONS

The United Nations flag code prescribes that the United Nations flag may be displayed as follows:

With one or more other flags, all flags should be displayed on the same level and be of approximately equal size.

On no occasion may any flag so displayed be larger than the UN flag.

On either side of any flag without being considered to be subordinated to any other flag.

Normally only on buildings and on stationary flagstaffs from sunrise to sunset.

The UN flag should not be displayed on days when the weather is inclement.

The UN flag should never be carried flat or horizontal, but always aloft and free. It should never be used as a drapery of any sort, festooned, drawn back, nor up in folds, but always allowed to fall free.

The United Nations flag may be displayed on the following occasions:

On all national and official holidays.

On United Nations Day, October 24.

On the occasion of any official event honoring the United Nations.

FLAG DESIGNATIONS

When the flag is carried by dismounted units it is known as the *colors*.

When flown from ships and boats, the flag is called an *ensign*.

When carried by tank, car, truck, or on horseback, the flag is called the *standard*.

HONORS TO THE NATIONAL ANTHEM

Outdoors: The following rules are customarily observed whenever and wherever the national anthem or "To the Colors" is played (not in formation):

At the first note, all dismounted personnel face the music, stand at attention, and render the prescribed salute; except at the "Escort of the Colors" or at "Retreat," you face toward the color or flag. The position of salute will be retained until the last note of the music is sounded.

Vehicles in motion should be brought to a halt. Persons riding in a passenger car or on a motorcycle dismount and salute as directed above. Occupants of other types of military vehicles remain seated at attention in the vehicle, the individual in charge of each vehicle dismounting and rendering the hand salute. Tank or armored car commanders salute from the vehicle.

During *colors*, a Navy boat under way within sight or hearing of the ceremony either lies to or proceeds at the slowest safe speed. The boat officer (or in his absence, the coxswain) stands and salutes— except when dangerous to do so. All other persons in the boat remain seated or standing, and do not salute.

The above marks of respect are shown the national anthem of any friendly country when played upon official occasions.

Indoors: When the national anthem is played indoors at a formal gathering, individuals will stand at attention and face the flag (if one is present), otherwise, face the music. Do not salute, unless covered or under arms.

Morning colors is the daily ceremony of raising the national flag. *Evening colors* or *retreat* is the ceremony of lowering the flag and putting it away for safekeeping.

Retreat is a daily ceremony at Army and Air Force posts and bases, and is held at a definite time in the late afternoon, usually 5 P.M. During bad weather or when a band is not present for the ceremony, a bugle call, "To the Colors," is played instead of the national anthem.

THE REVIEW

A review (or honors ceremony) may be held during a parade, when troops are ceremoniously paraded onto the field, and a person of distinction is on hand to "take the review." (In olden days, the dress parade was intended to impress visiting emissaries with the strength of the monarch's troops rather than to honor the visitor.) While a parade is in progress, stand quietly and do not smoke or talk.

When a dignitary or one or more individuals are to be honored during a parade, certain formalities are followed. At the service academies, for example at a Cadet Wing Parade, a senior government official may be asked to take the review, or one or more officers or senior professors who may be retiring.

The honored guest (or guests) is invited by the superintendent by formal invitation, and the invitation includes the guest's wife for both the parade and the reception that follows in the superintendent's quarters. Other guests are invited to sit in the superintendent's section on the parade ground and to attend the reception. Various officers and their wives from the station are also invited, and others, including the general public, may attend and sit in the stands.

After the cadets or midshipmen have marched by companies/squadrons onto the parade ground—each company with its own flag (guidon), and with all companies preceded by the Color Guard—the Brigade or Corps or Wing Commander gives the "Order Arms" and "Parade Rest."

The reviewing party will have already walked forward and taken a position facing the regimental officers, and an announcer will make the appropriate remarks about the honored guest. The Brigade or Wing or Corps Commander brings the companies to attention and announces, "Sir, the Brigade of Midshipmen (or Corps of Cadets or Cadet Wing)." The "Pass in Review" is spoken by the superintendent, and as each company marches by with flags momentarily dipped in salute to the honored guest and others in the reviewing group and stand, the salutes are returned by the honored guest and reviewing party.

Everyone stands during the review. Officers in uniform salute, but those out of uniform and civilian men face the flag, their right hand (with or without a hat) over their heart. Women guests stand quietly facing the flag; they wear suits or afternoon dress, and gloves. Civilian men and retired officers as well as officers out of uniform wear business suits.

OTHER HONORS

To colors: Military personnel passing an uncased color (standard) salute at a distance of six paces and hold the salute until they have passed six paces beyond it. Similarly, when an uncased color passes by, you salute when it is six paces away and hold the salute until it has passed six paces beyond you. Small flags carried by individuals are not saluted.

Personal honors: When personal honors are rendered, military personnel present salute at the first note of the music and hold the salute until the completion of the ruffles, flourishes, and march.

When a gun salute is rendered, military personnel being saluted and other persons in the ceremonial party render the hand salute throughout the firing of the gun salute. Other persons in the vicinity of the ceremonial party stand at attention.

Ackowledgment by persons in civilian dress may be made by standing at attention. A gun salute to the national flag requires no individual action. Other than standing at attention during dress parades—say, on the parade field at a service academy—all officers under the canopy are considered to be in the ceremonial party, and salute accordingly.

Military funerals: Military personnel salute during the passing of a caisson or hearse in a funeral procession. You salute whenever honors are rendered: when the body is removed from the hearse to the chapel, from the chapel to the hearse or caisson, and from the hearse or caisson to the grave. You salute when the volleys are fired and when "Taps" is sounded. In civilian dress, men stand at attention, uncovered, and hold their headdress over the left breast. (See Chapter 40, *The Military Funeral.*)

IN CIVILIAN DRESS

Outdoors: When facing the flag or music all men in civilian dress remove their hats or caps and hold them with their right hand over their heart. Ladies stand quietly.

Indoors: All men and women stand quietly, facing the flag/or music, with their hands free at their sides.

MOURNING FLAG

The colors are hoisted to the peak of the flagpole or staff, and then lowered halfway. When the flag is removed, it is again raised to the peak before being lowered. Where flags cannot be flown at half-staff, they should have a black streamer from the spearhead halfway down the flag. Flags hung horizontally or perpendicularly should bear a black bunting border of appropriate width.

INCLEMENT WEATHER

Flags are not usually flown at night or in inclement weather. A code of display adopted by Congress on 22 June 1942 states: "It is the universal custom to display the flag only from sunrise to sunset on buildings and on stationary flagstaffs in the open. However, the flag may be displayed at night upon special occasions when it is desired to produce a patriotic effect." The more modern trend is that a flag may be flown at night if it is lighted.

CHAPTER 43

Aboard Ship

LIFE ABOARD a naval vessel is completely different from regular duty in the other services. Therefore, some of the customs followed when an officer has sea duty are discussed here.

WARDROOM LIFE

Wardroom country aboard ship is said to be the naval officer's seagoing home where he may meet with his fellow officers for moments of relaxation.

Officers' country (the wardroom, staterooms, washrooms, assigned to officers) is out of bounds for enlisted personnel unless they are on official duty. The wardroom is normally not to be used as an office by any member, so contacts with enlisted personnel should be confined to their part of the ship or to the departmental office. On a small ship, this may be your stateroom.

Always remove your cap upon entering the wardroom. Never be boisterous; it is the home of all the officers, and their rights and privileges should be respected. You should keep the volume low when using the radio or television, and magazines and newspapers should not be left adrift; neither should they be removed from the wardroom where they have been placed for availability to all members. In the Navy, the expression is often heard: "The standards set in wardroom country are the standards found throughout the ship."

STATEROOM

An officer's stateroom should be orderly and clean at all times, and this the junior officer has to do himself. The mess specialist is responsible for cleaning the room and making the bunk for officers of the rank of commander and above—including the captain of a small ship who may be of less rank.

MEALS

The hours for wardroom meals are designated by the president of the mess, subject to the approval of the commanding officer. On small ships —destroyers and smaller—the president of the mess is usually the commanding officer. Breakfast hours may be shifted from time to time to conform to daily routine. In any event, except for Sundays and holidays, the wardroom should be cleared by 0800.

Lunch is usually served at 1130 underway and 1200 in port. Dinner normally is served at 1730 in port, or 1830 when in foreign ports. Other than at formal occasions, family-style meals are frequently served.

Seating arrangements are usually set up by the mess treasurer and approved by the executive officer. The president sits at the head of the senior table with the mess treasurer at the opposite end. Members are seated to the right and left of the president in order of seniority. This system is also followed in seating officers who are on temporary duty.

COURTESIES AT THE TABLE

The senior officer should be punctual in seating himself by the time the meal is scheduled to begin. In the event he is delayed, he should inform the next senior officer whether or not to proceed with the serving of the meal. Other members of the mess should arrive in the wardroom from three to five minutes prior to meals.

Never sit down before the senior officer takes his seat. If you are late for the meal, make apologies to the senior member at your table. If business unduly detains you, notify the senior officer present and eat later with the officers coming off watch.

The senior officer present usually makes any announcements. If you have something to bring before the members, request his permission and brief him on the subject. Officers going on watch should eat before regular meal hours and be clear of the wardroom prior to the regular meal.

It is everyone's duty to promote a cheerful atmosphere at the table. A good rule to follow is: "Don't talk shop during mealtime, but save it until after dessert and coffee." Wait until coffee is served before you light up.

GUESTS

The mess should have a written policy in regard to guests, which will ensure coverage of the following items: (a) How guests of any individual are to be distinguished from guests of the mess; (b) What charge, if any, is to be made for guests; and (c) What proportionate charge should be made for children as compared to adults.

Officers should be encouraged to bring their guests aboard ship for dinner, but not repeatedly. Each member should speak to the guests, and in a sense act as co-host.

Guests of senior officers usually sit at the senior table, with the honored guest on the right of the presiding officer, the host officer second, and other guests taking precedence over regular mess members. In large ships with a number of mess tables, the guests are seated next to their officer hosts and as close to the place of honor as possible. The space next to a guest should never be left unoccupied. At formal dinners, which are held less frequently today, the use of place cards is desirable.

These rules should be followed:

Inform the mess president beforehand of any plan to have guests.

Notify the mess treasurer of the number and names of the guests in order that any place cards and seating may be arranged.

Make certain that the guests understand the time the meal is to be served, and the formality or informality of the occasion. Casual dress may be worn, but not beach-style attire.

If the ship is at anchor, the host should be sure that guests are well informed as to the weather and the boat schedule.

Ensure by advance arrangements that the guests will not be unduly delayed at the naval base gate because of identification problems.

Be available on the quarterdeck to welcome guests aboard.

Designate a certain room for the use of women guests.

Introduce all members present to the guests (each member should come forward to meet them).

Ship talk should not be discussed in detail. Guests in any walk of life— teen-ager or oldster—should never be "talked down to" nor treated condescendingly just because they are unfamiliar with service customs.

Arrange for the guests to depart at a reasonable hour. Generally, dinner guests leave within an hour after the movie, smoker, or party.

Notify the officer of the deck well in advance as to the boat in which the guests are to depart.

If possible, accompany the women guests home, or have them accompanied by a fellow officer; otherwise, arrange for the women guests to return to their homes in groups.

EXCHANGE OF MEAL COURTESIES

It is courteous for the wardroom occasionally to invite the commanding officer—if he messes separately—to have a meal in the wardroom. The same courtesy is normally extended to the unit commander by the ship's mess president. The unit commander will appreciate an occasional invitation to a meal in the wardrooms of the ships of his command—particularly the flagship. Included with the unit commander in all such invitations, generally, is the chief of staff (chief staff officer). In some cases, as appropriate and desired, the senior officers of the unit commander's staff are also invited.

It is customary for unit commanders and commanding officers, if maintaining a separate mess, to return such meals as opportunity permits. The difficulty of an all-inclusive return of such courtesies to each individual in a mess should, however, be appreciated.

PAYMENT OF MESS BILL

Every officer attached to a ship belongs to one of the officers' messes and is required to pay to the mess treasurer the full amount of his mess bill monthly and in advance.

When you are ordered to detached duty, or sent to a hospital, you are entitled to a rebate of the full amount for the period of your absence, or as prescribed by the mess bylaws and these vary from ship to ship.

When in a transient or temporary duty status, you are not entitled to reimbursement for meals, but you will be charged at a rate prescribed by the president of the mess. Officers in such status may become temporary members of the mess if their temporary duty becomes of an extended nature.

SOCIAL ACTIVITY

There are many pleasant ways to build a ship's spirit, which require the interest and participation of all hands. Mess nights may be scheduled when guests gather aboard ship for dinner, and family nights may be planned with children attending. Cook-outs, dances ashore at beaches and in service clubs, tournaments such as golf, tennis, bridge, and chess, all are good ways to foster friendships and closeness of service ties.

Every wardroom mess should give a dinner for the commanding officer at some convenient time soon after his assuming command. In similar fashion, a farewell dinner should be held in his honor prior to being detached.

VISITS AND CALLS ABOARD SHIP

You are expected to make an official call on your commanding officer in his cabin within 48 hours after reporting in, and stay about 10 minutes unless asked to remain longer. Beforehand, ask the executive officer when it will be convenient for you to do so. In large ships, the CO may have definite arrangements for meeting and talking with newly assigned officers.

When an American warship calls at a foreign naval activity, the visited country's senior officer present usually sends a liaison officer to call upon the visiting ship's commander to offer courtesies and to exchange information as appropriate. This liaison officer is usually invited to the wardroom after his visit with the CO, and he will give pertinent information to those who are planning excursions.

After the prescribed exchange of official calls by senior officers, committees of the visiting ship's officers make calls on the wardrooms of the other foreign ships in port. For this purpose the wardroom should have cards for use in extending invitations for a meal, for movies in the mess, or for receptions.

The liaison officer may bring guest cards or invitations for honorary membership in the port's officers' club, or country club, as well as invitations to social functions. These invitations should be answered promptly, in handwritten replies.

When your ship is in a foreign port for several days, it is desirable that members of the mess give a dinner for their foreign hosts to repay their hospitality.

When a foreign ship visits your home port, a committee is sent to the visiting ship to extend hospitality. In some ports, the nearest ship of the home navy is designated as the "host ship," whose specific responsibility is to assist the visitor in any way possible. When more than one U.S. ship is present, the senior officer present designates a ship to send a committee; this precludes too many visits.

PIPING A VIP ABOARD

When a very important official visits a ship, he is piped on board. As his boat comes alongside, following a gun salute, if any, the piping commences by the boatswain's mate, lasts about 20 seconds, and ends as the visitor steps onto the lower gangway platform. Those on deck stand at attention until the VIP's head reaches the level of the deck as he ascends, then the boatswain's mate salutes with his left hand and commences piping the visitor aboard. All hands in the quarterdeck area salute and hold the salute for the full duration of the pipe—plus the ruffles and flourishes or music, whichever is last.

The visitor who is now on the upper gangway platform, pauses and faces aft and salutes the colors. He then turns, salutes again, holding his salute through the line of sideboys; then he halts, holding his salute until the end of the music, or to the end of the sideboys. Still holding the salute he looks at the officer of the deck or senior welcoming officer, and says "Sir, may I have (or, Sir I request) permission to come aboard?" He then completes the salute, the boatswain ends his piping, and all hands in the quarterdeck area complete their salute.

All hands stand at attention during the greeting ceremonies, which may include the inspection of the guard followed by the introduction of the VIP to the principal officers on deck.

Upon departure, notice is sent to the quarterdeck by the flag lieutenant, the sideboys are paraded, and in the quarterdeck area the visitor takes leave of his hosts, then says to the officer of the deck "Sir, may I have (or, I request) permission to leave the ship?" He holds his salute while proceeding through the line of sideboys, faces the national colors and pauses to end the salute, then goes down the gangway. The piping ends as the visitor's head passes below the level of the deck.

WOMEN GUESTS

When you bring a woman guest on board, she precedes you. If this is her first visit, it may be well to explain the proper procedure. Upon reaching the quarterdeck she should step quickly aboard—then step out of the way so that you—her officer escort—will be clear as you execute the ritual of saluting the colors aft, and then turn and salute the officer of the deck. She should be careful not to stand between you and the officer of the deck as you exchange salutes. You then introduce her to him.

If she wishes to make some recognition of the flag when coming on board or leaving a ship, she should hesitate at the top of the gangway and glance up for a moment at the flag. When women are not military personnel, they are not privileged to honor the flag with a salute.

Military women render the same salute and honors as their male counterparts.

Strangers to the Navy way of life should be told in advance of a visit that liquor and pets are not brought aboard ship. There are various rules about bringing cameras on board, and these should be determined beforehand. Nonmilitary women should use care in the type of dress worn.

SHIP LAUNCHING

After a ship is authorized by Congress, there are three ceremonial occasions during her construction and fitting out: the keel laying, the launch and christening, and the commissioning.

The construction of a large warship usually requires about three years from keel laying to launching. The name of the ship and its sponsors are chosen by the Secretary of the Navy upon the recommendation of the Chief of Naval Operations. There are over 125 types of ships whose name sources are not set by law but which have been standardized by tradition and approved by the Navy.

Although a ship is assigned a name long before she is launched, the ship does not receive her name until she is christened. Since mariners facing the unknown perils of the sea place their faith not only in a stout ship but in an unseen guiding spirit, the religious part of the christening ceremony is important.

Carriers are usually named for famous men, ships of the Old Navy, or historic battles; *cruisers* for cities; *submarines* for fish and other creatures of the sea and also for famous men; and *destroyers* for American heroes and Secretaries of the Navy.

Aircraft carriers are usually sponsored by the wives of naval personnel associated with aviation, and submarines are sponsored by wives of personnel in that service. Sponsors for vessels named in honor of particular persons are usually the nearest female relative of the honored person. Although women are sponsors nowadays, in early years men performed this honor. The first recorded christening of a U.S. ship is that of the frigate *Constitution* on 21 October 1797 by Captain James Sever, USN. One person usually christens a ship, but a co-sponsor may be named.

The mayor of a city is usually invited to nominate a sponsor for a cruiser named in honor of the city. The commandants of naval districts are authorized to designate sponsors for some of the smaller vessels built within their districts.

At the time of the launching, the sponsor, ship officers, officials of the shipbuilding company, and the commandant of the naval district in which the vessel has been built (or his representative), assemble on a flag-decorated platform erected for the occasion at the bow of the ship.

The chaplain of the naval shipyard or district will offer a prayer for the officers and men of the Navy and the ship. The band will play the national anthem, and as the ship begins to move down the ways, the sponsor will break a bottle of wine or water—usually champagne—across the ship's bow and say, "In the name of the United States I christen thee. . . ."

SHIP COMMISSIONING

The commissioning ceremony marks the initiation of a ship into the operating forces of the U.S. Navy. Until then, the ship has been the responsibility of the commandant of the naval district or of the naval shipyard where she was being built. Therefore, no ensign, jack, or commission pennant flies beforehand.

Guests are invited by card to the commissioning ceremony, and the invitation usually includes a reception or lunch following the ceremony, as well as an inspection of the ship. A printed program gives the ship's background, sponsors, officers, and crew. Officers wear dress uniform and ladies wear suits, or appropriate daytime dresses, and gloves. The ceremony lasts about an hour.

The crew is assembled on the quarterdeck or other open area, usually in two ranks facing inboard. Officers are assembled in two ranks athwartships facing aft, and there is a band and Marine or seaman guard. Distinguished guests and speakers, and other guests, will be seated nearby.

The first watch is on the quarterdeck and quartermasters are stationed at the national ensign, Union Jack, and commission pennant. When "Attention" is sounded, the national anthem is played and the flags and pennant are hoisted simultaneously.

The commandant formally turns the ship over to the prospective commanding officer, who reads his orders from the Navy Department. His first order is, "Set the watch." The presentation of a plaque or gift to the ship by a state, city, or sponsor, then takes place, followed by the benediction.

CHAPTER 44

The Dining-In &
Dining-Out

A DINING-IN is a formal dinner given by a wing, unit, or organization. It may honor a departing officer or welcome a new one. It may give recognition to a dignitary, or to individual and unit achievements. Or it may simply be a pleasant way for officers on a station to get better acquainted. Other than military women on the station, it is a stag affair. When nonmilitary women are invited, this is a "dining-out."

The term "dining-in" derives from an old Viking tradition of celebrating great battles and feats of heroes by formal ceremony, which spread to the monasteries and early-day universities, and to the military when the officers' mess was established.

Medals are worn by all members of the mess and the military guests, including retired officers. A civilian guest wears black tie or whatever is stated in the invitation, and officers wear the prescribed uniform—the Air Force mess dress, the Navy dinner dress, or whatever is prescribed by your service.

There are two officers of the mess: the president, who usually is the commanding officer of the station, and the vice, called "Mr. Vice." He is a junior officer in the command, chosen for his ability to speak well, and is in charge of innumerable details. All officers in the unit (organization, etc.) are expected to attend, but a written request to be excused may be accepted by the president.

GUESTS

Mess officers should arrive at least ten minutes before the hour of invitation in order to meet and talk with the guests of honor, and get acquainted with others. You do not leave until the guests have departed—unless you have been excused beforehand for a good reason.

Official guests are guests of the mess as a whole; their expenses are shared. The expenses of personal guests are paid by the one who invited them. This includes bar expenses. Cocktails are usually served about 45 minutes before dinner, and the cocktail time should be stated on the invitation.

THE PRESIDENT AND MR. VICE

The *president* sets the date and place of the dining-in, acquires the speaker, arranges for a chaplain to give the invocation, and greets all guests before dinner and all members of the mess if possible. He introduces the guest speaker and other honored guests to the mess. His duties include the appointment of Mr. Vice and various committees.

The *vice*, usually called Mr. Vice, is the first to arrive and the last to leave the mess. He makes the appropriate toasts, and should be prepared to make others if called upon. He sounds the dinner chimes at the designated time. Long before the night of the dining-in he should have checked on the reservations, musicians, and music, kept in touch with the mess manager concerning the menu and the cleaning of unit silver, the collection of any paintings or photographs to be shown, and made certain that all colors and standards to be used were in good order. The national and organizational colors are placed behind the president's chair.

The president appoints other mess officers as committee chairmen, such as: *table arrangements*, (place cards, seating, centerpiece, checking out the unit's silver, crystal, and china); and *dining room arrangements*, (the menu, coordination of serving time with the head waiter, a public address system if needed, the awards to be presented, flags and trophies, photographer, the payment of mess and bar charges).

The seating arrangement for the mess should be posted in the cocktail lounge in order that all hands know where they will be seated.

Hosts should be appointed to contact the invited guests in advance and inform them as to mess customs, dress, the agenda, the time allowed for speeches, and arrange for transportation and quarters when needed.

A *protocol* committee prepares invitations for the president's signature, provides biographical sketches, briefs the hosts when necessary, and has a thank-you letter ready for the president's signature, to be sent to the guest of honor following the dining-in.

PLANNING THE DINING-IN

Start early. Two weeks to a month before the time set for the dinner, send out invitations to the guests who are not members of the mess. The fill-in card is often used for the invitations, or they may be handwritten or printed. Since this is a formal occasion, formal wording is used. For example, the wording for official guests should include the phrase "the honor (or honour) of the presence of . . ." but for personal guests, would read "the pleasure of the company of . . ." or ". . . your company."

Invitations must state the type of uniform to be worn. When it is uncertain what a retired officer might have, it is correct to write "Military Evening Dress, if convenient" in the lower right-hand corner of the invitation. Mess officers wear the prescribed uniform. At a dining-out, women wear long dinner dresses.

The menu usually consists of four or five courses, with roast prime ribs of beef and Yorkshire pudding traditional but not a necessity. Wines may be served in decanters by waiters, or placed on the table and passed around, from left to right counterclockwise.

SEATING

At a dining-in, the guest of honor sits to the right of the president at the head table, with the next ranking guest on the president's left. Other guests are seated throughout the mess. The members of the mess are seated according to seniority, with Mr. Vice at the foot of the table.

At a dining-out, the guest of honor's wife is seated to the right of the president, and the second ranking woman to his left. The president's wife is seated to the right of the guest of honor. For variations in seating, *see* Chapter 18, Seating Plans & Precedence.

The tables should be set up in the manner most suitable to the dining area. The head table usually is a long single table, but side tables may be placed down each end in a modified "E"—with no seats off center. No one should be seated across from those at the head table. It is important that tables are not crowded, with everyone having plenty of elbow room.

SMOKING AND TOASTING

The table is cleared following dessert and coffee, with port—or the wine used—poured. But you do not drink the port, or smoke, even though cigarettes and ashtrays have been placed on the table and cigars passed—until the president announces, "Gentlemen, the smoking lamp is lighted."

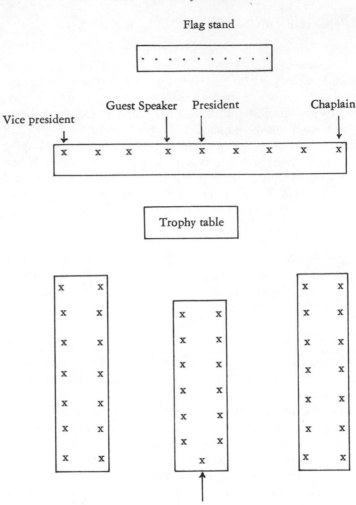

Air Force Plan for Table and Seating Arrangements

Now you may smoke. Mr. Vice will light the smoking lamp, when there is one, which is passed to the president who lights the guest of honor's cigar, if he smokes.

The president stands and proposes a toast to the Commander-in-Chief of the United States (when foreign guests are present, their head of state is toasted first) and each officer stands with raised glass. Other toasts will continue, but you must remember not to bottoms-up your glass on each toast, only on the final traditional toast. And you do not stand or drink a toast when you are the one toasted. (*See* Chapter 23, Toasts.)

AIR FORCE JOC DINING-OUT AGENDA

Date

Place

1900   Members and guests arrive.

1940   The bar closes. Members take their positions at the tables. (All remain standing). The after burner is off—no smoking.

1945   President calls mess to order with one rap of the gavel.

1946   President requests the flags. Colors are posted by the honor guard.

1950   Invocation.

1952   President proposes a toast to the Commander-In-Chief.
President: "To the President of the United States."
Members: "To President —."
Mr. Vice proposes a toast to the Secretary of the Air Force.
Mr. Vice: "To the Secretary of the Air Force."
Members: "To Secretary —."
Mr. Vice proposes a toast to the Chief of Staff, United States Air Force.
Mr. Vice: "To the Chief of Staff, United States Air Force."
Members: "To the Chief of Staff."

1955   President seats the mess.

1956   Welcoming remarks by the president of the mess.

1958   The president introduces each guest and wife at the head table. (Hold your applause as an appropriate toast will be rendered.)

1959   Mr. Vice proposes a toast. (Members stand, wives and guests remain seated.)
Mr. Vice: "To our distinguished guests."
Members: "Hear, hear."

2000   President seats the mess.

2001   Dinner is served. (Begin eating immediately.)
Dinner music is provided.

2040   President calls for a break with two raps of the gavel. Members adjourn to the bar.

2055   Members return to the mess and remain standing. President will seat the mess with one rap of the gavel. (Dessert is brought in to the sound of music.)

2100   Smoking lamp is lit.

2121   President introduces the distinguished speaker.

2122   Speech by Senator Doe.

2145   Mr. Vice proposes a toast to our distinguished speaker.
Everyone rises and picks up his wine glass.
Mr. Vice: "To our distinguished speaker."
Members: "Hear, hear."

2146   President calls for the retiring of the colors.

2147   President/commander renders closing remarks.

2148   President adjourns the mess by two raps of the gavel. (Members remain standing behind their chairs until the guests have left.)

2150   Dancing commences with music provided.

CHAPTER 45

When You Retire

A SERVICE MAN or servicewoman of retirement age has had plenty of time to decide what to do before the day of retirement arrives. The officer who must retire before the mandatory retirement age may not have had much time to plan for it—perhaps he or she is a young officer who has been passed over, or who unexpectedly is retired for physical disability.

PHYSICAL DISABILITY

Officers may be retired at any time, at any age, for physical disability. At first, they may be retired temporarily, and be examined regularly by doctors until the extent of the illness or injury is determined.

During this time they will receive disability retirement pay and other benefits of regular retirement. After the extent of the disability is known, they will be returned to active duty or retired permanently with benefits.

While the officer is ill or disabled, he or she will receive medical care at the nearest military hospital. For extended or specialized care, he or she may be taken to the National Medical Center at Bethesda, Maryland. Military hospitals have trained personnel to assist a member of the family in legal or everyday counseling. The Aid or Relief Society of each service and the Red Cross are ready to assist families when needed.

PLANNING FOR RETIREMENT

A wise man or woman will make plans for the future long before the necessity arises. When you are stationed in an area with a university or college nearby, night classes are available for the active-duty officer, with courses leading to a masters degree or a doctorate; business administration courses will take you into the business world. With your military background and specialized courses, your future should be secure—if you stay clear of conflict-of-interest jobs.

THE RÉSUMÉ

After you retire and you want a job, you may need to send out resumés to prospective employers. With the resumé—which may be several pages in length and photocopied—send an accompanying one-page cover letter —which must be original, *not* photocopied. The department head or president of the company to whom you send the resumé will not want to read through a lengthy cover letter *and* resumé; he wants to be able to go through the whole thing quickly, catch the gist of it immediately, feel that you truly want to work for *him*, know that you are qualified for his particular needs, and make an on-the-spot evaluation. When interested, he will re-examine your application and give it a thorough scrutiny.

In writing your cover letter, make it positive and concise. State why you want to work for this particular firm and mention any special abilities that make you eligible for this particular job. Do not use military terms that are not relevant to the business. This cover letter is your front, your personal advertisement. And like any good ad, it should be to the point.

In writing your resumé, employ the standard newspaper trick of writing the most important thing first, then the next most important, and so on. But remember that the most important thing is what the prospective employer is interested in—not what you may personally feel was the most important thing in your military career. Also remember that any employer (in a large firm particularly) wants only those who can get along together and can take orders as well as give them. If you have had leadership training or experience in some special program, be sure that you add this. Getting along with people is an art.

It is very important that all names and titles, including the name of the firm, and address, are absolutely correct. Do your homework before sending out the application; learn as much about the business as possible. When called in for an interview, you must be prepared for any question.

You should send out several letters and resumés to various firms, regardless of whether or not they need new people at that time. Something might turn up unexpectedly, and a check of the firm's files would turn up your application. Although you send original letters to each prospective place of employment, the same form can be used.

One of the best ways to learn about new jobs is through classmates and friends who are already employed by certain firms. Word-of-mouth frequently discloses a line on a new job that is just what you want.

RESTRICTED EMPLOYMENT

A retired officer must be alert to the type of conflict-of-interest employment that cannot be undertaken without the risk of losing retired pay or being prosecuted.

If you have any doubt concerning such restrictions you should write for an opinion to the office of the Judge Advocate General of your service in Washington, D.C. Some restrictions apply to regular retired officers, others to all retired personnel.

In your letter, give complete information about the type of work that you are interested in, the duties you will be expected to carry out, and any special provisions, as well as your retired status.

WEARING THE UNIFORM

Retired, reserve, or separated personnel are authorized to wear the uniform upon many occasions. You may wear it to memorial services, military weddings or funerals, military balls, and inaugurals. A separated person wears a uniform of the highest grade held during war service.

You may wear your uniform upon such patriotic occasions as parades, national holidays, or ceremonies when any active or reserve U.S. military unit is taking part.

Other occasions are meetings or functions of associations established for military purposes, or when the membership of a group is mainly or entirely made up of honorably discharged or retired veterans of the armed forces or of reserve personnel. The uniform may be worn when traveling to and from the place of the ceremony on the day of the occasion or within 24 hours of the time of the scheduled function.

Retired officers wear a uniform when engaged in some military activity, such as when engaged in military instruction or when responsible for military discipline at an educational institution.

You do not wear your uniform when you are visiting or living in a foreign country, except at a formal ceremony or social occasion as required in the invitation or the regulations or customs of the country.

You do not wear the uniform when conducting personal or business matters, or in any demonstration or activity of a political, economic, or religious nature—except upon bona fide authority.

Retired members may wear civilian clothing when riding in military aircraft, but their attire must reflect favorably on the military service.

MILITARY TITLES

You retain your military title following retirement, subject to certain restrictions. These restrictions are in connection with commercial enterprises when such use, intentionally or not, gives rise to any appearance of sanction, endorsement, sponsorship, or approval by any service department or the Department of Defense.

You do not use your official service title when making public appearances outside of this country unless authorized by the appropriate overseas commander.

RETIRED DESIGNATIONS

The word "Retired" (or "Ret.") is used by all regular and reserve personnel who retired because of age or physical disability, including those on the temporary disability retired list.

For example, when you retire from the Army or Army Reserve, you would write "USA, Retired" or "USAR Ret." On a business envelope this could be Colonel John E. Doe, USA (Ret.). Informally, Colonel would be abbreviated to Col.

DESIGNATIONS ON SOCIAL INVITATIONS, CARDS

Some people are unsure of the correct way to address or extend invitations to, or as, retired personnel. There is a misunderstanding, sometimes, in the wording of a formal wedding invitation.

There is no difference in the wording of active or retired *couples*. For example the traditional wording is:

COLONEL AND MRS. JOHN EARL DOE
REQUEST THE HONOUR OF THE PRESENCE OF
ETC.

But when a divorced or widowed officer sends the invitation in his (or her) name only, the wording includes the word retired after his or her name:

COLONEL JOHN EARL DOE
UNITED STATES ARMY, RETIRED
REQUESTS THE HONOUR OF THE PRESENCE OF
ETC.

In addressing the envelope you write "Colonel and Mrs. John Earl Doe," *never* adding "U.S. Army, Retired." The wife is *not* included in his military designation.

On personal (calling) cards, the retired single status is used in the same way as on the wedding invitation. But on joint cards, as with the wedding invitation, the word "Retired" is not designated. On joint cards only, rank abbreviations or a middle name initial may be used with a very long name.

RETIREMENT BENEFITS

Most officers retire between their 20th and 30th years of service—or at a little over 40 or 50 years of age. In case of war or national emergency, a retired officer may be recalled to active duty. Otherwise he or she may start a second career in order to put the children through college, or possibly retire to a life of ease on the golf course or in world travel.

As a retired officer, you will receive a retirement check for as long as you live. If you retire after 20 years, the amount is about half of your base pay at the time of retirement.

There are a number of benefits that you receive upon retirement: the continued use of the PX, commissary, the military hospitals and medical services, the officers' club, and recreational facilities, and you will retain your ID card. There are Social Security and Veterans Administration benefits. And there is space available in military aircraft for travel.

Space available means just that: surplus space aboard an aircraft of the Military Airlift Command (MAC) on scheduled overseas flights. Those eligible are retired regular members, reserve personnel who retired after 20 years or more of service or who retired for physical disability, or reservists who retired at age 60. Retired personnel who have an armed forces identification card (DD Form 2N, gray) may take eligible dependents with them—children under 21, and husbands or wives.

There is also space-available travel for retired personnel on unscheduled military aircraft flights within the continental United States. Before flight time, you and any dependents must sign certificates stating that the travel is not for personal gain, and waivers clearing the government for injury, property loss, or death incurred in connection with an MAC flight.

There are no reservations for such flights. You appear at the MAC Air Passenger Terminal and stand by; in heavily traveled areas it might be a long wait. Wear comfortable civilian clothing.

PREPARING FOR DEATH

There is no excuse for any officer to leave his or her family in poor financial circumstances after his death. The fact that a man or woman does not want to face the fact of death is no reason for putting off a plan that insures the security of the average family. Each member of the armed forces upon retirement has the opportunity to participate in this plan.

The *Survivor Benefit Plan* (SBP) will provide income of up to 55 percent of a retired member's pay to the surviving widow or widower; an additional plan includes dependent children. A third plan will provide for children only (if the spouse is deceased or divorced); when there is no spouse and there are no children, an alternate plan provides for another person with an insurable interest in the retiree.

When only the surviving wife or husband is covered, the formula for maximum protection (55 percent of retired pay) is 2½ percent of the first $300 of monthly retired pay, plus 10 percent of the remainder above that figure. For example, should your retired pay be $900 a month, the amount deducted each month for membership in the plan would be $67.50, with your wife or husband receiving $495 each month.

As you know, retired pay stops on the day a retiree dies. To ease the problem of service families without adequate income, Congress signed into law the SBP in 1972, with members automatically enrolled in the plan with maximum coverage if they have spouses or dependent children at retirement *unless* they choose a lesser coverage in writing, or decline participation.

DEPENDENCY AND INDEMNITY COMPENSATION (DIC)

The husband or wife of a member of the armed forces who dies while *in service or of a service-incurred cause after separation* is eligible for a monthly payment from the Veterans Administration. DIC can be paid for life if the spouse does not remarry. Supplemental payments are made for unmarried children under 18, or between 18 and 23 if attending VA-approved schools. Certain disabled children may be eligible for life benefits.

There has been some misunderstanding among wives of deceased retirees who think that all service people have DIC compensations, but it is only for families of those who die on active duty or in related causes.

SERVICEMEN'S GROUP LIFE INSURANCE (SGLI)

All members of the uniformed services are eligible for the Servicemen's Group Life Insurance low-cost coverage throughout their full-time active duty or active duty for training, and for 120 days following separation or release.

The uniformed services include: commissioned, warrant, and enlisted members of the Army, Navy, Marine Corps, Air Force, and Coast Guard; commissioned members of the National Oceanic and Atmospheric Administration and the Public Health Service; cadets or midshipmen at the service academies, and members of the ROTC; also, those in the ready reserve of a uniformed service on active training duty.

As amended by the Veterans Insurance Act of 1974, the maximum amount of insurance for all members is $20,000. Lesser amounts are available—or none at all, which must be put in writing. The low rate of $3.40 for the maximum amount is deducted from the paycheck of those on active duty. Ready reservists pay the same rates. There is limited coverage for National Guard and some reserve members.

The Veterans Group Life Insurance (VGLI) is administered by the Office of Servicemen's Life Insurance and is supervised by the VA. This provides for automatic conversion of SGLI to a five-year, nonrenewable term policy at reasonable rates and no physical examination. This means that the veteran is covered for a period immediately after separation or release from the service. The beneficiary features for both the SGLI and VGLI programs are identical.

SOCIAL SECURITY

Since January 1957, members of the armed forces have contributed to Social Security and are eligible to receive benefits in the same manner as civilian employees in various occupations. The amount of the benefit depends upon the contributor's average earnings over a specified time. No one can be fully insured who has credit for less than one and a half years of work. Any questions should be directed to the nearest office.

CHAMPUS

Congress in 1966 authorized a comprehensive health-care program using civilian facilities to meet the needs of service families. The Civilian

Health and Medical Program of the Uniformed Services (CHAMPUS) is the portion of the Uniformed Services Health Benefits Program (USHBP) that ensures medical and health facilities and services that cannot be obtained from a military hospital or facility, on a low cost-sharing basis. The address is: OCHAMPUS, Aurora, CO 80045.

Dependents of active-duty members of the uniformed services, retired members and their dependents, and dependents of deceased active or retired members are eligible for USHBP on a space-available basis.

At the age of 65, retirees and their dependents, and survivor beneficiaries entitled to Medicare lose the CHAMPUS portion of USHBP eligibility. You always need to show your ID card.

MAJORCARE 90

Majorcare 90 offers men and women leaving the armed forces a comprehensive protection against hospital and medical expenses. Benefits are payable for 52 weeks for covered expenses which might begin during the 90-day period following separation from active duty. Members of the family are also eligible. The plan will protect you in this country or anywhere in the world.

YOUR ASSETS

You should make a list of your assets and keep these records and all important papers in a safe place available to a member of your family or lawyer. These records must be updated as the need arises—cost of living changes, bonuses, new investments. You should keep any record of a financial setback such as a loss in bond or stock sales which may be deducted in the profit-loss evaluation of your IRS tax. There should be car, life, fire, property, and insurance records, and your all-important military records; any citizenship papers or change-of-name records; mortgages, abstracts, stocks or bonds, birth and death certificates of all members of the family, burial instructions, and your will.

This list should be talked over with your wife (or husband) in order that he or she fully understands what can or cannot be done later on. Some men, usually those of an older generation, have "protected" their wives from some of the realities of life—and this has done her no favor. When she cannot carry on by herself, then someone has to do it for her or help her on matters that she probably wishes she knew how to do herself.

PROOF OF AGE

Anyone who has lost a birth certificate, or who never received one, can apply for proof of age from the U.S. Bureau of the Census. When they find that the person's age was recorded during a certain year, a document will be sent showing the proper age. This can be used to get a delayed birth certificate from state officials. And it can also be used as a substitute that is now accepted by state or federal agencies and private industry. A fee of $7.50 is charged, plus $1 for each additional copy of the transcript.

When you need proof for Social Security, get an application at a local Social Security office. Otherwise write to: Personal Census Service Branch, Bureau of the Census, Pittsburg, Kansas 66762.

FUNERAL EXPENSES

For retired personnel, the Veterans Administration pays $250 when interment is in a national cemetery in a nonservice-connected death, or $400 in a private cemetery in a nonservice-connected death. When the cause of death was service connected, $800 is paid in either a national or private cemetery. Also, Social Security provides approximately $255 to the next of kin when the deceased was eligible.

Retired personnel do not receive transportation/costs either for the deceased or for themselves. The VA will pay the cost of transporting the remains of any veteran who was hospitalized or in a nursing home (or its equivalent) of a VA facility, or at VA expense, or was in transit to or from the hospital or facility.

A headstone or grave marker, or urn, and an American flag are provided for the service at a national cemetery. For the grave of a military man or woman in a civilian or private cemetery, a headstone or grave marker will be provided through the services of the Commanding Officer, United States Army, Memorial Affairs Agency, Washington, D.C. 20315.

YOUR WILL

A well-thought-out will is one of the most important legal papers that you will ever write. It must be witnessed. Your will gives you, the testator, the right to leave your property to whomever you wish.

When a person dies without a will, he is said to die intestate. This means that any property will be distributed in accordance with the laws of your state, with the court appointing an administrator for this purpose. This is both expensive and time consuming.

Some husbands and wives have joint wills, leaving their estate to each other. If you think that you do not need to make out a will— possibly having no children or great riches—then consider the fact that if you and your wife (or husband) were killed in an accident, your property would be disposed of by law in the line of descendancy, perhaps going to someone you may not know very well or care for.

When you make out a will before you retire, the legal assistance officer can help you. When you write it after retirement and live at a distance from a military installation, you may write to your military department which furnishes retirees with handbooks on this and many other subjects. Otherwise, a civilian attorney can help you; he will be up to date on the laws of your state.

In drawing up a will you name an executor or executrix (usually your spouse) to carry out its provisions. The will must be kept in a safe place known to the executor, your lawyer, or the person charged with this responsibility. In cases of emergency, say on a battlefield or following an accident, a will can be written and witnessed by those nearby. One or more witnesses are required; the number depends upon the laws of your state—of which you should be aware.

When the time comes, the will is probated. The executor or person named files the will in the office of the Clerk of the Probate Court, Orphans Court, or Register of Wills, as the office may be called in various parts of the country.

POWER OF ATTORNEY

A power of attorney is a legal document whereby you give another person the power to act for you either in a single transaction or in all transactions. He is known as your "attorney in fact." To grant this power is something you should carefully consider.

The occasions when you might need to appoint a power of attorney might be when you will be out of the state or country for a time and business must be attended to; in cases of serious illness, senility, blindness, or when you are living temporarily or permanently in a nursing home and are unable to handle business affairs.

Although almost all cases in connection with a power of attorney are honorable transactions, it is possible in extreme cases of abuse for your name to be pledged to loans or mortgages and your property sold for any amount regardless of its worth. Therefore, it is very important that you are careful in granting this power; when able, you should first discuss this with a legal assistance officer or civilian attorney.

THE LIVING WILL

The *living-will*—the right to die with dignity—is a document that you may sign, stating that you do not want to have your life prolonged artificially after a physician decides that there is no hope for recovery. Members of your family, your doctor, and your lawyer should have copies.

Such a document does *not* give anyone the right to end the life of another in a "mercy killing," but it does give permission to a doctor to stop using any artificial means, such as a machine attached to an electrical outlet, or medications, to prolong life.

Such a document is thus an act of compassion to spare the family the suffering, anguish, and expense of prolonging the heartbeat when death is inevitable. It is *not* a document of suicide, and should be written while you are in sound mind—preferably when in good health—to prevent questions being raised later.

You may receive a free copy of the Living Will by writing to: Concern For Dying, 250 West 57th Street, New York, N. Y. 10019. However, a dollar for each copy ordered would help defray Council expenses and would be appreciated.

In September 1976, California became the first state to legalize the "Right to Die" of a terminally ill patient.

Service Organization

CHAPTER 46

The Armed Forces

As a serviceman or servicewoman, you are thoroughly indoctrinated in the structure and customs and traditions of your own service. You know the general structure of the armed forces, and a great deal about the other services, since you all work together as a team for the security of this country. For those who have been out of uniform for some time, and for members of service families, the following should prove informative.

THE CHIEF EXECUTIVE

As the Chief Executive, the President of the United States is the Commander in Chief of the armed forces. In matters of national security he is advised by the Department of Defense which, in turn, is advised by several other agencies, including the National Security Council which directs the basic military legislation of the nation.

The total numerical strength of the armed forces is over 2,200,000 men and women on active duty, including cadets and midshipmen.

THE DEPARTMENT OF DEFENSE (DOD)

The Department of Defense is headed by the Secretary of Defense, a civilian of cabinet rank appointed by the President. There are three military departments—the Army, Navy, and Air Force. The Marines are an integral party of the Navy and in times of war the Coast Guard is under Navy jurisdiction. Each military department has a civilian secretary who is responsible for the personnel, equipment, and doctrine of his service. These are the Secretary of the Army, the Secretary of the Navy, and the Secretary of the Air Force. There are two Deputy Secretaries of Defense, and there are Assistant Secretaries for various agencies.

To the average person the obvious question might arise: how do the services avoid getting in each other's way and duplicating manpower or workloads?

One answer is the publication of a DoD document sometimes called the "functions paper" which furthers efficiency and planning in each of the services. The basic functions are stated in broad terms in federal law (Title 10 U.S.C.) stating that the Air Force is to be "organized, trained, and equipped primarily for prompt and sustained air offensive and defensive operations." The Army is for the operation on land and the Navy for sustained combat at sea. The major purpose of the law and the functions paper is to achieve the best possible combat effectiveness, economy, specialization, and unified control of the armed forces, without duplication.

THE NATIONAL SECURITY ACT

The National Security Act of 1947 was enacted after World War II for the purpose of reorganizing the military establishment of the United States, which was facing world-wide responsibilities following the war.

The Act established the Joint Chiefs of Staff as a permanent body within the military establishment; it established the Department of Defense; it separated the Air Force from the Army by forming the Department of the Air Force.

THE JOINT CHIEFS OF STAFF (JCS)

The group to be called the Joint Chiefs of Staff came into being shortly after Pearl Harbor. President Franklin D. Roosevelt and Prime Minister Winston Churchill made the decision to establish a supreme Anglo-American military body for the strategic direction of World War II. The American chiefs of staff needed to discuss procedures among themselves before meeting with the British officers, and they met regularly though informally. Soon the group became known as the "Joint Chiefs of Staff."

The JCS is composed of the Chief of Staff of the Army, the Chief of Staff of the Air Force, the Chief of Naval Operations. In June 1952 the Commandant of the Marine Corps was given co-equal status with other members of the JCS, on matters pertaining to the Corps.

The Chairman of the Joint Chiefs of Staff is appointed by the President on a rotating basis among the services. Each service chief is responsible for keeping the secretary of his military department fully informed about the activities of the JCS.

UNIFIED AND SPECIFIED COMMANDS

A unified command has a broad mission under a single commander with components from two or more services.

A specified command is composed of forces from one service. In the chain of command both commands are under the advice of the JCS.

UNIFIED COMMANDS

U.S. Alaskan Command has two components, the U.S. Army, Alaska, and the Alaskan Air Command. Its role is to safeguard the North American continent.

U.S. Atlantic Command is responsible for all joint U.S. military action in the Atlantic Ocean area. The Commander in Chief controls all U.S. Fleet and Fleet Marine Forces in the area, and is also Supreme Allied Commander, Atlantic. The command staff is composed of senior military officers from all services.

The *Continental Air Defense Command* is made up of U.S. air defense forces. CONAD and NORAD are under the command of the same Air Force general who also heads the Air Force Aerospace Defense Command. The North American Air Defense Command includes both the U.S. Air Force Aerospace Defense Command and the Canadian Forces Air Defense Command and is responsible for the air defense of the U.S. and Canada.

The *U.S. European Command* is located in Germany and is the senior military headquarters in Europe. It is composed of the U.S. Army Europe, the U.S. Air Forces Europe and the U.S. Naval Forces Europe. The Commander in Chief also commands assigned Military Assistance Advisory Groups (MAAG) and Missions in Europe and North Africa.

The *U.S. Pacific Command* has the responsibility of defending the U.S. against attack throughout the Pacific. The principal components are U.S. Army Pacific, U.S. Pacific Fleet, and Pacific Air Forces. There are subordinate unified commanders, also chiefs of U.S. Military Assistance and Advisory Groups.

U.S. Readiness Command is composed of six divisions of the Army Forces Command and about 50 tactical air squadrons of the Tactical Air

Command. They deal quickly and efficiently with any threat as it arises, and also are on call to respond to humanitarian and mercy missions anywhere and at any time.

The *U.S. Southern Command* provides the defense of the Panama Canal, and offers assistance to Latin American countries. The Commander in Chief has a joint staff of Army, Navy, Air Force, and Marine personnel.

SPECIFIED COMMAND

The Strategic Air Command, under the Air Force, maintains an airborne command post over the central U.S. which could take control of all bombers and missiles in the event underground and alternate command posts were destroyed. A flying command-post aircraft has been airborne around the clock since 3 February 1961.

COMMISSIONING PROGRAMS

There are several ways for men and women to acquire a commission in the armed forces: by attending one of the service academies; by joining an ROTC program in college; by attending one of the various officer candidate schools which are open to college graduates and qualified enlisted personnel; and by direct appointment—usually offered to highly trained professionals in the medical and allied health sciences and legal or religious fields.

WOMEN IN THE SERVICES

It took a very long time for women to be accepted in the armed forces. It took a long time for them to be integrated into the services, as they are today, with opportunity for advancement in rank and for commands once available only to men. Assignments are the same with the exception of those in direct or close combat areas, aboard ships, or in isolated stations. Today's servicewomen are an important part of the work force in the Department of Defense.

In 1968 women officers became eligible to attend the senior service colleges, such as the Army War College. Women are now selected in competition with their male counterparts for attendance at command and staff colleges as well as the senior service colleges.

In 1976 women were admitted to the service academies for the first time. The first women cadets to attend the Maritime academies entered Kings Point in 1974.

A limited number of qualified women are admitted to flight schools in the services. Upon graduation they are assigned to noncombat planes or areas. There are an estimated 175,000 women now serving in the four military services.

UNIFORMED SERVICES UNIVERSITY
OF THE HEALTH SCIENCE

A university for the purpose of training men and women to become military medical doctors and specialists is located on the grounds of the Naval Medical Center at Bethesda, Maryland.

The Uniformed Services University of the Health Sciences and its School of Medicine became a reality in September 1972, when the 92nd Congress passed an act establishing the university for the preparation of medical students to serve in the three military departments and the Public Health Service. Studies lead to the practice of curative and preventative medicine on a global scale in both peacetime and war.

The first class of 31 students entered in the fall of 1976, with studies at the Armed Forces Institute of Pathology, located at the Walter Reed Army Medical Center, until the facilities are completed in 1980.

College graduates not over 28 years of age are eligible for the School of Medicine. Upon graduation with a Doctor of Medicine degree, they spend their first year as interns in military hospitals and then take further specialty training. Graduates are obligated for seven years' duty as officers in the Medical Corps.

Most of the clinical experience is at the three military medical teaching facilities in the greater Washington area: the Walter Reed Army Medical Center, the National Naval Medical Center, and the Malcolm Grow USAF Medical Center. Clinical electives are provided by Wilford Hall USAF Medical Center in San Antonio, Texas. Additional educational and research training is available at leading research institutes.

CHAPTER 47

The U.S. Army

WHEN THE CONTINENTAL ARMY was established on 14 June 1775, it was already more than a year older than the Declaration of Independence. The Continental Congress appointed Colonel George Washington as Commander in Chief of the Regular Army and the volunteer militia. Farmers, merchants, and craftsmen were the first volunteers, carrying a variety of hunting weapons and family firearms. The original ten companies have grown to today's force of over 785,000 men and women on active duty.

Today, the Army's force of 16 combat divisions has no distance limitations. The Army is capable of airborne deployment to any location in the world within a matter of hours, with the most sophisticated equipment for infantry, airborne, mechanized, and amphibious operations.

DEPARTMENT OF THE ARMY

The Secretary of the Army is responsible for the Army establishment. There is an Under Secretary, and Assistant Secretaries for Financial Management, Installation and Logistics, Manpower and Reserve Affairs, Research and Development, and Civil Works. Also a General Counsel, Administrative Assistant, Chiefs of Information and Legislative Liaison, and various offices and assistants. His principal advisor is the Army Chief of Staff.

ORGANIZATION

The Army Chief of Staff is a member of the Joint Chiefs of Staff. In his office are a Vice Chief, the Director of the Army Staff, and the Ballistic Missile Defense Program Manager.

The Army division is the basic unit of ground combat power. There are five types: Infantry, Armor, Mechanized, Airborne, and Air Assault.

MAJOR U.S. COMMANDS

The following specialized commands are within the United States:

The *U.S. Army Forces Command* at Fort McPherson, Georgia. Under this command are the First U.S. Army at Fort Meade, Maryland; Fifth U.S. Army at Fort Sam Houston, Texas, and Sixth U.S. Army, Presidio of San Francisco, California.

U.S. Army Training and Doctrine Command at Fort Monroe, Virginia.

U.S. Army Health Services Command, Fort Sam Houston, Texas.

U.S. Army Materiel Command, Washington, D.C.

Military District of Washington, D.C.

U.S. Army Communications Command, Fort Huachuca, Arizona.

U.S. Army Criminal Investigation Command, Washington, D.C.

U.S. Army Recruiting Command, Fort Sheridan, Illinois.

OVERSEAS COMMANDS

The Army components of Unified Commands include: *U.S. Army Europe, U.S. Army Forces Readiness Command*, the *U.S. Army Japan*, and the *Eighth U.S. Army* in Korea.

THE U.S. MILITARY ACADEMY

On 4 July 1802, ten cadets enrolled in the U.S. Military Academy at West Point, New York, which had been established by an act of Congress and signed by President Jefferson the preceding March. Almost three decades earlier, the strategic importance of the location of West Point on the Hudson River had led General George Washington to place a garrison of American Revolutionary troops there to stop British efforts to control river navigation.

Today, approximately 4,800 young men and women compose the Corps of Cadets, with 118 women entering the academy for the first time in July 1976. Upon completion of the four-year course, the graduates receive Bachelor of Science degrees and commissions as second lieutenants in the U.S. Army. The academy colors are black, gold, and gray; the motto is *Duty, Honor, Country.* The official song is "Alma Mater," and the mascot is the army mule. The reservation encompasses 16,000 acres.

The fourth classmen (Plebes) have a continuous indoctrination course during their first year. By year's end the new third classman (Yearling) leaves the reservation immediately after Graduation Week and then returns to spend two months at Camp Buckner just outside West Point. There they are introduced to the modern Army and put to practice the unit tactics that have been taught.

Second classmen (Cows) undergo an intensive summer training program, with some cadets spending three weeks at Airborne School at Fort Benning, Georgia, which qualifies them as parachutists. Others enter Range School at Fort Benning, or attend Flight School at Fort Rucker, Alabama. Still others attend Jungle School in Alaska. A month is spent in the Army Orientation Program with active army units in this country, Europe, Panama, Alaska, and Hawaii.

The first classmen take over a number of responsibilities their final summer. Some help in the training of the plebes, while others aid in the training of the third class at Camp Buckner. The year brings to a conclusion the intensive courses of study in the sciences and humanities, with leadership stressed.

WOMEN IN THE ARMY

On 14 May 1942, Congress enacted a law establishing the Women's Army Auxiliary Corps because of the shortage of manpower in the Army. By a subsequent act, the name was changed to Women's Army Corps, and the women were called "Wacs."

During World War II, more than 140,000 women served in the Corps in this country, Europe, Africa, the Southwest Pacific, China, India, Hawaii, the Philippines, and Alaska.

At the end of the war, the Army was faced with the loss of its women soldiers and asked Congress to make the WAC a permanent part of the military establishment. By Public Law 625, the Women's Army Corps became a component of the regular Army and Army Reserve of the United States in 1947.

Twenty years later restrictions, which had been imposed earlier, were removed on strength, promotion, and length of service for retirement; and women were permitted to enter the National Guard. In 1972 the AROTC programs were opened to women.

Women officers are assigned to major headquarters such as Training and Doctrine Command at Fort Monroe; Forces Command at Fort McPherson; Health Services Command at Fort Sam Houston, and U.S. Army Europe and Pacific Commands. They are eligible to command any type of unit other than those having combat or direct combat-support missions.

A "FIRST"

The first women to serve officially in the armed forces were a group of nurses who were with the U.S. Army under contract in the Spanish American War, without military status. In 1901 Congress recognized the services of the nurses by establishing the Army Nurse Corps within the Medical Department of the Army, without rank, officer status, equal pay, retirement or veterans benefits. In World War I, the demands for manpower created the opportunity for women to do work other than nursing, which relieved men for combat.

CHAPTER 48

The U.S. Navy

A LITTLE-KNOWN GROUP of ships called "Washington's Navy" preceded the founding of the Continental Navy on 13 October 1775. General Washington was concerned with the need for supplies and ammunition to continue the siege of the British in Boston. By using funds provided for his Army, the future first President assembled a fleet of eight vessels to capture some urgently needed supplies.

After the Continental Congress authorized a Navy, a naval committee was ordered to fit out a number of ships, and the 24-gun ship *Alfred* and the 20-gun *Columbus* were ready in late December. The first Commander in Chief of the eight-ship fleet was Esek Hopkins, who put to sea in February 1776. Serving as first lieutenant aboard the flagship *Alfred* was John Paul Jones. In all, the Continental Navy never numbered more than 3,000 men at any one time, and had a total of 123 officers.

Today's electronic, supersonic, and nuclear Navy has come a long way from yesterday's sloops of war and ironclads. The *USS Nimitz* can accommodate over 6,000 men—twice the number who served at any one time in the Continental Navy. Today, some 540,000 officers and men are on active duty.

THE DEPARTMENT OF THE NAVY

The Secretary of the Navy heads the naval establishment. In his immediate office are the Under Secretary, and Assistant Secretaries for

Financial Management, Installations and Logistics, Manpower and Reserve Affairs, and Research and Development.

Command flows down from the Chief of Naval Operations through the Fleet Commanders to all bases and ships of the Fleet, and from the Commandant of the Marine Corps to the various forces and commands. The Marine Corps is an integral part of the U.S. Navy, and in times of war the U.S. Coast Guard comes under naval jurisdiction.

ORGANIZATION

The Chief of Naval Operations (CNO) is the principal naval adviser to the Secretary of the Navy; he is a member of the Joint Chiefs of Staff. The office of the CNO includes the Vice Chief and Deputy CNOs for Plans, Policy, and Operations; Air Warfare; Submarine Warfare; Surface Warfare; Logistics, and Manpower.

OPERATING FORCES AND COMMANDS

The Operating Forces of the Navy include the several fleets, seagoing forces, district forces, Fleet Marine Forces, and the Military Sealift Command. Ships of the Operating Forces are organized in three systems: Type Commands, Fleet Commands, and Task Forces.

Type Commands are the destroyers, submarines, mine and amphibious vessels, which are subdivided into flotillas, squadrons, and divisions. Fleet Commanders have charge of the Pacific and Atlantic Fleets; a Task Force is made up of fleets divided into units, forces, elements, groups.

The major Fleet Commands are U.S. Atlantic Fleet, U.S. Pacific Fleet, U.S. Naval Forces Europe, and Military Sealift Command. The Fleet Marine Forces are under the jurisdiction of naval officers, but the discipline and training remain with the Marines.

There are a number of shore commands, and naval districts inside as well as outside the continental United States.

THE U.S. NAVAL ACADEMY

The U.S. Naval Academy was founded as the Naval School in 1845 at Annapolis, Maryland. The 10-acre site along the Severn River was a near-abandoned Army post, Old Fort Severn. In 1850 the school received its present name, and a four-year course of study with summer cruises replaced the five-year program in which one year was spent at sea. During the Civil War the midshipmen were quartered at Newport, Rhode Island, and again the Academy compound was used by the Army.

Today, on 329 acres including considerable landfill, about 4,800 young men and women comprise the Brigade of Midshipmen. The first 81 women to enter came in July 1976. The Academy colors are navy blue and gold, the mascot is Bill the Goat. The official song is "Navy Blue and Gold."

The fourth classmen, or Plebes, undergo an indoctrination program their first year; the third classmen, or Youngsters, have six to eight weeks at sea training with the fleet their first summer. Second classmen receive professional training and familiarization in warfare specialities, with visits to the submarine school at New London, Connecticut, the Surface Warfare School at Newport, Rhode Island, and the air facility at Pensacola, Florida. Introduction to amphibious assault is provided by the Marines. During their last summer, first classmen perform the duties of junior officers with the fleet.

Graduates receive a Bachelor of Science degree and commissions as ensigns in the Navy, with a certain quota commissioned second lieutenants in the Marine Corps. The majority of ensigns are line officers, with duty in aircraft carriers, cruisers, destroyers, nuclear power programs, flight or submarine training.

WOMEN IN THE NAVY

At the height of World War II, some 86,000 women were serving in the Navy as Women Accepted for Volunteer Emergency Service—WAVES. The term is now inappropriate in its definition since women are a part of the regular Navy and not "accepted for volunteer service." However, the term remains popular if not official. Today, there are approximately 20,000 women on active duty, of which about 4,000 are officers.

In 1942, Congressional legislation authorized the enlistment and commissioning of women in the Naval Reserve, and two years later women were permitted to serve in Hawaii and Alaska. Since the Women's Armed Forces Integration Act of 1948, women have served not as a separate corps but as an integral part of the naval establishment. Legislation in 1967 repealed the restrictions on rank.

In World War I, by act of 29 August 1916 which set up the Naval Reserve Force, Navy and Coast Guard women were designated Yeoman (F), called "Yeomanette," and Marine (F) called "Marinette." They served in clerical and administrative duties as draftsmen, fingerprint experts, and recruiters.

Today a career progression plan for unrestricted line officers is: 1, basic management for lieutenants; 2, middle management for lieutenant commanders; 3, upper management for commanders, and 4, key management for captains whose commands would be at major shore establishments, project management, and Washington headquarters.

Women are interchangeable with men in most shore and overseas assignments, but may not serve in combat areas or ships of the fleet. Several women officers completed the first flight training as female naval aviators in 1973 when they flew helicopters and propeller-driven aircraft in noncombat search and rescue and transport missions.

CHAPTER 49

The U.S. Marines

PRIOR TO THE American Revolution able-bodied men from the colonies had been serving as Marines in America—but in support of British operations. Four colonial battalions were raised in 1740 to fight in England's war with Spain. During the Seven Years' War (French and Indian War), the colonials again served as Marines in support of the British against the French.

In October 1775, the Continental Congress directed General George Washington to secure two armed vessels from Massachusetts, place them on the "Continental risque and pay," and use them for the capture of ammunition. He was also to give orders for the "proper encouragement to the Marines and seamen" who served in the vessels. Records indicate that this is the first time that Congress ever mentioned "Marines."

Throughout the Revolution, three types of Marines fought for their country: the Continental or Regular Marines, Marines of the state navies, and Marines of the privateers. But it was the Continental Marines who were officially charged by Congress with fulfilling a military role in the fight for independence. This came about on 10 November 1775 by a resolution formally establishing two battalions of Marines to be distinguished by the name "American Marines."

Thus the Marine Corps was born almost eight months before the Declaration of Independence was signed. Then, as now, they were charged ". . . to serve to advantage by Sea when required. . . ." Some 196,000 men and women are on active duty today.

ORGANIZATION

The National Security Act reaffirmed the Marine Corps as a separate service within the Navy Department. The Commandant of the Marine Corps is a member of the Joint Chiefs of Staff on matters pertaining to the Marines. Marine Corps Headquarters is in Washington, D.C.

There is an Assistant Commandant; a Chief of Staff; a Sergeant Major; and a number of Deputy Chiefs of Staff and directors.

COMMANDS

The Marine Corps is composed of *Operating Forces* and a *Supporting Establishment* which emphasize air-ground operations both ashore and afloat. The Operating Forces include three active divisions, three aircraft wings, as well as combat and support units.

The largest of the Operating Forces is the Fleet Marine Force, Pacific which has two divisions, two aircraft wings, and a supporting Force Troops command. Fleet Marine Force, Atlantic commands the Operating Forces on the East Coast. This is made up of a division and aircraft wings and a supporting Force Troops command.

The Marine Corps Reserve includes the 4th Marine Division and the 4th Marine Aircraft Wing. This Division is the Corps reserve force in readiness and has cadre headquarters at Camp Pendleton, California.

The Supporting Establishment has these Districts: 1st, at Long Island, New York; 4th, at Philadelphia, Pennsylvania; 6th, at Atlanta, Georgia; 8th, at New Orleans, Louisiana; 9th, at Overland Park, Kansas, and 12th, at Treasure Island, San Francisco, California. Each District has bases, camps, and unit training centers which provide training and logistical support for the Corps.

OFFICER CANDIDATE PROGRAMS

Commissions in the Marine Corps are received in these areas:

1. *Marine Corps Officer Candidate Class* (OCC). For men and women college graduates. Qualified enlisted personnel are eligible.

2. *Marine Platoon Leaders Class.* For undergraduate college students.

3. *Naval Reserve Officer Training Corps* (NROTC). For undergraduate students at various colleges and universities.

4. *U.S. Naval Academy.* A limited number of midshipmen (16-2/3 percent of the graduating class) may elect to go into the Marine Corps upon graduation.

College graduates who want to be aviators or ground officers are eligible for a reserve commission after completing a 12-week training and screening course, followed by advanced flight training. Undergraduates may take the naval aviator or naval flight officer program open to both Navy and Marine candidates.

The Marine Corps Development and Education Command is located at Quantico, Virginia, and includes the Development Center, the Marine Corps Education Center, and Long Range Study Panel. All new Marine officers, both men and women, receive basic training there.

WOMEN IN THE MARINES

Over 300 Reservists (Female) called "Marinettes," served during World War I, mainly in clerical jobs at Marine Headquarters and at the Navy Department. Some were assigned to Marine recruiting. About 20,000 women served in World War II when, as now, they shared the name Marine with the men. Today 3,200 women are an integral part of the Corps.

Officers and enlisted women are now eligible for assignments until recently only available for men. This came about after a successful pilot program was conducted at 1st Marine Division, Camp Pendleton, California, and the 2nd Marine Aircraft Wing at Cherry Point, North Carolina.

Women Marines are assigned to stateside divisions, aircraft wings, force service regiments, and force troops headquarters in rear echelon billets. They serve overseas in many countries.

Ever-increasing numbers are assigned to such nontraditional jobs for women as engineering and electronics, with a captain currently serving as a military judge and a lieutenant commanding a military police platoon. The majority continue to serve in positions of administration, communications, supply, and disbursing.

THE U.S. MARINE BAND

Traditionally referred to as "The President's Own," the United States Marine Band dates from the birthday of the Marine Corps, although it technically came into existence a day later—on 11 July 1775, when in 1798, President John Adams signed a bill creating the Marine "Musicians," and the fife and drum were played when the Continental Marines were on the march. Generally, two drummers and one fifer were assigned to the Marine Guard in the ships of the early Navy.

The band made its first appearance in the White House at a New

Year's Day reception given by President Adams. Since Thomas Jefferson's day, the band has played at every presidential inauguration. Since 1805, the band has been quartered at Marine Barracks, and it was here that John Philip Sousa wrote many of his marches while leader of the band.

SILENT DRILL PLATOON

The Silent Drill Platoon, Marine Barracks, which is a part of the Ceremonial Guard Company, is made up of handpicked volunteers who perform precise military drills at evening parades and ceremonies.

The silent drill by 24 Marines is carried out without any verbal command with intricate movements in strict military cadence set by the crack of rifles when exchanged among the Marines. They perform regularly on Friday evenings at 9 P.M. in Washington, D.C., and these performances are frequently called "Moonlight Parades."

CHAPTER 50

The U.S. Air Force

THE U.S. AIR FORCE is the youngest member of the armed forces. The need for such a force was proven during World War II when the air offense and defense were major factors in the war's successful conclusion. About 590,000 men and women are now on active duty.

The Air Force started within the U.S. Army in August 1907, when one officer and two enlisted men were assigned to the newly established Aeronautical Division in the Office of the Chief Signal Officer. The division underwent a number of changes before being formally created in 1920 as the Air Service, a combatant arm of the Army. Six years later the service formally became the Army Air Corps.

Early in World War II, the corps became the Army Air Forces, with General H. H. Arnold the commanding general. Following the war, President Harry S. Truman signed the National Security Act of 1947, which not only established a new defense organization—the Department of Defense—but a separate Department of the Air Force coequal with the Army and Navy. Thus, there were established separate military departments for land, sea, and air.

ORGANIZATION

The Secretary of the Air Force is responsible for the affairs of the Department of the Air Force. His chief assistants are the Under Secretary and the Assistant Secretaries for Research and Development, Installations and Logistics, Financial Management, Manpower; an Administrative Assistant; General Counsel; and Directors of Information, Legislative Liaison, Space Systems, and Personnel Security.

The *Air Staff* consists of a Chief of Staff, a Vice Chief of Staff, and five Deputy Chiefs of Staff and other military and civilian specialists.

AIR FORCE STRUCTURE

The basic Air Force structure is: Flight (the lowest tactical echelon), Squadron, Group, Wing (the basic unit), Air Division, Numbered Air Force, and Major Command.

The major air commands and separate operating agencies under Headquarters, USAF, are:

Strategic Air Command (SAC), Offutt AFB, Omaha, Nebraska; the long-range strike force.

Aerospace Defense Command (ADC), at Ent AFB, Colorado Springs, Colorado; responsible for the air defense of the United States, and a component of the Joint USA-Canadian North American Air Defense Command (NORAD).

Tactical Air Command (TAC), Langley AFB, Hampton, Virginia; insures readiness in worldwide air operations.

Air Force Communications Service (AFCS), Richards-Gebaur AFB, Missouri; traffic control.

Air University (AU), Maxwell AFB, Montgomery, Alabama; prepares officers for command or staff duties.

Military Airlift Command (MAC), Scott AFB, Illinois; gives global air transportation for armed forces personnel, air rescue.

Air Force Logistics Command (AFLC), Wright-Patterson AFB, Ohio, provides materials and supplies around the world.

Air Training Command (ATC), Randolph AFB, San Antonio, Texas, procures airmen for training.

Air Force Systems Command (AFSC), Andrews AFB, Maryland; responsible for up-to-date aerospace systems.

U.S. Air Force Security Service (USAFSS), Kelly AFB, San Antonio, Texas; handles security.

U.S. Air Forces in Europe (USAFE), is located at Ramstein AB, Germany.

U.S.A.F. Southern Command (USAFSO), at Albrook AFB, Canal Zone.

Pacific Air Forces (PACAF), at Hickam AFB, Hawaii.

Alaskan Air Command (AAC), at Elmendorf AFB, Alaska.

U.S. AIR FORCE ACADEMY

The Air Force Academy is located 12 miles north of Colorado Springs on 18,000 acres bordered on the west by the Rocky Mountains. The Cadet Wing is composed of approximately 4,800 young men and women, with the first 158 women cadets entering in June 1976. Graduates receive a baccalaureate degree and commissions as second lieutenants in the Air Force.

The Academy was established by Congress on 1 April 1954. The first class of 306 cadets was sworn in on 11 July 1955 at Lowry Air Force Base, Denver, while new buildings were under construction. On 29 August 1958, cadets moved into their new quarters, and the first class graduated the following year.

The fourth classmen, Doolies, have an indoctrination period upon entering the academy. Third classmen have survival, resistance, and escape training. Parachuting, lightplane flying, underwater demolition, and scuba training are held during the final two years.

The academy has a planetarium and an observatory, and its own airstrip which serves the lightplane, sailplane, and parachuting activities. There are pilot and navigator indoctrination programs.

Academy colors are blue and silver, and their official song is "The Air Force Song." The falcon is the mascot.

AIR UNIVERSITY

The Air University is a vast complex responsible for the professional education and research in specific fields for Air Force officers. The major units are at Maxwell AFB, Montgomery, Alabama, the site of the Wright brothers early flying school.

Some of its schools are the Air War College, the Air Command and Staff College, the Squadron Officer School, the Air University Institute for Professional Development, and the Air Force Institute of Technology. The newest of the professional schools under the jurisdiction of the Air University is the Air Force Senior Noncommissioned Officer Academy, at Gunter AFB, which prepares chief and senior master sergeants for positions of greater responsibility.

WOMEN IN THE AIR FORCE

During World War II, before the U.S. Air Force was established, approximately 40,000 women served with the Army Air Force as Air-Wacs. More than 1,000 Women Air Service Pilots (WASPS) ferried aircraft, towed targets, and taught flying during the war.

The women's Armed Forces Integration Act of 18 June 1949 not only recognized the contributions of women in the services but separated the Air-Wacs from the Army by creating the Women in the Air Force as a part of the new U.S. Air Force. Today there are approximately 30,000 women in the service.

Women officers lead units comprised of both sexes, and are eligible for assignments as wing commander and recruiting group commander. They are assigned to such posts as space systems, nuclear research, computer technology, and are serving as instructors at the Air Force Academy. As in the other services, Air Force women are not assigned to combat areas.

CHAPTER 51

The U.S. Coast Guard

THE U.S. COAST GUARD is a branch of the armed forces of the United States. It is also the principal federal peacetime agency for maritime safety and law enforcement. It has a dual role: in peacetime the Coast Guard operates in the Department of Transportation; during times of war it is part of the Navy. But in war or peace, the Coast Guard remains an armed force at all times.

The history of the Coast Guard goes back to the beginning of this country when colonists settled along the coasts and constructed lighthouses for the safety of men and their boats. The oldest recorded lighthouse is the Boston Light built in 1716.

In terms of continuous service, the Coast Guard is the oldest of the nation's seagoing armed forces. Smuggling was widespread and Alexander Hamilton, the first Secretary of the Treasury, asked Congress for a fleet of armed revenue cutters for the collection of tonnage dues and import duties from ships entering American waters.

Hamilton, who is called the founder of the Coast Guard, requested "that there be ten boats, two for the coasts of Massachusetts and New Hampshire; one for Long Island Sound; one for New York; one for the Bay of Delaware; two for the Chesapeake; one for North Carolina; one for South Carolina; and one for Georgia." The bill was passed on 4 August 1790, with the ten heavy-keeled schooners each costing $1000. The service was called "The system of cutters."

For nearly eight years this fleet of cutters was the young nation's only navy. Then in 1798 the regular Navy was organized. The following

538

year, due to hostilities with French privateers, Congress ordained that "Revenue Cutters shall, whenever the President of the United States shall so direct, cooperate with the Navy of the United States."

Thus began the early association of the Coast Guard and the United States Navy.

In these early years the Coast Guard was known as the "Revenue Marine," the "Revenue-Marine Service," and the "Revenue Service." In 1863 the title became the Revenue Cutter Service. By 1915 the Life Saving Service was merged with the Revenue Cutter Service to form the U.S. Coast Guard.

By 1939, the Bureau of Lighthouses was transferred to the Coast Guard; a few years later the Bureau of Marine Inspection and Navigation became a part of the service. About 38,000 men and women are on active duty.

ORGANIZATION

During peacetime the Commandant of the Coast Guard is responsible to the Secretary of Transportation. On 1 April 1967, this responsibility—after 177 years—was transferred from the Treasury Department to the newly established Department of Transportation.

In times of national emergency the Commandant is responsible to the Secretary of the Navy and the Chief of Naval Operations. The Secretaries of Transportation and of the Navy are authorized to make available to each other such personnel, vessels, and equipment as are advisable.

Coast Guard Headquarters is located in Washington, D.C. There are two Area Offices, Atlantic and Pacific; 12 District Offices, and 15 Headquarters Units.

The Commandant is assisted by a Vice Commandant, a Chief of Staff, and several heads of offices. The peacetime manpower is about 40,000 active-duty men and women, both officers and enlisted personnel. Besides enforcing federal laws on shore and at sea the Coast Guard maintains constant readiness for times of emergency.

The marine safety of American vessels, including their construction and inspection, is a major responsibility of the service. Lifesaving operations have been in effect since 1785.

U.S. COAST GUARD ACADEMY

The U.S. Coast Guard Academy, founded in 1876, is located on a 110-acre site along the Thames River at New London, Connecticut. The first "school of instruction" in 1877 had nine cadets quartered in the old refitted schooner *Dobbin.* The following year the bark *Chase* was built as a cadet ship; when it put into winter quarters at New Bedford, Massachusetts, the school continued in a sail loft.

A few years later the *Chase* was winter quartered at Arundel Cove in Curtis Bay, Maryland, and a two-story wooden school was built in the repair yard. In 1910 the school moved into an old Army coastal defense post, Fort Trumbull, at New London.

The Corps of Cadets is composed of approximately 1100 young men and women. The first 40 women were admitted in July 1976. The academy motto is *Scientiae Cedit Mare* (The Sea Yields to Knowledge). Colors are royal blue and white. Their song is "Coast Guard Fore'er." During summer months the cadets train in the three-masted auxiliary bark *Eagle,* and in cutters. The *Eagle* was one of the many tall ships that took part in the 1976 Bicentennial celebration.

Upon graduation the cadets receive a Bachelor of Science degree and are commissioned ensigns in the U.S. Coast Guard, with a five-year service commitment. Appointments to the academy are made on the basis of an annual nationwide competitive examination; there are no Congressional appointments.

WOMEN IN THE COAST GUARD

Coast Guard women served with Navy women as Yeomanettes during World War I. But it was not until World War II that Coast Guard women came into their own. Then, 15 officers and 153 enlisted Navy women were trained at the Coast Guard Academy, making up the first contingent of SPARS.

In December 1973, legislation abolished the restriction that women could only serve in the Coast Guard Reserve, and a new program for enlistment and commissioning in the regular Coast Guard was begun.

Since 1974, the designation SPARS went out of official existence, but will not soon be forgotten. The designation was coined from the initial letters of the Coast Guard motto: *Semper Paratus*—Always Ready. A female Coast Guard Reserve captain currently is in an advisory capacity to the Commandant of the Coast Guard on matters pertaining to the Women in the Guard, as they are now called.

Women are eligible for assignment to all Coast Guard units other than floating units and isolated duty stations. They are serving at training commands, headquarters, district offices, and are among the first women from any service to be assigned to flight school at Pensacola, Florida. Upon completion of this training they are assigned to any operational aviation command in an unrestricted flying status.

CHAPTER 52

The Reserves

TODAY, THE SAFETY and defense of America depends upon its military and naval strength. In order to be prepared for any emergency at any time, the armed forces must have a backup of personnel trained for military duty as a bulwark to insure national and international security.

Fighting in the American Revolution lasted six years. After independence was won, the Army and Navy were so reduced that for a time the Continental Army had a strength of only 80 men and a few officers to guard the military supplies at West Point and Fort Pitt. The Navy fared no better.

RESERVE STRENGTH

Currently, there are approximately 260,000 men and women serving in the U.S. Army Reserve, and 400,000 in the National Guard; in the Navy there are 450, 000 Reserves; in the Marine Corps, 142,000; in the Air Force, 176,000 in the Reserve and about 95,000 in the Air National Guard. There are about 11,000 in the Coast Guard Reserve.

There are three categories of the Reserves: the Ready Reserve, with men and women available for immediate mobilization; the Standby Reserve, for those available only in times of national emergency; and the Retired Reserve who may be called back into service as needed.

Young men and women without prior military service may enlist in a reserve program by applying at any local organized reserve unit of the service of their choice. All programs require enlistees to serve some time on active duty for training, and upon completion of this basic training he or she returns to the local unit and attends training assemblies or drills throughout the year. There is a minimum of 48 assemblies/drills a year which usually are held on weekends or evenings; one weekend is the equivalent of four training drills; also a two-week summer refresher program is required. National Guard and Reserve pay is based on the armed forces pay scale for the grade and length of service.

THE NATIONAL GUARD

The Army and Air National Guards are volunteer military organizations within each state whose members train part-time for local and national protection. There are nearly 5,000 Guard units located in this country and in Puerto Rico, the District of Columbia, and the Virgin Islands.

The National Guard has a dual status: as a state organization its members can be ordered to active duty in times of local emergencies or disasters; and as reserve components of the U.S. Army and U.S. Air Force, they can be sent into active federal service as needed. Age limits for men and women are 17 to 34, and 17 to 35, respectively. Women may enter any Air or Army Guard unit that is not related to combat.

Intensive training—and later performance—include infantry, air defense, medical, and ordinance for the Army Guard; and air defense, air refueling, tactical fighter, and global training for the Air Guard. Officer candidates attend the ANG Academy of Military Science or the Army Guard OCS program.

COMMISSIONING PROGRAMS

There are several avenues leading to commissions in the services, other than the federal maritime (Merchant Marine) or service academies. Among them are the Officer Candidate Schools (OCS) for the Army, Navy, and Coast Guard; the Officer Training School (OTS) for the Air Force; the Marine Corps Officer Candidate Class (OCC); Aviation Officer Candidate (AOC) and Platoon Leaders Class (PLC) programs.

And there are the Reserve Officers Training Corps (ROTC) programs held in colleges and universities since 1916. In 1972 the programs were opened to women.

Currently, the ROTC consists of 528 Army, Navy, and Air Force units, with instruction in the Science or Aerospace Departments in the colleges or universities, military and private schools in this country and Puerto Rico and the District of Columbia. The training consists of two to five hours of military instruction each week while the students pursue an academic course leading to a baccalaureate degree. The cadets and midshipmen must be between 17 and 21 years of age, are subsidized, and wear uniforms in drills and at other military occasions.

There are various programs offered, both obligated and nonobligated. Students may compete nationally for a four-year scholarship, but there are also one-, two-, and three-year scholarships. The four-year program consists of a basic course for the first two years, and an advanced course for the junior and senior years. The purpose of the two-year course is to make eligible the transfer students from junior colleges or institutions where ROTC programs were not given. Then, the student may take a six-week summer training course in order to qualify for the advanced course.

Scholarship students are obligated to serve four years on active duty. Seniors may take flight training and go into the aviation program furnished by the service; upon graduation they serve three years. Nonobligated graduates serve three to six months on active duty, then join their reserve unit.

Army programs are held in some 287 colleges and universities. Air Force programs are held in some 173 institutions. The program for the Navy and Marines is the same for the first two years; then beginning with the junior year Marine courses are taught for those going into the Corps. Training is held in 58 colleges and universities.

Junior ROTC programs are available for high school students, and those in military schools at the secondary level. All services with the exception of the Coast Guard have student programs, with boys and girls required to be at least 14 years old and to complete at least 96 hours of training and study each year. There are approximately 180,000 students in the program.

WOMEN IN THE ROTC

The Air Force was the first to open the door for women in the ROTC in 1956. Due to the many restrictions—thus a low enrollment—the program ended in 1961.

Eight years later, the AFROTC again started a program for women, with fewer restrictions—such as those of marriage and pregnancy, which are no longer causes for disqualification. Also, there were opportunities for more challenging jobs. One of the first to enter the program when it opened at the University of Tennessee became a communications electronics engineer with the AF Communications Service at Richards-Gebaur AFB, Missouri.

Since then the enrollment of women in the ROTC programs has steadily increased. Today, women participate in 285 of the 287 host colleges that offer Army ROTC; 51 of the 58 colleges with Navy units, and 168 of the 173 Air Force units. Four-year scholarships, as well as the lesser scholarships, are offered to women as well as men.

THE CITADEL

It is not possible to list the many colleges and universities that have ROTC programs, but as an example, one college that has programs for all services is The Citadel, the Military College of South Carolina, located at Charleston.

The Citadel was founded in 1842 and derived its name from the old fortress in which it was first quartered. The fortress was first garrisoned by federal troops, then by state troops until they were replaced by 20 students who made up the first Corps of Cadets and who served as arsenal guards while pursuing their studies.

On 9 January 1861, before the firing on Fort Sumter, cadets manned the guns which drove back from the entrance to Charleston Harbor the *Star of the West*, a steamer sent by the federal government to relieve the fort. During the Civil War and afterwards the college buildings were used by troops, and not until 1882 did the rebuilt institution reopen. In 1918, the city of Charleston gave a tract of land adjacent to the Ashley River to the state for a greater Citadel, which was completed four years later on the present site. As the enrollment increased through the years, new buildings were added.

Citadel men have served in all wars since its founding. During World War II, over 99 percent of the approximately 4,000 undergraduates who attended the college during the war years served in the armed forces.

The Citadel is a liberal arts as well as a military college. It prepares young men for business or military careers, with Bachelor of Science, Art, or Engineering degrees granted. All cadets take four years of ROTC training—a requirement for graduation. To be eligible for a commission, the cadet must complete the basic course and then accept a contract during the advanced course in his third and fourth years. This contract is an agreement to serve on active duty up to two years or longer in the service of his choice. Cadets who major in chemistry, physics, or other highly specialized fields may receive a direct appointment.

In the Army military science program, senior cadets with ROTC contracts who demonstrate outstanding leadership and academic attributes are designated distinguished military students and offered commissions in the regular Army.

In the Air Force department of aerospace studies, the course covers the nature of war and traces the development of aerospace power during the first two years; during the last two years, the curriculum places additional emphasis on leadership and management.

In the Navy's department of naval science, the latest naval engineering, gun, missile, and underwater weapons systems are studied, as well as the principles of military leadership.

The social life of the cadets is varied. Parents Day and the ring hop are held in the fall; the Senior Week honors the graduates. The Summerall Guards, the precision drill platoon, highlights Corps Day which is held in honor of the birthday of the Corps of Cadets. A banquet for the fourth classmen is sponsored by the chaplain and the religious council, and there are mixers, harbor cruises in the college yawl, and varsity and intramural sports programs.

CHAPTER 53

The U.S. Merchant Marine

MERCHANT SHIPS have long plied the oceans of the world—long before organized navies were founded. During America's early years of growth between the Revolutionary and Civil Wars, much of the country's wealth was in its shipping and commerce. American ships were so numerous that England's supremacy of the sea was being challenged.

But the Civil War changed this growth. At the end of the war the merchant fleet, including coastwise shipping, was 60 percent of its pre-war size. Only 29 percent of the imports and exports were carried in American ships. Shipping had gone to foreign fleets and the American seamen were unprotected from exploitation by U.S. laws. For a long time the merchant marine was in the doldrums.

In a broad sense, the U.S. Merchant Marine is composed of all privately owned American flag vessels—both ocean-going and the smaller craft engaged in local river, harbor, and coastal work, and their personnel. At peace or in war, a strong Merchant Marine is vital in international commercial competition and for support of military forces which may be stationed throughout the world. During World War II, the Korean conflict, and in Vietnam over 98 percent of the troops and supplies reached the combat zone in ships—many of them merchant ships. The peak of participation was reached during WW II in the Murmansk run, when shipping lanes to Russia were cut off by the Germans, and American convoys were exposed to constant attack while carrying millions of tonnage across the oceans.

In 1970 a new federal program revitalized the U.S. Merchant Marine and today it is on the way to becoming one of the fastest and most efficient fleets in the world. The change is due to a subsidy program, with over 80 merchant ships under construction and an increase in industry employment.

MERCHANT MARINE OFFICERS

The responsibility for the safe operation of merchant vessels rests with the officers who are licensed in their specific capacity by the U.S. Coast Guard. A license is issued only after certain training or experience requirements are met, including a written examination.

After receiving his license, the new third mate or third assistant engineer may join a ship as a qualified junior officer. The third mate will progress by a licensing procedure to second mate, and eventually will become the ship's master; a third assistant engineer will become a second assistant engineer with the final step the chief engineer.

THE MARITIME SERVICE

The U.S. Maritime Service comes under the jurisdiction of the Department of Commerce. There is an Assistant Secretary of Commerce for Maritime Affairs, U.S. Maritime Administration, and a Deputy Assistant Secretary, with headquarters in Washington, D.C.

This service was a voluntary civilian training organization established in 1938 pursuant to the Merchant Marine Act of 1936, as amended, for the purpose of training licensed and unlicensed personnel for service in American merchant vessels. Although personnel were assigned ranks and ratings like members of the U.S. Coast Guard, they were not, and are not, members of the armed forces. At the present time the last vestiges of this program are the U.S. Merchant Marine Academy and the six State Maritime Academies.

These state academies are: California Maritime Academy, Maine Maritime Academy, Massachusetts Maritime Academy, State University of New York Maritime College, the Texas Maritime Academy of Texas A.&M. University, and the Great Lakes Maritime Academy of Northwestern Michigan College.

All academies combine formal academic studies with programs leading to careers as officers in the American Merchant Marine, career officers in the U.S. Navy and Coast Guard, or shore careers as admiralty lawyers, naval architects, marine insurance underwriters or oceanographers. At the conclusion of their training, a graduating midshipman or cadet receives a merchant marine license certifying his or her qualifications as a Third Mate, a Third Assistant Engineer, or in the case of a Dual License candidate, both. In addition, a graduate receives a Bachelor of Science degree and a commission as ensign in the U.S. Naval Reserve.

Specific Navy interest in maritime training stems from the national defense requirement that Merchant Marine officers are trained in naval procedures in order that they can work jointly in times of war—a "fourth arm of defense." The Navy provides naval science courses, the equivalent of the NROTC courses in colleges and universities. Federal authority and financial aid for the academies dates from the Act of Congress of 1874.

THE MARITIME ACADEMIES

THE STATE UNIVERSITY OF NEW YORK (SUNY) MARITIME COLLEGE

The New York Maritime College, located at Fort Schuyler, Bronx, New York, is the oldest of the maritime academies. Founded in 1875 as the Nautical School, it became so successful that the States of Pennsylvania, Massachusetts, California, Maine, Texas, and finally Michigan, founded their own academies.

The founding of this first maritime academy was due to a group of New York citizens who were alarmed at the worsening condition of the maritime service following the Civil War, and who appealed to the New York State Legislature. The first class of 26 young men—the required entrance age was between 15 and 19—boarded the sloop of war USS *St. Mary's*, berthed in the East River. The schoolship was later replaced by the USS *Newport*, both on loan from the Navy by Act of Congress.

Not until 1934 was a shore facility acquired, at the present site that once was an old pentagon-shaped Army post (the Pentagon in Washington, D.C. was later patterned after it). During World War II, the college was the training site for Naval Reserve officers and Merchant Marine cadets.

The Maritime College is one of 32 specialized colleges of the State University of New York. Most of the men and women students are enrolled in the four-year course as cadets in the Maritime Service program, with others in the NROTC unit that was established in 1974. A Master's Degree is available in transportation management or engineering. The curricula includes courses in meteorology, oceanography, nuclear science, and naval architecture. A multi-million dollar modernization program has been completed.

Cadets wear uniforms, participate in intercollegiate sports and in the intramural program, and have the advantage of cultural activities in New York City. On-the-job summer training is in the schoolship TS *Empire State.*

THE MASSACHUSETTS MARITIME ACADEMY

The second oldest of the maritime academies is the Massachusetts Maritime Academy, founded in 1891 as the Massachusetts Nautical Training School, located at Boston. In 1942 the school was moved to Buzzards Bay and given its present name. In 1964, legislation placed the academy within the Massachusetts State College system.

The first training ship was the USS *Enterprise,* loaned to the Commonwealth by the federal government in 1892, with the first class of 40 cadets going on board the following year.

The Corps of Cadets engage in varsity athletics and an intramural program. A new building program has been completed, and the enrollment has tripled in recent years. In 1975 the Academy was designated as a Commonwealth Marine Sciences Center. Cadets have summer training in TS *Bay State.*

THE CALIFORNIA MARITIME ACADEMY

In 1929 the California Maritime Academy was established as the California Nautical School. Located on the shores of the Carquinez Strait, the Academy has the advantage of being in the San Francisco Bay area with its cultural activities as well as the opportunity for the midshipmen to make trips in ocean-going vessels.

The Corps of Midshipmen includes women, and a four-year program leads to a baccalaureate degree and licensing. There are two core curricula—nautical industrial technology and marine engineering technology, as well as special schools and certifications in such fields as Navy firefighting and damage-control or as Coast Guard lifeboatmen or able seamen. The annual summer cruise is in TS *Golden Bear.*

THE MAINE MARITIME ACADEMY

The Maine Maritime Academy was founded in 1941 on the shores of Penobscot Bay at Castine, with the first class composed of 28 midshipmen. The Regiment of Midshipmen includes both men and women.

Following World War II the curriculum was expanded from 18 months to the present four-year program. Upon completion of the sophomore year, students in the nautical science and marine engineering programs may be assigned aboard merchant ships as cadets for a 60-day training period.

The midshipmen take part in team sports and such extracurricular activities as the scuba club, the propeller club, the precision drill team, or the "Singing Mariners," which makes an annual fall tour. Members of the faculty and the midshipmen, over a three-year period, built a tanker simulator for training in tanker operations, the only one of its kind in existence. This provides for the loading and discharging of liquid cargo under simulated shipboard conditions.

THE TEXAS MARITIME ACADEMY

The Texas Maritime Academy was established at Galveston in 1962. Since 1971 it has operated academically as a division of Moody College of Marine Sciences and Maritime Resources of Texas A.&M. University. Classes are held on Mitchell campus at Pelican Island as well as at Fort Crockett on Galveston Island.

The TS *Texas Clipper* serves uniformed cadets as classroom and dormitory both ashore and at sea. The converted cargo-passenger liner is berthed at Pelican Island during the regular school year and is manned by cadets each summer on a nine-week training cruise. The four-year course is co-educational, and high school graduates who are entering the University may earn six college semester hours aboard the clipper during the summer cruise.

Moody College of Marine Sciences and Maritime Resources offers only marine-related degree programs. Its two divisions, the Texas Maritime Academy and the Department of Marine Sciences, lead to a bachelor's degree in marine sciences. A third component is the research Galveston Coastal Zone Laboratory. All programs lead to a Bachelor of Science degree from Texas A.&M.

Students meeting Coast Guard requirements may take examinations for licensing.

GREAT LAKES MARITIME ACADEMY
OF NORTHWESTERN MICHIGAN COLLEGE

The youngest of the maritime academies is the Great Lakes Maritime Academy located at Traverse City, Michigan. This academy prepares young men to serve as officers aboard Great Lakes ships, and it is the only maritime academy to operate on fresh water. It was founded in 1969.

Cadets are part of the student body at NMC, live in the residence halls with other students, and wear uniforms only in marine classes, on cruises, or on other military occasions.

The Academy is a division of a community college that offers the Associate of Science Degree and qualifies cadets to be examined under Coast Guard regulations for either a first-class pilot license (Great Lakes) or third assistant engineer's license. Included in the three-year program is a minimum of nine months' training in basic seamanship and engine mechanics sailing in Great Lakes ships.

THE U.S. MERCHANT MARINE ACADEMY

The U.S. Merchant Marine Cadet Corps was established in March 1938, with training for the midshipmen held aboard merchant ships and later at temporary shore establishments. In 1942, permanent facilities were set up on the former Walter P. Chrysler estate at Kings Point, New York, overlooking Long Island Sound. Dedication services were held on the 68-acre campus in September 1943, when its present name was established. Recently, an additional eight-acre tract was acquired. In 1971 the National Maritime Research Center was located on the grounds.

During World War II the enrollment was increased, but the course of instruction reduced to two years. By the end of the war the four-year course as originally planned was instituted. During the war years the Academy graduated 6,634 officers.

Kings Point, as the Academy is referred to, was the first of the maritime or service academies to accept women—in 1974—with approximately 40 currently enrolled.

Midshipmen can choose from three basic curricula: Nautical Science for the preparation of deck officers who will receive a U.S. Coast Guard license; Marine Engineering for those who will become licensed as third assistant engineers, and a combined curriculum, the Dual License Program which leads to licenses in both specialties.

Sea training is a special feature of the Kings Point program, with each midshipman assigned with a fellow student to an operating vessel of the merchant fleet for two half-year intervals. A Bachelor of Science degree is granted to all graduates.

Due to its proximity to New York City, varied cultural programs are available. There is a full varsity and intramural program, and the sailing squadron participates in frequent races on Long Island Sound. The Academy yachts take part in the Marblehead to Halifax race, the Annapolis to Newport race, and several other ocean races.

Index